The
University of
Law

The University of Law
133 Great Hampton Street
Birmingham B18 6AQ
Telephone: 01483 216041
Email: library-birmingham@law.ac.uk

This book must be returned on or before the last date recorded below.

Birmingham I Bristol I Chester I Guildford I London I Manchester I York

WATSON-GANDY ON
PERSONAL INSOLVENCY PRACTICE

Second Edition

WATSON-GANDY ON PERSONAL INSOLVENCY PRACTICE LITIGATION, PROCEDURE AND PRECEDENTS

Second Edition

Professor Mark Watson-Gandy
Barrister, Three Stone Chambers

With thanks to
Robert Marr, Solicitor
Stephen Allinson, Solicitor and Licensed Insolvency
Practitioner, Chairman of the Board of The Insolvency Service

WS
&H

Wildy, Simmonds & Hill Publishing

© Mark Watson-Gandy, 2018

Contains public sector information licensed under the Open Government Licence v3.0

ISBN: 9780854902330

British Library Cataloguing in Publication Data

A catalogue record for this book is available from the British Library

First edition 2012

This edition published in 2018 by

Wildy, Simmonds & Hill Publishing
58–59 Carey Street
London WC2A 2JF
England
www.wildy.com

Typeset by Heather Jones, North Petherton, Somerset.
Printed in Great Britain by CPI Antony Rowe, Chippenham, Wiltshire.

Contents

Foreword to the Second Edition

Substantive and procedural insolvency law can be a complex affair. This much-needed book provides the reader with easy access to the processes. The style is easy to read, and relevant material is provided together with a worked precedent.

Professor Mark Watson-Gandy's second edition of *Personal Insolvency Practice* is a work of its time. The introduction of the Insolvency (England and Wales) Rules 2016, which took effect in April 2017, sought to achieve three objectives. First to consolidate the existing instruments which made up the Insolvency Rules 1986. Secondly, to update the Rules in terms of their structure, language and style of drafting. The modernisation of language is intended to make the Rules easier to read and understand. Time will tell whether this has been achieved. At the time of the first edition, Professor Watson-Gandy will have been able to direct readers to statutory forms in use. His task has become harder as that is no longer the case. The Insolvency Service has decided to abolish the statutory forms and prescribe the content for notices and documents in the Rules, making the Rules longer. The last objective for the Insolvency Rules Committee was to implement some policy changes. These changes mainly arose from the introduction of the Small Business, Enterprise and Employment Act 2015 and deregulatory initiatives. All these matters have had to be woven into the second edition studiously produced by the author. In addition, the author has updated the text to take account of recent Acts of Parliament and regulations such as the EU Regulation 2015/848 on Insolvency Proceedings 2015.

The first edition was said by Chief Registrar Baister to provide a 'practical guide to the bankruptcy process' and that readers would find the book 'an invaluable weapon in their legal armoury'. The second edition does not disappoint. The order of the chapters has altered slightly to follow what may be thought of as the usual run of events: statutory demand followed by bankruptcy petition followed by a myriad possible applications. I am delighted to see that the aptly named 'Toolkit' chapter providing practical guidance to court users remains.

Chief Registrar Briggs
21 September 2017

Table of Cases

References are to page numbers.

Table of Statutes

References are to page numbers.

Table of Statutory Instruments

References are to page numbers.

Pt 8 – Individual Voluntary Arrangements (IVA)
r 8.2(2)	191
r 8.4	183
r 8.8	188, 202
r 8.8(1)(a)–(e)	183, 188, 202
r 8.8(2)(a), (b)	183, 188, 202
r 8.8(3)	188, 202
r 8.8(4)	181, 184, 189, 190, 192, 203, 204
r 8.8(4)(a)–(c)	189, 203
r 8.8(5)	189, 203
r 8.9(1)	181, 189, 203
r 8.9(1)(a)	182, 189, 203
r 8.9(1)(b)	189, 203
r 8.9(2)	181, 189, 203
r 8.10	189, 203
r 8.10(a)–(d)	189, 203
r 8.11(1)–(3)	189, 203
r 8.12(a)–(i)	190, 204
r 8.13	190, 192
r 8.13(1)	184, 190, 204
r 8.13(2)	190, 204
r 8.13(2)(a)	190, 204
r 8.13(2)(b)	184, 190, 204
r 8.14(a)–(e)	190
r 8.14(f)–(i)	191
r 8.15	184, 191
r 8.15(1)	191
r 8.15(1)(a)–(c)	191
r 8.15(2)–(4)	191
r 8.15(5)	191
r 8.15(5)(a)–(c)	191
r 8.15(6)	191
r 8.16	191
r 8.16(a)–(e)	191
r 8.16(f), (g)	192
r 8.17(1)	192
r 8.17(2)	192
r 8.17(3)	192
r 8.17(3)(a), (b)	192
r 8.18(1)	192
r 8.18(2)	192
r 8.19	216
r 8.20(2)	216
r 8.22(1)	216
r 8.22(2)	216
r 8.22(3)	216
r 8.22(3)(a)–(d)	216
r 8.22(4)	216
r 8.22(5)	216
r 8.22(6)	216
r 8.22(6)(a)–(c)	217
r 8.22(7)	217
r 8.22(7)(a), (b)	217

Table of Practice Directions and Practice Notes

References are to page numbers.

Table of International Material

Table of Forms and Guides

References are to page numbers.

Chapter 1

STATUTORY DEMAND

OBJECTIVE

A person is deemed unable to pay his debts if a creditor (by assignment or otherwise) to whom that person is indebted in a sum exceeding £5,000[1] then due has served on him a statutory demand in the prescribed form requiring him to pay the sum so due, and he has for 3 weeks thereafter neglected to apply to set the demand aside or to pay the sum or to secure[2] or compound for it to the reasonable satisfaction of the creditor.

While creditors' petitions still require a petition to the court and a hearing, debtors now apply online for their own bankruptcy.

STATUTORY FORM

The statutory demand should be on:

- Form SD2[3] (for liquidated sums payable immediately);
- Form SD3 (for liquidated sums payable at a future date);
- Form SD4 (for liquidated sums payable immediately following a judgment or court order).

The statutory demand should set out:

- as the heading, either 'Statutory demand under section 268(1) (debt payable immediately) of the Insolvency Act 1986' or 'Statutory demand under section 268(2) (debt not immediately payable)';
- the amount of the debt;
- the debtor's full name;[4]

---

[1]   As at the date of writing, the sum is still £750 for companies.

[2]   Whilst no express provision exists equivalent to section 269(1) of the Insolvency Act 1986 allowing creditors to waive security to be able to serve a statutory demand, the Act is to be read as a whole and it should be interpreted as being possible: *Re Bartram* [2010] EWHC 2910 (Ch), [2011] BPIR 1.

[3]   Form SD1 is the form for companies.

[4]   Rule 1.6(2) of the Insolvency (England and Wales) Rules 2016.

- the debtor's residential address (unless an order limiting disclosure has been made);[5]
- the name of the creditor;
- the address of the creditor;
- whether it is made under section 268(1) (debt immediately payable) or section 268(2) (debt not immediately payable):[6]

  - if under section 268(1) and based on any court order or judgment:

    - the name of the court;
    - the date of the order or judgment;

  - if under section 268(2), the grounds upon which it is said that the debtor has no reasonable prospect of paying the debt;

- the amount of the debt;
- the consideration for the debt or, if none, how it arises;
- if the creditor is entitled to the debt by way of assignment, details of the original creditor and any intermediary assignees;
- a statement that if the debtor does not comply with the demand, bankruptcy proceedings may be commenced;
- the date by which the debtor must comply with the demand, if bankruptcy proceedings are to be avoided;
- a statement of the methods of compliance which are open to the debtor;
- a statement that the debtor has the right to apply to the court to have the demand set aside;
- a statement that:

  - rule 10.4(4) of the Insolvency (England and Wales) Rules 2016 sets out to which court such an application must be made;
  - the name of the court or hearing centre of the county court to which, according to the present information, the debtor must make the application (i.e. the High Court, the County Court at Central London or a named hearing centre of the county court, as the case may be);
  - if presented by a Minister of the Crown or a government department, the statutory demand must explain that the debtor may alternatively apply to set aside the demand to the High Court or the County Court at Central London (as the case may be) if the Minister or department intends to present a bankruptcy petition to one of them;

- a statement that any application to set aside the demand must be made within 18 days of service on the debtor;

---

[5] Rule 1.6(2) of the Insolvency (England and Wales) Rules 2016.
[6] Rule 10.1(1)(a) of the Insolvency (England and Wales) Rules 2016.

- a statement that if the debtor does not apply to set aside the demand within 18 days or otherwise deal with this demand within 21 days after its service, the debtor could be made bankrupt and the debtor's property and goods taken away;
- with regard to any charge by way of interest not previously notified to the bankrupt as included in his liability that has accrued at the date of the demand or any other charge accruing from time to time that has accrued at the date of the demand,[7] state:

  – the amount or rate of the charge or interest;
  – the grounds on which payment of any charge or interest is claimed;

- if the creditor holds any security:[8]

  – the nature of the security held by the creditor;
  – the value attributed by the creditor to that security at the date of the demand;
  – the amount claimed for payment in the demand shall be the full amount of the debt less the amount specified as the value of the security;[9]

- contact information for the creditor to enable the debtor to communicate with him, with a view to securing or compounding for the debt to the creditor's satisfaction or establishing to the creditor's satisfaction that there is a reasonable prospect that the debt will be paid when it falls due. This must include:

  – a named contact;
  – the contact's postal address;
  – the contact's telephone number;
  – the contact's electronic address;

- the date of the demand;
- be authenticated[10] by:

  – the creditor; or
  – someone authorised by the creditor to do so, stating:[11]

    – that the person is authorised to make the demand on the creditor's behalf;
    – the person's relationship to the creditor.

---

[7]   Rules 10.7 and 10.8 of the Insolvency (England and Wales) Rules 2016.

[8]   Rule 10.9 of the Insolvency (England and Wales) Rules 2016.

[9]   Rule 10.9 of the Insolvency (England and Wales) Rules 2016.

[10] Rule 10.5 of the Insolvency (England and Wales) Rules 2016. For what will suffice as to authentication, see rule 1.5. Hard copy documents must be signed: rule 1.5(2).

[11] Rule 10.6 of the Insolvency (England and Wales) Rules 2016.

SERVICE

The creditor is under an obligation to do all that is reasonable to bring the demand to the debtor's attention.[12] If practicable, the statutory demand should be personally served. Failure to serve personally is not, however, necessarily fatal to the statutory demand.[13] As a statutory demand is not a court document, permission to serve overseas is not required.[14]

EVIDENCE

A certificate should be prepared proving service (this will later need to be filed with any bankruptcy petition).[15] The deponent should be the process server who effected service or have direct knowledge of service and should be verified by a statement of truth.

This should address:

- how the deponent effected service of the demand, where he did it and on whom;
- the reaction (if any) to service;
- if the deponent did not effect service personally, the steps taken with a view to serving the demand personally;
- the means whereby the process server sought to bring the demand to the attention of the debtor (even if the same was ineffective);
- the date and time which to the best of the knowledge, information and belief of the process server the demand came to the attention of the debtor.

And should exhibit:

- the statutory demand;
- if service has been acknowledged in writing by the debtor or a person authorised to accept service on his behalf, a copy of the acknowledgement.[16]

---

[12] Rule 10.2 of the Insolvency (England and Wales) Rules 2016. *Omokwe v HFC Bank* [2007] BPIR 1157; *Yang v Official Receiver* [2013] EWHC 3577 (Ch), [2014] BPIR 826.

[13] *Bush v Bank Mandiri* [2011] BPIR 19.

[14] Paragraph 13.1.1 of the CPR Practice Direction – Insolvency Proceedings. For the procedure to be adopted when serving overseas, see paragraphs 13.1.1–13.1.7.

[15] Rule 10.3 of the Insolvency (England and Wales) Rules 2016.

[16] Rule 10.3(4) of the Insolvency (England and Wales) Rules 2016.

NOTES

Unlike a statutory demand presented against a company, a private individual may apply to set aside a statutory demand presented against him.

KEY MATERIALS

Section 268 of the Insolvency Act 1986

268 Definition of 'inability to pay', etc.; the statutory demand
(1) For the purposes of section 267(2)(c), the debtor appears to be unable to pay a debt if, but only if, the debt is payable immediately and either—

   (a) the petitioning creditor to whom the debt is owed has served on the debtor a demand (known as 'the statutory demand') in the prescribed form requiring him to pay the debt or to secure or compound for it to the satisfaction of the creditor, at least 3 weeks have elapsed since the demand was served and the demand has been neither complied with nor set aside in accordance with the rules, or
   (b) execution or other process issued in respect of the debt on a judgment or order of any court in favour of the petitioning creditor, or one or more of the petitioning creditors to whom the debt is owed, has been returned unsatisfied in whole or in part.

(2) For the purposes of section 267(2)(c) the debtor appears to have no reasonable prospect of being able to pay a debt if, but only if, the debt is not immediately payable and—

   (a) the petitioning creditor to whom it is owed has served on the debtor a demand (also known as 'the statutory demand') in the prescribed form requiring him to establish to the satisfaction of the creditor that there is a reasonable prospect that the debtor will be able to pay the debt when it falls due,
   (b) at least 3 weeks have elapsed since the demand was served, and
   (c) the demand has been neither complied with nor set aside in accordance with the rules.

Rules 10.1–10.3 of the Insolvency (England and Wales) Rules 2016

The statutory demand (section 268)
10.1.—(1) A statutory demand under section 268 must contain—

   (a) the heading either 'Statutory demand under section 268(1) (debt payable immediately) of the Insolvency Act 1986' or 'Statutory demand under section 268(2) (debt not immediately payable)';

    (b)   identification details for the debtor;

    (c)   the name and address of the creditor;

    (d)   a statement of the amount of the debt, and the consideration for it (or, if there is no consideration, the way in which it arises);

    (e)   if the demand is made under section 268(1) and founded on a judgment or order of a court, the date of the judgment or order and the court in which it was obtained;

    (f)   if the demand is made under section 268(2), a statement of the grounds on which it is alleged that the debtor appears to have no reasonable prospect of paying the debt;

    (g)   if the creditor is entitled to the debt by way of assignment, details of the original creditor and any intermediary assignees;

    (h)   a statement that if the debtor does not comply with the demand bankruptcy proceedings may be commenced;

    (i)   the date by which the debtor must comply with the demand, if bankruptcy proceedings are to be avoided;

    (j)   a statement of the methods of compliance which are open to the debtor;

    (k)   a statement that the debtor has the right to apply to the court to have the demand set aside;

    (l)   a statement that rule 10.4(4) of the Insolvency (England and Wales) Rules 2016 states to which court such an application must be made; and name the court or hearing centre of the County Court to which, according to the present information, the debtor must make the application (i.e. the High Court, the County Court at Central London or a named hearing centre of the County Court as the case may be);

    (m)   a statement that any application to set aside the demand must be made within 18 days of service on the debtor; and

    (n)   a statement that if the debtor does not apply to set aside the demand within 18 days or otherwise deal with this demand within 21 days after its service the debtor could be made bankrupt and the debtor's property and goods taken away.

(2)   Where the statutory demand is served by a Minister of the Crown or a Government Department the statutory demand must explain that the debtor may alternatively apply to set aside the demand to the High Court or the County Court at Central London (as the case may be) if the Minister or Department intends to present a bankruptcy petition to one of them.

(3)   A demand must name one or more individuals with whom the debtor may communicate with a view to—

    (a)   securing or compounding the debt to the satisfaction of the creditor; or

    (b)   establishing to the creditor's satisfaction that there is a reasonable prospect that the debt will be paid when it falls due.

(4)   The postal address, electronic address and telephone number (if any) of the named individual must be given.

(5)   A demand must be dated and authenticated either by the creditor or by a person who is authorised to make the demand on the creditor's behalf.

(6) A demand which is authenticated by a person other than the creditor must state that the person is authorised to make the demand on the creditor's behalf and state the person's relationship to the creditor.

(7) If the amount claimed in the demand includes—

(a) any charge by way of interest of which notice had not previously been delivered to the debtor as a liability of the debtor's; or

(b) any other charge accruing from time to time,

the amount or rate of the charge must be separately identified, and the grounds on which payment of it is claimed must be stated.

(8) The amount claimed for such charges must be limited to that which has accrued at the date of the demand.

(9) If the creditor holds any security in respect of the debt, the full amount of the debt must be specified, but—

(a) the demand must specify the nature of the security, and the value which the creditor puts upon it at the date of the demand; and

(b) the demand must claim payment of the full amount of the debt, less the specified value of the security.

Service of statutory demand
10.2. A creditor must do all that is reasonable to bring the statutory demand to the debtor's attention and, if practicable in the particular circumstances, serve the demand personally.

Proof of service of statutory demand
10.3.—(1) Where section 268 requires a statutory demand to be served before the petition, a certificate of service of the demand must be filed with the court with the petition.

(2) The certificate must be verified by a statement of truth and be accompanied by a copy of the demand served.

(3) If the demand has been served personally on the debtor, the statement of truth must be made by the person who served the demand unless service has been acknowledged in writing by the debtor or a person authorised to accept service.

(4) If service has been acknowledged in writing either by—

(a) the debtor; or

(b) a person who is authorised to accept service on the debtor's behalf and who has stated that this is the case in the acknowledgement of service;

then the certificate of service must be authenticated either by the creditor or by a person acting on the creditor's behalf, and the acknowledgement of service must accompany the certificate.

(5) If the demand has been served other than personally and there is no acknowledgement of service, the certificate must be authenticated by a person or persons having direct personal knowledge of the means adopted

for serving the statutory demand, and must contain the following information—

(a)   the steps taken to serve the demand; and
(b)   a date by which, to the best of the knowledge, information and belief of the person authenticating the certificate, the demand will have come to the debtor's attention.

(6)   Where paragraph (5) applies the statutory demand is deemed to have been served on the debtor on the date referred to in paragraph (5)(b) unless the court determines otherwise.

The relevant extracts of the CPR Practice Direction – Insolvency Proceedings are reproduced in Chapter 24.

1.1   CREDITOR'S STATUTORY DEMAND

Rule 10.1   **Statutory Demand under Section 268(1)(a) of the**
Form SD2   **Insolvency Act 1986. Debt for Liquidated Sum**
                   Payable Immediately

Warning
- This is an **important** document. You should refer to the notes below entitled 'How to comply with a statutory demand or have it set aside.'
- If you wish to have this demand set aside you must make application to do so **within 18 days** from its service on you.
- If you do not apply to set aside **within 18 days** or otherwise deal with this demand as set out in the notes **within 21 days** after its service on you, you could be made bankrupt and your property and goods taken away from you.
- Please read the demand and notes very carefully. If you are in doubt about your position you should seek advice **immediately** from a solicitor, a Citizens Advice Bureau or a licensed insolvency practitioner.

Notes for Creditor
- If the Creditor is entitled to the debt by way of assignment, details of the original creditor and any **intermediary** assignees should be given in part B on page 3.
- If the amount of debt includes interest not previously notified to the company as included in its liability, details should be given, including the grounds upon which interest is charged. The amount of interest must be shown separately.
- Any other charge accruing due from time to time may be claimed. The amount **or** rate of the charge must be identified and the grounds on which it is claimed must be stated.
- In either case the amount claimed must be limited to that which has accrued due at the date of the demand.
- If signatory of the demand is a solicitor or other agent of the creditor the name of his/her firm should be given

---

Demand

To   IAN FLAKEY

Address   1 GERANIUM COTTAGE, LONDON

This demand is served on you by the creditor:

Name   ANGRY PLC

Address   1 UNPAID BILL STREET, LONDON

The creditor claims that you own the sum of £2,045,687.50, full particulars of which are set out on page 2, and that it is payable immediately and, to the extent of the sum demanded, is unsecured.

The creditor demands that you pay the above debt or secure or compound for it to the creditor's satisfaction.

[The creditor making this demand is a Minister of the Crown or a Government Department, and it is intended to present a bankruptcy petition in the [High Court][County Court at Central London] [Delete as appropriate].

* Delete if signed by the creditor himself.

Signature of individual _____

Name   CLIVE CRABBY
          BLOCK LETTERS

Date   1ST APRIL 2020

*Position with or relationship to creditor
SOLICITOR

* I am authorised to make this demand on the creditor's behalf.

N.B. The person making this demand must complete the whole of pages 1, 2 and parts A, B and C (as applicable) on page 3.

* This is the address to which the court or the creditor will send any documents relating to this demand

Address   WIGG & CO, 1 LAW STREET, LONDON

_____

Tel. №   0207 666 6666

Ref.   CC/ANGRY/1

Details of Debt
(These details must include (a) when the debt was incurred, (b) the consideration for the debt (or if there is no consideration the way in which it arose) and (c) the amount due as at the date of this demand.)

THE DEBTOR IS INDEBTED TO THE CREDITOR IN THE SUM OF £2,000,000 FOR GOODS SOLD AND DELIVERED BY THE PETITIONER TO IAN FLAKEY UNDER A CONTRACT DATED 1ST DECEMBER 2010 AND EVIDENCED BY AN INVOICE NUMBER 001 TOGETHER WITH INTEREST IN THE SUM OF £45,687.50 IN CONTRACTUAL INTEREST CALCULATED AT A RATE OF 13.1% PER ANNUM FROM THE DATE OF DELIVERY OF THE INVOICE TO THE DATE OF DEMAND.

TOTAL £2,045,687.50

Note: If there is insufficient space, please continue on a separate sheet and clearly indicate on this page that you are doing so.

Part A
Appropriate Court for Setting Aside Demand

Rule 10.4(4) and 10.4(8) of the Insolvency Rules 2016 states that the appropriate court is the court to which you would have to present your own bankruptcy petition in accordance with Rule XXXXX. In accordance with those rules on present information the appropriate court is [the High Court] [the County Court at Central London] [or] [County Court Hearing Centre]
(address)

Any application by you to set aside this demand should be made to that court.

Part B
The individual or individuals to whom any communication regarding this demand may be addressed is/are:

Name   CLIVE CRABBY OF WIGG & CO
          (BLOCK LETTERS)
Address   1 LAW STREET, LONDON

Telephone Number   0207 666 6666

Reference   CC/ANGRY/1

Part C
For completion if the creditor is entitled to the debt by way of assignment.

	Name	Date(s) of Assignment
Original Creditor		
Assignees		

How to comply with a statutory demand or have it set aside (ACT WITHIN 18 DAYS)

If you wish to avoid a bankruptcy petition being presented against you, you must pay the debt shown on page 1, details of which are set out on page 2 of this notice, within the period of 21 days after its service upon you. Alternatively, you can attempt to come to a settlement with the creditor. To do this you should:

- Inform the individual (or one of the individuals) named in Part B above immediately that you are willing and able to offer security for the debt to the creditor's satisfaction; or
- Inform the individual (or one of the individuals) named in Part B immediately that you are willing and able to compound for the debt to the creditor's satisfaction.

If you dispute the demand in whole or in part you should:

- Contact the individual (or one of the individuals) named in Part B immediately.

If you consider that you have grounds to have this demand set aside or you do not quickly receive a satisfactory written reply from the individual named in Part B whom you have contacted, you should **apply within 18 days** from the date of service of this demand on you to the appropriate court shown in Part A above to have the demand set aside.

Any application to set aside the demand should be made within 18 days from the date of service upon you and be supported by a witness statement stating the grounds on which the demand be set aside. The forms may be obtained from the appropriate court when you attend to make the application.

REMEMBER! From the date of service on you of this document

(a)   you have only 18 days to apply to this court to have the demand set aside, and
(b)   you have only 21 days before the creditor may present a bankruptcy petition.

1.2   CERTIFICATE OF PERSONAL SERVICE

Rule 10.3   **Certificate of Personal Service of Statutory Demand**[17]

IN THE MATTER OF IAN FLAKEY

Date of Statutory Demand 1ST APRIL 2020

(a) Insert name, address and description of person making the statements in the Certificate and whether the creditor or a person acting on his behalf

I, (a) IAN FLINGITT-ANRUN of 1 Serve Street, London, Process Server

state as follows:

(b) Delete 'I' and insert name and address of person who effected service, if applicable
(c) Insert date
(d) Insert time which must be either before or after 16.00 hours Monday to Friday or before or after 12.00 hours Saturday
(e) Insert address

1. (b) [I][IAN FLINGITT-ANRUN]
did on (c) 1ST APRIL 2020
(d) [before] [after] 16.00   hours, at (e)
1 UNPAID BILL STREET, LONDON

personally serve the above-named debtor with the demand dated
1ST APRIL 2020

(f) Delete words in [ ] if no acknowledgement of service has been received
(g) Give particulars of the way in which the debtor acknowledged service of the demand

(f) [2. That on (c) 1ST APRIL 2020
the debtor acknowledged service of the demand by (g) SHOUTING 'IT'S A FAIR COP, GUV, YOU'VE CAUGHT ME AT LAST' AND SIGNING A NOTE ACKNOWLEDGING RECEIPT OF THE STATUTORY DEMAND DATED 1ST APRIL 2020]
3. A copy of the demand marked 'A' (f) [and the acknowledgment of service marked 'B'] is/are attached.
4. A copy of the written acknowledgment of receipt of the statutory demand sent by THE ABOVE-NAMED DEBTOR [or .... Who was authorised to accept service on the debtor's behalf] marked 'B' is/are attached.

STATEMENT OF TRUTH

I believe that the facts stated in this Certificate are true.

Full name IAN FLINGITT-ANRUN
....
Signed ....
Dated ....

[17]   Form 6.11 has not been replaced; however, this suggested precedent addresses the requirements of rule 10.3 of the Insolvency (England and Wales) Rules 2016.

Chapter 2

APPLICATION TO SET ASIDE A STATUTORY DEMAND

OBJECTIVE

A person is deemed unable to pay his debts if a creditor (by assignment or otherwise) to whom that person is indebted in a sum exceeding £5,000 then due has served on him a statutory demand in the prescribed form requiring him to pay the sum so due, and he has for 3 weeks thereafter neglected to apply to set the demand aside or to pay the sum or to secure or compound for it to the reasonable satisfaction of the creditor.

A statutory demand may, however, be set aside on one or more of the following grounds:[1]

- the debtor appears to have a counterclaim, set off or cross demand which equals or exceeds the amount of debt[2] specified in the statutory demand;
- the debt is disputed on grounds which appear to be substantial;
- it appears that the creditor holds some security in respect of the debt and either the creditor has failed to disclose its nature, value and the amount of the debt left unsecured[3] or the court is satisfied that the value of the security equals or exceeds the full value of the debt;
- the court is satisfied, on some other grounds, that the demand ought to be set aside.

The court's power to set aside the statutory demand is discretionary[4] and the mere presence of a defect does not make the setting aside of the demand inevitable.[5] The court will not look behind an earlier judgment. Where the court takes the view that the security is undervalued, the court may require the creditor to amend his statutory demand.[6]

---

[1]   Rule 10.5(5) of the Insolvency (England and Wales) Rules 2016.

[2]   Rule 10.5(5)(a) of the Insolvency (England and Wales) Rules 2016.

[3]   Rule 10.1(9) of the Insolvency (England and Wales) Rules 2016.

[4]   *Khan v Breezevale Sarl; sub nom Re a Debtor (No 106 of 1992)* [1996] BPIR 190.

[5]   *Coulter v Chief of Dorset Police* [2004] EWCA Civ 1259, [2005] BPIR 62.

[6]   Rule 10.5(7) of the Insolvency (England and Wales) Rules 2016.

APPLICATION

The application is made in the court the debtor would have petitioned for his own bankruptcy.[7] The exception to this rule is where the statutory demand is served by a government department or where the statutory demand is based on a judgment debt and specifies that the creditor intends to present his petition in the High Court when the application is to the High Court.

The application is made on Form IAA. The application should set out:

- that the application is made under the Insolvency Act 1986 or the Insolvency (England and Wales) Rules 2016 (as the case may be);[8]
- the section number or rule under which relief is sought;[9]
- the name of the parties;[10]
- the name of the bankrupt or debtor;[11]
- the court name;[12]
- the case number;[13]
- the remedy applied for or directions sought;[14]
- the name and address of each person to be served or, if none, stating that it is intended that no person will be served;[15]
- where there is a requirement for particular persons to be given notice of the application under the Act or Rules, stating the name and address of each such person;[16]
- the applicant's address for service.[17]

The application notice must be authenticated by the applicant or his solicitor.[18]

COURT FEES

A court fee of £155 is payable.[19]

---

[7] Rule 10.4(4) of the Insolvency (England and Wales) Rules 2016.

[8] Rule 1.35(2)(a) of the Insolvency (England and Wales) Rules 2016.

[9] Rule 1.35(2)(b) of the Insolvency (England and Wales) Rules 2016.

[10] Rule 1.35(2)(c) of the Insolvency (England and Wales) Rules 2016.

[11] Rule 1.35(2)(d) of the Insolvency (England and Wales) Rules 2016.

[12] Rule 1.35(2)(e) of the Insolvency (England and Wales) Rules 2016.

[13] Rule 1.35(2)(f) of the Insolvency (England and Wales) Rules 2016.

[14] Rule 1.35(2)(g) of the Insolvency (England and Wales) Rules 2016.

[15] Rule 1.35(2)(h) of the Insolvency (England and Wales) Rules 2016.

[16] Rule 1.35(2)(i) of the Insolvency (England and Wales) Rules 2016.

[17] Rule 1.35(2)(j) of the Insolvency (England and Wales) Rules 2016.

[18] Rule 1.35(3) of the Insolvency (England and Wales) Rules 2016. For what amounts to authentication, see rule 1.5. For hard copy applications, this means signed: rule 1.5(2).

[19] Paragraph 3.5 of Schedule 1 to the Civil Proceedings Fees (Amendment) Order 2011.

TIME LIMIT

An application to set aside must be made within 18 days of service or the date of its advertisement.[20]

EVIDENCE

The application should[21] state the date upon which the debtor first became aware of the statutory demand,[22] and state the grounds upon which the debtor asserts that the statutory demand should be set aside,[23] namely one or more of:

- the debtor has a counterclaim which equals or exceeds the amount of debt[24] specified in the statutory demand;
- the debtor has a set off which equals or exceeds the amount of debt[25] specified in the statutory demand;
- the debtor has a cross demand which equals or exceeds the amount of debt[26] specified in the statutory demand;
- the debt is disputed;
- the creditor holds security in respect of the debt which either:

  - the creditor has failed to disclose (accurately) its nature, value and the amount of the debt left unsecured; or
  - the value of the security equals or exceeds the full value of the debt;

- there are some other grounds that the demand ought to be set aside;
- state the short particulars of the facts and matters that found the grounds;
- exhibit the statutory demand.

The court has the power to determine the application on the first hearing, but more usually directions are given for the filing of further evidence.[27] Fresh evidence can be adduced and the parties are not limited to materials adduced in a previous hearing or constrained by the rule in *Ladd v Marshall* [1954] 1 WLR 1489.[28] If the opportunity has not been taken already, this opportunity should be taken to ensure that the matters in the witness statement are amplified in a further witness statement in traditional format. Care should be taken to ensure that the evidence filed is sufficient to establish the defence, that set off or cross claim is genuine,

---

[20] Rule 10.4(2) of the Insolvency (England and Wales) Rules 2016.

[21] Rule 10.4(3) of the Insolvency (England and Wales) Rules 2016.

[22] Rule 10.4(6)(a) of the Insolvency (England and Wales) Rules 2016.

[23] Rule 10.4(6)(b) of the Insolvency (England and Wales) Rules 2016.

[24] Rule 10.5(5)(a) of the Insolvency (England and Wales) Rules 2016.

[25] Rule 10.5(5)(a) of the Insolvency (England and Wales) Rules 2016.

[26] Rule 10.5(5)(a) of the Insolvency (England and Wales) Rules 2016.

[27] Rule 10.5(4) of the Insolvency (England and Wales) Rules 2016.

[28] *Royal Bank of Scotland v Binnell* [1996] BPIR 352.

serious and of substance. It would appear that any points based on jurisdiction should, more appropriately, be challenged at the petition stage.[29]

KEY MATERIALS

Rules 10.4 and 10.5 of the Insolvency (England and Wales) Rules 2016

Application to set aside statutory demand

10.4.—(1) The debtor may apply to the court for an order setting aside the statutory demand.

(2)   The application must be made within 18 days from the date of the service of the statutory demand.

(3)   The application must—

(a)   identify the debtor;

(b)   state that the application is for an order that the statutory demand be set aside;

(c)   state the date of the statutory demand; and

(d)   be dated and authenticated by the debtor, or by a person authorised to act on the debtor's behalf.

(4)   The application must be made to the court or hearing centre—

(a)   determined in accordance with rule 10.48; or

(b)   to which rule 10.11(1) requires a petition to be presented if—

(i)   the creditor serving the statutory demand is a Minister of the Crown or a government Department,

(ii)   the debt in respect of which the statutory demand is made, or part of it equal to or exceeding the bankruptcy level (within the meaning of section 267), is the subject of a judgment or order of a court, and

(iii)   the statutory demand—

(aa)   specifies the date of the judgment or order and the court in which it was obtained, and

(bb)   indicates the creditor's intention to present a bankruptcy petition against the debtor in the High Court or the County Court at Central London as the case may be.

---

[29]   See, for example, section 265(1)(b) of the Insolvency Act 1986 whereby jurisdiction on the basis of the personal presence of the debtor is to be assessed as at the date of the petition; and *Shierson v Vlieland-Boddy* [2005] EWCA Civ 974, [2005] 1 WLR 3966

(5) The time within which the debtor must comply with the statutory demand ceases to run on the date the application is filed with the court, subject to any order of the court under rule 10.5.

(6) The debtor's application must be accompanied by a copy of the statutory demand, where it is in the debtor's possession, and supported by a witness statement containing the following—

    (a) the date on which the debtor became aware of the statutory demand;

    (b) the grounds on which the debtor claims that it should be set aside; and

    (c) any evidence in support of the application.

Hearing of application to set aside

10.5.—(1) On receipt of an application to set aside a statutory demand, the court may, if satisfied that no sufficient cause is shown for it, dismiss it without giving notice of the application to the creditor.

(2) The time for complying with the statutory demand runs again from the date the application is dismissed under paragraph (1).

(3) Unless the application is dismissed under paragraph (1), the court must fix a venue for it to be heard, and must give at least five business days' notice to—

    (a) the debtor or, if the debtor's application was made by a solicitor acting for the debtor, to the solicitor;

    (b) the creditor; and

    (c) whoever is named in the statutory demand as the person with whom the debtor may communicate about the demand (or the first such if more than one).

(4) On the hearing of the application, the court must consider the evidence then available to it, and may either determine the application or adjourn it, giving such directions as it thinks appropriate.

(5) The court may grant the application if—

    (a) the debtor appears to have a counterclaim, set-off or cross demand which equals or exceeds the amount of the debt specified in the statutory demand;

    (b) the debt is disputed on grounds which appear to the court to be substantial;

    (c) it appears that the creditor holds some security in relation to the debt claimed by the demand, and either rule 10.1(9) is not complied with in relation to it, or the court is satisfied that the value of the security equals or exceeds the full amount of the debt; or

    (d) the court is satisfied, on other grounds, that the demand ought to be set aside.

(6) An order setting aside a statutory demand must contain—

    (a) identification details for the debtor;

    (b) the date of the hearing of the application;

   (c)   the date of the statutory demand;
   (d)   an order that the statutory demand be set aside;
   (e)   details of any further order in the matter; and
   (f)   the date of the order.

(7)   Where the creditor holds some security in relation to the debt and has complied with rule 10.1(9) but the court is satisfied that the statutory demand undervalues the security, the court may order the creditor to amend the demand (but without prejudice to the creditor's right to present a bankruptcy petition by reference to the original demand as so amended).

(8)   If the court dismisses the application, it must make an order authorising the creditor to present a bankruptcy petition either as soon as reasonably practicable, or on or after a date specified in the order.

(9)   The court must deliver a copy of any order under paragraphs (6) to (8) to the creditor as soon as reasonably practicable.

2.1 APPLICATION TO SET ASIDE A STATUTORY DEMAND

Form IAA   **Insolvency Act Application Notice**

IN THE HIGH COURT OF JUSTICE
BUSINESS AND PROPERTY COURTS OF ENGLAND AND WALES
INSOLVENCY AND COMPANIES LIST (ChD)
IN BANKRUPTCY

NO: 666 OF 2020

IN THE MATTER OF IAN FLAKEY
AND IN THE MATTER OF THE INSOLVENCY ACT 1986

BETWEEN:-

IAN FLAKEY

Applicant

and

ANGRY PLC

Respondent

Is this application within existing insolvency proceedings?   YES/~~NO~~

I (~~We~~), IAN FLAKEY of 1 Geranium Cottage, London intend to apply to the ~~Judge/District Judge~~/Registrar on:

Date: 1st April 2020

Time: 00:00 hours

Place: Royal Courts of Justice, 7 Rolls Buildings, Fetter Lane, London EC4A 1NL

This application having been issued at the RCJ, 7 Rolls Buildings, Fetter Lane, London, EC4A 1NL will be heard at the time and date pursuant to the endorsement underneath the Court Seal on the front page of this application.

FOR AN ORDER THAT:

1.   The statutory demand of the Respondent dated 1st April 2020 be set aside.

2.   The costs of this application be paid by the Petitioner.

Such further and other order and other relief as this Honourable Court thinks fit.

The grounds upon which I seek the above order are set out in the 1st witness statement of Ian Flakey dated 1st April 2020, a copy of which is annexed to this application.

THE NAMES AND ADDRESSES OF THE PERSON(S) UPON WHOM IT IS INTENDED TO SERVE THIS APPLICATION ARE:

Name: ANGRY PLC

Address: 1 UNPAID BILL STREET, LONDON

Name:

Address:

~~OR~~

~~IT IS NOT INTENDED TO SERVE ANY PERSON WITH THIS APPLICATION~~

Dated:

Signed:　　SNARKEY & SNYDE

Solicitors for the applicant ~~or Applicant~~
Address: 1 LAW STREET, LONDON
Telephone: 0207 666 6666
Email: law@snarkeysnyde.com

*This is the address which will be treated by Court as the Petitions address for service

If you do not attend, the court may make such order as it thinks just.

Applicant: I Flakey: 1st: IF1: [ ] 20[ ]

IN THE HIGH COURT OF JUSTICE
BUSINESS AND PROPERTY COURTS OF ENGLAND AND WALES
INSOLVENCY AND COMPANIES LIST (ChD)

NO: [ ] OF 20[ ]

IN THE MATTER OF IAN FLAKEY
AND IN BANKRUPTCY
AND IN THE MATTER OF THE INSOLVENCY ACT 1986

BETWEEN:-

IAN FLAKEY

Applicant

and

ANGRY PLC

Respondent

1ST WITNESS STATEMENT OF IAN FLAKEY

I, IAN FLAKEY of 1 Geranium Cottage, London, Businessman, STATE as follows:

1. I am the Applicant in this application to set aside the Respondent's statutory demand.

2. The matters set out in this witness statement are true and within my own knowledge except where otherwise indicated, in which case I have explained the source of my information or belief.

3. On 1st April 2020, I was served with a statutory demand by Angry plc claiming £2,045,687.50 based on an invoice for goods they say were sold and delivered to me. I refer to page [ ] of 'IF1' which is a true copy of the statutory demand.

4. I made no such order. I refer to page [ ] of 'IF1' which is a true copy of my records for purchases and deliveries for the periods alluded to by Angry plc.

5. Angry plc did however deliver 1,000 boxes of widgets contaminated with sulphuric acid. The acid not only corroded the widgets delivered, but also seeped into my own store of widgets rendering them corroded and unusable. I refer to page [ ] of 'IF1' which is a true copy of the photographs of the damaged widgets. Angry plc are in breach of contract as the widgets they supplied were not of satisfactory quality.

6. By reason of the matters I describe, not only do I not owe any money for the widgets delivered, but I have also suffered £100,000 of loss from the damage to my existing stock of widgets. I refer to page [ ] of 'IF1' which is a true copy of a report on the damage suffered by me by an independent valuer, Uther Unreliable.

7. In all the circumstances, I ask this Honourable Court that the statutory demand be set aside.

STATEMENT OF TRUTH

I believe that the facts stated in this Witness Statement are true.

Signed [ ]
Full name [*IAN FLAKEY*]
Dated [ ] 20[ ]

Chapter 3

CREDITOR'S BANKRUPTCY PETITION

OBJECTIVE

A bankruptcy petition can be presented if it can be shown that the statutory grounds under section 267 of the Insolvency Act 1986 are made out, namely there is an unsecured debt for a liquidated sum in excess of £5,000 payable to the petitioning creditor, either immediately or at some certain future date, and the debtor appears either to be unable to pay the debt or to have no reasonable prospect of paying the debt and there is no outstanding application to set aside the statutory demand.

A debtor is deemed to be unable to pay his debts:[1]

- if a creditor (by assignment or otherwise) to whom the debtor is indebted in a sum exceeding £5,000 has served on the debtor a statutory demand in the prescribed form requiring the debtor to pay the debt or secure or compound it, and the debtor has for 3 weeks thereafter neglected to pay the sum or to secure or compound for it to the reasonable satisfaction of the creditor or set the demand aside; or
- if execution or other process issued on a judgment, decree or order of any court in favour of the creditor against the debtor is returned unsatisfied in whole or in part.

Where the debt is not immediately payable, a debtor is deemed to be unable to pay his debts if a creditor to whom the debtor is indebted in a sum exceeding £5,000 has served on the debtor a statutory demand in the prescribed form requiring the debtor to establish to the satisfaction of the creditor that there is a reasonable prospect that the debt will be paid when it falls due, and the debtor has for 3 weeks thereafter neglected to comply with the demand or set the demand aside.[2]

Where the requirements of section 268 of the Insolvency Act 1986 have been met, it is no defence for a debtor to demonstrate that he was solvent at the time.[3]

In any event, the court will not make a bankruptcy order unless it is either satisfied that the debt, which is immediately payable, has not been paid, secured or

---

[1]   Section 268(1) of the Insolvency Act 1986.

[2]   Section 268(2) of the Insolvency Act 1986.

[3]   *Johnson v Tandridge District Council* [2007] EWHC 3325 (Ch), [2008] BPIR 405.

compounded, or that the debtor has no reasonable prospects of paying the debt when it falls due.[4] The court may dismiss the petition if it is satisfied that the debtor can pay all his debts or that the debtor has offered to secure or compound his debts, and that had the offer been accepted the petition would have been dismissed and that offer has been unreasonably refused.[5]

A debt is undisputed unless there is a dispute on a substantial ground. A petition may be brought on a secured debt provided that the creditor is willing to give up his security or if the petition is to be brought on the unsecured part of the debt and the secured part is valued.[6]

EXPEDITING THE PETITION AND THE HEARING

Where a petition is being presented on the basis of a statutory demand and there is a serious possibility that the debtor's property or its value will be seriously diminished during the 3-week period of the statutory demand, the court will allow the petition to be presented prematurely.[7] The statutory demand must have been served[8] and the petition and evidence will need to state the grounds for the early presentation.[9] The hearing of the bankruptcy petition will not in any event take place until at least 3 weeks have elapsed from the service of the statutory demand.[10] Any grounds for abridgement should be set out in the petition.[11]

The petition will not be heard unless at least 14 days have elapsed from the date it was served on the debtor. The court has the power to abridge this time if either the debtor consents or if it appears appropriate or if the debtor has absconded.[12]

PETITION

There are four possible forms for the petition:

- Form Bank 1 (on the failure to pay a statutory debt on a debt due immediately).
- Form Bank 2 (on the failure to pay a statutory debt on a debt due at a future date).

---

[4]　Section 271(1) of the Insolvency Act 1986.

[5]　Section 271(3) of the Insolvency Act 1986.

[6]　Section 269(1) of the Insolvency Act 1986, and *Zandfarid v BCCI* [1996] BPIR 501. Whilst there is no equivalent provision for waiving security for the purposes of a statutory demand, the Act is to be read as a whole and should be interpreted as being possible: *Re Bartram* [2010] EWHC 2910 (Ch), [2011] BPIR 1.

[7]　Section 270 of the Insolvency Act 1986.

[8]　*Wehmeyer v Wehmeyer* [2001] BPIR 548.

[9]　Section 270 of the Insolvency Act 1986.

[10]　Section 271(2) of the Insolvency Act 1986.

[11]　Section 270 of the Insolvency Act 1986.

[12]　Rule 10.21(2) of the Insolvency (England and Wales) Rules 2016.

- Form Bank 3 (where execution of a judgment is returned unsatisfied).
- Form Bank 4 (on the default of a voluntary arrangement).

Before presenting a petition, the petitioner must conduct a search at the Royal Courts of Justice, the Central London County Court and whichever county court is believed to be the debtor's own county court, and include the following certificate at the end of the petition:

> I/We certify that I/we have conducted a search for petitions presented against the debtor in the period of 18 months ending today and that [no prior petitions have been presented in the said period which are still pending] [a prior petition (No [ ]) has been presented and is pending in the [ ] Court and I am/we are issuing this petition at risk as to costs][13]

The petitioner will need to bring two (and possibly three) copies of the petition to the court for sealing. These will comprise:

- the original petition for the court;
- a copy for service on the debtor;
- a copy for service on the supervisor, if there is an individual voluntary arrangement (IVA) in force.

The court will endorse the date and time for the first hearing of the petition on the petition.

The petition must:

- state the name of the petitioner;[14]
- state the postal address of the petitioner;
- state the name of the petitioner's solicitor;
- state the postal address of the petitioner's solicitor;
- state the full name of the debtor;[15]
- state any other names the debtor is known by to the creditor's knowledge;[16]
- state the bankrupt's residential address (subject to any order for limited disclosure);[17]
- state that the petitioner requests that the court make a bankruptcy order against the debtor;
- state whether the debtor's centre of main interests is within a member state, the debtor's centre of main interests is not within a member state, or the debtor carries on business as an Article 1.2 undertaking;[18]
- state whether the debtor is (or is not) resident in England and Wales;

---

[13] Paragraph 14.3.1 of the CPR Practice Direction – Insolvency Proceedings.
[14] Rule 10.7(1) of the Insolvency (England and Wales) Rules 2016.
[15] Rules 1.6(2) and 10.8(1) of the Insolvency (England and Wales) Rules 2016.
[16] Rule 10.8(3) of the Insolvency (England and Wales) Rules 2016.
[17] Rules 1.6(2) and 10.8(1) of the Insolvency (England and Wales) Rules 2016.
[18] Rule 10.7(1) of the Insolvency (England and Wales) Rules 2016.

- state whether the petition is presented to the High Court, the County Court at Central London, or a specified hearing centre;[19]
- explain the reasons why the court to which the petition is presented is the correct court[20] (e.g. the High Court where the case is allocated to the London Insolvency District and the debt is over £50,000);
- if the petition is based on a statutory demand, and more than 4 months have elapsed between the service of the demand and the presentation of the petition, explain the reasons for the delay;[21]
- provide a blank box for the court to complete with the details of the venue for hearing the petition;[22]
- state the occupation (if any) of the debtor;[23]
- give the name or names in which the debtor carries on business, if other than the name of the debtor, and whether, in the case of any business of a specified nature, the debtor carries it on alone or with others;
- state the nature of the debtor's business, and the address or addresses at which it is carried on;
- state any name or names, other than the name of the debtor, in which the debtor has carried on business at or after the time when the debt was incurred, and whether the debtor has done so alone or with others;
- set out any address or addresses at which the debtor has resided or carried on business at or after that time, and the nature of that business;
- state whether the centre of main interests or an establishment of the debtor (as defined in Article 3.1 of the EU Regulation[24]) is in another member state;
- state the amount of the debt owed to the petitioner;[25]
- identify the consideration provided for the debt (or, if none, how the debt arises);
- give separate particulars of:

  - when the debt was incurred or became due;
  - any charges or interest not previously notified to the debtor;
  - any charges or interest accruing from time to time;
  - the rate or amount of the charges or interest
  - the grounds for imposing the charge or interest;

- state either:

  - that the debt is unsecured;[26]

---

[19] Rule 10.7(1) of the Insolvency (England and Wales) Rules 2016.

[20] For the basis of selection of the court, see rule 10.11 of the Insolvency (England and Wales) Rules 2016.

[21] Rule 10.7(2) of the Insolvency (England and Wales) Rules 2016.

[22] Rule 10.7(3) of the Insolvency (England and Wales) Rules 2016.

[23] Rule 10.8(1) of the Insolvency (England and Wales) Rules 2016.

[24] As amended by the Insolvency Amendment (EU 2015/848) Regulations 2017 (SI 2017/702).

[25] Rule 10.9(1) of the Insolvency (England and Wales) Rules 2016.

[26] Rule 10.9(1)(f) of the Insolvency (England and Wales) Rules 2016.

> – that if the creditor has security for the debt, the creditor is willing to give up his security for the benefit of all creditors; or
> – the petition is not made in respect of the secured part and an estimate of the secured part of the debt;[27]

- state:

> – that the debt is for a liquidated sum payable immediately, and the debtor appears to be unable to pay it; or
> – that the debt is for a liquidated sum payable at some certain, future time (that time to be specified), and the debtor appears to have no reasonable prospect of being able to pay it;

- as applicable, state:

> – that the petition was based upon a statutory demand which was served upon the debtor,[28] and:
>
> > – the date of service;[29]
> > – the manner of service;
> > – that the demand has neither been complied with nor set aside in accordance with the Rules;
> > – that there is no outstanding application to set the demand aside;
>
> – that the debt arises on a judgment,[30] and:
>
> > – the court dealing with enforcement;
> > – particulars of how the judgment has been returned unsatisfied;

- if not supported by witness statement verifying it, be verified by a statement of truth.[31]

If an IVA is in force, the petition should be presented before the court to which the nominee's report was presented.[32] The petition needs to be presented at or posted to the Chambers of the Bankruptcy Registrar, Royal Courts of Justice, 7 Rolls Buildings, Fetter Lane, London EC4A 1NL or at a Chancery District Registry if:[33]

---

[27] Section 269(1) of the Insolvency Act 1986.

[28] Rule 10.9(2) of the Insolvency (England and Wales) Rules 2016.

[29] For which, see paragraph 14.2.4 of the CPR Practice Direction – Insolvency Proceedings.

[30] Rule 10.9(3) of the Insolvency (England and Wales) Rules 2016.

[31] Rule 10.10(1) of the Insolvency (England and Wales) Rules 2016.

[32] Rule 10.11(6) of the Insolvency (England and Wales) Rules 2016.

[33] Rule 10.11 of the Insolvency (England and Wales) Rules 2016.

- the petition is:

    - for a debt over £50,000;[34]

- and either:

    - for most of the last 6 months or for a longer period than in any other
      insolvency district the debtor carried on business within the London
      Insolvency District or (if he was not in business) has been a resident in
      the London Insolvency District[35] or the petitioner is unable to ascertain
      the debtor's residence or place of business in England and Wales[36] or
      the petitioner has neither been resident nor had a place of business in
      England or Wales in the last 6 months; or
    - the petition is presented by a government department and the statutory
      demand has stated that the petition will be presented in that court or it
      is based on an unsatisfied court order.[37]

Otherwise the petition should be presented at the county court with insolvency
jurisdiction for the area in which the debtor has resided or carried on his principal
place of business for the longest period in the last 6 months.[38]

EVIDENCE

The petition should be verified by a statement of truth. This may be either set out
on the petition itself[39] or be in a separate document on Form Bank 5, which should
be filed at the same time and be deposed to by the petitioner (or one of its officers
if the petitioner is a company) or by a responsible person who is authorised to
make the witness statement and has the requisite knowledge.

The statement of truth should address:

- the name of the debtor;
- the name of the petitioner;
- the court at which the petition is presented;

---

[34] Rule 10.11(1)(a) of the Insolvency (England and Wales) Rules 2016. Below £50,000 and the case
is allocated to the County Court at Central London. This, a little confusingly, is situated in the
Thomas More Building of the Royal Courts of Justice on the Strand, London, whilst the High
Court Bankruptcy Registry is situated, two streets away, also at the Royal Courts of Justice, but
at 7 Rolls Buildings, Fetter Lane, London.

[35] Rule 10.11(2) of the Insolvency (England and Wales) Rules 2016.

[36] In which case, the debtor is deemed to reside in the London Insolvency District: rule 12.5(c) of
the Insolvency (England and Wales) Rules 2016.

[37] In which case, the debtor is deemed to reside in the London Insolvency District: rule 12.5(c) of
the Insolvency (England and Wales) Rules 2016.

[38] Rule 6.9A(2) and (4) of the Insolvency (England and Wales) Rules 2016.

[39] Rule 10.11(2) and (4) of the Insolvency (England and Wales) Rules 2016.

- that the deponent has the requisite knowledge of the matters referred to in the petition;
- how that knowledge was obtained;
- that the statements in the petition are true or true to the best of the deponent's knowledge, information or belief;[40]
- the date of the witness statement;
- be authenticated[41] by:

  - the creditor; or
  - someone authorised by the creditor to do so, stating:[42]

    - that the person is authorised to make the demand on the creditor's behalf;
    - the person's relationship to the creditor.

And should exhibit:

- the petition.[43]

COURT FEES

A court fee of £280[44] is payable, plus a deposit of £990,[45] which will be used to pay the Official Receiver if a bankruptcy order is made.

SERVICE

A sealed copy of the petition should be personally served on the debtor.[46]

Where service is not practicable in this way, an application should be made for substituted service.

A sealed copy of the petition should also be served, if applicable, on the supervisor of any existing voluntary arrangement and any member state liquidator who has been appointed.

A certificate should be prepared proving service. The deponent should be the process server who effected service.

---

[40] Rule 10.10(1) of the Insolvency (England and Wales) Rules 2016.

[41] Rule 10.10(4) of the Insolvency (England and Wales) Rules 2016. For what will suffice as to authentication, see rule 1.5. Hard copy documents must be signed: rule 1.5(2).

[42] Rule 10.10(4)–(5) of the Insolvency (England and Wales) Rules 2016.

[43] Rule 10.10(3) of the Insolvency (England and Wales) Rules 2016.

[44] Paragraph 3.1 of Schedule 1 to the Civil Proceedings Fees (Amendment) Order 2014.

[45] Rule 2(b) of the Insolvency Proceedings (Fees) (Amendment) Order 2016.

[46] Rule 10.14(1) of, and Schedule 3 to, the Insolvency (England and Wales) Rules 2016.

This should address:[47]

- the name of the debtor;
- the name of the creditor;
- the court in which the petition was filed;
- the court number of the petition;
- the date of the petition;
- whether the petition was a sealed copy;
- the date on which service was effected;
- how the deponent effected service of the petition;
- the reaction (if any) to service.

This should exhibit:

- a sealed copy of the petition;
- a sealed copy of any order for substituted service;[48]
- any document evidencing the debtor's acknowledgement of service.

HEARING

At the day of the hearing but before the petition is heard, the petitioner will need to file with the clerk of the court a certificate that the debt is continuing and a list of names and addresses of people who intend to appear on the petition on Form Bank 8 and whether they intend to support or oppose it.[49] Every creditor who intends to appear on the hearing of the petition needs to give to the petitioning creditor notice, giving his name and address and any telephone number, whether his intention is to support or oppose the petition and the amount and nature of his debt. The notice needs to have arrived no later than 4 pm on the business day before the forthcoming hearing.[50] If no notice of intention to appear has been given, then the creditor may only attend with the permission of the court.

The hearing is in chambers before the registrar or district judge. Advocates are not expected to robe. The parties should expect the hearing to be dealt with in a summary fashion and if the petition is opposed, for the petition to be adjourned for a contested hearing before the registrar or district judge. The creditor, the debtor, the supervisor and any creditor who has given notice of their intention to attend on Form Bank 7 may attend the hearing.[51] On each adjourned hearing, the petitioner's representative needs to certify that he has made enquiries of the petitioner within the last business day to confirm the debt is still owing.[52]

---

[47] Schedule 4, paragraph 6 to the Insolvency (England and Wales) Rules 2016.

[48] Schedule 4, paragraph 6(3) to the Insolvency (England and Wales) Rules 2016.

[49] Rule 10.20 of the Insolvency (England and Wales) Rules 2016.

[50] Rule 10.19 of the Insolvency (England and Wales) Rules 2016.

[51] Rule 10.21(3) of the Insolvency (England and Wales) Rules 2016.

[52] Paragraph 14.5 of the CPR Practice Direction – Insolvency Proceedings.

If the registrar adjourns the hearing the petitioning creditor needs to serve the debtor, and any creditors who have given notice of their intention to appear, notice of the adjourned hearing and its venue.[53]

WITHDRAWAL OR DISMISSAL

If the petitioner decides that he wishes to withdraw or seek that his own petition be dismissed, he must seek permission to withdraw it and, unless the court otherwise orders, he must a file a witness statement.[54] The application cannot be heard before the return date of the petition. The witness statement should explain:

- the capacity in which the deponent makes the witness statement;
- the authority the deponent has to make the witness statement;
- that the petitioner seeks permission to withdraw the petition or that the petition is dismissed;
- the grounds of the application;
- the circumstances in which it is made;
- if any payment has been made to settle the petitioner's debt or any arrangement entered into:

  - the dispositions of property made for the purposes of the settlement or arrangement;
  - whether it was the debtor's property or the property of some other person;
  - whether the disposition was made with the approval or ratification of the court.

KEY MATERIALS

Sections 264–271 of the Insolvency Act 1986

264 Who may present a bankruptcy petition
(1) A petition for a bankruptcy order to be made against an individual may be presented to the court in accordance with the following provisions of this Part—

    (a) by one of the individual's creditors or jointly by more than one of them,
    (b) ...
    [(ba) by a temporary administrator (within the meaning of [Article 52 of the EU Regulation]),]

---

[53] Rule 10.23 of the Insolvency (England and Wales) Rules 2016. Evidence of this needs to be filed with the court by the petitioner by certificate: paragraph 14.5.3 of the CPR Practice Direction – Insolvency Proceedings.

[54] Rule 10.30 of the Insolvency (England and Wales) Rules 2016.

[(bb) by an insolvency practitioner (within the meaning of Article 2(5) of the EU Regulation) appointed in proceedings by virtue of Article 3(1) of the EC Regulation,]

(c)   by the supervisor of, or any person (other than the individual) who is for the time being bound by, a voluntary arrangement proposed by the individual and approved under Part VIII, or

(d)   where a criminal bankruptcy order has been made against the individual, by the Official Petitioner or by any person specified in the order in pursuance of section 39(3)(b) of the Powers of Criminal Courts Act 1973.

(2)   Subject to those provisions, the court may make a bankruptcy order on any such petition.

[265 Creditor's petition: debtors against whom the court may make a bankruptcy order]

[(1)   A bankruptcy petition may be presented to the court under section 264(1)(a) only if—

(a)   the centre of the debtor's main interests is in England and Wales, or

(b)   the centre of the debtor's main interests is not in a member state of the European Union which has adopted the [EU Regulation], but the test in subsection (2) is met.

(2)   The test is that—

(a)   the debtor is domiciled in England and Wales, or

(b)   at any time in the period of three years ending with the day on which the petition is presented, the debtor—

(i)   has been ordinarily resident, or has had a place of residence, in England and Wales, or

(ii)   has carried on business in England and Wales.

(3)   The reference in subsection (2) to the debtor carrying on business includes—

(a)   the carrying on of business by a firm or partnership of which the debtor is a member, and

(b)   the carrying on of business by an agent or manager for the debtor or for such a firm or partnership.

(4)   In this section, references to the centre of the debtor's main interests have the same meaning as in Article 3 of the [EU Regulation].]

266 Other preliminary conditions

(1)   Where a bankruptcy petition relating to an individual is presented by a person who is entitled to present a petition under two or more paragraphs of section 264(1), the petition is to be treated for the purposes of this Part as a petition under such one of those paragraphs as may be specified in the petition.

(2)   A bankruptcy petition shall not be withdrawn without the leave of the court.

(3)   The court has a general power, if it appears to it appropriate to do so on the grounds that there has been a contravention of the rules or for any other reason, to dismiss a bankruptcy petition or to stay proceedings on such a petition; and, where it stays proceedings on a petition, it may do so on such terms and conditions as it thinks fit.

(4)   Without prejudice to subsection (3), where a petition under section 264(1)(a), (b) or (c) in respect of an individual is pending at a time when a criminal bankruptcy order is made against him, or is presented after such an order has been so made, the court may on the application of the Official Petitioner dismiss the petition if it appears to it appropriate to do so.

Creditor's petition

267 Grounds of creditor's petition

(1)   A creditor's petition must be in respect of one or more debts owed by the debtor, and the petitioning creditor or each of the petitioning creditors must be a person to whom the debt or (as the case may be) at least one of the debts is owed.

(2)   Subject to the next three sections, a creditor's petition may be presented to the court in respect of a debt or debts only if, at the time the petition is presented—

   (a)   the amount of the debt, or the aggregate amount of the debts, is equal to or exceeds the bankruptcy level,

   (b)   the debt, or each of the debts, is for a liquidated sum payable to the petitioning creditor, or one or more of the petitioning creditors, either immediately or at some certain, future time, and is unsecured,

   (c)   the debt, or each of the debts, is a debt which the debtor appears either to be unable to pay or to have no reasonable prospect of being able to pay, and

   (d)   there is no outstanding application to set aside a statutory demand served (under section 268 below) in respect of the debt or any of the debts.

(3)   A debt is not to be regarded for the purposes of subsection (2) as a debt for a liquidated sum by reason only that the amount of the debt is specified in a criminal bankruptcy order.

(4)   'The bankruptcy level' is £750; but the Secretary of State may by order in a statutory instrument substitute any amount specified in the order for that amount or (as the case may be) for the amount which by virtue of such an order is for the time being the amount of the bankruptcy level.

(5)   An order shall not be made under subsection (4) unless a draft of it has been laid before, and approved by a resolution of, each House of Parliament.

268 Definition of 'inability to pay', etc.; the statutory demand

(1)   For the purposes of section 267(2)(c), the debtor appears to be unable to pay a debt if, but only if, the debt is payable immediately and either—

   (a)   the petitioning creditor to whom the debt is owed has served on the debtor a demand (known as 'the statutory demand') in the prescribed form requiring him to pay the debt or to secure or compound for it to the satisfaction of the creditor, at least 3 weeks have elapsed since the demand was served and the demand has been neither complied with nor set aside in accordance with the rules, or

(b)   execution or other process issued in respect of the debt on a judgment or order of any court in favour of the petitioning creditor, or one or more of the petitioning creditors to whom the debt is owed, has been returned unsatisfied in whole or in part.

(2)   For the purposes of section 267(2)(c) the debtor appears to have no reasonable prospect of being able to pay a debt if, but only if, the debt is not immediately payable and—

(a)   the petitioning creditor to whom it is owed has served on the debtor a demand (also known as 'the statutory demand') in the prescribed form requiring him to establish to the satisfaction of the creditor that there is a reasonable prospect that the debtor will be able to pay the debt when it falls due,

(b)   at least 3 weeks have elapsed since the demand was served, and

(c)   the demand has been neither complied with nor set aside in accordance with the rules.

269 Creditor with security

(1)   A debt which is the debt, or one of the debts, in respect of which a creditor's petition is presented need not be unsecured if either—

(a)   the petition contains a statement by the person having the right to enforce the security that he is willing, in the event of a bankruptcy order being made, to give up his security for the benefit of all the bankrupt's creditors, or

(b)   the petition is expressed not to be made in respect of the secured part of the debt and contains a statement by that person of the estimated value at the date of the petition of the security for the secured part of the debt.

(2)   In a case falling within subsection (1)(b) the secured and unsecured parts of the debt are to be treated for the purposes of sections 267 and 270 as separate debts.

270 Expedited petition

In the case of a creditor's petition presented wholly or partly in respect of a debt which is the subject of a statutory demand under section 268, the petition may be presented before the end of the 3-week period there mentioned if there is a serious possibility that the debtor's property or the value of any of his property will be significantly diminished during that period and the petition contains a statement to that effect.

271 Proceedings on creditor's petition

(1) The court shall not make a bankruptcy order on a creditor's petition unless it is satisfied that the debt, or one of the debts, in respect of which the petition was presented is either—

  (a) a debt which, having been payable at the date of the petition or having since become payable, has been neither paid nor secured or compounded for, or

  (b) a debt which the debtor has no reasonable prospect of being able to pay when it falls due.

(2) In a case in which the petition contains such a statement as is required by section 270, the court shall not make a bankruptcy order until at least 3 weeks have elapsed since the service of any statutory demand under section 268.

(3) The court may dismiss the petition if it is satisfied that the debtor is able to pay all his debts or is satisfied—

  (a) that the debtor has made an offer to secure or compound for a debt in respect of which the petition is presented,

  (b) that the acceptance of that offer would have required the dismissal of the petition, and

  (c) that the offer has been unreasonably refused;
    and, in determining for the purposes of this subsection whether the debtor is able to pay all his debts, the court shall take into account his contingent and prospective liabilities.

(4) In determining for the purposes of this section what constitutes a reasonable prospect that a debtor will be able to pay a debt when it falls due, it is to be assumed that the prospect given by the facts and other matters known to the creditor at the time he entered into the transaction resulting in the debt was a reasonable prospect.

(5) Nothing in sections 267 to 271 prejudices the power of the court, in accordance with the rules, to authorise a creditor's petition to be amended by the omission of any creditor or debt and to be proceeded with as if things done for the purposes of those sections had been done only by or in relation to the remaining creditors or debts.

Rules 10.6–10.17, 10.20–10.26 and 10.30 of the Insolvency (England and Wales) Rules 2016

Application and interpretation

10.6.—(1) This Chapter relates to a creditor's petition and making a bankruptcy order on such a petition.

(2) In this Chapter 'the debt' means the debt in relation to which the petition is presented.

(3) This Chapter also applies to a petition under section 264(1)(c) by a supervisor of, or person bound by, an IVA, with any necessary modifications.

Contents of petition

10.7.—(1) The petition must state—

  (a) the name and postal address of the petitioner;
  (b) where the petitioner is represented by a solicitor, the name, postal address and telephone number of the solicitor;
  (c) that the petitioner requests that the court make a bankruptcy order against the debtor;
  (d) whether—

    (i) the debtor's centre of main interests is within a member State,
    (ii) the debtor's centre of main interests is not within a member State, or
    (iii) the debtor carries on business as an Article 1.2 undertaking;

  (e) whether the debtor—

    (i) is resident in England and Wales, or
    (ii) is not resident in England and Wales;

  (f) whether the petition is presented to—

    (i) the High Court,
    (ii) the County Court at Central London, or
    (iii) a specified hearing centre; and

  (g) the reasons why the court or hearing centre to which the petition is presented is the correct court or hearing centre under rule 10.11.

(2) If the petition is based on a statutory demand, and more than four months have elapsed between the service of the demand and the presentation of the petition, the petition must explain the reasons for the delay.
(3) The petition must also contain a blank box for the court to complete with the details of the venue for hearing the petition.

Identification of debtor

10.8.—(1) The petition must state the following matters about the debtor, so far as they are within the petitioner's knowledge—

  (a) the debtor's identification details;
  (b) the occupation (if any) of the debtor;
  (c) the name or names in which the debtor carries on business, if other than the name of the debtor, and whether, in the case of any business of a specified nature, the debtor carries it on alone or with others;

(d) the nature of the debtor's business, and the address or addresses at which it is carried on;

(e) any name or names, other than the name of the debtor, in which the debtor has carried on business at or after the time when the debt was incurred, and whether the debtor has done so alone or with others;

(f) any address or addresses at which the debtor has resided or carried on business at or after that time, and the nature of that business; and

(g) whether the centre of main interests or an establishment of the debtor (as defined in Article 3.1 of the EU Regulation) is in another member State.[55]

(2) The particulars of the debtor given under this rule determine the title of the proceedings.

(3) If to the petitioner's knowledge the debtor has used any name other than the one specified under paragraph (1)(a), that fact must be stated in the petition.

Identification of debt

10.9.—(1) The petition must state for each debt in relation to which it is presented—

(a) the amount of the debt, the consideration for it (or, if there is no consideration, the way in which it arises) and the fact that it is owed to the petitioner;

(b) when the debt was incurred or became due;

(c) if the amount of the debt includes any charge by way of interest not previously notified to the debtor as a liability of the debtor's, the amount or rate of the charge (separately identified);

(d) if the amount of the debt includes any other charge accruing from time to time, the amount or rate of the charge (separately identified);

(e) the grounds on which any such a charge is claimed to form part of the debt, provided that the amount or rate must, in the case of a petition based on a statutory demand, be limited to that claimed in the demand;

(f) that the debt is unsecured (subject to section 269); and

(g) either—

(i) that the debt is for a liquidated sum payable immediately, and the debtor appears to be unable to pay it, or

(ii) that the debt is for a liquidated sum payable at some certain, future time (that time to be specified), and the debtor appears to have no reasonable prospect of being able to pay it.

(2) Where the debt is one for which, under section 268, a statutory demand must have been served on the debtor, the petition must—

(a) specify the date and manner of service of the statutory demand; and

(b) state that, to the best of the creditor's knowledge and belief—

---

[55] As amended by the Insolvency Amendment (EU 2015/848) Regulations 2017.

      (i)   the demand has been neither complied with nor set aside in accordance with these Rules, and

      (ii) that no application to set it aside is outstanding.

(3)   If the case is within section 268(1)(b) (unsatisfied execution or process in respect of judgment debt, etc.) the petition must state which court issued the execution or other process and give particulars of the return.

Verification of petition

10.10.—(1) The petition must be verified by a statement of truth.

(2)   If the petition relates to debts to different creditors, the debt to each creditor must be separately verified.

(3)   A statement of truth which is not contained in or endorsed upon the petition which it verifies must be sufficient to identify the petition and must contain—

      (a)   the name of the debtor;

      (b)   the name of the petitioner; and

      (c)   the court or hearing centre in which the petition is to be presented.

(4)   The statement of truth must be authenticated and dated by or on behalf of the petitioner.

(5)   Where the person authenticating the statement of truth is not the petitioner, or one of the petitioners, the statement of truth must state—

      (a)   the name and postal address of the authenticating person;

      (b)   the capacity in which, and the authority by which, that person authenticates the statement of truth; and

      (c)   the means of the authenticating person's knowledge of the matters verified.

Court in which petition is to be presented

10.11.—(1) Where the proceedings are allocated to the London Insolvency District under rule 12.5(a)(i) to (iv) or (b), the creditor must present the petition to—

      (a)   the High Court where the debt is £50,000 or more; or

      (b)   the County Court at Central London where the debt is less than £50,000.

(2)   Where the proceedings are allocated to the London Insolvency District under rule 12.5(a)(v), (c) or (d), the creditor must present the petition to the High Court.

(3)   Where the debtor is resident in England and Wales and the proceedings are not allocated to the London Insolvency District, the creditor must present the petition to the debtor's own hearing centre.

(4)   The debtor's own hearing centre is—

(a) where the debtor has carried on business in England and Wales within the six months immediately preceding the presentation of the petition, the hearing centre for the insolvency district where for the longest period during those six months—

(i) the debtor carried on business, or
(ii) the principal place of business was located, if business was carried on in more than one insolvency district; or

(b) where the debtor has not carried on business in England and Wales within the six months immediately preceding the presentation of the petition, the hearing centre for the insolvency district where the debtor resided for the longest period during those six months.

(5) If the debtor is not resident in England and Wales but was resident or carried on business in England and Wales within the six months immediately preceding the presentation of the petition and the proceedings are not allocated to the London Insolvency District, the petition may be presented either to the debtor's own hearing centre or to the High Court.

(6) Unless paragraph (2) applies, where to the petitioner's knowledge there is in force for the debtor an IVA under Part 8 of the Act, the petition must be presented to the court or hearing centre—

(a) to which the nominee's report under section 256 was submitted;
(b) to which an application has been made, where a nominee has made a report under section 256A(3); or
(c) as determined under paragraphs (1) to (5) in any other case.

(7) The petition must contain sufficient information to establish that it is presented in the appropriate court and, where the court is the County Court, the appropriate hearing centre.

10.12.—(1) The petition must be filed with the court.
(2) A petition may not be filed unless—

(a) a receipt for the deposit payable to the official receiver is produced on presentation of the petition; or
(b) the Secretary of State has given notice to the court that the petitioner has made suitable alternative arrangements in accordance with an order made under section 415(3) for the payment of the deposit and that notice has not been revoked.

(3) A notice of alternative arrangements for the deposit may be revoked by a further notice filed with the court.
(4) The following copies of the petition must also be filed with the court with the petition—

(a) one for service on the debtor;

(b)   one copy for the supervisor, if to the petitioner's knowledge there is in force for the debtor an IVA under Part 8 of the Act, and the petitioner is not the supervisor of the IVA; and

(c)   one copy for the liquidator, if to the petitioner's knowledge there is a member State liquidator appointed in main proceedings in relation to the debtor.

(5)   The date and time of filing the petition must be endorsed on the petition and on the copies.

(6)   The court must fix a venue for hearing the petition, and this must also be endorsed on the petition and the copies.

(7)   Each copy of the petition must have the seal of the court applied to it and must be delivered to the petitioner.

10.13.—(1) When the petition is filed, the court must as soon as reasonably practicable deliver to the Chief Land Registrar an application for registration of the petition in the register of pending actions.

(2)   The application must contain—

(a)   a statement that the court is applying for registration of a petition in bankruptcy proceedings as a pending action with the Chief Land Registrar under section 5 of the Land Charges Act 1972;

(b)   the debtor's name;

(c)   the debtor's gender, if known;

(d)   details of the debtor's trade, profession or occupation, including any trading name and, in the case of a partnership, the name and gender, if known, of each of the other partners;

(e)   the postal address for each known place of residence of the debtor, including the debtor's business address where the court considers it to be appropriate for the purpose of the notice;

(f)   the relevant key number allocated by the Land Charges Department;

(g)   the name of the court (and hearing centre if applicable);

(h)   the number and date of the petition; and

(i)   the name and postal address of the petitioner.

(3)   The application must be sealed and dated by the court.

(4)   A separate application must be completed for each debtor and for any alternative name by which the debtor has been or is known (other than any trading name).

Service of petition and delivery of copies

10.14.—(1) The petitioner must serve the petition on the debtor in accordance with Schedule 4 (Service of documents).

(2)   If to the petitioner's knowledge there is in force for the debtor an IVA, and the petitioner is not the supervisor of the IVA, a copy of the petition must be delivered by the petitioner to the supervisor.

(3) If to the petitioner's knowledge, there is a member State liquidator appointed in main proceedings in relation to the debtor, a copy of the petition must be delivered by the petitioner to the member State liquidator.

Death of debtor before service
10.15 If the debtor dies before service of the petition, the court may order service to be effected on the debtor's personal representative, or on such other person as it thinks just.

Amendment of petition
10.16. The petition may be amended at any time after presentation with the court's permission.

Security for costs
10.17.—(1) This rule applies where the debt is a liquidated sum payable at some future time, it being claimed in the petition that the debtor appears to have no reasonable prospect of being able to pay it.

(2) The debtor may apply for an order that the petitioning creditor give security for the debtor's costs.

(3) The nature and amount of the security to be ordered is in the court's discretion.

(4) If an order for security is made then the petition may not be heard until the whole amount of the security has been given.

List of appearances
10.20.—(1) The petitioner must prepare for the court a list of the persons who have delivered a notice under rule 10.19 of their intention to appear.

(2) The list must contain—

(a) the date of the presentation of the bankruptcy petition;

(b) the date of the hearing of the petition;

(c) a statement that the persons listed have delivered notice that they intend to appear at the hearing of the petition;

(d) the name and address of each person who has delivered notice of intention to appear;

(e) in the case of creditors, the amount owed to each such creditor;

(f) the name and postal address of any solicitor for a person listed; and

(g) whether each person listed intends to support the petition, or to oppose it.

(3) On the day appointed for hearing the petition, a copy of the list must be handed to the court before the hearing commences.

(4) If the court gives a person permission to appear under rule 10.19(6) then the petitioner must add that person to the list with the same particulars.

Hearing of petition
10.21.—(1) The petition may not be heard until at least 14 days have elapsed since it was served on the debtor.

(2) However the court may, on such terms as it thinks just, hear the petition at an earlier date, if—

    (a)   it appears that the debtor has absconded;
    (b)   the court is satisfied that it is a proper case for an expedited hearing; or
    (c)   the debtor consents to a hearing within the 14 days.

(3) The following persons may appear and be heard—

    (a)   the petitioning creditor;
    (b)   the debtor;
    (c)   the supervisor of any IVA in force for the debtor; and
    (d)   any person who has delivered a notice under rule 10.19.

Postponement of hearing

10.22.—(1) The petitioner may, if the petition has not been served, apply to the court to appoint another day for the hearing.

(2) The application must state the reasons why the petition has not been served.

(3) Costs of the application may not be allowed in the proceedings except by order of the court.

(4) If the court appoints another day for the hearing, the petitioner must as soon as reasonably practicable deliver notice of that day to any person who delivered notice of intention to appear under rule 10.19 and to any person who must be served with a copy of the petition under rule 10.14.

Adjournment of the hearing

10.23.—(1) This rule applies if the court adjourns the hearing of a bankruptcy petition.

(2) The order of adjournment must identify the proceedings and contain—

    (a)   the date of the presentation of the petition;
    (b)   the order that the further hearing of the petition be adjourned to the venue specified in the order;
    (c)   the venue of the adjourned hearing; and
    (d)   the date of the order.

(3) Unless the court otherwise directs, the petitioner must as soon as reasonably practicable deliver a notice of the order of adjournment to—

    (a)   the debtor; and
    (b)   any person who has delivered a notice of intention to appear under rule 10.19 but was not present at the hearing.

(4) The notice of the order of adjournment must identify the proceedings and—

(a) contain—

    (i)   the date of the presentation of the petition,

     (ii)   the date the order of adjournment was made, and

     (iii) the venue for the adjourned hearing; and

  (b)   be authenticated and dated by the petitioner or the petitioner's solicitor.

Decision on the hearing

10.24.—(1) On the hearing of the petition, the court may make a bankruptcy order if satisfied that the statements in the petition are true, and that the debt on which it is founded has not been paid, or secured or compounded.

(2)   If the petition is brought in relation to a judgment debt, or a sum ordered by any court to be paid, the court may stay or dismiss the petition on the ground that an appeal is pending from the judgment or order, or that execution of the judgment has been stayed.

(3)   An order dismissing or giving permission to withdraw a bankruptcy petition must contain—

  (a)   identification details for the proceedings;

  (b)   the date of the presentation of the bankruptcy petition;

  (c)   the name, postal address and description of the applicant;

  (d)   a statement that the petition has been heard;

  (e)   the order that the petition be dismissed or that, with the permission of the court, the petition is withdrawn;

  (f)   details of any further terms of the order;

  (g)   the date and reference number of the registration of the petition as a pending action with the Chief Land Registrar;

  (h)   an order that the entry relating to the petition in the register of pending actions be vacated on the debtor's application; and

  (i)   the date of the order.

(4)   The order must notify the debtor that it is the debtor's responsibility and in the debtor's interest to ensure that the registration of the petition as an entry, both with the Chief Land Registrar and in the title register of any property owned by the debtor, is cancelled.

(5)   In the case of a petition preceded by a statutory demand, the petition will not be dismissed on the ground only that the amount of the debt was over-stated in the demand, unless the debtor, within the time allowed for complying with the demand, delivered a notice to the creditor disputing the validity of the demand on that ground; but, in the absence of such notice, the debtor is deemed to have complied with the demand if the correct amount is paid within the time allowed.

Vacating registration on withdrawal of petition

10.25. If the petition is withdrawn by permission of the court, the court must deliver to the debtor two sealed copies of the order (one for the Chief Land Registrar).

Non-appearance of petitioning creditor

10.26. A petitioning creditor who fails to appear on the hearing of the petition may not present a petition either alone or jointly with any other person against the same debtor in respect of the same debt without the permission of the court to which the previous petition was presented.

Petitioner seeking dismissal or permission to withdraw

[Note. See rule 10.24 for the contents of an order dismissing or giving permission to withdraw a petition.]

10.30.—(1) Where the petitioner applies to the court for the petition to be dismissed, or for permission to withdraw it, the petitioner must file with the court a witness statement specifying the grounds of the application and the circumstances in which it is made if —

    (a)   a person has delivered notice under rule 10.19 of intention to appear at the hearing of the petition; or

    (b)   the court so orders.

(2)   If any payment has been made to the petitioner since the petition was filed by way of settlement (in whole or in part) of the debt or any arrangement has been entered into for securing or compounding the debt, the witness statement must also state—

    (a)   what dispositions of property have been made for the purposes of the settlement or arrangement;

    (b)   whether, in the case of any disposition, it was property of the debtor, or of some other person; and

    (c)   whether, if it was property of the debtor, the disposition was made with the approval of, or has been ratified by, the court (if so, specifying the relevant court order).

(3)   An order giving permission to withdraw a petition must not be made before the petition is heard.

(4)   The order of dismissal or granting permission to withdraw a bankruptcy petition must contain—

    (a)   identification details for the proceedings;

    (b)   the date of the filing of the bankruptcy petition;

    (c)   the name, postal address and description of the applicant;

    (d)   a statement that the petition has been heard;

    (e)   the order that the petition be dismissed or that, with the permission of the court, the petition is withdrawn;

    (f)   details of any further terms of the order;

    (g)   the date and reference number of the registration of the petition as a pending action with the Chief Land Registrar;

    (h)   an order that the entry relating to the petition in the register of pending actions be vacated on the debtor's application; and

    (i)   the date of the order.

Article 3 of the EU Regulation 2015/848 on Insolvency Proceedings 2015

Article 3
International jurisdiction

1. The courts of the Member State within the territory of which the centre of the debtor's main interests is situated shall have jurisdiction to open insolvency proceedings ('main insolvency proceedings'). The centre of main interests shall be the place where the debtor conducts the administration of its interests on a regular basis and which is ascertainable by third parties.

    In the case of a company or legal person, the place of the registered office shall be presumed to be the centre of its main interests in the absence of proof to the contrary. That presumption shall only apply if the registered office has not been moved to another Member State within the 3-month period prior to the request for the opening of insolvency proceedings.

    In the case of an individual exercising an independent business or professional activity, the centre of main interests shall be presumed to be that individual's principal place of business in the absence of proof to the contrary. That presumption shall only apply if the individual's principal place of business has not been moved to another Member State within the 3-month period prior to the request for the opening of insolvency proceedings.

    In the case of any other individual, the centre of main interests shall be presumed to be the place of the individual's habitual residence in the absence of proof to the contrary. This presumption shall only apply if the habitual residence has not been moved to another Member State within the 6-month period prior to the request for the opening of insolvency proceedings.

2. Where the centre of the debtor's main interests is situated within the territory of a Member State, the courts of another Member State shall have jurisdiction to open insolvency proceedings against that debtor only if it possesses an establishment within the territory of that other Member State. The effects of those proceedings shall be restricted to the assets of the debtor situated in the territory of the latter Member State.

3. Where insolvency proceedings have been opened in accordance with paragraph 1, any proceedings opened subsequently in accordance with paragraph 2 shall be secondary insolvency proceedings.

4. The territorial insolvency proceedings referred to in paragraph 2 may only be opened prior to the opening of main insolvency proceedings in accordance with paragraph 1 where

    (a) insolvency proceedings under paragraph 1 cannot be opened because of the conditions laid down by the law of the Member State within the territory of which the centre of the debtor's main interests is situated; or

    (b) the opening of territorial insolvency proceedings is requested by:

(i)   a creditor whose claim arises from or is in connection with the operation of an establishment situated within the territory of the Member State where the opening of territorial proceedings is requested; or

(ii)   a public authority which, under the law of the Member State within the territory of which the establishment is situated, has the right to request the opening of insolvency proceedings.

When main insolvency proceedings are opened, the territorial insolvency proceedings shall become secondary insolvency proceedings.

The relevant extracts of the CPR Practice Direction – Insolvency Proceedings are reproduced in Chapter 24.

3.1   BANKRUPTCY PETITION

Rules 10.7–10.9
Form Bank 1

Creditor's Bankruptcy Petition on Failure to Comply with a Statutory Demand for a Liquidated Sum Payable Immediately

IN THE HIGH COURT OF JUSTICE
IN BANKRUPTCY

IN THE MATTER OF IAN FLAKEY
AND IN THE MATTER OF THE INSOLVENCY ACT 1986

(a) Insert full name(s) and address(es) of petitioner(s)

I/We (a) ANGRY PLC of 1 Unpaid Bill Street, London

(b) Insert full name, place of residence and occupation (if any) of debtor

petition the court that a bankruptcy order may be made against (b)
IAN FLAKEY

(c) Insert in full any other name(s) by which the debtor is or has been known
(d) Insert trading name (adding 'with another or others', if this is so), business address and nature of business

[also known as (c)   ]
[and carrying on business as (d) FLAKEY ENTERPRISES   ]

(e) Insert any other address or addresses at which the debtor has resided at or after the time the petition debt was incurred
(f) Give the same details as specified in note (d) above for any other businesses which have been carried on at or after the time the petition debt was incurred

[and lately residing at (e) 1 GERANIUM COTTAGE, LONDON
      ]
[and lately carrying on business as (f) WIDGET SELLER

(g) Delete as applicable

and say as follows:—
1. (g) [the debtor's centre of main interests is in England and Wales][the debtor has an establishment in England and Wales.]
OR
The debtor carries on business as an insurance undertaking; a credit institution; an investment undertaking providing services involving the holding of funds or securities for third parties; or a collective investment undertaking as referred to in Article 2.2 of the EU Regulation on Insolvency Proceedings
OR
The debtor's centre of main interests is not within a member State(h)

(h) State how the test in s265 (2) of the IA86 is met

2. The debtor is (g)[not] resident in England and Wales. I am presenting this petition to the (g)[High Court][Central London County Court] because (g)[the proceedings are allocated to the London Insolvency District as][(g)Rule

10.11[(1)[~~(a)~~][(b)]][~~(2)][(5)][(6)~~] applies][and the petition debt is (g)[£50,000 or more]~~[less than £50,000]~~][and within the 6 months immediately preceding its presentation (g)[the debtor carried on business in England and Wales and the debtor carried on business within the area of the London Insolvency District (g)[for the greater part of that period of 6 months]~~[for a longer period than in any other insolvency district]][the debtor has not carried on business in England and Wales but has resided in England and Wales and the debtor resided within the area of the London Insolvency District (g)[for the greater part of that period of 6 months][for a longer period than in any other insolvency district]]~~.

~~OR~~

~~The debtor is (g)[not] resident in England and Wales. I am presenting this petition to this county court because (g)Rule 10.11[(3)][(4)][(a)][(b)] applies [and within the 6 months immediately preceding its presentation (g)[the debtor has carried on business in England and Wales and for the longest part of the period during which the debtor carried on business within that period of 6 months, the [principal] place of business has been situated in the district of this county court][the debtor has not carried on business in England and Wales, but has resided in England and Wales and for the longest part of the period during which the debtor was resident in England and Wales within that period of 6 months, the debtor resided in the Insolvency district of this county court]].~~

(j) Please give the amount of debt(s), what they relate to and when they were incurred. Please show separately the amount or rate of any interest or other charge not previously notified to the debtor **and the reasons why you are claiming it**

(k) Insert date of service of a statutory demand

(l) State manner of service of demand

(m) If 3 weeks have not elapsed since service of statutory demand give reasons for earlier presentation of petition

3. The debtor is justly and truly indebted to us in the aggregate sum of £(j)2,000,000

4. The above-mentioned debt is for a liquidated sum payable immediately and the debtor appears to be unable to pay it.

5. On (k) 1ST APRIL 2020 a statutory demand was served upon the debtor by (l) I FLINGITT-ANRUN in respect of the above-mentioned debt. To the best of my knowledge and belief the demand has neither been complied with nor set aside in accordance with the Insolvency Rules and no application to set it aside is outstanding

(m)

6. I/We do not, nor does any person on our behalf, hold any security on the debtor's estate, or any part thereof, for the payment of the above-mentioned sum

OR

~~I/We hold security for the payment of (g) [part of] the above-mentioned sum.~~

~~I/We will give up such security for the benefit of all the creditors in the event of a bankruptcy order being made.~~

~~OR~~

~~I/We hold security for the payment of part of the above-mentioned sum and we estimate the value of such security to be £   . This petition is not made in respect of the secured part of our debt.~~

Endorsement

This Petition having been issued at the RCJ, 7 Rolls Buildings, Fetter Lane, London, EC4A 1NL will be heard at the time and date pursuant to the endorsement underneath the Court Seal on the front page of this Petition

OR

This petition having been presented to the court on 1ST JUNE 2020
it is ordered that the petition shall be heard as follows:—
Date
Time hours
Place

(n) Insert name of debtor

and you, the above-named (n) IAN FLAKEY , are to take notice that if you intend to oppose the petition you must not later than 7 days before the day fixed for the next hearing
(i) file in court a notice specifying the grounds on which you object to the making of a bankruptcy order; and
(ii) send a copy of the notice to the petitioner or his solicitor. The solicitor to the petitioning creditor is:—(o)

(o) This is the address which will be treated by Court as the Petitions address for service.

Name WIGG & CO
Address 1 LAW STREET, LONDON
Email
Telephone Number   0207 666 6666
Reference DUFFDEBT/1

3.2   WITNESS STATEMENT VERIFYING THE BANKRUPTCY PETITION

Rule 10.10   **Verification of the Petition**
Form Bank 5

IN THE HIGH COURT OF JUSTICE
IN BANKRUPTCY

NO: 666 OF 20[ ]

IN THE MATTER OF IAN FLAKEY

AND

IN THE MATTER OF THE INSOLVENCY ACT 1986

~~I, [Insert Name] of [Insert Address, and occupation, or if none description] say as follows:~~

1. ~~I am the Petitioner.~~
2. ~~The statements in this Petition are made from my own knowledge except where otherwise indicated, in which case I have explained the source of my information and belief.~~
3. ~~The statement in the Petition are true to the best of my knowledge, information and belief.~~
4. ~~(a) I consider the Company's centre of main interest is at OR the Company has an establishment at [Insert address]. Accordingly the EU Regulation on Insolvency Proceedings will apply and these will be main/secondary/territorial proceedings OR the EU Regulation on Insolvency Proceedings will not apply to these proceedings.~~

~~OR~~

I, {GERRY PINK-RIBBON of Wigg & Co, 1 Law Street, London, Solicitor say as follows:

1. I am [~~a director or company secretary or an office holder or~~ the solicitor] of the Petitioner.
2. I am duly authorised by the Petitioner to make this witness statement on it's behalf. The statements in this Petition are made from my own knowledge except where otherwise indicated, in which case I have explained the source of my information and belief.
3. I have been concerned in the matters referred to in the Petition because [~~state source of knowledge of matters referred to~~] I HAVE HAD AT ALL MATERIAL TIMES CONDUCT OF THE CASE ON BEHALF OF THE PETITIONER.
4. the statements in the Petition are true to the best of my knowledge, information and belief.
5. (a) I consider the BANKRUPT's centre of main interest is at 1 GERANIUM COTTAGE, LONDON. Accordingly the EU Regulation on Insolvency Proceedings will apply and these will be main~~/secondary/territorial~~ proceedings ~~OR the EU Regulation on Insolvency Proceedings will not apply to these proceedings.~~

Signed ....
Name: GERRY PINK-RIBBON
Dated: 1st April 2020

(a) Delete as applicable.

3.3   LIST OF APPEARANCES

Rule 10.10   **List of Appearances**
Form Bank 8

IN THE HIGH COURT OF JUSTICE
IN BANKRUPTCY

                                                        NO: 666 OF 20[ ]
IN THE MATTER OF IAN FLAKEY

AND

IN THE MATTER OF THE INSOLVENCY ACT 1986

Bankruptcy Petition presented on 1ST APRIL 2019

To be heard on 1ST MAY 2019

The following persons have given notice that they intend to appear on the hearing of the above-mentioned petition

Name and Address	Name and Address of Solicitors if any	Amount owed to Creditor £	Whether supporting or opposing the petition

3.4   CERTIFICATE OF CONTINUING DEBT

<u>IN THE HIGH COURT OF JUSTICE</u>
<u>IN BANKRUPTCY</u>

<u>NO: 666 OF 20[ ]</u>

IN THE MATTER OF IAN FLAKEY

AND

IN THE MATTER OF THE INSOLVENCY ACT 1986

Bankruptcy Petition presented on 1ST APRIL 2019

CERTIFICATE OF CONTINUING DEBT

I certify that I have/my firm has made enquiries of the petitioning creditor(s) within the last business day prior to the hearing/adjourned hearing and to the best of my knowledge and belief the debt on which the petition is founded is still due and owing and has not been paid or secured or compounded for save as to ...

Signed ....
SNARKEY & SNYDE SOLICITORS

Dated ....

Chapter 4

RESPONDING TO A CREDITOR'S PETITION: NOTICE TO ATTEND AT THE HEARING OF A PETITION

OBJECTIVE

At the day of the hearing but before the petition is heard, the petitioner will need to file with the clerk of the court a list of names and addresses of people who intend to appear on the petition and whether they intend to support or oppose it.[1] Provided a notice has been served, the creditors can be heard on the petition. If no notice of intention to appear has been given, then the list of appearances should state so, and a person who has failed to give notice of his intention to appear will not be heard without the court's permission.[2]

The petitioner will also need to file certificates that the debt is still due and that the debtor and creditors who have given notice have been given notice of the hearing.

NOTICE OF INTENTION TO APPEAR

The notice, on Form Bank 7, must set out:[3]

- the name of the party on behalf of whom it is to be filed;
- the address of the party on behalf of whom it is to be filed;
- the telephone number of the party on behalf of whom it is to be filed;
- the date of the presentation of the bankruptcy petition and a statement that the notice relates to a matter of that petition;
- the date of the hearing of the petition;
- the reference of the party on behalf of whom it is to be filed;
- the name of any other person authorised to speak on his behalf;
- whether that person intends to support or oppose the petition;
- the amount and nature of the debtor's debt (if any).

---

[1]   Rule 10.20 of the Insolvency (England and Wales) Rules 2016.

[2]   Rule 10.19(6) of the Insolvency (England and Wales) Rules 2016.

[3]   Rule 10.19(2) of the Insolvency (England and Wales) Rules 2016.

COURT FEES

No fee is payable simply to respond to a petition.

SERVICE

The notice of intention to appear must be sent so as to reach the petitioner not later than 4 pm on the business day before the hearing. For the computation of business days, Saturdays, Sundays, Good Friday, Christmas Day and bank holidays are excluded.

KEY MATERIALS

Rules 10.17–10.19 and 10.29–10.30 of the Insolvency (England and Wales) Rules 2016

10.17.—(1) This rule applies where the debt is a liquidated sum payable at some future time, it being claimed in the petition that the debtor appears to have no reasonable prospect of being able to pay it.

(2) The debtor may apply for an order that the petitioning creditor give security for the debtor's costs.

(3) The nature and amount of the security to be ordered is in the court's discretion.

(4) If an order for security is made then the petition may not be heard until the whole amount of the security has been given.

Debtor's notice of opposition to petition

10.18.—(1) A debtor who intends to oppose the making of a bankruptcy order must not less than five business days before the day fixed for the hearing—

(a) file a notice with the court; and

(b) deliver a copy of the notice to the petitioning creditor or the petitioner's solicitor.

(2) The notice must—

(a) identify the proceedings;

(b) state that the debtor intends to oppose the making of a bankruptcy order; and

(c) state the grounds on which the debtor opposes the making of the order.

Notice by persons intending to appear

10.19.—(1) A creditor or a member State liquidator appointed in main proceedings in relation to the debtor who intends to appear on the hearing of the petition must deliver a notice of intention to appear to the petitioner.

(2) The notice must contain the following—

    (a)   the name and address of the person, and any telephone number and reference which may be required for communication with that creditor or with any other person (also to be specified in the notice) authorised to speak or act on the person's behalf;

    (b)   the date of the presentation of the bankruptcy petition and a statement that the notice relates to the matter of that petition;

    (c)   the date of the hearing of the petition;

    (d)   in the case of a creditor, the amount and nature of the debt due from the debtor to the creditor;

    (e)   whether the person intends to support or oppose the petition;

    (f)   where the person is represented by a solicitor or other agent, the name, postal address, telephone number and reference number (if any) of that person and details of that person's position with or relationship to the creditor or member State liquidator; and

    (g)   the name and postal address of the petitioner.

(3) The notice must be authenticated and dated by the person delivering it.

(4) The notice must be delivered to the petitioner or the petitioner's solicitor at the address shown in the court records.

(5) The notice must be delivered so as to reach the petitioner (or the petitioner's solicitor) not later than 4 pm on the business day before that which is appointed for the hearing (or, where the hearing has been adjourned, for the adjourned hearing).

(6) A person who fails to comply with this rule may appear and be heard on the hearing of the petition only with the permission of the court.

Substitution of petitioner

10.27.—(1) This rule applies where the petitioner—

    (a)   is subsequently found not to have been entitled to present the petition;

    (b)   consents to withdraw the petition or to allow it to be dismissed;

    (c)   consents to an adjournment;

    (d)   fails to appear in support of the petition when it is called on in court on the day originally fixed for the hearing, or on a day to which it is adjourned; or

    (e)   appears, but does not apply for an order in the terms of the petition.

(2) The court may, on such terms as it thinks just, substitute as petitioner a person who—

    (a)   has delivered a notice under rule 10.19 of intention to appear at the hearing;

    (b)   is willing to prosecute the petition; and

    (c)   was, in the case of a creditor, at the date on which the petition was presented, in such a position in relation to the debtor as would have enabled the creditor on that date to present a bankruptcy petition in relation to a debt or debts owed to that creditor by the debtor, paragraphs (a) to (d) of section 267(2) being satisfied in relation to that debt or those debts.

Change of carriage of petition

10.29.—(1) On the hearing of the petition, a person who has delivered notice under rule 10.19 of intention to appear at the hearing, may apply to the court for an order giving that person carriage of the petition in place of the petitioner, but without requiring any amendment of the petition.

(2) The court may, on such terms as it thinks just, make a change of carriage order if satisfied that—

  (a) the applicant is an unpaid and unsecured creditor of the debtor or a member State liquidator appointed in main proceedings in relation to the debtor; and

  (b) the petitioner either—

    (i)   intends by any means to secure the postponement, adjournment, dismissal or withdrawal of the petition, or

    (ii) does not intend to prosecute the petition, either diligently or at all.

(3) The court must not make such an order if satisfied that the petitioner's debt has been paid, secured or compounded by means of—

  (a) a disposition of property made by some person other than the debtor; or

  (b) a disposition of the debtor's own property made with the approval of, or ratified by, the court.

(4) A change of carriage order may be made whether or not the petitioner appears at the hearing.

(5) If the order is made, the person given the carriage of the petition is entitled to rely on all evidence previously provided in the proceedings.

(6) The change of carriage order will contain—

  (a) identification details for the proceedings;

  (b) the date of the hearing of the petition;

  (c) the name of the person who is willing to be given carriage of the petition ('the relevant person');

  (d) a statement that the relevant person is a creditor of the debtor or a member State liquidator appointed in main proceedings in relation to the debtor;

  (e) the name of the original petitioner;

  (f) a statement that the relevant person has applied for an order under this rule to have carriage of the petition in place of the original petitioner;

  (g) the order that the relevant person must within a period which is specified in the order serve upon the debtor and the original petitioner a sealed copy of the order;

  (h) the order that the further hearing of the petition be adjourned to the venue specified in the order;

(i)   the venue of the adjourned hearing;

(j)   the order that the question of the costs of the original petitioner be reserved until the final determination of the petition; and

(k)   the date of the order.

Petitioner seeking dismissal or permission to withdraw

10.30.—(1) Where the petitioner applies to the court for the petition to be dismissed, or for permission to withdraw it, the petitioner must file with the court a witness statement specifying the grounds of the application and the circumstances in which it is made if—

(a)   a person has delivered notice under rule 10.19 of intention to appear at the hearing of the petition; or

(b)   the court so orders.

(2)   If any payment has been made to the petitioner since the petition was filed by way of settlement (in whole or in part) of the debt or any arrangement has been entered into for securing or compounding the debt, the witness statement must also state—

(a)   what dispositions of property have been made for the purposes of the settlement or arrangement;

(b)   whether, in the case of any disposition, it was property of the debtor, or of some other person; and

(c)   whether, if it was property of the debtor, the disposition was made with the approval of, or has been ratified by, the court (if so, specifying the relevant court order).

(3)   An order giving permission to withdraw a petition must not be made before the petition is heard.

(4)   The order of dismissal or granting permission to withdraw a bankruptcy petition must contain—

(a)   identification details for the proceedings;

(b)   the date of the filing of the bankruptcy petition;

(c)   the name, postal address and description of the applicant;

(d)   a statement that the petition has been heard;

(e)   the order that the petition be dismissed or that, with the permission of the court, the petition is withdrawn;

(f)   details of any further terms of the order;

(g)   the date and reference number of the registration of the petition as a pending action with the Chief Land Registrar;

(h)   an order that the entry relating to the petition in the register of pending actions be vacated on the debtor's application; and

(i)   the date of the order.

The relevant extracts of the CPR Practice Direction – Insolvency Proceedings are reproduced in Chapter 24.

4.1   NOTICE BY DEBTOR OF INTENTION TO OPPOSE BANKRUPTCY PETITION

Rule 10.18   **Debtor's Notice of Opposition to Petition**
Form Bank 6

<u>IN THE HIGH COURT OF JUSTICE</u>
<u>IN BANKRUPTCY</u>

IN THE MATTER OF IAN FLAKEY

AND

IN THE MATTER OF THE INSOLVENCY ACT 1986

(a) Insert name and address   Take not that I (a)
which will be used for service by   intend to oppose the application to make a bankruptcy order
the court   on the following grounds:–
                                     THE DEBT IS BONA FIDE DISPUTED AND I HAVE A
                                     COUNTERCLAIM WORTH
                                     £3,000,000 WHICH IS IN EXCESS OF THE CLAIM MADE

Dated   _____
To the   HIGH COURT OF JUSTICE   court
and to the [solicitors for] the petitioner.

4.2   WITNESS STATEMENT IN OPPOSITION TO THE PETITION FOR BANKRUPTCY

Applicant: I Flakey: 1st: IF1: [ ] 20[ ]

IN THE HIGH COURT OF JUSTICE
BUSINESS AND PROPERTY COURTS OF ENGLAND AND WALES
INSOLVENCY AND COMPANIES LIST (ChD)

NO: [ ] OF 20[ ]

IN THE MATTER OF IAN FLAKEY
AND IN BANKRUPTCY
AND IN THE MATTER OF THE INSOLVENCY ACT 1986

BETWEEN:-

IAN FLAKEY

Applicant

and

ANGRY PLC

Respondent

1ST WITNESS STATEMENT OF IAN FLAKEY

I, IAN FLAKEY of 1 Geranium Cottage, London, Businessman, STATE as follows:

1.   I am the Applicant in this application and the respondent to the Petitioner Company's petition for my bankruptcy.

2.   The matters set out in this witness statement are true and within my own knowledge except where otherwise indicated, in which case I have explained the source of my information or belief.

3.   There is now produced and shown to me a bundle consisting of true copies of the documents I will refer to in my witness statement marked 'IF1'.

4.   I make this witness statement in support of my application to dismiss the said Petition.

5.   On 1st April 2020, I was served with a statutory demand by Angry plc claiming £2,045,687.50 based on an invoice for goods they say were sold and delivered to me. I refer to page [ ] of 'IF1' which is a true copy of the statutory demand.

6.   I made no such order. I refer to page [ ] of 'IF1' which is a true copy of my records for purchases and deliveries for the periods alluded to by Angry plc.

7.   Angry plc did however deliver 1,000 boxes of widgets contaminated with sulphuric acid. The acid not only corroded the widgets delivered but seeped into my own store of widgets rendering them corroded and unusable. I refer to page [ ] of 'IF1' which is a true copy of the photographs of the damaged widgets.

8.   By reason of the matters I describe, not only do I not owe any money for the widgets delivered but I have suffered £100,000 of loss from the damage to my

existing stock of widgets. I refer to page [ ] of 'IF1' which is a true copy of a report on the damage suffered by me by an independent valuer, Uther Unreliable.

9.   In all the circumstances, I ask this Honourable Court that this petition be dismissed.

STATEMENT OF TRUTH

I believe that the facts stated in this Witness Statement are true.

Signed [ ]
Full name [*IAN FLAKEY*]
Dated [ ] 20[ ]

Chapter 5

RESPONDING TO A PETITION: APPLICATION FOR A VALIDATION ORDER

OBJECTIVE

In a bankruptcy, any disposition of the bankrupt's property made after the date of the presentation of the bankruptcy petition until the property vests in his trustee is, unless the court otherwise orders, void.[1] A defence exists, however, for third parties where the payment or property is received before the commencement of the bankruptcy in good faith, for value and without notice of the presentation of the petition.[2]

The effect of this in practice is to sterilise the debtor's ability to trade or make payments and his bankers, as soon as they become aware of the petition, will freeze his bank account. This is because payments into or out of the debtor's bank account are dispositions of property, irrespective of whether the account is in credit or overdrawn.[3]

A validation order is necessary to allow the debtor to use his funds for legal advice and representation.[4]

The debtor may apply to the court for a validation order which operates to allow the debtor to continue to trade by:

- validating dispositions of property in the debtor's ordinary course of business;
- validating payments to and from the debtor's bank account in the ordinary course of business;
- validating specific isolated transactions beneficial to the debtor.

The court is cautious about making such an order and credible evidence needs to be shown that it would benefit all creditors.[5] The court will seek to ensure the

---

[1] Section 284(1)–(3), of the Insolvency Act 1986. It is void not merely voidable: *Bateman v Hyde* [2009] EWHC 81 (Ch), [2009] BPIR 737.

[2] Section 284(4) of the Insolvency Act 1986.

[3] *Re Tain Construction Ltd, Rose v AIB Group (UK) plc* [2003] EWHC 1737 (Ch), [2003] 1 WLR 2791, *Re McGuinness Bros (UK) Ltd* (1987) 3 BCC 571.

[4] *Pettit v Novakovic* [2007] BCC 462.

[5] *Re Fairways Graphics* [1991] BCLC 468.

interests of unsecured creditors are not prejudiced.[6] Transactions which have the effect of reducing the assets available to creditors will not be validated.

APPLICATION

Each application should set out:

- that the application is made under the Insolvency Act 1986 or the Insolvency (England and Wales) Rules 2016 (as the case may be);[7]
- the section number or rule under which relief is sought;[8]
- the name of the parties;[9]
- the name of the bankrupt or debtor;[10]
- the court name;[11]
- the case number;[12]
- the remedy applied for or directions sought;[13]
- the name and address of each person to be served or, if none, stating that that it is intended that no person will be served;[14]
- where there is a requirement for particular persons to be given notice of the application under the Act or Rules, stating the name and address of each such person;[15]
- the applicant's address for service.[16]

The application notice must be authenticated by the applicant or his solicitor.[17]

Any person interested in the transaction (in practice, the application is usually made by the debtor) may apply on notice by application notice Form IAA made to the registrar or district judge. An application should be made to the High Court judge only: (a) where it is urgent and no registrar or district judge is available to hear it; or (b) where it is complex or raises new or controversial points of law; or (c) where it is estimated to last longer than 30 minutes. The application can be made without notice if urgent. Three copies of the application are needed. A draft of the order sought should be attached to the application.

---

[6]   *Re Gray's Inn Construction Co* [1980] 1 WLR 711.

[7]   Rule 1.35(2)(a) of the Insolvency (England and Wales) Rules 2016.

[8]   Rule 1.35(2)(b) of the Insolvency (England and Wales) Rules 2016.

[9]   Rule 1.35(2)(c) of the Insolvency (England and Wales) Rules 2016.

[10] Rule 1.35(2)(d) of the Insolvency (England and Wales) Rules 2016.

[11] Rule 1.35(2)(e) of the Insolvency (England and Wales) Rules 2016.

[12] Rule 1.35(2)(f) of the Insolvency (England and Wales) Rules 2016.

[13] Rule 1.35(2)(g) of the Insolvency (England and Wales) Rules 2016.

[14] Rule 1.35(2)(h) of the Insolvency (England and Wales) Rules 2016.

[15] Rule 1.35(2)(i) of the Insolvency (England and Wales) Rules 2016.

[16] Rule 1.35(2)(j) of the Insolvency (England and Wales) Rules 2016.

[17] Rule 1.35(3) of the Insolvency (England and Wales) Rules 2016. For what amounts to authentication, see rule 1.5. For hard copy applications, this means signed: rule 1.5(2).

COURT FEES

Where the application is made by ordinary application on notice to other parties, a court fee of £155 is payable.[18] Where the application is made by consent or without notice in existing proceedings, a court fee of £50 is payable.[19]

EVIDENCE

The application should be supported by a witness statement from the debtor himself.[20] This should address:

- the debtor's name and address;
- on whom the applicant has given notice of this application and how and when notice was provided;
- the date on which the petition was presented;
- the details of the circumstances leading to the presentation of the petition;
- how and when the applicant became aware of the presentation of the petition;
- whether the bank or the payee is aware the petition has been presented;
- whether the petition debt is admitted or disputed and, if the latter, brief details of the basis on which the debt is disputed;
- full details of the debtor's financial position including details of his assets and liabilities and security upon those assets;
- details of any relevant bank account, including account number, sort code, bank name and branch address;
- the credit (or debit) balance on each account;
- a cash flow forecast and profit and loss projection for the period for which the order is sought;
- details of the dispositions or payments in respect of which an order is sought;
- the reasons relied on in support of the need for such dispositions or payments to be made;
- the effect on the debtor's financial position if the transaction for which permission is sought goes ahead;
- any other factors that might be thought to be relevant to the exercise of the court's discretion;
- details of any consents obtained from the persons affected by the transaction or served with notice of the application;
- details of any property to be sold, mortgaged or re-mortgaged (including its title number);
- the value of the property and the proposed sale price, or details of the mortgage or re-mortgage;

---

[18] Paragraph 3.12 of Schedule 1 to the Civil Proceedings Fees (Amendment) Order 2014.

[19] Paragraph 3.11 of Schedule 1 to the Civil Proceedings Fees (Amendment) Order 2014.

[20] Paragraph 14.8 of the CPR Practice Direction – Insolvency Proceedings.

- details of any existing mortgages or charges on the property and redemption figures;
- the costs of sale (e.g. solicitors' or agents' costs);
- how and by whom any net proceeds of sale (or sums coming into the debtor's hands as a result of any mortgage or re-mortgage) are to be held pending the final hearing of the petition;
- whether the proposed transactions were in good faith and in the ordinary course of business;
- that there was no basis for considering that the transaction might operate to prefer a creditor or guarantor;
- any facts demonstrating the benefit of the transaction to creditors as a whole;
- any facts demonstrating that there is no prejudice to the creditors as a whole by the transaction taking place;
- the detail of the debtor's financial position showing the debtor's trading is profitable.

And should exhibit:

- evidence of the debtor's assets (including details of any security and the amounts secured) and liabilities (e.g. the most recent tax and management accounts and estimated statement of affairs);
- a cash flow forecast and profit and loss projection for the period for which the order is sought;
- evidence of any consents obtained from:

  - the petitioning creditor;
  - any creditor substituted as petitioner;
  - any creditor who has been given carriage of the petition;
  - any creditor who has given notice to the petitioner of his intention to appear on the hearing of the petition pursuant to rule 10.19 of the Insolvency (England and Wales) Rules 2016;

- any draft agreement for any proposed transactions;
- an independent valuation of the property to be disposed of.

If appropriate, this should be supported by a witness statement from the debtor's accountant.[21] This should confirm:

- the financial information given by the debtor;
- that the debtor is solvent and able to pay his debts as they fall due;
- that the proposed transaction or series of transactions in respect of which the order is sought will be beneficial to or will not prejudice the interests of all the unsecured creditors as a class;[22]
- the effect of the transaction on the debtor's financial position.

---

[21] Paragraph 14.8.3 of the CPR Practice Direction – Insolvency Proceedings.

[22] *Denney v John Hudson & Co Ltd* [1992] BCLC 901, CA, *Re Fairway Graphics Ltd* [1991] BCLC 468.

And should exhibit:

- evidence of the bankrupt's assets (including details of any security and the amounts secured) and liabilities, e.g. the latest filed accounts, any draft accounts and estimated statement of affairs);
- a cash flow forecast and profit and loss projection for the period for which the order is sought.

SERVICE

The application should be served on:

- the petitioning creditor;
- any creditor substituted as petitioner;
- any creditor who has been given carriage of the petition;
- any creditor who has given notice to the petitioner of his intention to appear on the hearing of the petition pursuant to rule 10.19 of the Insolvency (England and Wales) Rules 2016.

The application and the evidence in support will need to be filed at court and served on the respondent as soon as practicable after it is filed and in any event, unless it is necessary to apply without notice or on short notice, at least 14 days before the date fixed for the hearing.[23]

The usual rule is that, subject to any other express provision, the application must be served at least 14 days before the date fixed for the hearing.[24] However, the court does have power, in cases of urgency, to hear an application immediately with or without notice to the other parties.[25]

Service may be effected personally[26] or by post on the respondent (Part 6 of the Civil Procedure Rules (CPR) applies for these purposes)[27] or, where they have authority to accept service, on the respondent's solicitors.[28] Electronic service of documents is now permissible under the Rules, providing the respondent currently consents to service in that way and has provided an email address for service in that way.

---

[23] Rule 12.9(3) of the Insolvency (England and Wales) Rules 2016.

[24] Rule 12.9(3) of the Insolvency (England and Wales) Rules 2016.

[25] Rule 12.10 of the Insolvency (England and Wales) Rules 2016.

[26] Rule 1.44 of the Insolvency (England and Wales) Rules 2016.

[27] Schedule 4, paragraph 1(2) to the Insolvency (England and Wales) Rules 2016.

[28] Rule 1.40 of the Insolvency (England and Wales) Rules 2016.

KEY MATERIALS

Section 284 of the Insolvency Act 1986

284 Restrictions on dispositions of property

(1) Where a person is adjudged bankrupt, any disposition of property made by that person in the period to which this section applies is void except to the extent that it is or was made with the consent of the court, or is or was subsequently ratified by the court.

(2) Subsection (1) applies to a payment (whether in cash or otherwise) as it applies to a disposition of property and, accordingly, where any payment is void by virtue of that subsection, the person paid shall hold the sum paid for the bankrupt as part of his estate.

(3) This section applies to the period beginning with the day of the presentation of the petition for the bankruptcy order and ending with the vesting, under Chapter IV of this Part, of the bankrupt's estate in a trustee.

(4) The preceding provisions of this section do not give a remedy against any person—

  (a) in respect of any property or payment which he received before the commencement of the bankruptcy in good faith, for value and without notice that the petition had been presented, or

  (b) in respect of any interest in property which derives from an interest in respect of which there is, by virtue of this subsection, no remedy.

(5) Where after the commencement of his bankruptcy the bankrupt has incurred a debt to a banker or other person by reason of the making of a payment which is void under this section, that debt is deemed for the purposes of any of this Group of Parts to have been incurred before the commencement of the bankruptcy unless—

  (a) that banker or person had notice of the bankruptcy before the debt was incurred, or

  (b) it is not reasonably practicable for the amount of the payment to be recovered from the person to whom it was made.

(6) A disposition of property is void under this section notwithstanding that the property is not or, as the case may be, would not be comprised in the bankrupt's estate; but nothing in this section affects any disposition made by a person of property held by him on trust for any other person.

Paragraph 14.8 of the CPR Practice Direction – Insolvency Proceedings

14.8 Validation orders

14.8.1 A person against whom a bankruptcy petition has been presented ('the debtor') may apply to the court after presentation of the petition for relief from the effects of section 284(1)–(3) of the Act by seeking an order that any disposition of his assets or payment made out of his funds, including any bank account (whether it is in credit or overdrawn) shall not be void in the event of a bankruptcy order being made on the petition (a 'validation order').

14.8.2 Save in exceptional circumstances, notice of the making of the application should be given to (a) the petitioning creditor(s) or other petitioner, (b) any creditor who has given notice to the petitioner of his intention to appear on the hearing of the petition pursuant to r 6.23 1986, (c) any creditor who has been substituted as petitioner pursuant to r 6.30 Insolvency Rules 1986 and (d) any creditor who has carriage of the petition pursuant to r 6.31 Insolvency Rules 1986.

14.8.3 The application should be supported by a witness statement which, save in exceptional circumstances, should be made by the debtor. If appropriate, supporting evidence in the form of a witness statement from the debtor's accountant should also be produced.

14.8.4 The extent and contents of the evidence will vary according to the circumstances and the nature of the relief sought, but in a case where the debtor is trading or carrying on business it should include, as a minimum, the following information:

(1) when and to whom notice has been given in accordance with paragraph 14.8.2 above;
(2) brief details of the circumstances leading to presentation of the petition;
(3) how the debtor became aware of the presentation of the petition;
(4) whether the petition debt is admitted or disputed and, if the latter, brief details of the basis on which the debt is disputed;
(5) full details of the debtor's financial position including details of his assets (including details of any security and the amount(s) secured) and liabilities, which should be supported, as far as possible, by documentary evidence, e.g. accounts, draft accounts, management accounts or estimated statement of affairs;
(6) a cash flow forecast and profit and loss projection for the period for which the order is sought;
(7) details of the dispositions or payments in respect of which an order is sought;
(8) the reasons relied on in support of the need for such dispositions or payments to be made;
(9) any other information relevant to the exercise of the court's discretion;
(10) details of any consents obtained from the persons mentioned in paragraph 14.8.2 above (supported by documentary evidence where appropriate);
(11) details of any relevant bank account, including its number and the address and sort code of the bank at which such account is held.

14.8.5 Where an application is made urgently to enable payments to be made which are essential to continued trading (e.g. wages) and it is not possible to assemble all the evidence listed above, the court may consider granting limited relief for a short period, but there must be sufficient evidence to satisfy the court that the interests of creditors are unlikely to be prejudiced.

14.8.6 Where the debtor is not trading or carrying on business and the application relates only to a proposed sale, mortgage or re-mortgage of the debtor's home evidence of the following will generally suffice:

(1)   when and to whom notice has been given in accordance with 14.8.2 above;
(2)   whether the petition debt is admitted or disputed and, if the latter, brief details of the basis on which the debt is disputed;
(3)   details of the property to be sold, mortgaged or re-mortgaged (including its title number);
(4)   the value of the property and the proposed sale price, or details of the mortgage or re-mortgage;
(5)   details of any existing mortgages or charges on the property and redemption figures;
(6)   the costs of sale (e.g. solicitors' or agents' costs);
(7)   how and by whom any net proceeds of sale (or sums coming into the debtor's hands as a result of any mortgage or re-mortgage) are to be held pending the final hearing of the petition;
(8)   any other information relevant to the exercise of the court's discretion;
(9)   details of any consents obtained from the persons mentioned in 14.8.2 above (supported by documentary evidence where appropriate).

14.8.7 Whether or not the debtor is trading or carrying on business, where the application involves a disposition of property the court will need to be satisfied that any proposed disposal will be at a proper value. Accordingly an independent valuation should be obtained and exhibited to the evidence.

14.8.8 The court will need to be satisfied by credible evidence that the debtor is solvent and able to pay his debts as they fall due or that a particular transaction or series of transactions in respect of which the order is sought will be beneficial to or will not prejudice the interests of all the unsecured creditors as a class (*Denney v John Hudson & Co Ltd* [1992] BCLC 901, [1992] BCC 503, CA; *Re Fairway Graphics Ltd* [1991] BCLC 468).

14.8.9 A draft of the order sought should be attached to the application.

14.8.10 Similar considerations to those set out above are likely to apply to applications seeking ratification of a transaction or payment after the making of a bankruptcy order.

5.1 ORDINARY APPLICATION FOR A VALIDATION ORDER PURSUANT TO SECTION 284 OF THE INSOLVENCY ACT 1986

Form IAA   **Insolvency Act Application Notice**

IN THE HIGH COURT OF JUSTICE
BUSINESS AND PROPERTY COURTS OF ENGLAND AND WALES
INSOLVENCY AND COMPANIES LIST (ChD)
IN BANKRUPTCY

NO: 666 OF 2020

IN THE MATTER OF IAN FLAKEY
AND IN THE MATTER OF THE INSOLVENCY ACT 1986

BETWEEN:-

IAN FLAKEY

Applicant

and

ANGRY PLC

Respondent

Is this application within existing insolvency proceedings? YES/~~NO~~

I (~~We~~), IAN FLAKEY of 1 Geranium Cottage, London intend to apply to the ~~Judge/District Judge~~/Registrar on:

Date: 1st April 2020

Time: 00:00 hours

Place: Royal Courts of Justice, 7 Rolls Buildings, Fetter Lane, London EC4A 1NL

This application having been issued at the RCJ, 7 Rolls Buildings, Fetter Lane, London, EC4A 1NL will be heard at the time and date pursuant to the endorsement underneath the Court Seal on the front page of this application.

FOR AN ORDER THAT:

1. Notwithstanding the presentation of the said Petition:

   a. payments made into or out of the bank accounts of the Applicant at Brassic Bank plc in the ordinary course of his business, and
   b. dispositions of the property of the Applicant made in the ordinary course of his business for proper value (for the avoidance of doubt, including the proposed sale of the van, registration mark 'REK 1' to Foxy Motors Limited for £2,000),

   between the date of presentation of the Petition and the date of judgment on the Petition or further order in the meantime shall not be void by virtue of the provisions of section 284 of the Insolvency Act 1986 in the event of an Order for the Bankruptcy of the Applicant being made on the said Petition provided that Brassic Bank plc shall be under no obligation to verify for itself whether any transaction through the Bankrupt's bank accounts is in the ordinary course of business, or that it represents full market value for the relevant transaction.

2.   The costs of this application be paid by the Petitioner.

Such further and other order and other relief as this Honourable Court thinks fit.

The grounds upon which I seek the above order are set out in the 1st witness statement of Ian Flakey dated 1st April 2020, a copy of which is annexed to this application.

THE NAMES AND ADDRESSES OF THE PERSON(S) UPON WHOM IT IS INTENDED TO SERVE THIS APPLICATION ARE:

Name: ANGRY PLC

Address: 1 UNPAID BILL STREET, LONDON

Name:

Address:

~~OR~~

~~IT IS NOT INTENDED TO SERVE ANY PERSON WITH THIS APPLICATION~~

Dated:

Signed: SNARKEY & SNYDE

Solicitors for the applicant ~~or Applicant~~   *This is the address
Address: 1 LAW STREET, LONDON   which will be treated
Telephone: 0207 666 6666   by Court as the
Email: law@snarkeysnyde.com   Petitions address for
                                                service

If you do not attend, the court may make such order as it thinks just.

5.2   DRAFT VALIDATION ORDER

IN THE HIGH COURT OF JUSTICE
BUSINESS AND PROPERTY COURTS OF ENGLAND AND WALES
INSOLVENCY AND COMPANIES LIST (ChD)

IN THE MATTER OF IAN FLAKEY
IN BANKRUPTCY
AND IN THE MATTER OF THE INSOLVENCY ACT 1986

NO: [ ] OF 20[ ]

BEFORE MR REGISTRAR WISE
DATED: [ ] OF 20[ ]

BETWEEN:-

ANGRY PLC

Petitioner

and

IAN FLAKEY

Respondent

DRAFT MINUTE OF ORDER

UPON the Respondent's application dated [ ]

AND UPON HEARING Counsel for the Petitioner and the Respondent

AND UPON READING the evidence noted as having been read

IT IS ORDERED THAT:

1.   Notwithstanding the presentation of the said Petition:

   a.   payments made into or out of the bank accounts of the Applicant in the ordinary course of his business, and

   b.   dispositions of the property of the Applicant made in the ordinary course of his business for proper value (for the avoidance of doubt, including the proposed sale of the Bankrupt's van, registration mark 'REK 1' to Foxy Motors Limited for £2,000),

   between the date of presentation of the Petition and the date of judgment on the Petition or further order in the meantime shall not be void by virtue of the provisions of section 284 of the Insolvency Act 1986 in the event of an Order for the Bankruptcy of the Applicant being made on the said Petition provided that Brassic Bank plc shall be under no obligation to verify for itself whether any transaction through the Bankrupt's bank accounts is in the ordinary course of business, or that it represents full market value for the relevant transaction.

2.   The costs of this application be paid by the Petitioner.

Dated: [ ] 20[ ]

Service of this order

The Court has provided a sealed copy of this order to the serving party:

SNARKEY & SNYDE
1 LAW STREET
LONDON

5.3 DEBTOR'S WITNESS STATEMENT IN SUPPORT OF AN APPLICATION FOR A VALIDATION ORDER

Applicant: I Flakey: 1st: IF1: [ ] 20[ ]

IN THE HIGH COURT OF JUSTICE
BUSINESS AND PROPERTY COURTS OF ENGLAND AND WALES
INSOLVENCY AND COMPANIES LIST (ChD)

NO: [ ] OF 20[ ]

IN THE MATTER OF IAN FLAKEY
IN BANKRUPTCY
AND IN THE MATTER OF THE INSOLVENCY ACT 1986

BETWEEN:-

IAN FLAKEY

Applicant

and

ANGRY PLC

Respondent

_____

1ST WITNESS STATEMENT OF IAN FLAKEY
_____

I, IAN FLAKEY of 1 Geranium Cottage, London, Businessman, STATE as follows:

1. I am the Applicant in this application and the respondent to the Petitioner Company's petition for my bankruptcy.

2. The matters set out in this witness statement are true and within my own knowledge except where otherwise indicated, in which case I have explained the source of my information or belief.

3. There is now produced and shown to me a bundle consisting of true copies of the documents I will refer to in my witness statement marked 'IF1'.

4. I make this witness statement in support of my application for an order that notwithstanding the presentation of the said Petition:

    a. payments made into or out of my bank accounts at Brassic Bank plc in the ordinary course of my business, and
    b. dispositions of my property made in the ordinary course of my business for proper value (for the avoidance of doubt, including the proposed sale of my van, registration mark 'REK 1' to Foxy Motors Limited for £2,000),

    between the date of presentation of the Petition and the date of judgment on the Petition or further order in the meantime shall not be void by virtue of the provisions of section 284 of the Insolvency Act 1986 in the event of an Order for my bankruptcy being made on the said Petition provided that Brassic Bank plc shall be under no obligation to verify for itself whether any transaction through my bank accounts is in the ordinary course of business, or that it represents full market value for the relevant transaction.

5.   On 1st April 2020, I was served with a statutory demand by Angry plc claiming
      £2,045,687.50 based on an invoice for goods they say were sold and delivered to
      me. I refer to page [ ] of 'IF1' which is a true copy of the statutory demand.

6.   I made no such order and was never delivered any such goods. I refer to page [ ]
      of 'IF1' which is a true copy of my records for purchases and deliveries for the
      periods alluded to by Angry plc.

7.   Upon discovering the statutory demand on my return from the Christmas vacation
      on 5th January 2020, I instructed my solicitors, Silk & Co, to write to Angry plc to
      explain that the debt was disputed.

8.   On 5th January 2020, my solicitors, Silk & Co, wrote to Angry plc explaining that I
      had first seen the statutory demand today, the basis on which the alleged debt is
      disputed and inviting them to withdraw it. They warned that any petition would
      be an abuse of process as the debt was disputed. I refer to page [ ] of 'IF1' which is
      a true copy of my solicitor's letter.

9.   Instead of replying to my solicitor's letter, on 6th January 2020, Gustav Grim of
      Angry plc served me with a bankruptcy petition. I refer to page [ ] of 'IF1' which is
      a true copy of the petition.

10.   Angry plc appears to have told my bank about the petition and my bank, Brassic
      Bank plc, has frozen my account and refused either to accept my customers'
      money or pay out on my cheques.

11.   I trade as sole proprietor of a profitable business and am able to pay my debts as
      they fall due. I refer to page [ ] of 'IF1' which is a true copy of a letter from my
      accountant, Derek Devious, setting out my latest accounts and confirming my
      solvency and setting out of list of my principal assets and their book valuations,
      my liabilities and the mortgage and other securities secured upon them.

12.   I presently hold £50,000 in credit in my bank account and a further £20,000 in
      cheques I have been unable to present at the Bank because of the petition. At
      page [ ] of 'IF1' is a true copy of the most recent statement of my bank account.

13.   But for the presentation of the petition I would have paid £10,000 this month in
      wages, national insurance contributions and PAYE to my employees. I have the
      same liability each month I trade. I would also have wished to pay a further £5,000
      to my suppliers and £1,000 in business rates, electricity and water (I have no
      obligation to pay rent as I own my own premises). As with the wage cost, these
      are monthly outgoings. Next month the VAT quarter falls due and I will have to
      pay an additional £9,000 to HM Revenue & Customs. I refer to page [ ] of 'IF1'
      which is a true copy of a list of payments I would wish to make each month for the
      next three months.

14.   Whilst this would in theory diminish the amount available in my bank account, it
      would allow me to continue to trade. As I have said my business is profitable and
      allowing me to continue to trade would swell the resources available to my
      creditors. I refer to page [ ] of 'IF1' which is a true copy of projections prepared by
      my accountant, Derek Devious, showing my monthly projected profit and loss and
      cashflow if I was allowed to trade over the next quarter.

15.   Before the petition was presented I had agreed to sell my Nogo van, registration mark 'REK 1' to Foxy Motors Limited for £2,000. I refer to page [ ] of 'IF1' which is a true copy of the proposed sale agreement. I had proposed to make the sale because I had discovered it was more cost effective to outsource my deliveries. I refer to page [ ] of 'IF1' which is a true copy of the extract from the current edition of *Glasser's Guide* which shows Nogo vans of the age and condition of ours have a resale value of £2,000. I am anxious to resell the van now because Foxy may withdraw from the sale if I do not complete it soon and if I retain it much longer I will have to be put to the extra expense of an MOT and new tax disk as these fall due next month. In short, the sale benefits not only me but any creditors I may have.

16.   The proposed transactions and payments are to be made in good faith and in the ordinary course of my business. There is no basis for considering that the payments or transaction might operate to prefer some creditor or guarantor over any others. Indeed, this Honourable Court will appreciate that there is no prejudice to the creditors as a whole by the order being granted.

STATEMENT OF TRUTH

I believe that the facts stated in this Witness Statement are true.

Signed [ ]
Full name [*IAN FLAKEY*]
Dated [ ] 20[ ]

5.4 ACCOUNTANT'S WITNESS STATEMENT IN SUPPORT OF AN APPLICATION FOR A VALIDATION ORDER

Applicant: D Devious: 1st: DD1: [ ] 20[ ]

IN THE HIGH COURT OF JUSTICE
BUSINESS AND PROPERTY COURTS OF ENGLAND AND WALES
INSOLVENCY AND COMPANIES LIST (ChD)

NO: [ ] OF 20[ ]

IN THE MATTER OF IAN FLAKEY
IN BANKRUPTCY
AND IN THE MATTER OF THE INSOLVENCY ACT 1986

BETWEEN:-

IAN FLAKEY

Applicant

and

ANGRY PLC

Respondent

1ST WITNESS STATEMENT OF DEREK DEVIOUS

I, DEREK DEVIOUS, Botch Buildings, London, a Certifiable Accountant, STATE as follows:

1.   I am the accountant of the Applicant and I am authorised to make this witness statement on his behalf.

2.   The matters set out in this witness statement are true and within my own knowledge except where otherwise indicated, in which case I have explained the source of my information or belief.

3.   There is now produced and shown to me a bundle consisting of true copies of the documents I will refer to in my witness statements marked 'DD1'.

4.   I make this witness statement in support of Ian Flakey's application for an order that notwithstanding the presentation of the said Petition:

   (a)   payments made into or out of his bank accounts in the ordinary course of his business, and

   (b)   dispositions of his property made in the ordinary course of its business for proper value (including the proposed sale of the company van, registration mark 'REK 1' to Foxy Motors Limited for £2,000),

   between the date of presentation of the Petition and the date of judgment on the Petition or further order in the meantime shall not be void by virtue of the provisions of section 284 of the Insolvency Act 1986 in the event of an Order for his bankruptcy being made on the said Petition provided that (the relevant bank) shall be under no obligation to verify for itself whether any transaction through his bank accounts is in the ordinary course of business, or that it represents full market value for the relevant transaction.

5.   I have read the witness statement of Ian Flakey. I am able to confirm that the financial information set out in the witness statement of Ian Flakey represents an accurate statement of his affairs at the date of this statement and that he is solvent and able to pay his debts as they fall due.

6.   I am able to confirm for the reasons set out in the witness statement of Ian Flakey that the proposed payments described in his witness statement and the sale of Bustco Ltd's Nogo van, registration mark 'REK 1' to Foxy Motors Limited for £2,000 are not prejudicial to the interests of all the unsecured creditors as a class

7.   In reaching this view, I refer to page [ ] of 'DD1' which is a true copy of an estimated statement of affairs I have prepared of his assets and liabilities as at the date of this witness statement (including details of any security and the amounts secured). I refer to pages [ ] to [ ] of 'DD1' which is a true copy of the documents I have relied on as evidence of such assets and liabilities.

8.   I also refer to:

   a)   page [ ] of 'DD1' which is a true copy of his latest personal accounts
   b)   page [ ] of 'DD1' which is a true copy of a cash flow forecast for the period for which the order is sought which I prepared for Mr Flakey
   c)   page [ ] of 'DD1' which is a true copy of a cash flow and profit and loss projection for the period for which the order is sought which I prepared for Mr Flakey.

STATEMENT OF TRUTH

I believe that the facts stated in this Witness Statement are true.

Signed [ ]
Full name [*DEREK DEVIOUS*]
Dated [ ] 20[ ]

Chapter 6

APPLICATION TO ANNUL A BANKRUPTCY ORDER

OBJECTIVE

Bankruptcy will normally end on discharge; however, this does not reverse the vesting of the bankrupt's estate upon his trustee. Annulment, by contrast, renders the bankruptcy order as if it had never been made. An order for annulment may be made whether or not the bankruptcy order has been discharged.[1]

Further, the court will annul a bankruptcy if it is satisfied that an IVA has been approved in respect of the bankrupt.[2]

The court may[3] annul a bankruptcy order if it at any time appears to the court either:

- that, on the grounds existing at the time the order was made, the order ought not to have been made;[4] or
- that, to the extent required by the rules, the bankruptcy debts and the expenses of the bankruptcy have all, since the making of the order, been either paid or secured for to the satisfaction of the court.[5]

Demonstrating that the bankruptcy order ought not to have been made needs to be done on the grounds that existed at the time the order was made. The basis must be the facts existing at the time. It does not matter that those facts were unknown to the debtor at the time.[6] Thus if at the time of the petition the debt did not exist, was illegal or otherwise unenforceable, it could not support a bankruptcy order.[7]

---

[1] Section 282(3) of the Insolvency Act 1986.

[2] Section 261(2) of the Insolvency Act 1986.

[3] Annulment under these grounds is discretionary and it is within the court's powers to refuse an annulment: *Omokwe v HFC* [2007] BPIR 1157. The discretion to refuse, however, does not arise where it is clear that the court lacks jurisdiction to make a bankruptcy order in the first place: *Raiffeisenlandesbank Oberoisterreich v Meyben* [2016] EWHC 414 (Ch), [2016] BPIR 697.

[4] Section 282(1)(a) of the Insolvency Act 1986.

[5] Section 282(1)(b) of the Insolvency Act 1986.

[6] *Henwood v Customs & Excise* [1998] BPIR 339.

[7] *Royal Bank of Scotland v Farley* [1996] BPIR 638.

Payment of the bankruptcy debts means not just the petition debt but: (a) any debt or liability to which the bankrupt is subject at the commencement of the bankruptcy; (b) any debt or liability to which he may become subject after the commencement of the bankruptcy (including after his discharge from bankruptcy) by reason of any obligation incurred before the commencement of the bankruptcy; and (c) any interest provable as set out in section 322(2) in Chapter IV of Part IX of the Insolvency Act 1986. It is important to remember that the bankrupt has no title to his property until the bankruptcy order is annulled as he is unable to offer the property within the bankruptcy estate as security until it is re-vested upon him. Further provision needs to be made to secure not only the debt but also the Official Receiver's costs to the close of the date of the annulment hearing. It is possible for the court to make an order for annulment but to direct that the order is not to be drawn until the Official Receiver has notified the court that debts in the sum specified in the bankruptcy order have been paid, and that there is security in relation to any other unproven sums.

APPLICATION

The application is made on Form IAA. The application should set out:

- that the application is made under the Insolvency Act 1986 or the Insolvency (England and Wales) Rules 2016 (as the case may be);[8]
- the section number or rule under which relief is sought;[9]
- the name of the parties;[10]
- the name of the bankrupt or debtor;[11]
- the court name;[12]
- the case number;[13]
- the remedy applied for or directions sought;[14]
- the name and address of each person to be served or, if none, stating that that it is intended that no person will be served;[15]
- where there is a requirement for particular persons to be given notice of the application under the Act or Rules, stating the name and address of each such person;[16]
- the applicant's address for service.[17]

---

[8] Rule 1.35(2)(a) of the Insolvency (England and Wales) Rules 2016.
[9] Rule 1.35(2)(b) of the Insolvency (England and Wales) Rules 2016.
[10] Rule 1.35(2)(c) of the Insolvency (England and Wales) Rules 2016.
[11] Rule 1.35(2)(d) of the Insolvency (England and Wales) Rules 2016.
[12] Rule 1.35(2)(e) of the Insolvency (England and Wales) Rules 2016.
[13] Rule 1.35(2)(f) of the Insolvency (England and Wales) Rules 2016.
[14] Rule 1.35(2)(g) of the Insolvency (England and Wales) Rules 2016.
[15] Rule 1.35(2)(h) of the Insolvency (England and Wales) Rules 2016.
[16] Rule 1.35(2)(i) of the Insolvency (England and Wales) Rules 2016.
[17] Rule 1.35(2)(j) of the Insolvency (England and Wales) Rules 2016.

The application notice must be authenticated by the applicant or his solicitor.[18]

Any person interested[19] (in practice, the application is usually made by the bankrupt) may apply on notice by ordinary application to the registrar or district judge. The application under section 282(1) of the Insolvency Act 1986 must state if annulment is being sought under section 282(1)(a) or section 282(1)(b).

COURT FEES

Where the application is made by ordinary application on notice to other parties, a court fee of £155 is payable.[20] Where the application is made by consent or without notice in existing proceedings, a court fee of £50 is payable.[21]

EVIDENCE

The application should be supported by a witness statement. This should address:[22]

- the debtor's name and address;
- the date on which the petition was presented;
- the date on which the bankruptcy order was made;
- the grounds upon which the applicant relies (i.e that the order ought not to have been made or that the debts and expenses of the bankruptcy have all been paid or secured or that an IVA has been approved);
- every fact relied on to establish that the ground is made out;
- if the application is under section 282(1)(b), evidence that:

  - all bankruptcy debts which have been proved have been either paid in full, or secured in full to the satisfaction of the court;
  - interest has been paid on the bankruptcy debts where appropriate (giving details of how much);
  - if a debt is disputed, or a creditor who has proved can no longer be traced, sufficient security has been given (in the form of money paid into court, or a bond entered into with approved sureties) to satisfy any sum that may subsequently be proved to be due to the creditor concerned and costs.

---

18 Rule 1.35(3) of the Insolvency (England and Wales) Rules 2016. For what amounts to authentication, see rule 1.5. For hard copy applications, this means signed: rule 1.5(2).

19 See, for example, *Paulin v Paulin* [2009] EWCA Civ 221, [2009] BPIR 572, where a wife applied for the annulment of her husband's bankruptcy on the basis that it was being deployed as a tactic to defeat her matrimonial proceedings.

20 Paragraph 3.12 of Schedule 1 to the Civil Proceedings Fees (Amendment) Order 2014.

21 Paragraph 3.11 of Schedule 1 to the Civil Proceedings Fees (Amendment) Order 2014.

22 Rule 10.132, (2) and (3) of the Insolvency (England and Wales) Rules 2016.

And should exhibit:

- any correspondence from the trustee;
- any evidence supporting the claim:

  - for example, proof of the indebtedness and of payment.

SERVICE

The application should be served on:

- the trustee in bankruptcy;[23]
- the Official Receiver;[24]
- the petitioning creditor, where the application is made under section 282(1)(a);[25]
- the bankrupt, where the application is made by a person other than the bankrupt.[26]

The application and the evidence in support will need to be filed at court and served on the respondent as soon as practicable after it is filed and in any event, unless it is necessary to apply without notice or on short notice, at least 14 days before the date fixed for the hearing.[27]

The usual rule is that, subject to any other express provision, the application must be served at least 14 days before the date fixed for the hearing.[28] However, the court does have power, in cases of urgency, to hear an application immediately with or without notice to the other parties.[29] Where the application is made under section 282(1)(b) of the Insolvency Act 1986, the application notice and supporting evidence must be served at least 28 days before the date of the hearing.[30]

Service may be effected personally[31] or by post on the respondent (Part 6 of the CPR applies for these purposes)[32] or, where they have authority to accept service, on the respondent's solicitors.[33] Electronic service of documents is now

---

[23] Rules 10.132(6) and 10.132(7) of the Insolvency (England and Wales) Rules 2016.

[24] Rules 10.132(6) and 10.132(7) of the Insolvency (England and Wales) Rules 2016.

[25] Rule 10.132(6) of the Insolvency (England and Wales) Rules 2016.

[26] Rule 10.132(8) of the Insolvency (England and Wales) Rules 2016.

[27] Rule 12.9(3) of the Insolvency (England and Wales) Rules 2016.

[28] Rule 12.9(3) of the Insolvency (England and Wales) Rules 2016.

[29] Rule 12.10(1) of the Insolvency (England and Wales) Rules 2016.

[30] Rule 10.132(7) of the Insolvency (England and Wales) Rules 2016.

[31] Rule 1.44 of the Insolvency (England and Wales) Rules 2016.

[32] Schedule 4, paragraph 1(2) to the Insolvency (England and Wales) Rules 2016.

[33] Rule 1.40 of the Insolvency (England and Wales) Rules 2016.

permissible under the Rules, providing the respondent currently consents to service in that way and has provided an email address for service in that way.[34]

REPORT BY TRUSTEE

Not less than 21 days before the date fixed for the hearing, the trustee or the Official Receiver sends to the applicant and files at court a report dealing with: (a) the circumstances leading to the bankruptcy; (b) the extent of the bankrupt's assets and liabilities at the date of the bankruptcy order and at the date of the present application; (c) details of creditors (if any) who are known to him to have claims, but have not proved; (d) such other matters as the person making the report considers to be, in the circumstances, necessary for the information of the court; (e) particulars of the extent (if any) to which, and the manner in which, the debts and expenses of the bankruptcy have been paid or secured; and (f) in so far as debts and expenses are unpaid but secured, the person making the report shall state in it whether and to what extent he considers the security to be satisfactory.

It will also include a statement of: (a) the trustee's remuneration; (b) the basis fixed for the trustee's remuneration; and (c) the expenses incurred by the trustee.

APPLICANT'S CLAIM THAT REMUNERATION IS OR EXPENSES ARE EXCESSIVE

If an application for annulment is made under section 282(1)(b) of the Insolvency Act 1986, the applicant may also apply to the court no later than 5 business days before the date fixed for the annulment hearing for an order reducing the trustee in bankruptcy fees and/or requiring their repayment on the ground that the remuneration charged or expenses incurred by the trustee is or are, in all the circumstances, excessive.[35] The application must be accompanied by a copy of any evidence which the applicant intends to adduce in support.

HEARING

Where the application for annulment is made under section 282(1)(b) of the Insolvency Act 1986 and it has been reported that there are known creditors of the bankrupt who have not proved, the court may give directions to allow them an opportunity to prove their debts.

The trustee will attend the hearing of the application. The Official Receiver may attend, but is not required to do so unless he has filed a report under rule 10.134 of the Insolvency (England and Wales) Rules 2016.

---

[34] Rule 1.45(2) of the Insolvency (England and Wales) Rules 2016.

[35] Rule 10.134 of the Insolvency (England and Wales) Rules 2016.

KEY MATERIALS

Sections 261 and 282 of the Insolvency Act 1986

261 Additional effect on undischarged bankrupt
(1) This section applies where—

    (a) the creditors' meeting summoned under section 257 approves the proposed voluntary arrangement (with or without modifications), and

    (b) the debtor is an undischarged bankrupt.

(2) Where this section applies the court shall annul the bankruptcy order on an application made—

    (a) by the bankrupt, or

    (b) where the bankrupt has not made an application within the prescribed period, by the official receiver.

(3) An application under subsection (2) may not be made—

    (a) during the period specified in section 262(3)(a) during which the decision of the creditors' meeting can be challenged by application under section 262,

    (b) while an application under that section is pending, or

    (c) while an appeal in respect of an application under that section is pending or may be brought.

(4) Where this section applies the court may give such directions about the conduct of the bankruptcy and the administration of the bankrupt's estate as it thinks appropriate for facilitating the implementation of the approved voluntary arrangement.

282 Court's power to annul bankruptcy order
(1) The court may annul a bankruptcy order if it at any time appears to the court—

    (a) that, on the grounds existing at the time the order was made, the order ought not to have been made, or

    (b) that, to the extent required by the rules, the bankruptcy debts and the expenses of the bankruptcy have all, since the making of the order, been either paid or secured for to the satisfaction of the court.

(2) The court may annul a bankruptcy order made against an individual on a petition under paragraph (a), (b) or (c) of section 264(1) if it at any time appears to the court, on an application by the Official Petitioner—

    (a) that the petition was pending at a time when a criminal bankruptcy order was made against the individual or was presented after such an order was so made, and

(b)   no appeal is pending (within the meaning of section 277) against the individual's conviction of any offence by virtue of which the criminal bankruptcy order was made;

and the court shall annul a bankruptcy order made on a petition under section 264(1)(d) if it at any time appears to the court that the criminal bankruptcy order on which the petition was based has been rescinded in consequence of an appeal.

(3)   The court may annul a bankruptcy order whether or not the bankrupt has been discharged from the bankruptcy.

(4)   Where the court annuls a bankruptcy order (whether under this section or under section 261 or 263D in Part VIII)—

(a)   any sale or other disposition of property, payment made or other thing duly done, under any provision in this Group of Parts, by or under the authority of the official receiver or a trustee of the bankrupt's estate or by the court is valid, but

(b)   if any of the bankrupt's estate is then vested, under any such provision, in such a trustee, it shall vest in such person as the court may appoint or, in default of any such appointment, revert to the bankrupt on such terms (if any) as the court may direct;

and the court may include in its order such supplemental provisions as may be authorised by the rules.

(5)   . . .

Rules 10.132–10.141 of the Insolvency (England and Wales) Rules 2016

Application for annulment

10.132.—(1) An application to the court under section 282(1) for the annulment of a bankruptcy order must specify whether it is made—

(a)   under subsection (1)(a) (claim that the order ought not to have been made); or

(b)   under subsection (1)(b) (debts and expenses of the bankruptcy all paid or secured).

(2)   The application must be supported by a witness statement stating the grounds on which it is made.

(3)   Where the application is made under section 282(1)(b), the witness statement must contain all the facts by reference to which, under the Act and these Rules, the court may be satisfied that the condition in section 282(1)(b) applies before annulling the bankruptcy order.

(4)   A copy of the application and the witness statement in support must be filed with the court.

(5)   The court must deliver notice of the venue fixed for the hearing to the applicant.

(6) Where the application is made under section 282(1)(a) the applicant must deliver notice of the venue, accompanied by copies of the application and the supporting witness statement, to the official receiver, the trustee (if different), and the person on whose petition the bankruptcy order was made in sufficient time to enable them to be present at the hearing.

(7) Where the application is made under section 282(1)(b) the applicant must deliver notice of the venue, accompanied by copies of the application and the supporting witness statement, to the official receiver and the trustee (if different) not less than 28 days before the hearing.

(8) Where the applicant is not the bankrupt, all notices, documents and evidence required by this Chapter to be delivered to another party by the applicant must also be delivered to the bankrupt.

Report by trustee

10.133.—(1) The following applies where the application is made under section 282(1)(b) (debts and expenses of the bankruptcy all paid or secured).

(2) Not less than 21 days before the date fixed for the hearing, the trustee must file with the court a report relating to the following matters—

    (a) the circumstances leading to the bankruptcy;

    (b) a summary of the bankrupt's assets and liabilities at the date of the bankruptcy order and at the date of the application;

    (c) details of any creditors who are known to the trustee to have claims, but have not proved; and

    (d) such other matters as the person making the report considers to be, in the circumstances, necessary for the information of the court.

(3) Where the trustee is other than the official receiver, the report must also include a statement of—

    (a) the trustee's remuneration;

    (b) the basis fixed for the trustee's remuneration under rule 18.16; and

    (c) the expenses incurred by the trustee.

(4) The report must include particulars of the extent to which, and the manner in which, the debts and expenses of the bankruptcy have been paid or secured.

(5) In so far as debts and expenses are unpaid but secured, the person making the report must state in it whether and to what extent that person considers the security to be satisfactory.

(6) A copy of the report must be delivered to the applicant as soon as reasonably practicable after it is filed with the court and the applicant may file a further witness statement in answer to statements made in the report.

(7) Copies of any such witness statement must be delivered by the applicant to the official receiver and the trustee (if different).

(8) If the trustee is other than the official receiver, a copy of the trustee's report must be delivered to the official receiver at least 21 days before the hearing.

(9) The official receiver may then file an additional report, a copy of which must be delivered to the applicant and the trustee (if not the official receiver) at least five business days before the hearing.

Applicant's claim that remuneration or expenses are excessive

10.134.—(1) Where the trustee is other than the official receiver and application for annulment is made under section 282(1)(b), the applicant may also apply to the court for one or more of the orders in paragraph (4) on the ground that the remuneration charged, or expenses incurred, by the trustee are in all the circumstances excessive.

(2) Application for such an order must be made no later than five business days before the date fixed for the hearing of the application for annulment and be accompanied by a copy of any evidence which the applicant intends to provide in support.

(3) The applicant must deliver a copy of the application and of any evidence accompanying it to the trustee as soon as reasonably practicable after the application is made.

(4) If the court annuls the bankruptcy order under section 282(1)(b) and considers the application to be well-founded, it must also make one or more of the following orders—

  (a) an order reducing the amount of remuneration which the trustee was entitled to charge;
  (b) an order that some or all of the remuneration or expenses in question be treated as not being bankruptcy expenses;
  (c) an order that the trustee or the trustee's personal representative pay to the applicant the amount of the excess of remuneration or expenses or such part of the excess as the court may specify; and
  (d) any other order that the court thinks just.

Power of court to stay proceedings

10.135.—(1) The court may, in advance of the hearing, make an order staying any proceedings which it thinks ought, in the circumstances of the application, to be stayed.

(2) Except in relation to an application for an order staying all or any part of the proceedings in the bankruptcy, application for an order under this rule may be made without notice to any other party.

(3) Where an application is made under this rule for an order staying all or any part of the proceedings in the bankruptcy, the applicant must deliver copies of the application to the official receiver and the trustee, if other than the official receiver, in sufficient time to enable them to be present at the hearing and make representations.

(4) Where the court makes an order under this rule staying all or any part of the proceedings in the bankruptcy, the rules in this Chapter nevertheless continue to apply to any application for, or other matters in connection with, the annulment of the bankruptcy order.

(5) If the court makes an order under this rule, it must deliver copies of the order to the applicant, the official receiver and the trustee (if different).

Notice to creditors who have not proved

10.136. Where the application for annulment is made under section 282(1)(b) and it has been reported to the court under rule 10.133(2)(c) that there are known creditors of the bankrupt who have not proved, the court may—

    (a) direct the trustee or, if no trustee has been appointed, the official receiver to deliver notice of the application to such of those creditors as the court thinks ought to be informed of it, with a view to their proving for their debts within 21 days;

    (b) direct the trustee or, if no trustee has been appointed, the official receiver to advertise the fact that the application has been made, so that creditors who have not proved may do so within a specified time; and

    (c) adjourn the application meanwhile, for any period not less than 35 days.

The hearing

10.137.—(1) The trustee must attend the hearing of the application under section 282(1) unless the court directs otherwise.

(2) The official receiver, if not the trustee, may attend, but is not required to do so unless the official receiver has filed a report under rule 10.133.

(3) If the court makes an order on the application or on an application under rule 10.134, it must deliver copies of the order to the applicant, the official receiver and (if other) the trustee.

(4) An order of annulment under section 282 must contain—

    (a) identification details for the proceedings;

    (b) the name and address of the applicant;

    (c) the date of the bankruptcy order;

    (d) the date of the filing of the bankruptcy petition or the making of the bankruptcy application;

    (e) the date and reference number of the registration of the bankruptcy petition or bankruptcy application as a pending action with the Chief Land Registrar;

    (f) the date and reference number of the registration of the bankruptcy order on the register of writs and orders affecting land with the Chief Land Registrar;

    (g) a statement that it appears to the court that—

        (i) the bankruptcy order ought not to have been made, or

        (ii) the bankruptcy debts and expenses of the bankruptcy have all been paid or secured to the satisfaction of the court;

    and that under section 282(2) the bankruptcy order ought to be annulled;

    (h) an order—

        (i) that the bankruptcy order specified in the order is annulled,

        (ii) that the bankruptcy petition or bankruptcy application specified in the order be dismissed, and

      (iii) that the registration of the petition or the bankruptcy application as a pending action with the Chief Land Registrar and of the bankruptcy order with the Chief Land Registrar specified in the order be vacated upon application made by the bankrupt; and

    (i)   the date of the order.

(5)   The order must contain a notice to the bankrupt stating—

    (a)   should the bankrupt require notice of the order to be gazetted and to be advertised in the same manner as the bankruptcy order was advertised, the bankrupt must within 28 days deliver notice of that requirement to the official receiver; and

    (b)   it is the bankrupt's responsibility and in the bankrupt's interest to ensure that the registration of the petition or bankruptcy application and of the bankruptcy order with the Chief Land Registrar are cancelled.

Matters to be proved under section 282(1)(b)

10.138.—(1) This rule applies in relation to the matters which—

    (a)   must, in an application under section 282(1)(b), be proved to the satisfaction of the court; and

    (b)   may be taken into account by the court on hearing such an application.

(2)   Subject to the following paragraph, all bankruptcy debts which have been proved must have been—

    (a)   paid in full; or

    (b)   secured in full to the satisfaction of the court.

(3)   If a debt is disputed, or a creditor who has proved can no longer be traced, the bankrupt must have given such security (in the form of money paid into court, or a bond entered into with approved sureties) as the court considers adequate to satisfy any sum that may subsequently be proved to be due to the creditor concerned and (if the court thinks just) costs.

(4)   Where such security has been given in the case of an untraced creditor, the court may direct that particulars of the alleged debt, and the security, be advertised in such manner as it thinks just.

(5)   If the court directs such advertisement and no claim on the security is made within 12 months from the date of the advertisement (or the first advertisement, if more than one), the court must, on application, order the security to be released.

(6)   In determining whether to annul a bankruptcy order under section 282(1)(b), the court may, if it thinks just and without prejudice to the generality of its discretion under section 282(1), take into account whether any sums have been paid or payment of any sums has been secured in respect of post-commencement interest on the bankruptcy debts which have been proved.

(7) For the purposes of paragraphs (2) and (6), security includes an undertaking given by a solicitor and accepted by the court.

(8) For the purposes of paragraph (6), 'post-commencement interest' means interest on the bankruptcy debts at the rate specified in section 328(5) in relation to periods during which those debts have been outstanding since the commencement of the bankruptcy.

Notice to creditors

10.139.—(1) Where the official receiver has delivered notice of the debtor's bankruptcy to the creditors and the bankruptcy order is annulled, the official receiver must as soon as reasonably practicable deliver notice of the annulment to them.

(2) Expenses incurred by the official receiver in delivering such notice are a charge in the official receiver's favour on the property of the former bankrupt, whether or not the property is actually in the official receiver's hands.

(3) Where any property is in the hands of a trustee or any person other than the former bankrupt, the official receiver's charge is subject to any costs that may be incurred by the trustee or that other person in effecting realisation of the property for the purpose of satisfying the charge.

Other matters arising on annulment

10.140.—(1) Within 28 days of the making of an order under section 282, the former bankrupt may require the official receiver to publish a notice of the making of the order in accordance with paragraphs (2) and (3).

(2) As soon as reasonably practicable the notice must be—

(a) gazetted; and
(b) advertised in the same manner as the bankruptcy order to which it relates was advertised.

(3) The notice must state—

(a) the name of the former bankrupt;
(b) the date on which the bankruptcy order was made;
(c) that the bankruptcy order against the former bankrupt has been annulled under section 282(1); and
(d) the date of the annulment.

(4) Where the former bankrupt—

(a) has died; or
(b) is a person lacking capacity to manage the person's own affairs (within the meaning of the Mental Capacity Act 2005);

the reference to the former bankrupt in paragraph (1) is to be read as referring to the former bankrupt's personal representative or, as the case may be, a person appointed by the court to represent or act for the former bankrupt.

Trustee's final account

10.141.—(1) Where a bankruptcy order is annulled under section 282, this does not of itself release the trustee from any duty or obligation, imposed on the trustee by or under the Act or these Rules, to account for all of the trustee's transactions in connection with the former bankrupt's estate.

(2) The trustee must deliver a copy of the trustee's final account to the Secretary of State as soon as practicable after the court's order annulling the bankruptcy order.

(3) The trustee must file a copy of the final account with the court.

(4) The final account must include a summary of the trustee's receipts and payments in the administration, and contain a statement to the effect that the trustee has reconciled the account with that which is held by the Secretary of State in respect of the bankruptcy.

(5) The trustee is released from such time as the court may determine, having regard to whether—

(a) the trustee has delivered the final accounts under paragraph (2); and

(b) any security given under rule 10.138 has been, or will be, released.

6.1   APPLICATION FOR ANNULMENT UNDER SECTION 282(1)(B) OF THE INSOLVENCY ACT 1986

Form IAA   **Insolvency Act Application Notice**

IN THE HIGH COURT OF JUSTICE
BUSINESS AND PROPERTY COURTS OF ENGLAND AND WALES
INSOLVENCY AND COMPANIES LIST (ChD)
IN BANKRUPTCY

NO: 666 OF 2020

IN THE MATTER OF IAN FLAKEY
AND IN THE MATTER OF THE INSOLVENCY ACT 1986

BETWEEN:-

IAN FLAKEY
(a bankrupt)

Applicant

and

(1) THE OFFICIAL RECEIVER
(2) GILES GRABBER
(Trustee in Bankruptcy)

Respondents

Is this application within existing insolvency proceedings?   YES/~~NO~~

I (~~We~~), IAN FLAKEY of 1 Geranium Cottage, London intend to apply to the ~~Judge/District Judge~~/Registrar on:

Date: 1st April 2020

Time: 00:00 hours

Place: Royal Courts of Justice, 7 Rolls Buildings, Fetter Lane, London EC4A 1NL

This application having been issued at the RCJ, 7 Rolls Buildings, Fetter Lane, London, EC4A 1NL will be heard at the time and date pursuant to the endorsement underneath the Court Seal on the front page of this application.

FOR AN ORDER THAT:

1.   The Applicant's bankruptcy be annulled under section 282(1)(b) of the Insolvency Act 1986 and that the bankruptcy petition be dismissed.

2.   Costs be provided for.

The grounds of this application are set out in the 1st witness statement of Ian Flakey dated 1st April 2020, a copy of which is served herewith.

THE NAMES AND ADDRESSES OF THE PERSON(S) UPON WHOM IT IS INTENDED TO SERVE THIS APPLICATION ARE:

Name: GILES GRABBER

Address: 1 VULTURE STREET, LONDON

Name: THE OFFICIAL RECEIVER

Address: 5TH FLOOR, ZONE B, 21 BLOOMSBURY STREET, LONDON WC1B 3SS

~~OR~~

~~IT IS NOT INTENDED TO SERVE ANY PERSON WITH THIS APPLICATION~~

Dated:

Signed: SNARKEY & SNYDE

Solicitors for the applicant ~~or Applicant~~   *This is the address
Address: 1 LAW STREET, LONDON   which will be treated
Telephone: 0207 666 6666   by Court as the
Email: law@snarkeysnyde.com   Petitions address for
                                             service

If you do not attend, the court may make such order as it thinks just.

6.2   DRAFT ORDER FOR ANNULMENT UNDER SECTION 282(1)(B) OF THE INSOLVENCY ACT 1986

IN THE HIGH COURT OF JUSTICE
BUSINESS AND PROPERTY COURTS OF ENGLAND AND WALES
INSOLVENCY AND COMPANIES LIST (ChD)

IN THE MATTER OF IAN FLAKEY
IN BANKRUPTCY
AND IN THE MATTER OF THE INSOLVENCY ACT 1986

NO: [ ] OF 20[ ]

BEFORE MR REGISTRAR WISE
DATED: [ ] 20[ ]

BETWEEN:-

IAN FLAKEY

Applicant

and

(1) GILES GRABBER
(as Trustee in Bankruptcy of IAN FLAKEY)
(2) THE OFFICIAL RECEIVER

Respondents

_____
DRAFT MINUTE OF ORDER
_____

UPON the Applicant's application dated [ ] and upon a bankruptcy petition filed on [ ]

AND UPON HEARING Counsel for the Petitioner and for Mr Grabber, the applicant's Trustee in Bankruptcy, and the Official Receiver in person

AND UPON READING the evidence noted as having been read

AND it appearing to the court [that the bankruptcy order ought not to have been made] [The bankruptcy debts and expenses of the bankruptcy have all been paid or resolved to the satisfaction of the court] and that under section 282 of the Insolvency Act 1986 the bankruptcy order ought to be annulled

IT IS ORDERED THAT:

1.   The Applicant's bankruptcy order dated 27 August 2020 be annulled under section 282(1)(b) of the Insolvency Act 1986 and that the bankruptcy petition presented on [ ] be dismissed.

2.   The costs of the Trustee in Bankruptcy and the Official Receiver of and occasioned by this application be paid by the Applicant.

Dated [ ] 20[ ]

Service of this order

The Court has provided a sealed copy of this order to the serving party:

SNARKEY & SNYDE
1 LAW STREET
LONDON

6.3   WITNESS STATEMENT IN SUPPORT OF AN APPLICATION FOR ANNULMENT UNDER SECTION 282(1)(B) OF THE INSOLVENCY ACT 1986

Applicant: I Flakey: 1st: IF1: [ ] 20[ ]

IN THE HIGH COURT OF JUSTICE
BUSINESS AND PROPERTY COURTS OF ENGLAND AND WALES
INSOLVENCY AND COMPANIES LIST (ChD)

AND IN THE MATTER OF THE INSOLVENCY ACT 1986

NO: [ ] OF 20[ ]

IN THE MATTER OF IAN FLAKEY
AND IN BANKRUPTCY

BETWEEN:-

IAN FLAKEY

Applicant

and

(1) GILES GRABBER
(as Trustee in Bankruptcy of IAN FLAKEY)
(2) THE OFFICIAL RECEIVER

Respondents

1ST WITNESS STATEMENT OF IAN FLAKEY

I, IAN FLAKEY of 1 Geranium Cottage, London, Businessman, STATE as follows:

1.   I am the Bankrupt and the Applicant in this application.

2.   The matters set out in this witness statement are true and within my own knowledge except where otherwise indicated, in which case I have explained the source of my information or belief.

3.   There is now produced and shown to me a bundle consisting of true copies of the documents I will refer to in my witness statement marked 'IF1'.

4.   I make this witness statement in support of my application to annul my bankruptcy.

5.   On 4th June 2020, a petition was filed against me in this Court upon which on 27th August 2020 a Bankruptcy Order was made.

6.   On 1st December 2020, I filed a statement of my affairs setting out the whole of my assets and liabilities. I refer to page [ ] of the exhibit marked 'IF1' which is a true copy of my statement of affairs.

7.   On 1st January 2021, my wife discharged my liabilities to the satisfaction of my Trustee in Bankruptcy by making a payment of £6 million to him. I refer to page [ ] of the exhibit marked 'IF1' which is a true copy of the cheque and a bank

statement showing that payment has cleared. I refer to page [ ] of the exhibit marked 'IF1' which is a true copy of a letter from my Trustee in Bankruptcy confirming the sum needed to discharge my liabilities.

8. On 2nd January 2021, my wife lodged with my Trustee a further sum of £5,000 which my Trustee in Bankruptcy had previously indicated would be sufficient to pay all my debts and expenses up to the date of this hearing in full. I refer to page [ ] of the exhibit marked 'IF1' which is a true copy of the cheque and a bank statement showing that payment has cleared. I refer to page [ ] of the exhibit marked 'IF1' which is a true copy of a letter from my Trustee in Bankruptcy confirming his estimation of the sum needed.

9. I respectfully ask that the said Bankruptcy Order be annulled and the petition be dismissed.

STATEMENT OF TRUTH

I believe that the facts stated in this Witness Statement are true.

Signed [ ]
Full name [*IAN FLAKEY*]
Dated [ ] 20[ ]

Chapter 7

APPLICATION TO RESCIND A BANKRUPTCY ORDER

OBJECTIVE

The bankruptcy court has the power to review, vary or rescind any order it has made in the exercise of its jurisdiction.[1] The court can properly consider this as an alternative to annulment.[2] An application to rescind is not an appeal. The bankruptcy registrar is free to consider any new material which was not before the court on the occasion the order was made.[3] Unlike with an application to annul, new circumstances can be relied upon before the court to persuade it to exercise its discretion to rescind the bankruptcy order.[4] The burden of proof is on the applicant.

The test for rescission is whether there are exceptional circumstances justifying an exercise of the court's discretion in the applicant's favour and that there is a material difference to the position which was before the court on the date of the order.[5] Where evidence adds little or there are no good grounds to explain why it had not been put before the court at the time of the original hearing, the application is likely to be refused.[6]

APPLICATION

The application is made on Form IAA. The application should set out:

- that the application is made under the Insolvency Act 1986 or the Insolvency (England and Wales) Rules 2016 (as the case may be);[7]

---

[1] Section 375 of the Insolvency Act 1986; *Crammer v West Bromwich Building Society* [2012] EWCA Civ 517, [2012] BPIR 963.

[2] *Fitch v Official Receiver* [1996] 1 WLR 242.

[3] *Re a debtor (No 32/SD/1991)* [1993] 1 WLR 314; *Ross v Revenue Commissioners* [2012] EWHC 1054 (Ch), [2012] BPIR 843.

[4] *Fitch v Official Receiver* [1996] 1 WLR 242.

[5] *Papanicola (as trustee in bankruptcy for Mak) v Humphreys* [2005] EWHC 335 (Ch), [2005] 2 All ER 418.

[6] *Official Receiver v Cooksey* [2013] BPIR 526.

[7] Rule 1.35(2)(a) of the Insolvency (England and Wales) Rules 2016.

- the section number or rule under which relief is sought;[8]
- the name of the parties;[9]
- the name of the bankrupt or debtor;[10]
- the court name;[11]
- the case number;[12]
- the remedy applied for or directions sought;[13]
- the name and address of each person to be served, or if none, stating that that it is intended that no person will be served;[14]
- where there is a requirement for particular persons to be given notice of the application under the Act or Rules, stating the name and address of each such person;[15]
- the applicant's address for service.[16]

The application notice must be authenticated by the applicant or his solicitor.[17]

Any person interested (in practice, the application is usually made by the bankrupt) may apply on notice by application notice made to the registrar or district judge.

COURT FEES

Where the application is made by ordinary application on notice to other parties, a court fee of £155 is payable.[18] Where the application is made by consent or without notice in existing proceedings, a court fee of £50 is payable.[19]

EVIDENCE

The application should be supported by a witness statement. This should address:

- the debtor's name and address;
- the date on which the petition was presented;
- the date on which the bankruptcy order was made;

---

[8] Rule 1.35(2)(b) of the Insolvency (England and Wales) Rules 2016.
[9] Rule 1.35(2)(c) of the Insolvency (England and Wales) Rules 2016.
[10] Rule 1.35(2)(d) of the Insolvency (England and Wales) Rules 2016.
[11] Rule 1.35(2)(e) of the Insolvency (England and Wales) Rules 2016.
[12] Rule 1.35(2)(f) of the Insolvency (England and Wales) Rules 2016.
[13] Rule 1.35(2)(g) of the Insolvency (England and Wales) Rules 2016.
[14] Rule 1.35(2)(h) of the Insolvency (England and Wales) Rules 2016.
[15] Rule 1.35(2)(i) of the Insolvency (England and Wales) Rules 2016.
[16] Rule 1.35(2)(j) of the Insolvency (England and Wales) Rules 2016.
[17] Rule 1.35(3) of the Insolvency (England and Wales) Rules 2016. For what amounts to authentication, see rule 1.5. For hard copy applications, this means signed: rule 1.5(2).
[18] Paragraph 3.12 of Schedule 1 to the Civil Proceedings Fees (Amendment) Order 2014.
[19] Paragraph 3.11 of Schedule 1 to the Civil Proceedings Fees (Amendment) Order 2014.

- how the applicant became aware of the bankruptcy order;
- that the application was made promptly once the applicant knew of the order;
- that, if the applicant was absent from the hearing, he had a good reason for not being present;
- that there has been some change of circumstances or new evidence justifying the rescission;[20]
- that the circumstances are exceptional;[21]
- that these matters demonstrate a material difference to the position before the court when the bankruptcy order was made.[22]

And should exhibit:

- the bankruptcy order;
- any evidence supporting the application.

SERVICE

Where the application is to rescind the bankruptcy order, notice of any such proposed application and a copy of the evidence relied on must be given to:

- the Official Receiver;
- the petitioner;
- any supporting creditors who were heard on the petition;
- the trustee in bankruptcy;
- the bankrupt, where the application is made by a person other than the bankrupt.

The application and the evidence in support will need to be filed at court and served on the respondent as soon as practicable after it is filed and in any event, unless it is necessary to apply without notice or on short notice, at least 14 days before the date fixed for the hearing.[23]

The usual rule is that, subject to any other express provision, the application must be served at least 14 days before the date fixed for the hearing.[24] However, the court does have power, in cases of urgency, to hear an application immediately with or without notice to the other parties.[25]

---

[20] *Papanicola (as trustee in bankruptcy for Mak) v Humphreys* [2005] EWHC 335 (Ch), [2005] 2 All ER 418.

[21] *Papanicola (as trustee in bankruptcy for Mak) v Humphreys* [2005] EWHC 335 (Ch), [2005] 2 All ER 418.

[22] *Papanicola (as trustee in bankruptcy for Mak) v Humphreys* [2005] EWHC 335 (Ch), [2005] 2 All ER 418.

[23] Rule 12.9(3) of the Insolvency (England and Wales) Rules 2016.

[24] Rule 12.9(3) of the Insolvency (England and Wales) Rules 2016.

[25] Rule 12.10(1) of the Insolvency (England and Wales) Rules 2016.

Service may be effected personally[26] or by post on the respondent (Part 6 of the CPR applies for these purposes)[27] or, where they have authority to accept service, on the respondent's solicitors.[28] Electronic service of documents is now permissible under the Rules, providing the respondent currently consents to service in that way and has provided an email address for service in that way.[29]

KEY MATERIALS

Section 375 of the Insolvency Act 1986

375 Appeals etc. from courts exercising insolvency jurisdiction

(1)   Every court having jurisdiction for the purposes of the Parts in this Group may review, rescind or vary any order made by it in the exercise of that jurisdiction.

(2)   An appeal from a decision made in the exercise of jurisdiction for the purposes of those Parts by a county court or by a registrar in bankruptcy of the High Court lies to a single judge of the High Court; and an appeal from a decision of that judge on such an appeal lies . . . to the Court of Appeal.

(3)   A county court is not, in the exercise of its jurisdiction for the purposes of those Parts, to be subject to be restrained by the order of any other court, and no appeal lies from its decision in the exercise of that jurisdiction except as provided by this section.

---

[26]   Rule 1.44 of the Insolvency (England and Wales) Rules 2016.

[27]   Schedule 4, paragraph 1(2) to the Insolvency (England and Wales) Rules 2016.

[28]   Rule 1.40 of the Insolvency (England and Wales) Rules 2016.

[29]   Rule 1.45 of the Insolvency (England and Wales) Rules 2016.

7.1   APPLICATION FOR RESCISSION UNDER SECTION 375 OF THE INSOLVENCY ACT 1986

Form IAA   **Insolvency Act Application Notice**

IN THE HIGH COURT OF JUSTICE
BUSINESS AND PROPERTY COURTS OF ENGLAND AND WALES
INSOLVENCY AND COMPANIES LIST (ChD)
IN BANKRUPTCY

NO: 666 OF 2020

IN THE MATTER OF IAN FLAKEY
AND IN THE MATTER OF THE INSOLVENCY ACT 1986

BETWEEN:-

IAN FLAKEY

Applicant

and

(1) THE OFFICIAL RECEIVER
(2) GILES GRABBER
(Trustee in Bankruptcy of IAN FLAKEY)
(3) ANGRY PLC

Respondents

Is this application within existing insolvency proceedings? YES/~~NO~~

I (~~We~~), IAN FLAKEY of 1 Geranium Cottage, London intend to apply to the ~~Judge/District Judge~~/Registrar on:

Date: 1st April 2020

Time: 00:00 hours

Place: Royal Courts of Justice, 7 Rolls Buildings, Fetter Lane, London EC4A 1NL

This application having been issued at the RCJ, 7 Rolls Buildings, Fetter Lane, London, EC4A 1NL will be heard at the time and date pursuant to the endorsement underneath the Court Seal on the front page of this application.

FOR AN ORDER THAT:

1.   The order for the Applicant's bankruptcy be rescinded under section 375 of the Insolvency Act 1986 and that the bankruptcy petition be dismissed.

2.   Costs be provided for.

The grounds of this application are set out in the 1st witness statement of Ian Flakey dated 1st April 2020, a copy of which is annexed to this application.

THE NAMES AND ADDRESSES OF THE PERSON(S) UPON WHOM IT IS INTENDED TO SERVE THIS APPLICATION ARE:

Name: THE OFFICIAL RECEIVER

Address: 5TH FLOOR, ZONE B, 21 BLOOMSBURY STREET, LONDON WC1B 3SS

Name: GILES GRABBER

Address: 1 VULTURE STREET, LONDON

Name: ANGRY PLC

Address: 1 UNPAID BILL STREET, LONDON

~~OR~~

~~IT IS NOT INTENDED TO SERVE ANY PERSON WITH THIS APPLICATION~~

Dated:

Signed: SNARKEY & SNYDE

Solicitors for the applicant ~~or Applicant~~   *This is the address
Address: 1 LAW STREET, LONDON   which will be treated
Telephone: 0207 666 6666   by Court as the
Email: law@snarkeysnyde.com   Petitions address for
                                                  service

If you do not attend, the court may make such order as it thinks just.

7.2 DRAFT ORDER FOR RESCISSION UNDER SECTION 375 OF THE INSOLVENCY ACT 1986

IN THE HIGH COURT OF JUSTICE
BUSINESS AND PROPERTY COURTS OF ENGLAND AND WALES
INSOLVENCY AND COMPANIES LIST (ChD)

IN THE MATTER OF IAN FLAKEY
IN BANKRUPTCY
AND IN THE MATTER OF THE INSOLVENCY ACT 1986

NO: [ ] OF 20[ ]

BEFORE MR REGISTRAR WISE
DATED: [ ] 20[ ]

BETWEEN:-

IAN FLAKEY

Applicant

and

(1) GILES GRABBER
(as Trustee in Bankruptcy of IAN FLAKEY)
(2) THE OFFICIAL RECEIVER
(3) ANGRY PLC

Respondents

DRAFT MINUTE OF ORDER

UPON the Applicant's application dated [ ]

AND UPON HEARING Counsel for the Petitioner and for Mr Grabber, the applicant's Trustee in Bankruptcy, and the Official Receiver in person

AND UPON READING the evidence noted as having been read

IT IS ORDERED THAT:

1. The order for the Applicant's bankruptcy dated 1st April 2020 be rescinded under section 375 of the Insolvency Act 1986 and that the bankruptcy petition presented on [ ] be dismissed.

2. [Provision for costs.]

Dated [ ] 20[ ]

Service of this order

The Court has provided a sealed copy of this order to the serving party:

SNARKEY & SNYDE
1 LAW STREET
LONDON

7.3   WITNESS STATEMENT IN SUPPORT OF AN APPLICATION FOR RESCISSION UNDER SECTION 375 OF THE INSOLVENCY ACT 1986

Applicant: I Flakey: 1st: IF1: [ ] 20[ ]

IN THE HIGH COURT OF JUSTICE
BUSINESS AND PROPERTY COURTS OF ENGLAND AND WALES
INSOLVENCY AND COMPANIES LIST (ChD)

AND IN THE MATTER OF THE INSOLVENCY ACT 1986

NO: [ ] OF 20[ ]

IN THE MATTER OF IAN FLAKEY
AND IN BANKRUPTCY

BETWEEN:-

IAN FLAKEY

Applicant

and

(1) GILES GRABBER
(as Trustee in Bankruptcy of IAN FLAKEY)
(2) THE OFFICIAL RECEIVER
(3) ANGRY PLC

Respondents

1ST WITNESS STATEMENT OF IAN FLAKEY

I, IAN FLAKEY of 1 Geranium Cottage, London, Businessman, STATE as follows:

1.   I am the Bankrupt and the Applicant in this application.

2.   The matters set out in this witness statement are true and within my own knowledge except where otherwise indicated, in which case I have explained the source of my information or belief.

3.   There is now produced and shown to me a bundle consisting of true copies of the documents I will refer to in my witness statement marked 'IF1'.

4.   I make this witness statement in support of my application to rescind my bankruptcy.

5.   On 4th June 2020, a petition was filed against me by Angry plc in this Court upon which on 27th August 2020 a Bankruptcy Order was made. I refer to page [ ] and page [ ] of my exhibit 'IF1' which is a true copy respectively of the petition and of the order. Both documents were only recently provided to me by Mr Grabber.

6.   I was wholly unaware of the petition or the statutory demand referred to in it or indeed to the making of the bankruptcy order until last Tuesday, 1st April 2020, when I was contacted by my Trustee in Bankruptcy, Mr Grabber.

7.   Neither the petition, nor the statutory demand, nor any order of the court was served on me.

8.   Indeed, the petition I refer to above shows my address as 1 Geronimo Cottage. My address is in fact 1 Geranium Cottage. It seems reasonable to infer from this that both the statutory demand, petition and any correspondence from the Court were sent to the wrong address. If someone accepted service at Geronimo Cottage it would not have been me as I live at 1 Geranium Cottage. I refer to page [ ] of my exhibit 'IF1' which is a true copy of the petition provided to me by Mr Grabber. I also refer to page [ ] of my exhibit 'IF1' which is a true copy of an electricity bill which shows my correct address.

9.   Obviously, I had no opportunity to set aside the statutory demand or to attend and resist the petition on the hearing at which the bankruptcy order was made.

10. Had I known of this we could have simply paid this sum by return. I refer to page [ ] of my exhibit 'IF1' which is a true copy of a letter from my accountant, Sibelius Shadey, which sets out my assets and liabilities. This Honourable Court will note at page [ ] that my assets include a bank account which showed £4 million in credit from which this debt could have readily be paid had I known about it.

11. Immediately upon discovering the matters set out above, I instructed my present lawyers to make this application.

12. Plainly, these are exceptional circumstances and no doubt had the Honourable Court had the benefit of this information or indeed had I had any opportunity to be represented before it, it is likely that a different order would have been made.

13. I respectfully ask that the said Bankruptcy Order be rescinded and the petition be dismissed.

STATEMENT OF TRUTH

I believe that the facts stated in this Witness Statement are true.

Signed [ ]
Full name [*IAN FLAKEY*]
Dated [ ] 20[ ]

Chapter 8

APPLICATION FOR PERMISSION TO ACT AS A DIRECTOR OF A COMPANY NOTWITHSTANDING BANKRUPTCY

OBJECTIVE

There is an automatic prohibition on an individual from being a director of a company or from directly or indirectly taking part in the promotion, formation or management of a company during the period from the making of the bankruptcy order against him until the date he receives his discharge from bankruptcy.[1] There are both criminal and civil sanctions if an undischarged bankrupt or a person who is subject to a Bankruptcy Restriction Order or Bankruptcy Restriction Undertaking acts in contravention of the automatic restrictions imposed on him. In summary, a person acting in breach:

- commits a criminal offence and is liable on conviction on indictment to imprisonment for not more than 2 years or a fine or both, and on summary conviction to imprisonment for not more than 6 months or a fine not exceeding the statutory maximum or both;[2]
- is personally liable for all the relevant debts of a company if he is involved in the management of that company.[3]

It is no defence that the bankruptcy was later annulled because of the payment of his debts or discharged.[4]

However, such a person is able to apply for the permission of the court to act in any of these capacities.[5] The discretion to grant permission is very wide and is considered on the facts. The court is concerned to protect the public from harm from the management of a company by a person who has been guilty of lack of probity or financial irresponsibility in the management of his own affairs or circumventing restrictions on him as a bankrupt by using a company.[6] The reasons

---

[1]   Section 11(1)(a) of the Company Directors Disqualification Act 1986.

[2]   Section 11(1) of the Company Directors Disqualification Act 1986. There is no requirement of *mens rea*: *R v Doring* [2002] EWCA Crim 1695, [2002] BCC 838.

[3]   Section 15(1)(a) of the Company Directors Disqualification Act 1986.

[4]   *IRC v McEnteggart* [2004] EWHC 3431 (Ch), [2007] 1 BCC 260.

[5]   Section 11(1) and (3) of the Company Directors Disqualification Act 1986.

[6]   *R v Brockley* [1994] 1 BCLC 606.

for the bankruptcy order in so far as they affect the bankrupt's ability to run a company are germane,[7] as are the existing and future business of the company.

Other factors that may be relevant for the court when considering whether or not to grant permission include:

- the beneficial effects of granting permission;
- the general reputation of the bankrupt;
- the age and health of the bankrupt;
- whether interested parties are aware that the application for permission has been made;
- the conditions/undertakings offered by the bankrupt;
- the duration and scope of the permission sought;
- the level of involvement the bankrupt will have in the company;[8]
- whether the shareholders have limited liability.

APPLICATION

The bankrupt may apply on notice to the registrar or district judge. The application must be made to the court in which the person was adjudged bankrupt.[9]

The application is made on Form IAA. The application should set out:

- that the application is made under the Insolvency Act 1986 or the Insolvency (England and Wales) Rules 2016 (as the case may be);[10]
- the section number or rule under which relief is sought;[11]
- the name of the parties;[12]
- the name of the bankrupt or debtor;[13]
- the court name;[14]
- the case number;[15]
- the remedy applied for or directions sought;[16]
- the name and address of each person to be served or, if none, stating that that it is intended that no person will be served;[17]

---

[7] *Re Barings plc (no 4)* [1999] BCLC 317.

[8] *Re Britannia Homes Centres* [2001] 2 BCLC 63.

[9] Section 11(2) of the Company Directors Disqualification Act 1986.

[10] Rule 1.35(2)(a) of the Insolvency (England and Wales) Rules 2016.

[11] Rule 1.35(2)(b) of the Insolvency (England and Wales) Rules 2016.

[12] Rule 1.35(2)(c) of the Insolvency (England and Wales) Rules 2016.

[13] Rule 1.35(2)(d) of the Insolvency (England and Wales) Rules 2016.

[14] Rule 1.35(2)(e) of the Insolvency (England and Wales) Rules 2016.

[15] Rule 1.35(2)(f) of the Insolvency (England and Wales) Rules 2016.

[16] Rule 1.35(2)(g) of the Insolvency (England and Wales) Rules 2016.

[17] Rule 1.35(2)(h) of the Insolvency (England and Wales) Rules 2016.

- where there is a requirement for particular persons to be given notice of the application under the Act or Rules, stating the name and address of each such person;[18]
- the applicant's address for service.[19]

The application notice must be authenticated by the applicant or his solicitor.[20]

COURT FEES

Where the application is made on notice to other parties, a court fee of £155 is payable.[21] Where the application is made by consent or without notice in existing proceedings, a court fee of £50 is payable.[22]

EVIDENCE

The application should be supported by a witness statement. This should address:

- the debtor's name and address;
- the date on which the petition was presented;
- the date on which the bankruptcy order was made;
- the reasons why the bankruptcy order was made;
- the nature of relief sought;
- the name of the company in respect of which relief is sought;[23]
- the company's registered address;
- if the company is incorporated in England and Wales, the company's registered number;[24]
- if the company is incorporated outside the United Kingdom:[25]

  - the country in which it is incorporated;
  - the company's registered company number in that country;
  - its overseas registered company number under Part 34 of the Companies Act 2006;

- if the company is unincorporated in England and Wales, the company's postal address;[26]

---

[18] Rule 1.35(2)(i) of the Insolvency (England and Wales) Rules 2016.

[19] Rule 1.35(2)(j) of the Insolvency (England and Wales) Rules 2016.

[20] Rule 1.35(3) of the Insolvency (England and Wales) Rules 2016. For what amounts to authentication, see rule 1.5. For hard copy applications, this means signed: rule 1.5(2).

[21] Paragraph 3.12 of Schedule 1 to the Civil Proceedings Fees (Amendment) Order 2014.

[22] Paragraph 3.11 of Schedule 1 to the Civil Proceedings Fees (Amendment) Order 2014.

[23] Rule 1.35(2) of the Insolvency (England and Wales) Rules 2016.

[24] Rule 1.6 of the Insolvency (England and Wales) Rules 2016.

[25] Rule 1.6 of the Insolvency (England and Wales) Rules 2016.

[26] Rule 1.6 of the Insolvency (England and Wales) Rules 2016.

- if the company has yet to be incorporated, whether it is to be a public/ private company;
- the debtor's past and present role in the company;
- that the directors are aware that the debtor is bankrupt;
- the nature of the company's business or intended business;[27]
- the place or places where the company's business is, or is to be, carried on;[28]
- whether it is a private or a public company;
- the persons who are, or are to be, principally responsible for the conduct of the company's affairs (whether as directors, shadow directors, managers or otherwise);[29]
- the manner and capacity in which the applicant proposes to take part or be concerned in the promotion or formation of the company or, as the case may be, its management;[30]
- the emoluments and other benefits to be obtained by the applicant from the directorship;[31]
- any hardship caused to the company by the debtor being unable to fulfill his role as a director or be involved in the management of the company;
- any facts about the company which might address any concerns that it would not be in the public interest for relief to be granted (e.g. supervision and financial control by a professionally qualified director, limited role undertaken by the bankrupt, bankrupt not a cheque signatory);
- any undertakings or conditions offered to address concerns about the protection of the public interest.

And should exhibit:

- any correspondence with the Official Receiver;
- the certificate of incorporation of the company;
- the memorandum and articles of association of the company;
- the annual returns of the company;
- the last filed accounts of the company.

SERVICE

The application should be served on:

- the trustee in bankruptcy;
- the Official Receiver.[32]

---

[27] Rule 9.25(2)(a) of the Insolvency (England and Wales) Rules 2016.

[28] Rule 9.25(2)(a) of the Insolvency (England and Wales) Rules 2016.

[29] Rule 9.25(2)(b) of the Insolvency (England and Wales) Rules 2016.

[30] Rule 9.25(2)(c) of the Insolvency (England and Wales) Rules 2016.

[31] Rule 9.25(2)(d) of the Insolvency (England and Wales) Rules 2016.

[32] Section 11(3) of the Company Directors Disqualification Act 1986.

The application and the evidence in support will need to be filed at court and served on the Official Receiver and the trustee accompanied by notice of the venue of the hearing not less than 28 days before the date fixed for the hearing.[33]

Service may be effected personally[34] or by post on the respondent (Part 6 of the CPR applies for these purposes)[35] or, where they have authority to accept service, on the respondent's solicitors.[36] Electronic service of documents is now permissible under the Rules, providing the respondent currently consents to service in that way and has provided an email address for service in that way.[37]

OFFICIAL RECEIVER'S REPORT

Not less than 14 days before the date fixed for the hearing the Official Receiver may file at court a report of any matters which he considers ought to be drawn to the court's attention. A copy of the report shall be sent by him, as soon as reasonably practicable after it is filed, to the bankrupt and to the trustee.

If the bankrupt wishes to deny or dispute any part of the report he must, no later than 5 business days before the date of the hearing, file in court a notice specifying which statements in the Official Receiver's report he intends to deny or dispute.[38] If he gives notice under this paragraph, he must send copies of it, not less than 4 days before the date of the hearing, to the Official Receiver and the trustee.

HEARING

The district judge or registrar will need to be satisfied that the Official Receiver and trustee in bankruptcy has been served with the application[39] and that permitting the bankrupt to act as a director or be involved in the management of a company would not be contrary to the public interest. Concerns may be addressed by offering undertakings or making the order conditional on precautions being implemented.

Consideration needs to be given by the bankrupt to the possibility of an income payment order being made at the hearing in the light of any salary he may gain as a result of permission being given; the court is given express power to consider this at the permission hearing.[40]

---

[33] Rule 9.26(1) of the Insolvency (England and Wales) Rules 2016.

[34] Rule 1.44 of the Insolvency (England and Wales) Rules 2016.

[35] Schedule 4, paragraph 1(2) to the Insolvency (England and Wales) Rules 2016.

[36] Rule 1.40 of the Insolvency (England and Wales) Rules 2016.

[37] Rule 1.45 of the Insolvency (England and Wales) Rules 2016.

[38] Rule 9.26(4) of the Insolvency (England and Wales) Rules 2016.

[39] Section 11(3) of the Company Directors Disqualification Act 1986.

[40] Rule 9.27 of the Insolvency (England and Wales) Rules 2016.

Both the Official Receiver and the trustee may appear on the hearing of the application and may make representations and cross examine the bankrupt.[41]

The Official Receiver is required to attend if he is of the view that it is contrary to the public interest that the application be granted.[42]

KEY MATERIALS

Section 11 of the Company Directors Disqualification Act 1986

11 Undischarged bankrupts
(1) It is an offence for a person to act as director of a company or directly or indirectly to take part in or be concerned in the promotion, formation or management of a company, without the leave of the court, at a time when—

  (a) he is an undischarged bankrupt,
  (aa) a moratorium period under a debt relief order applies in relation to him, or
  (b) a bankruptcy restrictions order or a debt relief restrictions order is in force in respect of him.

(2) 'The court' for this purpose is the court by which the person was adjudged bankrupt or, in Scotland, sequestration of his estates was awarded.
(3) In England and Wales, the leave of the court shall not be given unless notice of intention to apply for it has been served on the official receiver; and it is the latter's duty, if he is of opinion that it is contrary to the public interest that the application should be granted, to attend on the hearing of the application and oppose it.
(4) In this section 'company' includes a company incorporated outside Great Britain that has an established place of business in Great Britain.

Rules 9.25–9.27 of the Insolvency (England and Wales) Rules 2016

Application for permission under the Company Directors Disqualification Act 1986
9.25.—(1) This rule relates to an application for permission under section 11 of the Company Directors Disqualification Act 1986, to act as director of, or to take part or be concerned in the promotion, formation or management of a company by a person—

  (a) in relation to whom a moratorium period under a debt relief order applies; or

---

41 Rule 9.26(6) of the Insolvency (England and Wales) Rules 2016.
42 Section 11(3) of the Company Directors Disqualification Act 1986.

(b)   in relation to whom a debt relief restrictions order or undertaking is in force.

(2)   The application must be supported by a witness statement which must contain identification details for the company and specify—

(a)   the nature of its business or intended business, and the place or places where that business is, or is to be, carried on;

(b)   in the case of a company which has not yet been incorporated, whether it is, or is to be, a private or a public company;

(c)   the persons who are, or are to be, principally responsible for the conduct of its affairs (whether as directors, shadow directors, managers or otherwise);

(d)   the manner and capacity in which the applicant for permission proposes to take part or be concerned in the promotion or formation of the company or, as the case may be, its management; and

(e)   the emoluments and other benefits to be obtained by virtue of the matters referred to in paragraph (d).

(3)   The court must fix a venue for the hearing of the application, and must deliver a notice to the applicant for permission accordingly.

Report of official receiver

9.26.—(1) The applicant for permission must, not less than 28 days before the date fixed for the hearing, deliver to the official receiver, notice of the venue, accompanied by copies of the application and the witness statement under rule 9.25.

(2)   The official receiver may, not less than 14 days before the date fixed for the hearing, file with the court a report of any matters which the official receiver considers ought to be drawn to the court's attention.

(3)   A copy of the report must be delivered by the official receiver, as soon as reasonably practicable after it is filed, to the applicant for permission.

(4)   The applicant for permission may, not later than five business days before the date of the hearing, file with the court a notice specifying any statements in the official receiver's report which are to be denied or disputed.

(5)   If a notice is filed under paragraph (4), the applicant for permission must deliver copies of it, not less than three business days before the date of the hearing, to the official receiver.

(6)   The official receiver may appear on the hearing of the application, and may make representations and put to the applicant for permission such questions as the court may allow.

Court's order on application

9.27.—(1) If the court grants the application for permission under section 11 of the Company Directors Disqualification Act 1986, its order must specify that which by virtue of the order the applicant has permission to do.

(2)   The court may at the same time, having regard to any representations made by the official receiver on the hearing of the application, exercise in relation

to the moratorium period or the debt relief order to which the applicant for permission is subject, any power which it has under section 251M.

(3) Whether or not the application is granted, copies of the order must be delivered by the court to the applicant and the official receiver.

8.1   APPLICATION FOR PERMISSION UNDER SECTION 11 OF THE COMPANY DIRECTORS DISQUALIFICATION ACT 1986

Form IAA   **Insolvency Act Application Notice**

IN THE HIGH COURT OF JUSTICE
BUSINESS AND PROPERTY COURTS OF ENGLAND AND WALES
INSOLVENCY AND COMPANIES LIST (ChD)
IN BANKRUPTCY

NO: 666 OF 2020

IN THE MATTER OF IAN FLAKEY
AND IN THE MATTER OF THE INSOLVENCY ACT 1986
AND IN THE MATTER OF THE COMPANY DIRECTORS DISQUALIFICATION ACT 1986

BETWEEN:-

IAN FLAKEY

Applicant

and

(1) THE OFFICIAL RECEIVER
(2) GILES GRABBER
(Trustee in Bankruptcy of IAN FLAKEY)

Respondents

Is this application within existing insolvency proceedings?   YES/~~NO~~

I (~~We~~), IAN FLAKEY of 1 Geranium Cottage, London intend to apply to the ~~Judge/District Judge~~/Registrar on:

Date: 1st April 2020

Time: 00:00 hours

Place: Royal Courts of Justice, 7 Rolls Buildings, Fetter Lane, London EC4A 1NL

This application having been issued at the RCJ, 7 Rolls Buildings, Fetter Lane, London, EC4A 1NL will be heard at the time and date pursuant to the endorsement underneath the Court Seal on the front page of this application.

FOR AN ORDER THAT:

Pursuant to section 11 of the Company Directors Disqualification Act 1986 the Applicant, the above-named Bankrupt, has permission of the Court to act as a director of and/or take part and be concerned in the management of FLAKEY ENTERPRISES LIMITED, a private limited company incorporated under the Companies Act 1985 under company number 2222.

The grounds on which the Applicant claims to be entitled to the Order are set out in the witness statement of Ian Flakey dated 1st April 2020.

THE NAMES AND ADDRESSES OF THE PERSON(S) UPON WHOM IT IS INTENDED TO SERVE THIS APPLICATION ARE:

Name: THE OFFICIAL RECEIVER

Address: 5TH FLOOR, ZONE B, 21 BLOOMSBURY STREET, LONDON WC1B 3SS

Name: GILES GRABBER

Address: 1 VULTURE STREET, LONDON

~~OR~~

~~IT IS NOT INTENDED TO SERVE ANY PERSON WITH THIS APPLICATION~~

Dated:

Signed: SNARKEY & SNYDE

Solicitors for the applicant ~~or Applicant~~
Address: 1 LAW STREET, LONDON
Telephone: 0207 666 6666
Email: law@snarkeysnyde.com

*This is the address which will be treated by Court as the Petitions address for service

If you do not attend, the court may make such order as it thinks just.

8.2 DRAFT ORDER FOR PERMISSION UNDER SECTION 11 OF THE COMPANY DIRECTORS DISQUALIFICATION ACT 1986

IN THE HIGH COURT OF JUSTICE
BUSINESS AND PROPERTY COURTS OF ENGLAND AND WALES
INSOLVENCY AND COMPANIES LIST (ChD)

IN THE MATTER OF IAN FLAKEY
IN BANKRUPTCY

AND IN THE MATTER OF THE COMPANY DIRECTORS
DISQUALIFICATION ACT 1986
AND IN THE MATTER OF THE INSOLVENCY ACT 1986

NO: [ ] OF 20[ ]

BEFORE MR REGISTRAR WISE
DATED: [ ] 20[ ]

BETWEEN:-

IAN FLAKEY

Applicant

and

(1) GILES GRABBER
(as Trustee in Bankruptcy of IAN FLAKEY)
(2) THE OFFICIAL RECEIVER

Respondents

DRAFT MINUTE OF ORDER

UPON the Applicant's application dated [ ]

AND UPON HEARING Counsel for the Petitioner and for Mr Grabber, the applicant's Trustee in Bankruptcy, and the Official Receiver in person

AND UPON the Applicant giving the undertakings set out in the Schedule hereto

AND UPON READING the evidence noted as having been read

IT IS ORDERED THAT:

1. Permission be granted to the said IAN FLAKEY to act as director of and/or take part in the management of FLAKEY ENTERPRISES LIMITED ['the Company'].

2. The costs of the Trustee in Bankruptcy and the Official Receiver of and occasioned by this application be paid by the Applicant.

Service of this order

The Court has provided a sealed copy of this order to the serving party:

SNARKEY & SNYDE
1 LAW STREET
LONDON

THE SCHEDULE

The Applicant is granted permission to act as a director upon his undertaking to the Court that for so long as he is a director or takes part and be concerned in the management of the Company:

1.　　The Applicant will procure the holding of monthly board meetings of the Company at which both directors shall be present;

2.　　The Applicant will procure and ensure that all board meetings will be minuted;

3.　　The Applicant will procure and ensure that management accounts will be produced monthly for presentation at each board meeting;

4.　　The Applicant will procure and ensure that all returns in respect of the Company to HM Revenue & Customs for PAYE, corporation tax, NIC and VAT will be submitted on their due date and any payment due in respect of any liability for such tax will be paid on or before the due date of payment thereof;

5.　　The Applicant will not become a signatory for the Company's cheques;

6.　　The Applicant shall only be entitled to be paid a salary by the Company at a rate that is agreed by the Company and approved by the Board of the Company as being an amount which the Company is properly able to pay.

8.3 WITNESS STATEMENT IN SUPPORT OF AN APPLICATION FOR PERMISSION UNDER SECTION 11 OF THE COMPANY DIRECTORS DISQUALIFICATION ACT 1986

Applicant: I Flakey: 1st: IF1: [ ] 20[ ]

IN THE HIGH COURT OF JUSTICE
BUSINESS AND PROPERTY COURTS OF ENGLAND AND WALES
INSOLVENCY AND COMPANIES LIST (ChD)

NO: [ ] OF 20[ ]

IN THE MATTER OF IAN FLAKEY
AND IN BANKRUPTCY
AND IN THE MATTER OF THE COMPANY DIRECTORS
DISQUALIFICATION ACT 1986
AND IN THE MATTER OF THE INSOLVENCY ACT 1986

BETWEEN:-

IAN FLAKEY

Applicant

and

(1) GILES GRABBER
(as Trustee in Bankruptcy of IAN FLAKEY)
(2) THE OFFICIAL RECEIVER

Respondents

1ST WITNESS STATEMENT OF IAN FLAKEY

I, IAN FLAKEY of 1 Geranium Cottage, London, Businessman, STATE as follows:

1.   I am the Bankrupt and the Applicant in this application.

2.   The matters set out in this witness statement are true and within my own knowledge except where otherwise indicated, in which case I have explained the source of my information or belief.

3.   There is now produced and shown to me a bundle consisting of true copies of the documents I will refer to in my witness statement marked 'IF1'.

4.   I make this witness statement in support of my application for an Order pursuant to section 11 of the Company Directors Disqualification Act 1986 that I have permission of the Court to act as a director of and/or take part and be concerned in the management of FLAKEY ENTERPRISES LIMITED, a private limited company incorporated under the Companies Act 1985 under company number 2222 ['the Company'] notwithstanding my bankruptcy.

5.   On 4th June 2019, a petition was filed against me in this Court by Angry plc upon which on 27th August 2019 a Bankruptcy Order was made in respect of an unpaid bill for widgets. This does not relate to any business of the Company.

6.   On 1st December 2019, I filed a statement of my affairs setting out the whole of my assets and liabilities. I refer to page [ ] of the exhibit marked 'IF1' which is a

true copy of my statement of affairs. This Honourable Court will note that Angry plc is the principal creditor.

7. The Company is a private company limited by shares and was incorporated on 1st April 1999 by myself and Hieronymus Muddles and commenced trading that same month.

8. The Company has an issued share capital of £100 of which all are fully paid up. The shares are owned by Mr Muddles and my mother, Ermintrude Flakey, who each provided half the start-up capital.

9. The company trades from 4 Snoods Corner, London E1, which is its registered office.

10. The principal objects set out in the memorandum of association of the Company are to be a general trading company. I refer to pages [ ] of the exhibit marked 'IF1' which is a true copy of the Company's certificate of incorporation and memorandum and articles of association.

11. The Company's principal business is as a wholesaler of yo-yos.

12. I was skilled in sales and marketing whilst Mr Muddles, a qualified accountant of 40 years' experience, was able to provide the management and financial skills I lacked. We took on roles within the Company reflecting our skills with myself acting as Sales Director and Mr Muddles acting as Financial Director. We were the sole directors.

13. Mr Muddles is the sole cheque signatory.

14. I resigned as director of the Company immediately upon the making of the bankruptcy order against me. Before the bankruptcy order was made, as Sales Director, I was responsible for all the sales and negotiations of sales contracts of the Company.

15. Since my bankruptcy of which Mr Muddles is aware, Mr Muddles continues to act as its financial director. I would hope to resume my role as described in this paragraph in the event that permission is given by the Court for me to do so. I refer to page [ ] of the exhibit marked 'IF1' which is a true copy of a letter from Mr Muddles confirming that he is aware of my bankruptcy and of this application and his agreement with it.

16. The Company's filings of annual returns and accounts are up to date. I refer to page [ ] of the exhibit marked 'IF1' which is a true copy of all the information filed with the Registrar of Companies in respect of the Company.

17. Since the Company commenced trading in 1999 it has returned a healthy profit each year. I refer to page [ ] of the exhibit marked 'IF1' which is a true copy of the Company's annual accounts to date.

18. Notwithstanding my bankruptcy, my ongoing involvement as a director of the Company, and in the management of its affairs, is vital to the continued success of the Company's business. I am the sole person involved in the company with any experience of sales and marketing and clients expect that any negotiations for the bulk sale of yo-yos should be conducted at board level.

19.   The accountants of the Company have prepared a short report in connection with my application for permission to act as a director of the Company despite my bankruptcy. This report deals with the impact of my no longer acting as a director or being involved in the management of the Company's affairs. I refer to page [ ] of the exhibit marked 'IF1' which is a true copy of the report. As is apparent from the report, my non-availability to act as a director of the Company since the date of my bankruptcy order has adversely affected turnover. Repeat business is not being placed by existing customers because I am no longer available to service the customer's requirements. Mr Muddles has neither skill nor experience in sales or marketing. New business is therefore not being attracted because of my absence as the Company's sales director.

20.   Were I to able to be take reappointment as sales director, Mr Muddles has confirmed to me that I would receive my former salary of £100,000 per annum and take on my former role as being responsible for the sales and marketing of yo-yos for the Company. Taking this employment would be substantially to the benefit of the creditors in my bankruptcy.

21.   Were an order to be made, any concerns the Court might have as regards my acting as a company director might be addressed by my offering the following undertakings which are to have effect for so long as I am a director or take part in and am concerned in the management of the Company:

a.   I will procure the holding of monthly board meetings of the Company at which both directors shall be present;

b.   I will procure and ensure that all board meetings will be minuted;

c.   I will procure and ensure that management accounts will be produced monthly for presentation at each board meeting;

d.   I will procure and ensure that all returns in respect of the Company to the HM Revenue & Customs for PAYE, corporation tax, NIC and VAT will be submitted on their due date and any payment due in respect of any liability for such tax will be paid on or before the due date of payment thereof;

e.   I will not become a signatory for the Company's cheques;

f.   I shall only be entitled to be paid a salary by the Company at a rate that is agreed by the Company and approved by the Board of the Company as being an amount which the Company is properly able to pay.

22.   Mr Muddles has already confirmed he is prepared to ensure my undertakings are carried out. I refer to page [ ] of the exhibit marked 'IF1' which is a true copy of Mr Muddles' letter.

23.   Before my bankruptcy, I acted as a director of the Company and I dealt with the affairs of the Company in a satisfactory manner over that period. The continued success of the Company largely depends upon whether I am able to act as one of its directors and to be involved in the management of its affairs.

24.   I respectfully ask that the Order be granted in the terms sought.

STATEMENT OF TRUTH

I believe that the facts stated in this Witness Statement are true.

Signed [ ]
Full name [*IAN FLAKEY*]
Dated [ ] 20[ ]

Chapter 9

APPLICATION FOR DIRECTIONS BY A TRUSTEE IN BANKRUPTCY

OBJECTIVE

A trustee may apply for directions from the court in relation to any matter arising under the bankruptcy,[1] for example as to the appropriate approach to the validity of a charge or where he is concerned that there may be issues about the validity of his appointment.

APPLICATION

The application is made by application notice returnable to the district judge or registrar. A copy of the application should be filed at court with one additional copy for each party to be served.[2]

The application is made on Form IAA. The application should set out:

- that the application is made under the Insolvency Act 1986 or the Insolvency (England and Wales) Rules 2016 (as the case may be);[3]
- the section number or rule under which relief is sought;[4]
- the name of the parties;[5]
- the name of the bankrupt or debtor;[6]
- the court name;[7]
- the case number;[8]
- the remedy applied for or directions sought;[9]
- the name and address of each person to be served or, if none, stating that that it is intended that no person will be served;[10]

---

[1]   Section 303(2) of the Insolvency Act 1986.
[2]   Rule 12.7 of the Insolvency (England and Wales) Rules 2016.
[3]   Rule 1.35(2)(a) of the Insolvency (England and Wales) Rules 2016.
[4]   Rule 1.35(2)(b) of the Insolvency (England and Wales) Rules 2016.
[5]   Rule 1.35(2)(c) of the Insolvency (England and Wales) Rules 2016.
[6]   Rule 1.35(2)(d) of the Insolvency (England and Wales) Rules 2016.
[7]   Rule 1.35(2)(e) of the Insolvency (England and Wales) Rules 2016.
[8]   Rule 1.35(2)(f) of the Insolvency (England and Wales) Rules 2016.
[9]   Rule 1.35(2)(g) of the Insolvency (England and Wales) Rules 2016.
[10] Rule 1.35(2)(h) of the Insolvency (England and Wales) Rules 2016.

- where there is a requirement for particular persons to be given notice of the application under the Act or Rules, stating the name and address of each such person;[11]
- the applicant's address for service.[12]

The application notice must be authenticated by the applicant or his solicitor.[13]

The application should be made on notice to the parties interested in the decision.

COURT FEES

Where the application is made on notice to other parties, a court fee of £155 is payable.[14] Where the application is made by consent or without notice in existing proceedings, a court fee of £50 is payable.[15]

EVIDENCE

The trustee should file a witness statement in support. This should address:

- that the trustee makes this application as trustee in bankruptcy;
- that the trustee seeks the court's directions;
- the date of the bankruptcy;
- the date of the trustee's appointment;
- the question the trustee wants the court to answer;
- why the question needs to be answered;
- the background facts upon which the issue arises;
- the opposing contentions on the question.

The trustee should exhibit:

- evidence of the trustee's appointment;
- any documents relevant to the issue;
- any documents relevant to the facts upon which the issue arises.

SERVICE

The application should be served on:

---

[11] Rule 1.35(2)(i) of the Insolvency (England and Wales) Rules 2016.

[12] Rule 1.35(2)(j) of the Insolvency (England and Wales) Rules 2016.

[13] Rule 1.35(3) of the Insolvency (England and Wales) Rules 2016. For what amounts to authentication, see rule 1.5. For hard copy applications, this means signed: rule 1.5(2).

[14] Paragraph 3.12 of Schedule 1 to the Civil Proceedings Fees (Amendment) Order 2014.

[15] Paragraph 3.11 of Schedule 1 to the Civil Proceedings Fees (Amendment) Order 2014.

- the bankrupt;
- any party interested in the decision.

Service may be effected personally[16] or by post on the respondent (Part 6 of the CPR applies for these purposes)[17] or, where they have authority to accept service, on the respondent's solicitors.[18] Electronic service of documents is now permissible under the Rules, providing the respondent currently consents to service in that way and has provided an email address for service in that way.[19]

FIRST HEARING

The first hearing is before the registrar or district judge. Advocates are not expected to robe. The registrar may adjourn the case to the judge or give directions himself.

KEY MATERIALS

Section 303(2) of the Insolvency Act 1986

303 General control of trustee by the court
(2)   The trustee of a bankrupt's estate may apply to the court for directions in relation to any particular matter arising under the bankruptcy.
(2A) Where at any time after a bankruptcy petition has been presented to the court against any person, whether under the provisions of the Insolvent Partnerships Order 1994 or not, the attention of the court is drawn to the fact that the person in question is a member of an insolvent partnership, the court may make an order as to the future conduct of the insolvency proceedings and any such order may apply any provisions of that Order with any necessary modifications.
(2B) Where a bankruptcy petition has been presented against more than one individual in the circumstances mentioned in subsection (2A) above, the court may give such directions for consolidating the proceedings, or any of them, as it thinks just.
(2C) Any order or directions under subsection (2A) or (2B) may be made or given on the application of the official receiver, any responsible insolvency practitioner, the trustee of the partnership or any other interested person and may include provisions as to the administration of the joint estate of the partnership, and in particular how it and the separate estate of any member are to be administered.

---

[16] Rule 1.44 of the Insolvency (England and Wales) Rules 2016.
[17] Schedule 4, paragraph 1(2) to the Insolvency (England and Wales) Rules 2016.
[18] Rule 1.40 of the Insolvency (England and Wales) Rules 2016.
[19] Rule 1.45 of the Insolvency (England and Wales) Rules 2016.

9.1   ORDINARY APPLICATION FOR DIRECTIONS BY THE TRUSTEE IN BANKRUPTCY

Form IAA   **Insolvency Act Application Notice**

IN THE HIGH COURT OF JUSTICE
BUSINESS AND PROPERTY COURTS OF ENGLAND AND WALES
INSOLVENCY AND COMPANIES LIST (ChD)
IN BANKRUPTCY

NO: 666 OF 2020

IN THE MATTER OF IAN FLAKEY
AND IN THE MATTER OF THE INSOLVENCY ACT 1986

BETWEEN:-

GILES GRABBER
(Trustee in Bankruptcy of IAN FLAKEY)

Applicant

and

(1) BRASSIC BANK PLC
(2) IAN FLAKEY
(a bankrupt)

Respondents

Is this application within existing insolvency proceedings?   YES/~~NO~~

I (~~We~~), IAN FLAKEY of 1 Geranium Cottage, London intend to apply to the ~~Judge/District Judge~~/Registrar on:

Date: 1st April 2020

Time: 00:00 hours

Place: Royal Courts of Justice, 7 Rolls Buildings, Fetter Lane, London EC4A 1NL

This application having been issued at the RCJ, 7 Rolls Buildings, Fetter Lane, London, EC4A 1NL will be heard at the time and date pursuant to the endorsement underneath the Court Seal on the front page of this application.

FOR AN ORDER THAT:

1.   A declaration be made under section 303 of the Insolvency Act 1986 as to whether the Bankrupt has a debt in law to Brassic Bank.

2.   A declaration be made under section 303 of the Insolvency Act 1986 as to whether and if so to what extent does the mortgage created on 1st April 2019 by the Bankrupt in favour of Brassic Bank create a valid and enforceable security over the assets of the Bankrupt.

3.   Such further or other directions as shall to the Court seem fit.

4.   Costs be provided for.

5.   Any costs of the application that are not payable by the 1st Respondent or not recovered from it should be paid to the Applicant as the Bankrupt's trustee out of the assets of the bankruptcy as an expense of the bankruptcy within rule 10.149(a) of the Insolvency (England and Wales) Rules 2016.

6.   There be general liberty to apply.

The grounds upon which I seek the above relief are set out in the 1st witness statement of Giles Grabber dated 1st April 2020, a true copy of which is served herewith.

THE NAMES AND ADDRESSES OF THE PERSON(S) UPON WHOM IT IS INTENDED TO SERVE THIS APPLICATION ARE:

Name: IAN FLAKEY

Address: 1 GERANIUM COTTAGE, LONDON

Name: BRASSIC BANK PLC

Address: 26 LUCRE, LONDON

~~OR~~

~~IT IS NOT INTENDED TO SERVE ANY PERSON WITH THIS APPLICATION~~

Dated:

Signed: SNARKEY & SNYDE

Solicitors for the applicant ~~or Applicant~~   *This is the address
Address: 1 LAW STREET, LONDON   which will be treated
Telephone: 0207 666 6666   by Court as the
Email: law@snarkeysnyde.com   Petitions address for
                                                 service

If you do not attend, the court may make such order as it thinks just.

9.2   WITNESS STATEMENT IN SUPPORT OF AN APPLICATION FOR DIRECTIONS

Applicant: G Grabber: 1st: GG1: [ ] 20[ ]

NO: [ ] OF 20[ ]

IN THE MATTER OF IAN FLAKEY
IN BANKRUPTCY
AND IN THE MATTER OF THE INSOLVENCY ACT 1986

BETWEEN:-

GILES GRABBER
(as Trustee in Bankruptcy of Ian Flakey)

Applicant

and

(1) BRASSIC BANK PLC
(2) IAN FLAKEY

Respondents

1ST WITNESS STATEMENT OF GILES GRABBER

I, GILES GRABBER of Grabbers LLP, of 1 Vulture Street, London, Trustee in Bankruptcy of Ian Flakey, STATE as follows:

1.   I am the Applicant in this application.

2.   I make this witness statement in support of my application for directions as to whether the Bankrupt has a debt in law to Brassic Bank and as to the validity of a mortgage over the freehold property known as and situate at 1 Geranium Cottage, London, registered with Her Majesty's Land Registry under title number 1223345 ['the property'] between IAN FLAKEY and BRASSIC BANK PLC.

3.   The matters set out in this witness statement are true and within my own knowledge except where otherwise indicated, in which case I have explained the source of my information or belief.

4.   There is now produced and shown to me a bundle consisting of true copies of the documents I will refer to in my witness statement marked 'GG1'.

5.   A bankruptcy order was made against Ian Flakey ('the Bankrupt') on 1st March 2020. I refer to page [ ] of 'GG1' which is a true copy of the bankruptcy order.

6.   I was appointed as the Trustee in Bankruptcy of the Bankrupt on 1st April 2020. I refer to page [ ] of 'GG1' which is a true copy of my certificate of appointment.

7.   The Bankrupt's statement of affairs show that he was insolvent as at 31st December 2019 with a deficiency in the sum of £2,000,000. I refer to page [ ] of 'GG1' which is a true copy of the trading accounts of the Bankrupt and his

statement of affairs. Creditors' claims lodged in the bankruptcy amount to £3,500,000. I refer to page [ ] of 'GG1' which is a true copy of the proofs of debt evidencing the creditors' claims.

8.   Following my appointment, I began to investigate the affairs of the Bankrupt. The following matters became apparent.

9.   The Bankrupt's principal asset is the freehold property at 1 Geranium Cottage, London.

10.   The Bankrupt appears to have granted Brassic Bank plc a first legal mortgage over 1 Geranium Cottage, London. I refer to page [ ] of 'GG1' which is a true copy of a document which purports to be the legal mortgage and to page [ ] of 'GG1' the loan document under which the mortgage was granted. This Honourable Court will notice that these are not in a conventional format and the loan does not appear to relate to the Bankrupt at all.

11.   I also refer to page [ ] of 'GG1' which is a true copy of the entries in the land registry affecting the title of the property which shows the legal mortgage.

12.   Despite the registration of the mortgage, the bankrupt, Ian Flakey, disputes that the legal mortgage was validly executed and registered. I also refer to page [ ] of 'GG1' which is a true copy of the correspondence on this issue before my appointment which sets out the detailed legal arguments from the solicitors on both sides. Mr Flakey's contention appears to be that the underlying loan is not his and that the absence of the formality of his signature being on the mortgage is fatal to it.

13.   The property at 1 Geranium Cottage is the Bankrupt's principal asset and the issue of whether or not the mortgage is valid will affect the distribution to both Brassic Bank plc and the unsecured creditors.

14.   I therefore ask this Honourable Court for directions as to how I should approach the issue of the validity of the debt and the mortgage over the freehold property known as and situate at 1 Geranium Cottage, London.

STATEMENT OF TRUTH

I believe that the facts stated in this Witness Statement are true.

Signed [ ]
Full name [*GILES GRABBER*]
Dated [ ] 20[ ]

9.3   ORDER ON THE TRUSTEE'S APPLICATION FOR DIRECTIONS

IN THE HIGH COURT OF JUSTICE
BUSINESS AND PROPERTY COURTS OF ENGLAND AND WALES
INSOLVENCY AND COMPANIES LIST (ChD)

NO: [ ] OF 20[ ]

IN THE MATTER OF IAN FLAKEY
IN BANKRUPTCY
AND IN THE MATTER OF THE INSOLVENCY ACT 1986

BEFORE MR REGISTRAR WISE
DATED: [ ] OF 20[ ]

BETWEEN:-

GILES GRABBER
(as Trustee in Bankruptcy of Ian Flakey)

Applicant

and

(1) BRASSIC BANK PLC
(2) IAN FLAKEY

Respondents

_____

DRAFT MINUTE OF ORDER

_____

UPON THE APPLICATION of Giles Grabber dated [ ]

UPON HEARING Counsel for the Applicant and Counsel for Brassic Bank plc, the Respondent

AND UPON READING the evidence noted as being read

IT IS DIRECTED THAT

(1)   The Bankrupt [*is/is not*] indebted to Brassic Bank plc in the sum of £1 million

(2)   Brassic Bank plc's mortgage [*is a nullity and does not operate to charge/does take effect and rank as a first legal mortgage*] over the freehold property known as and situate at 1 Geranium Cottage, London, registered with Her Majesty's Land Registry under title number 1223345

AND IT IS ORDERED THAT:

1.   [Provision as to costs.]

2.   Any costs of the application that are not payable by the 1st Respondent or not recovered from it should be paid to the Applicant as such trustee out of the assets of the bankruptcy as an expense of the bankruptcy within rule 10.149(a) of the Insolvency (England and Wales) Rules 2016.

Service of this order

The Court has provided a sealed copy of this order to the serving party:

SNARKEY & SNYDE
1 LAW STREET
LONDON

Chapter 10

APPLICATION TO APPOINT AN INTERIM RECEIVER

OBJECTIVE

After presentation of the bankruptcy petition but while waiting for it to be heard, an interested party may apply to the court for the Official Receiver to be appointed as an interim receiver of the debtor's property if it is necessary to protect the bankrupt's property.[1] An interim receiver is the equivalent of a provisional liquidator in corporate liquidation.[2]

APPLICATION

The application is made by application notice on notice and should be made to the registrar or district judge.

An application to the court for the appointment of an interim receiver may be made by a creditor, the debtor, an insolvency practitioner appointed under section 273(2) of the Insolvency Act 1986 to prepare a report on a debtor's bankruptcy petition, a temporary administrator or a member state liquidator appointed in main proceedings.[3]

The application is made on Form IAA. The application should set out:

- that the application is made under the Insolvency Act 1986 or the Insolvency (England and Wales) Rules 2016 (as the case may be);[4]
- the section number or rule under which relief is sought;[5]
- the name of the parties;[6]
- the name of the bankrupt or debtor;[7]

---

[1]   Section 286 of the Insolvency Act 1986.
[2]   *Re Baars* [2003] BPIR 523; *Dadourian Group International v Simms* [2007] EWHC 723 (Ch), [2008] BPIR 508.
[3]   Rule 10.49 of the Insolvency (England and Wales) Rules 2016.
[4]   Rule 1.35(2)(a) of the Insolvency (England and Wales) Rules 2016.
[5]   Rule 1.35(2)(b) of the Insolvency (England and Wales) Rules 2016.
[6]   Rule 1.35(2)(c) of the Insolvency (England and Wales) Rules 2016.
[7]   Rule 1.35(2)(d) of the Insolvency (England and Wales) Rules 2016.

- the court name;[8]
- the case number;[9]
- the remedy applied for or directions sought;[10]
- the name and address of each person to be served or, if none, stating that that it is intended that no person will be served;[11]
- where there is a requirement for particular persons to be given notice of the application under the Act or Rules, stating the name and address of each such person;[12]
- the applicant's address for service.[13]

The application notice must be authenticated by the applicant or his solicitor.[14]

COURT FEES

A court fee of £155 is payable.[15] Before an order appointing the Official Receiver as interim receiver is issued, the applicant for it must deposit with him, or otherwise secure to his satisfaction, such sum as the court directs to cover his remuneration and expenses.

EVIDENCE

The application should be supported by a witness statement. This should address:

- the capacity in which the applicant makes the application;
- the debtor in respect of whom the application is being made;
- that an order for the appointment of an interim receiver is sought;
- the grounds as to why the interim receiver should be appointed;[16]
- whether or not the Official Receiver has been informed of the application and, if so, has been furnished with a copy of it;[17]
- if an insolvency practitioner has been appointed under section 273 of the Insolvency Act 1986, and it is proposed that he (and not the Official Receiver) should be appointed interim receiver, and it is not the insolvency practitioner himself who is the applicant under this Rule, that he has consented to act;[18]

---

[8]   Rule 1.35(2)(e) of the Insolvency (England and Wales) Rules 2016.
[9]   Rule 1.35(2)(f) of the Insolvency (England and Wales) Rules 2016.
[10] Rule 1.35(2)(g) of the Insolvency (England and Wales) Rules 2016.
[11] Rule 1.35(2)(h) of the Insolvency (England and Wales) Rules 2016.
[12] Rule 1.35(2)(i) of the Insolvency (England and Wales) Rules 2016.
[13] Rule 1.35(2)(j) of the Insolvency (England and Wales) Rules 2016.
[14] Rule 1.35(3) of the Insolvency (England and Wales) Rules 2016. For what amounts to authentication, see rule 1.5. For hard copy applications, this means signed: rule 1.5(2).
[15] Paragraph 3.12 of Schedule 1 to the Civil Proceedings Fees (Amendment) Order 2014.
[16] Rule 10.49 of the Insolvency (England and Wales) Rules 2016.
[17] Rule 10.49 of the Insolvency (England and Wales) Rules 2016.
[18] Rule 10.49(2)(c) of the Insolvency (England and Wales) Rules 2016.

- whether to the applicant's knowledge there has been proposed or is in force an IVA;[19]
- the applicant's estimate of the value of the property or business in respect of which the interim receiver is to be appointed;[20]
- the security being provided.

The applicant should exhibit:

- evidence supporting the application;
- correspondence disclosing the proposed application to the Official Receiver and his response;
- consent of the proposed interim receiver (if not the Official Receiver);
- evidence of the security provided.

SERVICE

The applicant shall send copies of the application and the witness statement to the person proposed to be appointed interim receiver.[21] If that person is the Official Receiver and an insolvency practitioner has been appointed under section 273 of the Insolvency Act 1986 (and he is not himself the applicant), copies of the application and witness statement shall be sent by the applicant to the insolvency practitioner.[22]

If, in any case where a copy of the application is to be sent to a person under this paragraph, it is for any reason not practicable to send a copy, that person must be informed of the application in sufficient time to enable him to be present at the hearing.

Service may be effected personally[23] or by post on the respondent (Part 6 of the CPR applies for these purposes)[24] or, where they have authority to accept service, on the respondent's solicitors.[25] Electronic service of documents is now permissible under the Rules, providing the respondent currently consents to service in that way and has provided an email address for service in that way.[26]

---

[19] Rule 10.49(2)(d) of the Insolvency (England and Wales) Rules 2016.

[20] Rule 10.49(2)(e) of the Insolvency (England and Wales) Rules 2016.

[21] Rule 10.49(3) of the Insolvency (England and Wales) Rules 2016.

[22] Rule 10.49(3) of the Insolvency (England and Wales) Rules 2016.

[23] Rule 1.44 of the Insolvency (England and Wales) Rules 2016.

[24] Schedule 4, paragraph 1(2) to the Insolvency (England and Wales) Rules 2016.

[25] Rule 1.40 of the Insolvency (England and Wales) Rules 2016.

[26] Rule 1.45 of the Insolvency (England and Wales) Rules 2016.

HEARING

The Official Receiver and (if appointed) the insolvency practitioner may attend the hearing of the application and make representations.[27]

The order appointing the interim receiver will state the nature and a short description of the property of which the person appointed is to take possession, and the duties to be performed by him in relation to the debtor's affairs.[28]

KEY MATERIALS

Section 286 of the Insolvency Act 1986

286 Power to appoint interim receiver
(1) The court may, if it is shown to be necessary for the protection of the debtor's property, at any time after the presentation of a bankruptcy petition and before making a bankruptcy order, appoint the official receiver to be interim receiver of the debtor's property.
(2) Where the court has, on a debtor's petition, appointed an insolvency practitioner under section 273 and it is shown to the court as mentioned in subsection (1) of this section, the court may, without making a bankruptcy order, appoint that practitioner, instead of the official receiver, to be interim receiver of the debtor's property.
(3) The court may by an order appointing any person to be an interim receiver direct that his powers shall be limited or restricted in any respect; but, save as so directed, an interim receiver has, in relation to the debtor's property, all the rights, powers, duties and immunities of a receiver and manager under the next section.
(4) An order of the court appointing any person to be an interim receiver shall require that person to take immediate possession of the debtor's property or, as the case may be, the part of it to which his powers as interim receiver are limited.
(5) Where an interim receiver has been appointed, the debtor shall give him such inventory of his property and such other information, and shall attend on the interim receiver at such times, as the latter may for the purpose of carrying out his functions under this section reasonably require.
(6) Where an interim receiver is appointed, section 285(3) applies for the period between the appointment and the making of a bankruptcy order on the petition, or the dismissal of the petition, as if the appointment were the making of such an order.
(7) A person ceases to be interim receiver of a debtor's property if the bankruptcy petition relating to the debtor is dismissed, if a bankruptcy order is made on the petition or if the court by order otherwise terminates the appointment.

---

[27] Rule 10.49(5) of the Insolvency (England and Wales) Rules 2016.
[28] Rule 10.51 of the Insolvency (England and Wales) Rules 2016.

(8) References in this section to the debtor's property are to all his property, whether or not it would be comprised in his estate if he were adjudged bankrupt.

Rules 10.49–10.54 of the Insolvency (England and Wales) Rules 2016

Application for appointment of interim receiver (section 286)

10.49.—(1) An application to the court under section 286 for the appointment of the official receiver or an insolvency practitioner as interim receiver may be made by—

(a) a creditor;
(b) the debtor;
(c) a temporary administrator; or
(d) a member State liquidator appointed in main proceedings (including in accordance with [Article 37 of the EU Regulation]).

(2) The application must be supported by a witness statement stating—

(a) the grounds on which it is proposed that the interim receiver should be appointed;
(b) whether or not the official receiver has been informed of the application and, if so, whether a copy of it has been delivered to that person;
(c) if the proposed interim receiver is an insolvency practitioner, that the insolvency practitioner has consented to act;
(d) whether to the applicant's knowledge there has been proposed or is in force an IVA; and
(e) the applicant's estimate of the value of the property or business in relation to which the interim receiver is to be appointed.

(3) The applicant must deliver copies of the application and the witness statement to the proposed interim receiver and to the official receiver.
(4) If for any reason it is not practicable to deliver a copy of the application to the proposed interim receiver that person must be informed of the application in sufficient time to be able to be present at the hearing.
(5) The official receiver may attend the hearing of the application and make representations.
(6) If satisfied that sufficient grounds are shown for the appointment, the court may appoint an interim receiver on such terms as it thinks just.

Deposit

10.50.—(1) An applicant for an order appointing the official receiver as interim receiver must, before the order is made, deposit with the official receiver, or otherwise secure to the official receiver's satisfaction, such sum as the court directs to cover the official receiver's remuneration and expenses.
(2) If the sum proves to be insufficient, the court may, on the application of the official receiver, order the applicant to deposit or secure an additional sum.

(3) If such additional sum is not deposited or secured within two business days after service of the order on the applicant the court may discharge the order appointing the official receiver as interim receiver.

(4) If a bankruptcy order is made after an interim receiver has been appointed, any money deposited under this rule must (unless it is required because the assets are insufficient to pay the remuneration and expenses of the interim receiver, or the deposit was made by the debtor out of the debtor's own property) be repaid to the person depositing it (or as that person may direct) out of the bankrupt's estate, in the prescribed order of priority.

Order of appointment

10.51.—(1) The order appointing the interim receiver must contain—

  (a) identification details for the proceedings;
  (b) the name and title of the judge making the order;
  (c) the name and postal address of the applicant;
  (d) identification details for the debtor;
  (e) the statement that the court is satisfied—

      (i)   that the debtor is unable to pay the debtor's debts, and
      (ii) that the proceedings are main, secondary, territorial or non-EC proceedings (as the case may be);

  (f) the order either that—

      (i)   upon the applicant depositing the sum specified in the order with the official receiver, the official receiver is appointed interim receiver of the property of the debtor, or
      (ii) the person specified in the order is appointed interim receiver of the property of the debtor;

  (g) identification and contact details for the interim receiver, where the interim receiver is not the official receiver;
  (h) details of the nature, together with a short description, of the property of which the interim receiver is to take possession;
  (i) details of the duties to be carried out by the interim receiver in relation to the debtor's affairs;
  (j) a notice to the debtor stating that the debtor must give the interim receiver all the information about the debtor's property that the interim receiver may require in order to carry out the functions imposed on the interim receiver by the order; and
  (k) the date of the order.

(2) The court must, as soon as reasonably practicable after the order is made, deliver two sealed copies of the order to the person appointed interim receiver.

(3) The interim receiver must as soon as reasonably practicable deliver a sealed copy of the order to the debtor.

Security

10.52.—(1) This rule applies where an insolvency practitioner is appointed as interim receiver under section 286.

(2) The cost of providing the security required under the Act must be paid in the first instance by the interim receiver.

(3) If a bankruptcy order is not made, the person so appointed is entitled to be reimbursed out of the property of the debtor, and the court may make an order on the debtor accordingly.

(4) If a bankruptcy order is made, the person so appointed is entitled to be reimbursed out of the bankrupt's estate in the prescribed order of priority.

(5) If the interim receiver fails to give or keep up the required security, the court may remove the interim receiver, and make such order as it thinks just as to costs.

(6) If an order is made under this rule removing the interim receiver, or discharging the order appointing the interim receiver, the court must give directions as to whether any, and if so what, steps should be taken for the appointment of another person as interim receiver.

Remuneration

10.53.—(1) The remuneration of an interim receiver (other than the official receiver) must be fixed by the court from time to time on application of the interim receiver.

(2) In fixing the remuneration of the interim receiver, the court must take into account—

(a) the time properly given by the interim receiver and staff of the interim receiver in attending to the debtor's affairs;

(b) the complexity of the case;

(c) any respects in which, in connection with the debtor's affairs, there falls on the interim receiver any responsibility of an exceptional kind or degree;

(d) the effectiveness with which the interim receiver appears to be carrying out, or to have carried out, the duties of the interim receiver; and

(e) the value and nature of the property with which the interim receiver has to deal.

(3) Without prejudice to any order the court may make as to costs, the interim receiver's remuneration (whether the official receiver or another) must be paid to the interim receiver, and the amount of any expenses incurred by the interim receiver (including the remuneration and expenses of any special manager appointed under section 370) reimbursed—

(a) if a bankruptcy order is not made, out of the property of the debtor; and

(b) if a bankruptcy order is made, out of the bankrupt's estate in the prescribed order of priority; or

(c) in either case (the relevant funds being insufficient), out of any deposit under rule 10.50.

(4) Unless the court otherwise directs, if a bankruptcy order is not made, the interim receiver may retain out of the debtor's property such sums or

property as are or may be required for meeting the remuneration and expenses of the interim receiver.

(5)   Where a person other than the official receiver has been appointed interim receiver, and the official receiver has taken any steps for the purpose of obtaining a statement of affairs or has performed any other duty under these Rules, the interim receiver must pay the official receiver such sum (if any) as the court may direct.

Termination of appointment

10.54.—(1) The appointment of the interim receiver may be terminated by the court on the application of the interim receiver, or a person specified in rule 10.49(1).

(2)   If the interim receiver's appointment terminates, in consequence of the dismissal of the bankruptcy petition or otherwise, the court may give such directions as it thinks just relating to the accounts of the interim receiver's administration and any other matters which it thinks appropriate.

10.1 APPLICATION FOR THE APPOINTMENT OF AN INTERIM RECEIVER

Form IAA   **Insolvency Act Application Notice**

IN THE HIGH COURT OF JUSTICE
BUSINESS AND PROPERTY COURTS OF ENGLAND AND WALES
INSOLVENCY AND COMPANIES LIST (ChD)
IN BANKRUPTCY

NO: 666 OF 2020

IN THE MATTER OF IAN FLAKEY
AND IN THE MATTER OF THE INSOLVENCY ACT 1986

BETWEEN:-

ANGRY PLC

Applicant

and

(1) IAN FLAKEY
(2) THE OFFICIAL RECEIVER

Respondents

Is this application within existing insolvency proceedings?   YES/~~NO~~

I (We), ANGRY PLC of 1 Unpaid Bill Street, London intend to apply to the ~~Judge/District Judge~~/Registrar on:

Date: 1st April 2020

Time: 00:00 hours

Place: Royal Courts of Justice, 7 Rolls Buildings, Fetter Lane, London EC4A 1NL

This application having been issued at the RCJ, 7 Rolls Buildings, Fetter Lane, London, EC4A 1NL will be heard at the time and date pursuant to the endorsement underneath the Court Seal on the front page of this application.

FOR AN ORDER THAT:

1.   The Official Receiver be appointed as interim receiver in respect of all of the property of Ian Flakey under section 286 of the Insolvency Act 1986.

2.   Such further and other order and other relief as this Honourable Court thinks fit.

The applicant is resident in and has carried on business in the London Insolvency District for the greater part of the 6 months prior to this application.

The applicant relies on the witness statement of Freddy Furious dated 1st April 2017 which sets out the grounds of this application.

THE NAMES AND ADDRESSES OF THE PERSON(S) UPON WHOM IT IS INTENDED TO
SERVE THIS APPLICATION ARE:

Name: IAN FLAKEY

Address: 1 GERANIUM COTTAGE, LONDON

Name: THE OFFICIAL RECEIVER

Address: 5TH FLOOR, ZONE B, 21 BLOOMSBURY STREET, LONDON WC1B 3SS

~~OR~~

~~IT IS NOT INTENDED TO SERVE ANY PERSON WITH THIS APPLICATION~~

Dated:

Signed: SNARKEY & SNYDE

Solicitors for the applicant ~~or Applicant~~   *This is the address
Address: 1 LAW STREET, LONDON   which will be treated
Telephone: 0207 666 6666   by Court as the
Email: law@snarkeysnyde.com   Petitions address for
                                             service

If you do not attend, the court may make such order as it thinks just.

10.2 WITNESS STATEMENT IN SUPPORT OF AN APPLICATION FOR AN INTERIM RECEIVER

Applicant: F Furious: 1st: FF1: [ ] 20[ ]

IN THE HIGH COURT OF JUSTICE
BUSINESS AND PROPERTY COURTS OF ENGLAND AND WALES
INSOLVENCY AND COMPANIES LIST (ChD)

NO: [ ] OF 20[ ]

IN THE MATTER OF IAN FLAKEY
AND IN BANKRUPTCY
AND IN THE MATTER OF THE INSOLVENCY ACT 1986

BETWEEN:-

ANGRY PLC

Applicant

and

(1) IAN FLAKEY
(2) THE OFFICIAL RECEIVER

Respondents

1ST WITNESS STATEMENT OF FREDDY FURIOUS

I, FREDDY FURIOUS, of Angry plc, 1 Unpaid Bill Street, London, Company Director, STATE as follows:

1. I am a director of the Applicant company. I am duly authorised to make this witness statement on its behalf.

2. I make this witness statement in support of the Applicant's application for an order:

   a. That the Official Receiver be appointed as interim receiver in respect of all of the property of Ian Flakey under section 286 of the Insolvency Act 1986;
   b. Such further and other relief as this Honourable Court thinks fit.

3. The matters stated in this witness statement are true and made from my own knowledge except where otherwise indicated, in which I case I explain the source of my information and belief.

4. There is now produced and shown to me a bundle marked 'FF1' which contains true copies of the documents I will refer to in support of this application.

5. On 1st April 2019, Angry plc sold Ian Flakey 100 boxes of widgets for £11,100. I refer to page [ ] of 'FF1' which is a true copy of the invoice.

6. To date no payments have been made for the widgets and Ian Flakey owes Angry plc £11,100.

7. On 1st May 2020, a process server, acting on my behalf, served a statutory demand for this unpaid debt by handing it to Mr Flakey. I refer to page [ ] of 'FF1' which is a true copy of the statutory demand. There has been no application to set the statutory demand aside.

8. On 1st June 2020, a process server, acting on my behalf, served a bankruptcy petition on Mr Flakey. I refer to page [ ] of the exhibit marked 'FF1' which is a true copy of the petition. This Honourable Court will see that the first hearing on this petition is listed for 1st November 2020.

9. On 2nd June 2020, I was walking past Mr Flakey's premises at 1 Geranium Cottage. I was horrified to see a large pile of widgets displayed outside 1 Geranium Cottage on which was fixed a large sign bearing the words 'Any Offers Accepted – Fleeing to Spain to evade my creditors – must take cash'. I refer to page [ ] of 'FF1' which is a true copy of a photograph I took of the sign.

10. I would ask that an interim receiver be appointed over all of Mr Flakey's business and assets. I do not know the full extent or value of his assets, however I would estimate that the stock alone owned by Mr Flakey was worth £20,000. I saw a rare vintage motorcar, registration mark 'Banger 1', parked outside which I would estimate as being worth in the region of £250,000.

11. I have notified the Official Receiver of Angry plc's intention to make this application and the Official Receiver has written back to say that he is willing to take this appointment but would expect £1,000 to be lodged as security for his fees. Angry plc has confirmed that it would be prepared to meet this sum. I can confirm on behalf of Angry plc that this remains the case if an order is made. I refer to page [ ] of my exhibit marked 'FF1' which is a true copy of this correspondence.

12. I believe that no individual voluntary arrangement is in force in respect of Mr Flakey.

13. In all the circumstances, I believe that Mr Flakey's assets are being dissipated to the detriment of his creditors and that the appointment of an interim receiver is necessary to protect them.

14. I therefore ask this Honourable Court to make the order in the terms sought.

STATEMENT OF TRUTH

I believe the facts stated in this Witness Statement are true.

Signed [ ]
Full name [*FREDDY FURIOUS*]
Dated [ ] 20[ ]

10.3   DRAFT ORDER APPOINTING AN INTERIM RECEIVER

IN THE HIGH COURT OF JUSTICE
BUSINESS AND PROPERTY COURTS OF ENGLAND AND WALES
INSOLVENCY AND COMPANIES LIST (ChD)

NO: [ ] OF 20[ ]

IN THE MATTER OF IAN FLAKEY
AND IN BANKRUPTCY

BEFORE MR REGISTRAR WISE
DATED: [ ] OF 20[ ]

BETWEEN:-

ANGRY PLC

Applicant

and

(1) IAN FLAKEY
(2) THE OFFICIAL RECEIVER

Respondents

_____
DRAFT ORDER
_____

UPON THE APPLICATION of Angry plc, a company registered in England and Wales number 666 whose registered office is 1 Unpaid Bill Street, London, a creditor

AND UPON HEARING Counsel for the parties

AND UPON reading the evidence noted as being read

And the court being satisfied that the debtor is unable to pay his debts

And the court being satisfied that the EU Regulation (a) does/does not apply (b) and that these proceedings are main proceedings as defined in Article 3 of the EU Regulation

IT IS ORDERED THAT upon the sum of £[ ] being deposited by the applicant with the Official Receiver the following person is appointed interim receiver of the property of the above-named debtor.

Name of interim receiver: The Official Receiver
Address: 5th Floor, Zone B, 21 Bloomsbury Street, London
                              WC1B 3SS

AND IT IS ORDERED THAT:

The Interim Receiver do
(1)   locate, protect, secure, take possession of, collect and get in all property or assets (of whatever nature) to which Ian Flakey of 1 Geranium Cottage, London is or appears to be entitled, such assets and that such property is not to be distributed

or parted with by the Interim Receiver until further order except pursuant to the functions hereby conferred

(2)   locate, protect, secure, take possession of, collect and get in the books, papers and records of Ian Flakey

(3)   investigate the affairs of Ian Flakey

(4)   do all such things as may be necessary or expedient for the protection of Ian Flakey's property or assets

(5)   without prejudice to the generality of the foregoing, bring or defend or proceed with any action or other legal proceedings on behalf of Ian Flakey and in his name or Ian Flakey's name as appropriate for the purpose of exercising the above functions, and, if so advised, compromise such proceedings

(6)   to do all things necessary or incidental to the foregoing functions, duties and powers.

Dated

NOTICE TO DEBTOR
You must give the interim receiver all the information he may require relating to your property and affairs in order for him to carry out the functions imposed on him by the terms of the above order.

Service of this order

The Court has provided a sealed copy of this order to the serving party:

SNARKEY & SNYDE
1 LAW STREET
LONDON

Chapter 11

APPLICATION FOR COMPENSATION AGAINST A TRUSTEE IN BANKRUPTCY

OBJECTIVE

The court has the power to require a trustee in bankruptcy who has misapplied or retained or become accountable for any money or property of the bankrupt or has been guilty of misfeasance or breach of any fiduciary or other duty in respect of the bankrupt's estate to compensate the estate and to repay, restore and account for property and money.[1] The court can award interest.

The trustee is not liable for any loss or damage for incorrectly seizing property if he reasonably believes it to form part of the bankrupt's estate and he was, at the time, entitled to do so. Indeed, he is treated as having a lien on such property or its proceeds of sale for his expenses.[2] Nor is he liable if acting under a court order.[3]

APPLICATION

The claim is made by application notice on notice to the trustee. It can be made by:

- the Official Receiver;
- the Secretary of State;
- a creditor of the bankrupt;
- the bankrupt, if there is likely to be a surplus on final distribution.[4]

The court's permission is required if the application is to be made by the bankrupt or the application is made after the trustee has had his release.[5]

The application is made on Form IAA. The application should set out:

---

[1]   Section 304(1) of the Insolvency Act 1986. For the test for liability, see *Katz v Oldham* [2016] BPIR 83.

[2]   Section 304(3) of the Insolvency Act 1986.

[3]   *Chapper v Jackson* [2012] EWHC 3897 (Ch), [2012] BPIR 257.

[4]   Section 304(2) of the Insolvency Act 1986. Once the trustee has had his release, a bankrupt can only apply with the permission of the court: *Re Borodzicz* [2016] BPIR 24.

[5]   Section 304(2) of the Insolvency Act 1986.

- that the application is made under the Insolvency Act 1986 or the Insolvency (England and Wales) Rules 2016 (as the case may be);[6]
- the section number or rule under which relief is sought;[7]
- the name of the parties;[8]
- the name of the bankrupt or debtor;[9]
- the court name;[10]
- the case number;[11]
- the remedy applied for or directions sought;[12]
- the name and address of each person to be served or, if none, stating that that it is intended that no person will be served;[13]
- where there is a requirement for particular persons to be given notice of the application under the Act or Rules, stating the name and address of each such person;[14]
- the applicant's address for service.[15]

The application notice must be authenticated by the applicant or his solicitor.[16]

The application should be returnable to the registrar or to the district judge in a Chancery District Registry or county court with insolvency jurisdiction.

COURT FEES

Where the application is made on notice to other parties, a court fee of £155 is payable.[17] Where the application is made by consent or without notice in existing proceedings, a court fee of £50 is payable.[18]

EVIDENCE

The application should be supported by a witness statement by the applicant. This should address:

---

[6] Rule 1.35(2)(a) of the Insolvency (England and Wales) Rules 2016.

[7] Rule 1.35(2)(b) of the Insolvency (England and Wales) Rules 2016.

[8] Rule 1.35(2)(c) of the Insolvency (England and Wales) Rules 2016.

[9] Rule 1.35(2)(d) of the Insolvency (England and Wales) Rules 2016.

[10] Rule 1.35(2)(e) of the Insolvency (England and Wales) Rules 2016.

[11] Rule 1.35(2)(f) of the Insolvency (England and Wales) Rules 2016.

[12] Rule 1.35(2)(g) of the Insolvency (England and Wales) Rules 2016.

[13] Rule 1.35(2)(h) of the Insolvency (England and Wales) Rules 2016.

[14] Rule 1.35(2)(i) of the Insolvency (England and Wales) Rules 2016.

[15] Rule 1.35(2)(j) of the Insolvency (England and Wales) Rules 2016.

[16] Rule 1.35(3) of the Insolvency (England and Wales) Rules 2016. For what amounts to authentication, see rule 1.5. For hard copy applications, this means signed: rule 1.5(2).

[17] Paragraph 3.12 of Schedule 1 to the Civil Proceedings Fees (Amendment) Order 2014.

[18] Paragraph 3.11 of Schedule 1 to the Civil Proceedings Fees (Amendment) Order 2014.

- the basis upon which the applicant has the right to bring the claim;
- the order the applicant seeks;
- whether permission is required and the reasons why it should be granted;
- the date of the bankruptcy;
- the date of the trustee's appointment;
- the nature of the duty the trustee owes to the estate in bankruptcy;
- full particulars of the matters how and when it is said the trustee has misapplied or retained or become accountable for any money or property of the estate in bankruptcy or has been guilty of misfeasance or breach of any fiduciary or other duty in respect of the bankruptcy estate;
- the fact that the arrangement operated to cause loss to the estate in bankruptcy and its creditors;
- particulars of the loss caused.

And should exhibit:

- evidence of the locus of the applicant;
- the bankruptcy order;
- the certificate of the trustee's appointment;
- evidence showing the respondent has misapplied or retained or become accountable for any money or property of the bankrupt or has been guilty of misfeasance or breach of any fiduciary or other duty to the bankruptcy's estate;
- evidence of the loss caused by the respondent's involvement.

SERVICE

The application should be served on:

- the trustee in bankruptcy.

The application and the evidence in support will need to be filed at court and served on the respondent as soon as practicable after it is filed and in any event, unless it is necessary to apply without notice or on short notice, at least 14 days before the date fixed for the hearing.[19]

The usual rule is that, subject to any other express provision, the application must be served at least 14 days before the date fixed for the hearing.[20] However, the court does have power, in cases of urgency, to hear an application immediately with or without notice to the other parties.[21]

---

[19] Rule 12.9(3) of the Insolvency (England and Wales) Rules 2016.

[20] Rule 12.9(3) of the Insolvency (England and Wales) Rules 2016.

[21] Rule 12.10(1) of the Insolvency (England and Wales) Rules 2016.

Service may be effected personally[22] or by post on the respondent (Part 6 of the CPR applies for these purposes)[23] or, where they have authority to accept service, on the respondent's solicitors.[24] Electronic service of documents is now permissible under the Rules, providing the respondent currently consents to service in that way and has provided an email address for service in that way.[25]

FIRST HEARING

At the first hearing, the registrar or district judge will give directions as to whether points of claim are needed and for the filing of evidence. He may also require the application to be served on other people. He may give directions as to whether witnesses are to attend for cross examination. The first hearing is likely to be in chambers and the advocates will not be expected to robe.

KEY MATERIALS

Section 304 of the Insolvency Act 1986

304 Liability of trustee

(1)   Where on an application under this section the court is satisfied—

(a)   that the trustee of a bankrupt's estate has misapplied or retained, or become accountable for, any money or other property comprised in the bankrupt's estate, or

(b)   that a bankrupt's estate has suffered any loss in consequence of any misfeasance or breach of fiduciary or other duty by a trustee of the estate in the carrying out of his functions,

the court may order the trustee, for the benefit of the estate, to repay, restore or account for money or other property (together with interest at such rate as the court thinks just) or, as the case may require, to pay such sum by way of compensation in respect of the misfeasance or breach of fiduciary or other duty as the court thinks just.

This is without prejudice to any liability arising apart from this section.

(2)   An application under this section may be made by the official receiver, the Secretary of State, a creditor of the bankrupt or (whether or not there is, or is likely to be, a surplus for the purposes of section 330(5) (final distribution)) the bankrupt himself.

But the leave of the court is required for the making of an application if it is to be made by the bankrupt or if it is to be made after the trustee has had his release under section 299.

---

[22]   Rule 1.44 of the Insolvency (England and Wales) Rules 2016.

[23]   Schedule 4, paragraph 1(2) to the Insolvency (England and Wales) Rules 2016.

[24]   Rule 1.40 of the Insolvency (England and Wales) Rules 2016.

[25]   Rule 1.45 of the Insolvency (England and Wales) Rules 2016.

(3)   Where—

   (a)   the trustee seizes or disposes of any property which is not comprised in the bankrupt's estate, and
   (b)   at the time of the seizure or disposal the trustee believes, and has reasonable grounds for believing, that he is entitled (whether in pursuance of an order of the court or otherwise) to seize or dispose of that property,

the trustee is not liable to any person (whether under this section or otherwise) in respect of any loss or damage resulting from the seizure or disposal except in so far as that loss or damage is caused by the negligence of the trustee; and he has a lien on the property, or the proceeds of its sale, for such of the expenses of the bankruptcy as were incurred in connection with the seizure or disposal.

11.1   APPLICATION FOR COMPENSATION AGAINST A TRUSTEE IN BANKRUPTCY

Form IAA   **Insolvency Act Application Notice**

IN THE HIGH COURT OF JUSTICE
BUSINESS AND PROPERTY COURTS OF ENGLAND AND WALES
INSOLVENCY AND COMPANIES LIST (ChD)
IN BANKRUPTCY

NO: 666 OF 2020

IN THE MATTER OF IAN FLAKEY
AND IN THE MATTER OF THE INSOLVENCY ACT 1986

BETWEEN:-

FREDDY FURIOUS

Applicant

and

GILES GRABBER
(Trustee in Bankruptcy of IAN FLAKEY)

Respondent

Is this application within existing insolvency proceedings?   YES/~~NO~~

I (~~We~~), FREDDY FURIOUS of 1 Grumpy Street, London intend to apply to the ~~Judge/District Judge~~/Registrar on:

Date: 1st April 2020

Time: 00:00 hours

Place: Royal Courts of Justice, 7 Rolls Buildings, Fetter Lane, London EC4A 1NL

This application having been issued at the RCJ, 7 Rolls Buildings, Fetter Lane, London, EC4A 1NL will be heard at the time and date pursuant to the endorsement underneath the Court Seal on the front page of this application.

FOR A DECLARATION THAT:

1.   The Respondent acted in breach of fiduciary duty and/or in breach of trust and/or was guilty of misfeasance within the meaning of section 304 of the Insolvency Act 1986 by making a payment of £2,500 to Samesburys to pay for the Respondent's grocery shopping on or around 1st April 2020, and/or

FOR AN ORDER THAT:

2.   The Respondent do pay to the Applicant the sum of £2,500 and/or such compensation or make such contribution to the estate in bankruptcy of Ian Flakey as this Honourable Court thinks fit, and/or

3.   There is an enquiry as to what property in the hands of the Respondent represents the payment of the £2,500.

4.   Interest is paid, whether or not compounded, on all sums found due from the Respondent at such rates as the Court thinks fit pursuant to the Court's equitable jurisdiction and/or section 35A of the Senior Courts Act 1981.

5.   The Respondent do pay the Applicant's costs of and incidental to this application.

6.   Such further and other order and other relief as this Honourable Court thinks fit.

The grounds upon which I seek the above order are set out in the 1st witness statement of Freddy Furious dated 1st April 2020, a true copy of which is served herewith.

THE NAMES AND ADDRESSES OF THE PERSON(S) UPON WHOM IT IS INTENDED TO SERVE THIS APPLICATION ARE:

Name: GILES GRABBER

Address: 1 VULTURE STREET, LONDON

Name:

Address:

~~OR~~

~~IT IS NOT INTENDED TO SERVE ANY PERSON WITH THIS APPLICATION~~

Dated:

Signed: SNARKEY & SNYDE

Solicitors for the applicant ~~or Applicant~~   *This is the address
Address: 1 LAW STREET, LONDON   which will be treated
Telephone: 0207 666 6666   by Court as the
Email: law@snarkeysnyde.com   Petitions address for
                                                              service

If you do not attend, the court may make such order as it thinks just.

11.2   WITNESS STATEMENT IN SUPPORT OF AN APPLICATION FOR COMPENSATION AGAINST A TRUSTEE IN BANKRUPTCY

Applicant: F Furious: 1st: FF1: [ ] 20[ ]

IN THE HIGH COURT OF JUSTICE
BUSINESS AND PROPERTY COURTS OF ENGLAND AND WALES
INSOLVENCY AND COMPANIES LIST (ChD)

NO: [ ] OF 20[ ]

IN THE MATTER OF IAN FLAKEY
AND IN BANKRUPTCY
AND IN THE MATTER OF THE INSOLVENCY ACT 1986

BETWEEN:-

FREDDY FURIOUS

Applicant

and

GILES GRABBER
(as Trustee in Bankruptcy of IAN FLAKEY)

Respondent

_____
1ST WITNESS STATEMENT OF FREDDY FURIOUS
_____

I, FREDDY FURIOUS of 1 Grumpy Street, London, Company Director, STATE as follows:

1.   I am the Applicant in this application and an unsecured creditor of the Bankrupt.

2.   The matters set out in this witness statement are true and within my own knowledge except where otherwise indicated, in which case I have explained the source of my information or belief.

3.   There is now produced and shown to me a bundle consisting of true copies of the documents I will refer to in my witness statement marked 'FF1'.

4.   I make this witness statement in support of my application for:

   a.   A declaration that the Respondent acted in breach of fiduciary duty and/or in breach of trust and/or was guilty of misfeasance within the meaning of section 304 of the Insolvency Act 1986 by making a payment of £2,500 to Samesburys to pay for the Respondent's grocery shopping on or around 1st April 2020, and/or

   b.   An order that the Respondent do pay to the Applicant the sum of £2,500 and/or such compensation or make such contribution to the estate in bankruptcy of Ian Flakey as this Honourable Court thinks fit, and/or

   c.   An enquiry as to what property in the hands of the Respondent represents the payment of the £2,500,

   d.   An order for interest, whether or not compounded, on all sums found due from the Respondent at such rates as the Court thinks fit pursuant to the Court's equitable jurisdiction and/or section 35A of the Senior Courts Act 1981,

   e.   An order that the Respondent do pay the Applicant's costs of and incidental to this application,

f.   Such further and other order and other relief as this Honourable Court thinks fit.

5.   On 27th August 2019, a Bankruptcy Order was made against the Bankrupt. I refer to page [ ] of the exhibit marked 'FF1' which is a true copy of the order.

6.   On 1st December 2019, the Respondent was appointed the Bankrupt's Trustee in Bankruptcy. I refer to page [ ] of the exhibit marked 'FF1' which is a true copy of his certificate of appointment.

7.   I proved in the bankruptcy in the sum of £4,000 representing an unpaid consignment of chrome pins which the Bankrupt had ordered and I had delivered but which had never been paid for.

8.   When on 1st April 2020, I was delivering my proof of debt to the offices of the Trustee, I noticed that he was receiving a large delivery from Samesburys, a supermarket, which seemed to comprise numerous boxes of triple chocolate chip biscuits. I jokingly remarked to Mr Grabber that I hoped the cost of this wasn't coming out of the estate.

9.   To my astonishment, Mr Grabber replied that it was and said that he indeed considered it something of a bargain as it only cost £2,500.

10.   When I expressed my outrage that the creditors' money should be used in this profligacy, Mr Grabber simply responded that 'Man cannot live by bread alone' and then added 'I'm not going to eat all of it myself. I will be using a few boxes to sell tea and biscuits at the local fete. Being an insolvency practitioner is not what it used to be'. I refer to page [ ] of 'FF1' which is a true copy of a note I made of the conversation shortly after.

11.   Mr Grabber is and was the Trustee in Bankruptcy of Mr Ian Flakey at all relevant times and owed fiduciary duties to act in the best interests of the estate and not to make secret profits. As trustee, he is accountable for his dealings with the estate's assets.

12.   In the light of the above, I am advised that by using the estate's money to make the payment to Samesburys Supermarket for his own grocery bill or to use the estate's money to buy stock to sell for his own benefit at his local fete, the Respondent acted in breach of his fiduciary duty and/or was in breach of trust and/or was guilty of misfeasance.

13.   In the circumstances Mr Flakey holds the £2,500 or the triple chocolate chip biscuits or the proceeds of sale he purchased with it on trust for the estate and he is liable to account to me and the other creditors for the same. I require an account of what happened to the triple chocolate chip biscuits.

14.   I respectfully ask that the Order be granted in the terms sought.

STATEMENT OF TRUTH

I believe that the facts stated in this Witness Statement are true.

Signed [ ]
Full name [*FREDDY FURIOUS*]
Dated [ ] 20 [ ]

11.3   DECLARATION THAT THERE HAS BEEN A BREACH OF DUTY BY A TRUSTEE IN BANKRUPTCY

IN THE HIGH COURT OF JUSTICE
BUSINESS AND PROPERTY COURTS OF ENGLAND AND WALES
INSOLVENCY AND COMPANIES LIST (ChD)

NO: [ ] OF 20[ ]

IN THE MATTER OF IAN FLAKEY
AND IN BANKRUPTCY
AND IN THE MATTER OF THE INSOLVENCY ACT 1986

BEFORE MR REGISTRAR WISE
DATED: [ ] OF 20[ ]

BETWEEN:-

FREDDY FURIOUS

Applicant

and

GILES GRABBER
(as Trustee in Bankruptcy of IAN FLAKEY)

Respondent

DRAFT MINUTE OF ORDER

UPON THE APPLICATION of Freddy Furious dated [ ]

UPON HEARING Counsel for the Applicant and for the Respondent

AND UPON READING the evidence noted as being read

IT IS DECLARED THAT the Respondent acted in breach of fiduciary duty and/or in breach of trust and/or was guilty of misfeasance by making a payment of £2,500 to Samesburys to pay for the Respondent's grocery shopping on or around 1st April 2020 within the meaning of section 304 of the Insolvency Act 1986

AND IT IS ORDERED THAT the Respondent do by 4 pm on 1st August 2021 repay to the estate in bankruptcy the sum of £2,500 in respect of the sum the Respondent in breach of fiduciary duty and/or in breach of trust and/or was guilty of misfeasance caused the Company to pay to Samesburys to pay for the Respondent's grocery shopping on or around 1st April 2020 together with interest in the sum of £250 to the date of this Order

AND IT IS ORDERED THAT the Respondent do pay the Applicant's costs of and incidental to this application, such costs to be assessed on a standard basis if not agreed

Service of this order

The Court has provided a sealed copy of this order to the serving party:

SNARKEY & SNYDE
1 LAW STREET
LONDON

Chapter 12

APPLICATION FOR AN ORDER FOR THE SALE OF THE BANKRUPT'S HOME

OBJECTIVE

The bankrupt's property vests in his trustee upon the trustee's appointment.[1] Often the bankrupt's matrimonial home will, however, be jointly owned with his spouse. The bankruptcy court[2] has powers to determine the interests of the beneficial owners and order the sale of property.[3]

There are two important provisos. First, the court will dismiss any application for an order for sale if the value of the bankrupt's interest is below £1,000.[4] Second, any interest the bankrupt has in his principal residence re-vests automatically on the bankrupt at the end of the period of 3 years of the bankruptcy unless the trustee has realised the interest, applied for an order for sale or possession or charge, or reached an agreement with the bankrupt to re-vest it.[5]

On an application for an order for sale, the court has a discretion to make such order as it thinks just and reasonable having regard to: (a) the interests of the bankrupt's creditors; (b) where the application is made in respect of land which includes a dwelling house which is or has been the home of the bankrupt or the bankrupt's spouse or civil partner or former spouse or former civil partner: (i) the conduct of the spouse, civil partner, former spouse or former civil partner, so far as contributing to the bankruptcy; (ii) the needs and financial resources of the spouse, civil partner, former spouse or former civil partner; and (iii) the needs of any children; and (c) all the circumstances of the case other than the needs of the bankrupt.[6]

However, where such an application is made after the end of the period of one year beginning with the first vesting of the bankrupt's estate in a trustee, the court will assume that the interests of the bankrupt's creditors outweigh all other considerations unless the circumstances of the case are exceptional.[7] The fact that

---

[1]   Section 306(1) of the Insolvency Act 1986.

[2]   Section 335A of the Insolvency Act 1986.

[3]   Section 14 of the Trusts of Land and Appointment of Trustees Act 1996.

[4]   Section 313A of the Insolvency Act 1986.

[5]   Section 283A of the Insolvency Act 1986.

[6]   Section 335A(2) of the Insolvency Act 1986.

[7]   Section 335A(3) of the Insolvency Act 1986.

a wife and children would be deprived of their home does not amount to exceptional circumstances but is considered merely to be a normal incident of bankruptcy.[8]

APPLICATION

The application is by application on notice on Form 7.1A for declarations and for an order for possession and sale. The application should be made on notice with the bankrupt and any person who it is thought might assert an interest in the property named as respondents.

The application is made on Form IAA. The application should set out:

- that the application is made under the Insolvency Act 1986 or the Insolvency (England and Wales) Rules 2016 (as the case may be);[9]
- the section number or rule under which relief is sought;[10]
- the name of the parties;[11]
- the name of the bankrupt or debtor;[12]
- the court name;[13]
- the case number;[14]
- the remedy applied for or directions sought;[15]
- the name and address of each person to be served or, if none, stating that that it is intended that no person will be served;[16]
- where there is a requirement for particular persons to be given notice of the application under the Act or Rules, stating the name and address of each such person;[17]
- the applicant's address for service.[18]

The application notice must be authenticated by the applicant or his solicitor.[19]

The application should be returnable to the registrar in the Bankruptcy Registry or to the district judge in a Chancery District Registry or county court with insolvency jurisdiction.

---

[8]   *Donoghue v Ingram* [2006] EWHC 282 (Ch), [2006] BPIR 417; *Dean v Stout* [2004] EWHC 3315 (Ch), [2005] BPIR 1113; *Turner v Avis* [2008] BPIR 1143; *Grant v Baker* [2016] EWHC 1782 (Ch), [2016] BPIR 1409.

[9]   Rule 1.35(2)(a) of the Insolvency (England and Wales) Rules 2016.

[10] Rule 1.35(2)(b) of the Insolvency (England and Wales) Rules 2016.

[11] Rule 1.35(2)(c) of the Insolvency (England and Wales) Rules 2016.

[12] Rule 1.35(2)(d) of the Insolvency (England and Wales) Rules 2016.

[13] Rule 1.35(2)(e) of the Insolvency (England and Wales) Rules 2016.

[14] Rule 1.35(2)(f) of the Insolvency (England and Wales) Rules 2016.

[15] Rule 1.35(2)(g) of the Insolvency (England and Wales) Rules 2016.

[16] Rule 1.35(2)(h) of the Insolvency (England and Wales) Rules 2016.

[17] Rule 1.35(2)(i) of the Insolvency (England and Wales) Rules 2016.

[18] Rule 1.35(2)(j) of the Insolvency (England and Wales) Rules 2016.

[19] Rule 1.35(3) of the Insolvency (England and Wales) Rules 2016. For what amounts to authentication, see rule 1.5. For hard copy applications, this means signed: rule 1.5(2).

COURT FEES

Where the application is made by ordinary application on notice to other parties, a court fee of £155 is payable.[20] Where the application is made by consent or without notice in existing proceedings, a court fee of £50 is payable.[21]

EVIDENCE

The application should be supported by a witness statement. This should address:

- the capacity in which the deponent makes this application;
- the order the deponent seeks;
- the date of the petition;
- the date of the bankruptcy order;
- the date upon which the trustee was appointed;
- the address and land registry number of the property;
- whether the property is residential or commercial;
- whether the property is freehold or leasehold (and if the latter the nature of the bankrupt's interest);
- whether the property is the bankrupt's principal dwelling house;
- whether the property is the principal dwelling house of the bankrupt's spouse or civil partner or former spouse or former civil partner;
- the bankrupt's indebtedness in the bankruptcy;
- the value of the bankrupt's other assets;
- the value of the property vested on the trustee;
- any mortgages secured on the property and their redemption value;
- that the value of the bankrupt's interest exceeds £1,000;[22]
- the conduct of the spouse, civil partner, former spouse or former civil partner, so far as contributing to the bankruptcy (so far as it is known);
- the needs and financial resources of the spouse, civil partner, former spouse or former civil partner (so far as it is known);
- the needs of any children (so far as it is known);
- the circumstances of the case other than the needs of the bankrupt;
- whether the application has been made after the end of the period of one year beginning with the first vesting of the bankrupt's estate in a trustee and (if so) that the interests of the bankrupt's creditors outweigh all other considerations unless the circumstances of the case are exceptional.[23]

And should exhibit:

- the bankruptcy order;
- the notice of the trustee's appointment;

---

[20] Paragraph 3.12 of Schedule 1 to the Civil Proceedings Fees (Amendment) Order 2014.

[21] Paragraph 3.11 of Schedule 1 to the Civil Proceedings Fees (Amendment) Order 2014.

[22] Section 313A of the Insolvency Act 1986.

[23] Section 335A(3) of the Insolvency Act 1986.

- the entry at Her Majesty's Land Registry;
- any documents available which tend to show the bankrupt's beneficial interest (for example Land Registry Form TR1);
- the bankrupt's statement of affairs;
- an independent valuation of the property to be disposed of.

FIRST HEARING

At the first hearing, the registrar or district judge will give directions as to whether points of claim are needed and for the filing of evidence. He may also require the application to be served on other people. He may give directions as to whether witnesses are to attend for cross examination. The first hearing is likely to be heard in chambers and the advocates are not expected to robe.

SERVICE

The application and the evidence in support should be filed at court and served on the respondent as soon as practicable after it is filed and in any event, unless it is necessary to apply without notice or on short notice, at least 14 days before the date fixed for the hearing.[24]

The usual rule is that, subject to any other express provision, the application must be served at least 14 days before the date fixed for the hearing.[25] However, the court does have power, in cases of urgency, to hear an application immediately with or without notice to the other parties.[26]

Service may be effected personally[27] or by post on the respondent (Part 6 of the CPR applies for these purposes)[28] or, where they have authority to accept service, on the respondent's solicitors.[29] Electronic service of documents is now permissible under the Rules, providing the respondent currently consents to service in that way and has provided an email address for service in that way.[30]

---

[24] Rule 7.4(5) of the Insolvency (England and Wales) Rules 2016.

[25] Rule 7.4(5) of the Insolvency (England and Wales) Rules 2016.

[26] Rule 7.4(6) of the Insolvency (England and Wales) Rules 2016.

[27] Rule 1.44 of the Insolvency (England and Wales) Rules 2016.

[28] Paragraph 1(2) of Schedule 4 to the Insolvency (England and Wales) Rules 2016.

[29] Rule 1.40 of the Insolvency (England and Wales) Rules 2016.

[30] Rule 1.45 of the Insolvency (England and Wales) Rules 2016.

KEY MATERIALS

Sections 283A, 313A, 335A, 336, 337 and 338 of the Insolvency Act 1986

283A Bankrupt's home ceasing to form part of estate

(1) This section applies where property comprised in the bankrupt's estate consists of an interest in a dwelling-house which at the date of the bankruptcy was the sole or principal residence of—

    (a) the bankrupt,

    (b) the bankrupt's spouse or civil partner, or

    (c) a former spouse or former civil partner of the bankrupt.

(2) At the end of the period of three years beginning with the date of the bankruptcy the interest mentioned in subsection (1) shall—

    (a) cease to be comprised in the bankrupt's estate, and

    (b) vest in the bankrupt (without conveyance, assignment or transfer).

(3) Subsection (2) shall not apply if during the period mentioned in that subsection—

    (a) the trustee realises the interest mentioned in subsection (1),

    (b) the trustee applies for an order for sale in respect of the dwelling-house,

    (c) the trustee applies for an order for possession of the dwelling-house,

    (d) the trustee applies for an order under section 313 in Chapter IV in respect of that interest, or

    (e) the trustee and the bankrupt agree that the bankrupt shall incur a specified liability to his estate (with or without the addition of interest from the date of the agreement) in consideration of which the interest mentioned in subsection (1) shall cease to form part of the estate.

(4) Where an application of a kind described in subsection (3)(b) to (d) is made during the period mentioned in subsection (2) and is dismissed, unless the court orders otherwise the interest to which the application relates shall on the dismissal of the application—

    (a) cease to be comprised in the bankrupt's estate, and

    (b) vest in the bankrupt (without conveyance, assignment or transfer).

(5) If the bankrupt does not inform the trustee or the official receiver of his interest in a property before the end of the period of three months beginning with the date of the bankruptcy, the period of three years mentioned in subsection (2)—

    (a) shall not begin with the date of the bankruptcy, but

    (b) shall begin with the date on which the trustee or official receiver becomes aware of the bankrupt's interest.

(6)   The court may substitute for the period of three years mentioned in subsection (2) a longer period—

    (a)   in prescribed circumstances, and
    (b)   in such other circumstances as the court thinks appropriate.

(7)   The rules may make provision for this section to have effect with the substitution of a shorter period for the period of three years mentioned in subsection (2) in specified circumstances (which may be described by reference to action to be taken by a trustee in bankruptcy).

(8)   The rules may also, in particular, make provision—

    (a)   requiring or enabling the trustee of a bankrupt's estate to give notice that this section applies or does not apply;
    (b)   about the effect of a notice under paragraph (a);
    (c)   requiring the trustee of a bankrupt's estate to make an application to the Chief Land Registrar.

(9)   Rules under subsection (8)(b) may, in particular—

    (a)   disapply this section;
    (b)   enable a court to disapply this section;
    (c)   make provision in consequence of a disapplication of this section;
    (d)   enable a court to make provision in consequence of a disapplication of this section;
    (e)   make provision (which may include provision conferring jurisdiction on a court or tribunal) about compensation.

313A Low value home: application for sale, possession or charge
(1)   This section applies where—

    (a)   property comprised in the bankrupt's estate consists of an interest in a dwelling-house which at the date of the bankruptcy was the sole or principal residence of—

      (i)   the bankrupt,
      (ii)   the bankrupt's spouse or civil partner, or
      (iii) a former spouse or former civil partner of the bankrupt, and

    (b)   the trustee applies for an order for the sale of the property, for an order for possession of the property or for an order under section 313 in respect of the property.

(2)   The court shall dismiss the application if the value of the interest is below the amount prescribed for the purposes of this subsection.
(3)   In determining the value of an interest for the purposes of this section the court shall disregard any matter which it is required to disregard by the order which prescribes the amount for the purposes of subsection (2).

335A Rights under trusts of land

(1) Any application by a trustee of a bankrupt's estate under section 14 of the Trusts of Land and Appointment of Trustees Act 1996 (powers of court in relation to trusts of land) for an order under that section for the sale of land shall be made to the court having jurisdiction in relation to the bankruptcy.

(2) On such an application the court shall make such order as it thinks just and reasonable having regard to—

  (a) the interests of the bankrupt's creditors;
  (b) where the application is made in respect of land which includes a dwelling house which is or has been the home of the bankrupt or the bankrupt's spouse or civil partner or former spouse or former civil partner—

    (i) the conduct of the spouse, civil partner, former spouse or former civil partner, so far as contributing to the bankruptcy,
    (ii) the needs and financial resources of the spouse, civil partner, former spouse or former civil partner, and
    (iii) the needs of any children; and

  (c) all the circumstances of the case other than the needs of the bankrupt.

(3) Where such an application is made after the end of the period of one year beginning with the first vesting under Chapter IV of this Part of the bankrupt's estate in a trustee, the court shall assume, unless the circumstances of the case are exceptional, that the interests of the bankrupt's creditors outweigh all other considerations.

(4) The powers conferred on the court by this section are exercisable on an application whether it is made before or after the commencement of this section.

336 Rights of occupation etc. of bankrupt's spouse

(1) Nothing occurring in the initial period of the bankruptcy (that is to say, the period beginning with the day of the presentation of the petition for the bankruptcy order and ending with the vesting of the bankrupt's estate in a trustee) is to be taken as having given rise to any rights of occupation under the Matrimonial Homes Act 1983 in relation to a dwelling house comprised in the bankrupt's estate.

(2) Where a spouse's rights of occupation under the Act of 1983 are a charge on the estate or interest of the other spouse, or of trustees for the other spouse, and the other spouse is adjudged bankrupt—

  (a) the charge continues to subsist notwithstanding the bankruptcy and, subject to the provisions of that Act, binds the trustee of the bankrupt's estate and persons deriving title under that trustee, and
  (b) any application for an order under section 1 of that Act shall be made to the court having jurisdiction in relation to the bankruptcy.

(3) Where a person and his spouse or former spouse are trustees for sale of a
dwelling house and that person is adjudged bankrupt, any application by the
trustee of the bankrupt's estate for an order under section 30 of the Law of
Property Act 1925 (powers of court where trustees for sale refuse to act)
shall be made to the court having jurisdiction in relation to the bankruptcy.

(4) On such an application as is mentioned in subsection (2) or (3) the court
shall make such order under section 1 of the Act of 1983 or section 30 of the
Act of 1925 as it thinks just and reasonable having regard to—

  (a) the interests of the bankrupt's creditors,
  (b) the conduct of the spouse or former spouse, so far as contributing to
      the bankruptcy,
  (c) the needs and financial resources of the spouse or former spouse,
  (d) the needs of any children, and
  (e) all the circumstances of the case other than the needs of the bankrupt.

(5) Where such an application is made after the end of the period of one year
beginning with the first vesting under Chapter IV of this Part of the
bankrupt's estate in a trustee, the court shall assume, unless the
circumstances of the case are exceptional, that the interests of the bankrupt's
creditors outweigh all other considerations.

337 Rights of occupation of bankrupt
(1) This section applies where—

  (a) a person who is entitled to occupy a dwelling house by virtue of a
      beneficial estate or interest is adjudged bankrupt, and
  (b) any persons under the age of 18 with whom that person had at some
      time occupied that dwelling house had their home with that person at
      the time when the bankruptcy petition was presented and at the
      commencement of the bankruptcy.

(2) Whether or not the bankrupt's spouse (if any) has rights of occupation under
the Matrimonial Homes Act 1983—

  (a) the bankrupt has the following rights as against the trustee of his
      estate—

      (i) if in occupation, a right not to be evicted or excluded from the
          dwelling house or any part of it, except with the leave of the court,
      (ii) if not in occupation, a right with the leave of the court to enter
          into and occupy the dwelling house, and

  (b) the bankrupt's rights are a charge, having the like priority as an
      equitable interest created immediately before the commencement of
      the bankruptcy, on so much of his estate or interest in the dwelling
      house as vests in the trustee.

(3) The Act of 1983 has effect, with the necessary modifications, as if—

    (a)   the rights conferred by paragraph (a) of subsection (2) were rights of occupation under that Act,

    (b)   any application for leave such as is mentioned in that paragraph were an application for an order under section 1 of that Act, and

    (c)   any charge under paragraph (b) of that subsection on the estate or interest of the trustee were a charge under that Act on the estate or interest of a spouse.

(4)   Any application for leave such as is mentioned in subsection (2)(a) or otherwise by virtue of this section for an order under section 1 of the Act of 1983 shall be made to the court having jurisdiction in relation to the bankruptcy.

(5)   On such an application the court shall make such order under section 1 of the Act of 1983 as it thinks just and reasonable having regard to the interests of the creditors, to the bankrupt's financial resources, to the needs of the children and to all the circumstances of the case other than the needs of the bankrupt.

(6)   Where such an application is made after the end of the period of one year beginning with the first vesting (under Chapter IV of this Part) of the bankrupt's estate in a trustee, the court shall assume, unless the circumstances of the case are exceptional, that the interests of the bankrupt's creditors outweigh all other considerations.

338 Payments in respect of premises occupied by bankrupt

Where any premises comprised in a bankrupt's estate are occupied by him (whether by virtue of the preceding section or otherwise) on condition that he makes payments towards satisfying any liability arising under a mortgage of the premises or otherwise towards the outgoings of the premises, the bankrupt does not, by virtue of those payments, acquire any interest in the premises.

Rules 10.121–10.124 and 10.167–10.170 of the Insolvency (England and Wales) Rules 2016

Interpretation

10.121 For the purposes of this Chapter 'and' includes any interest in, or right over, land.

Claim by mortgagee of land

10.122(1) Any person claiming to be the legal or equitable mortgagee of land belonging to the bankrupt may apply to the court for an order directing that the land be sold.

(2)   The court, if satisfied as to the applicant's title, may direct accounts to be taken and enquiries made to ascertain—

    (a)   the principal, interest and costs due under the mortgage; and

    (b)   where the mortgagee has been in possession of the land or any part of it, the rents and profits, dividends, interest, or other proceeds received by the mortgagee or on the mortgagee's behalf.

(3)   The court may also give directions in relation to any mortgage (whether prior or subsequent) on the same property, other than that of the applicant.

(4)   For the purpose of those accounts and enquiries, and of making title to the purchaser, any of the parties may be examined by the court, and must produce on oath before the court all such documents in their custody or under their control relating to the bankrupt's estate as the court may direct.

(5)   The court may under paragraph (4) order any of the parties to clarify any matter which is in dispute in the proceedings or give additional information in relation to any such matter and CPR Part 18 (further information) applies to any such order.

(6)   In any proceedings between a mortgagor and mortgagee, or the trustee of either of them, the court may order accounts to be taken and enquiries made in like manner as in the Chancery Division of the High Court.

Power of court to order sale

10.123.—(1) The court may order that the land, or any specified part of it, be sold and any party bound by the order and in possession of the land or part, or in receipt of the rents and profits from it, may be ordered to deliver possession or receipt to the purchaser or to such other person as the court may direct.

(2)   The court may—

    (a)   permit the person having the conduct of the sale to sell the land in such manner as that person thinks fit; or

    (b)   direct that the land be sold as directed by the order.

(3)   The court's order may contain directions—

    (a)   appointing the person to have the conduct of the sale;

    (b)   fixing the manner of sale (whether by contract conditional on the court's approval, private treaty, public auction, or otherwise);

    (c)   settling the particulars and conditions of sale;

    (d)   for obtaining evidence of the value of the property and for fixing a reserve or minimum price;

    (e)   requiring particular persons to join in the sale and conveyance;

    (f)   requiring the payment of the purchase money into court, or to trustees or others; or

    (g)   if the sale is to be by public auction, fixing the security (if any) to be given by the auctioneer, and the auctioneer's remuneration.

(4)   The court may direct that, if the sale is to be by public auction, the mortgagee may bid on the mortgagee's own behalf.

(5)   Nothing in this rule or rule 10.124 affects the rights in rem of creditors or third parties protected under Article 8 of the EU Regulation.

Proceeds of sale

10.124.—(1) The proceeds of sale must be applied as follows—

    (a)   first in payment of—

(i)   the trustee's expenses in relation to the application to the court,
(ii)   the trustee's expenses of the sale and attendance at it, and
(iii) any costs of the trustee arising from the taking of accounts, and making of enquiries, as directed by the court under rule 10.122;

(b) secondly, in payment of the amount found due to any mortgagee, for principal, interest and costs; and
(c) the balance must be retained by or paid to the trustee.

(2)   Where the proceeds of the sale are insufficient to pay in full the amount found due to any mortgagee, the mortgagee is entitled to prove as a creditor for any deficiency, and to receive dividends rateably with other creditors, but not so as to disturb any dividend already declared.

Bankrupt's home: property falling within section 283A
10.167.—(1) Where it appears to a trustee that section 283A(1) applies, the trustee must deliver notice as soon as reasonably practicable to—

(a) the bankrupt;
(b) the bankrupt's spouse or civil partner (in a case falling within section 283A(1)(b)); and
(c) the former spouse or former civil partner of the bankrupt (in a case falling within section 283A(1)(c)).

(2)   Such a notice must contain—

(a) the name of the bankrupt;
(b) the address of the dwelling-house;
(c) if the dwelling-house is registered land, the title number; and
(d) the date by which the trustee must have delivered the notice.

(3)   A trustee must not deliver such a notice any later than 14 days before the third anniversary of the bankruptcy order or, 14 days before the third anniversary of when the official receiver or trustee became aware of the property.

Application in relation to the vesting of an interest in a dwelling-house (registered land)
10.168.—(1) This rule applies where—

(a) the bankrupt's estate includes an interest in a dwelling-house which at the date of bankruptcy was the sole or principal residence of—

(i)   the bankrupt,
(ii)   the bankrupt's spouse or civil partner, or
(iii) a former spouse or former civil partner of the bankrupt; and

(b) the dwelling-house is registered land; and

(c)   an entry has been made relating to the bankruptcy in the individual register of the dwelling-house or the register has been altered to reflect the vesting of the bankrupt's interest in a trustee in bankruptcy.

(2)   Where such an interest ceases to be comprised in the bankrupt's estate and vests in the bankrupt under either section 283A(2) or 283A(4) of the Act, or under section 261(8) of the Enterprise Act 2002, the trustee must, within five business days of the vesting, make such application to the Chief Land Registrar as is necessary to show in the individual register of the dwelling-house that the interest has vested in the bankrupt.

(3)   The trustee's application must be made in accordance with the Land Registration Act 2002 and must be accompanied by—

(a)   evidence of the trustee's appointment (where not previously provided to the Chief Land Registrar); and
(b)   a certificate from the trustee stating that the interest has vested in the bankrupt under section 283A(2) or 283A(4) of the Act or section 261(8) of the Enterprise Act 2002 (whichever is appropriate).

(4)   As soon as reasonably practicable after making such an application, the trustee must deliver notice of the application—

(a)   to the bankrupt; and
(b)   to the bankrupt's spouse, former spouse, civil partner or former civil partner if the dwelling-house was the sole or principal residence of that person.

(5)   The trustee must deliver notice of the application to every person who (to the trustee's knowledge) claims an interest in, or is under any liability in relation to, the dwelling-house.

Vesting of bankrupt's interest (unregistered land)
10.169.—(1) Where an interest in a dwelling-house which at the date of the bankruptcy was the sole or principal residence of—

(a)   the bankrupt;
(b)   the bankrupt's spouse or civil partner; or
(c)   a former spouse or former civil partner of the bankrupt;

ceases to be comprised in the bankrupt's estate and vests in the bankrupt under either section 283A(2) or 283A(4) of the Act or section 261(8) of the Enterprise Act 2002 and the dwelling-house is unregistered land, the trustee must as soon as reasonably practicable deliver to the bankrupt a certificate as to the vesting.

(2)   Such a certificate is conclusive proof that the interest mentioned in paragraph (1) has vested in the bankrupt.

(3)   As soon as reasonably practicable after delivering the certificate, the trustee must deliver a copy of the certificate to the bankrupt's spouse, former

spouse, civil partner or former civil partner if the dwelling-house was the sole or principal residence of that person.

(4)   The trustee must deliver a copy of the certificate to every person who (to the trustee's knowledge) claims an interest in, or is under any liability relating to, the dwelling-house.

Vesting of bankrupt's estate: substituted period

10.170.—(1) For the purposes of section 283A(2) the period of one month is substituted for the period of three years set out in that section where the trustee has delivered notice to the bankrupt that the trustee considers—

(a)   the continued vesting of the property in the bankrupt's estate to be of no benefit to creditors; or

(b)   the re-vesting to the bankrupt will make dealing with the bankrupt's estate more efficient.

(2)   The one month period starts from the date of the notice.

12.1 APPLICATION FOR A DECLARATION OF INTEREST AND ORDER FOR SALE OF THE BANKRUPT'S MATRIMONIAL HOME

Form IAA   **Insolvency Act Application Notice**

IN THE HIGH COURT OF JUSTICE
BUSINESS AND PROPERTY COURTS OF ENGLAND AND WALES
INSOLVENCY AND COMPANIES LIST (ChD)
IN BANKRUPTCY

NO: 666 OF 2020

IN THE MATTER OF IAN FLAKEY
AND IN THE MATTER OF THE INSOLVENCY ACT 1986

BETWEEN:-

GILES GRABBER
(Trustee in Bankruptcy of IAN FLAKEY)

Applicant

and

(1) MRS TABITHA FLAKEY
(2) IAN FLAKEY

Respondents

Is this application within existing insolvency proceedings?   YES/~~NO~~

I (~~We~~), IAN FLAKEY of 1 Geranium Cottage, London intend to apply to the ~~Judge/District Judge~~/Registrar on:

Date: 1st April 2020

Time: 00:00 hours

Place: Royal Courts of Justice, 7 Rolls Buildings, Fetter Lane, London EC4A 1NL

This application having been issued at the RCJ, 7 Rolls Buildings, Fetter Lane, London, EC4A 1NL will be heard at the time and date pursuant to the endorsement underneath the Court Seal on the front page of this application.

FOR AN ORDER THAT:

See attached sheet.

THE NAMES AND ADDRESSES OF THE PERSON(S) UPON WHOM IT IS INTENDED TO SERVE THIS APPLICATION ARE:

Name: IAN FLAKEY

Address: 1 GERANIUM COTTAGE, LONDON

Name: TABITHA FLAKEY

Address: 1 GERANIUM COTTAGE, LONDON

~~OR~~

~~IT IS NOT INTENDED TO SERVE ANY PERSON WITH THIS APPLICATION~~

Dated:

Signed: SNARKEY & SNYDE

Solicitors for the applicant ~~or Applicant~~
Address: 1 LAW STREET, LONDON
Telephone: 0207 666 6666
Email: law@snarkeysnyde.com

*This is the address
which will be treated
by Court as the
Petitions address for
service

If you do not attend, the court may make such order as it thinks just.

Continuation

Under section 335A of the Insolvency Act 1986:

1.   A declaration that the 1st Respondent holds the beneficial interest in the freehold property known as and situate at 1 Geranium Cottage, London, Land Registry Title number 1234, ['1 Geranium Cottage'] on trust as to 50% for herself and as to 50% for the Applicant.

2.   An order that 1 Geranium Cottage be sold with vacant possession and that the 1st Respondent do concur in such sale.

3.   An order that the conduct of such sale of 1 Geranium Cottage be given to the Applicant as Trustee in Bankruptcy of the estate of the Bankrupt.

4.   An order that the 1st Respondent should join with the Applicant and do all such things as may be necessary to procure the said sale of 1 Geranium Cottage with vacant possession.

5.   An order that the 1st Respondent do within 28 days deliver up vacant possession of 1 Geranium Cottage to the Applicant.

6.   An order that the 1st Respondent shall be removed forthwith as trustee for sale and that the Applicant be appointed in her place under section 41 of the Trustee Act 1925 and that the Applicant shall have power as Trustee to execute all necessary deeds, documents and instruments relating to the said sale.

7.   An order that upon sale the proceeds of sale of 1 Geranium Cottage be applied in the following manner: (1) to the expenses of sale be discharged out of the proceeds of sale, (2) to discharge the mortgage in favour of Brassic Bank plc, (3) the balance of the proceeds of sale shall be paid in equal shares to the 1st Respondent and the Applicant as Trustee in Bankruptcy of the estate of the 2nd Respondent, (4) there shall be deducted from the 1st Respondent's entitlement and added to the Applicant's entitlement of the net proceeds: (i) Any sum ordered by way of costs under this Order, (ii) a sum in respect of the 1st Respondent's use and occupation of 1 Geranium Cottage since the date of the Bankruptcy Order at £200 per week.

8.   An order that in the event that the aggregate amount to be deducted from the 1st Respondent's share is found to exceed the value of the 1st Respondent's share, the 1st Respondent do pay to the Applicant such balance within 28 days of it being demanded by the Applicant.

9.   An order that the 1st Respondent do pay the costs of and incidental to this Application.

10. Any costs of the application that are not payable by the 1st Respondent or not recovered from her should be paid to the Applicant as such trustee out of the assets of the bankruptcy as an expense of the bankruptcy within rule 10.149(a) of the Insolvency (England and Wales) Rules 2016.

11. Such further and other order and other relief as this Honourable Court thinks fit.

The grounds of this application are set out in the witness statement of Giles Grabber dated [ ].

12.2 WITNESS STATEMENT IN SUPPORT OF AN APPLICATION FOR A DECLARATION OF INTEREST IN AND ORDER FOR SALE OF THE BANKRUPT'S MATRIMONIAL HOME

Applicant: G Grabber: 1st: GG1: [ ] 20[ ]

IN THE HIGH COURT OF JUSTICE
BUSINESS AND PROPERTY COURTS OF ENGLAND AND WALES
INSOLVENCY AND COMPANIES LIST (ChD)

NO: [ ] OF 20[ ]

IN THE MATTER OF IAN FLAKEY
IN BANKRUPTCY
AND IN THE MATTER OF THE INSOLVENCY ACT 1986

BETWEEN:-

GILES GRABBER
(as Trustee in Bankruptcy of IAN FLAKEY)

Applicant

and

(1) TABITHA FLAKEY
(2) IAN FLAKEY

Respondents

1ST WITNESS STATEMENT OF GILES GRABBER

I, GILES GRABBER of Grabbers LLP, of 1 Vulture Street, London, Trustee in Bankruptcy of Ian Flakey, STATE as follows:

1.   I am the Applicant in this application. I am the Trustee in Bankruptcy of Ian Flakey.

2.   I make this witness statement in support of my application for:

   a.   A declaration that the 1st Respondent holds the beneficial interest in the freehold property known as and situate at 1 Geranium Cottage, London, Land Registry Title number 1234, ['1 Geranium Cottage'] on trust as to 50% for herself and as to 50% for the Applicant.

   b.   An order that 1 Geranium Cottage be sold with vacant possession and that the 1st Respondent do concur in such sale.

   c.   An order that the conduct of such sale of 1 Geranium Cottage be given to the Applicant as Trustee in Bankruptcy of the estate of the Bankrupt.

   d.   An order that the 1st Respondent should join with the Applicant and do all such things as may be necessary to procure the said sale of 1 Geranium Cottage with vacant possession.

   e.   An order that the 1st Respondent do within 28 days deliver up vacant possession of 1 Geranium Cottage to the Applicant.

   f.   An order that the 1st Respondent shall be removed forthwith as trustee for sale and that the Applicant be appointed in her place under section 41 of the Trustee Act 1925 and that the Applicant shall have power as Trustee to execute all necessary deeds, documents and instruments relating to the said sale.

g.   An order that upon sale the proceeds of sale of 1 Geranium Cottage be applied in the following manner: (1) the expenses of sale be discharged out of the proceeds of sale; (2) to discharge the mortgage in favour of Brassic Bank plc; (3) the balance of the proceeds of sale shall be paid in equal shares to the 1st Respondent and the Applicant as Trustee in Bankruptcy of the estate of the 2nd Respondent; (4) there shall be deducted from the 1st Respondent's entitlement and added to the Applicant's entitlement of the net proceeds: (i) Any sum ordered by way of costs under this Order; (ii) a sum in respect of the 1st Respondent's use and occupation of 1 Geranium Cottage since the date of the Bankruptcy Order at £200 per week.

h.   An order that in the event that the aggregate amount to be deducted from the 1st Respondent's share is found to exceed the value of the 1st Respondent's share, the 1st Respondent do pay to the Applicant such balance within 28 days of it being demanded by the Applicant.

i.   An order that the 1st Respondent do pay the costs of and incidental to this Application.

j.   Any costs of the application that are not payable by the 1st Respondent or not recovered from her should be paid to the Applicant as such trustee out of the assets of the bankruptcy as an expense of the bankruptcy within rule 10.149(a) of the Insolvency (England and Wales) Rules 2016.

k.   Such further and other order and other relief as this Honourable Court thinks fit.

3.   The matters set out in this witness statement are true and within my own knowledge except where otherwise indicated, in which case I have explained the source of my information or belief.

4.   There is now produced and shown to me a bundle consisting of true copies of the documents I will refer to in my witness statement marked 'GG1'.

5.   A bankruptcy order was made against the Bankrupt on 1st March 2020. I refer to page [ ] of 'GG1' which is a true copy of the bankruptcy order.

6.   I was appointed as the Trustee in Bankruptcy of the Bankrupt on 1st April 2020. I refer to page [ ] of 'GG1' which is a true copy of my certificate of appointment.

7.   The Bankrupt's statement of affairs show that he was insolvent as at 31st December 2020 with a deficiency in the sum of £2,000,000. I refer to page [ ] of 'GG1' which is a true copy of the trading accounts of the Bankrupt and his statement of affairs. Creditors' claims lodged in the bankruptcy amount to £3,500,000. I refer to page [ ] of 'GG1' which is a true copy of the proofs of debt evidencing the creditors' claims.

8.   Following my appointment, I began to investigate the affairs of the Bankrupt. The following matters became apparent.

9.   The Bankrupt's principal asset is his interest in 1 Geranium Cottage, London. I refer to page [ ] of 'GG1' which is a true copy of an extract in respect of the property at HM Land Registry.

10.   The property is held in the name of the 1st Respondent, however it is clear from the conveyancing files and land registry entry that it is held in equal shares for her and the Bankrupt. I refer to page [ ] of 'GG1' which is a true copy of the

conveyancing files I have been able to obtain from the Bankrupt's solicitors, Fudgit & Co which shows that the purchase price was paid for equally by the Bankrupt and the 1st Respondent.

11.   I understand that the property is the principal dwelling house of the Bankrupt and the 1st Respondent, his wife. They continue to enjoy this property and have made to date no payment to the estate in bankruptcy for their use of the property.

12.   The property is worth £500,000. I refer to page [ ] of 'GG1' which is a true copy of a drive-by valuation from Foxy Estate Agents. The valuation estimates that the rental value of the property is £200 per week.

13.   There is a mortgage on the property in the sum of £160,000. This would mean the Bankrupt's interest is worth £200,000 before sale cost. The Bankrupt has no other assets.

14.   This application is made more than one year after my appointment as trustee and the interests of the bankrupt's creditors outweigh all other considerations.

15.   I therefore ask that this Honourable Court make the declaration and order for sale sought. I am not aware of any exceptional circumstances which might militate against making such an order and the value of the Bankrupt's interest, even allowing for the costs of sale, plainly exceeds £1,000.

STATEMENT OF TRUTH

I believe that the facts stated in this Witness Statement are true.

Signed [ ]
Full name [*GILES GRABBER*]
Dated [ ] 20[ ]

12.3   DECLARATION OF INTEREST AND ORDER FOR SALE OF THE BANKRUPT'S MATRIMONIAL HOME

IN THE HIGH COURT OF JUSTICE
BUSINESS AND PROPERTY COURTS OF ENGLAND AND WALES
INSOLVENCY AND COMPANIES LIST (ChD)

NO: [ ] OF 20[ ]

IN THE MATTER OF IAN FLAKEY
IN BANKRUPTCY
AND IN THE MATTER OF THE INSOLVENCY ACT 1986

BEFORE MR REGISTRAR WISE
DATED: [ ] OF 20[ ]

BETWEEN:-

GILES GRABBER
(as Trustee in Bankruptcy of IAN FLAKEY)

Applicant

and

(1) TABITHA FLAKEY
(2) IAN FLAKEY

Respondents

DRAFT MINUTE OF ORDER

UPON THE APPLICATION of Giles Grabber of Grabbers LLP, Trustee in Bankruptcy of the above named IAN FLAKEY ('the Bankrupt')

UPON HEARING Counsel for the Applicant and Counsel for the 1st and 2nd Respondents

AND UPON READING the evidence noted as being read

IT IS DECLARED THAT the 1st Respondent holds the beneficial interest in the freehold property known as and situate at 1 Geranium Cottage, London, Land Registry Title number 1234, ['1 Geranium Cottage'] on bare trust as to 50% for herself and as to 50% for the Applicant

IT IS ORDERED THAT:

1.   1 Geranium Cottage be sold with vacant possession and that the 1st Respondent do concur in such sale.

2.   The conduct of such sale of 1 Geranium Cottage be given to the Applicant as Trustee in Bankruptcy of the estate of the Bankrupt.

3.   The 1st Respondent should join with the Applicant and do all such things as may be necessary to procure the said sale of 1 Geranium Cottage with vacant possession.

4.   The 1st Respondent do within 28 days deliver up vacant possession of 1 Geranium Cottage to the Applicant.

5.   The 1st Respondent shall be removed forthwith as trustee for sale and that the Applicant be appointed in her place under section 41 of the Trustee Act 1925 and that the Applicant shall have power as Trustee to execute all necessary deeds, documents and instruments relating to the said sale.

6.   Upon sale the proceeds of sale of 1 Geranium Cottage be applied in the following manner: (1) the expenses of sale to be discharged out of the proceeds of sale; (2) to discharge the mortgage in favour of Brassic Bank plc; (3) the balance of the proceeds of sale shall be paid in equal shares to the 1st Respondent and the Applicant as Trustee in Bankruptcy of the estate of the 2nd Respondent; (4) there shall be deducted from the 1st Respondent's entitlement and added to the Applicant's entitlement of the net proceeds: (i) any sum ordered by way of costs under this Order; (ii) a sum in respect of the 1st Respondent's use and occupation of 1 Geranium Cottage since the date of the Bankruptcy Order at £200 per week.

7.   In the event that the aggregate amount to be deducted from the 1st Respondent's share is found to exceed the value of the 1st Respondent's share, the 1st Respondent do pay to the Applicant such balance within 28 days of it being demanded by the Applicant.

8.   The 1st Respondent do pay the costs of and incidental to this Application.

9.   Any costs of the application that are not payable by the 1st Respondent or not recovered from her should be paid to the Applicant as such trustee out of the assets of the bankruptcy as an expense of the bankruptcy within rule 10.149(a) of the Insolvency (England and Wales) Rules 2016.

Service of this order

The Court has provided a sealed copy of this order to the serving party:

SNARKEY & SNYDE
1 LAW STREET
LONDON

Chapter 13

APPLICATION FOR AN INTERIM ORDER IN SUPPORT OF AN INDIVIDUAL VOLUNTARY ARRANGEMENT

OBJECTIVE

The effect of an interim order is to provide a moratorium during which a debtor may make a proposal to his creditors for an IVA. During the moratorium and absent the permission of the court, no bankruptcy petition may be presented or proceeded with, a landlord cannot forfeit his lease by peaceable re-entry, security cannot be enforced, goods cannot be repossessed, legal proceedings or process cannot be instituted or proceeded with and execution and distress cannot be levied against the debtor or his property.[1] The order will be granted if the court considers the IVA proposal is serious and viable.[2]

APPLICATION

The application is made by application notice on notice and should be made to the registrar or district judge.

Where no bankruptcy order has been made, the application for the interim order may be made by the debtor only.[3] The application should be made to a court in which the debtor would be entitled to present his own petition in bankruptcy under rule 10.48 of the Insolvency (England and Wales) Rules 2016[4] and contain sufficient information to establish that it is brought in the appropriate court.[5]

Where a bankruptcy order has been made, an application for an interim order may be made by an undischarged bankrupt, by his trustee in bankruptcy or by the Official Receiver.[6] Any application by an undischarged bankrupt must be on at least 2 business days' notice to his trustee or the Official Receiver.[7] The

---

[1] Section 252 of the Insolvency Act 1986.

[2] *Singh v Singh* [2013] EWHC 4783 (Ch), [2014] BPIR 1555; *Tucker v Atkins* [2014] BPIR 1569.

[3] Section 253(2) of the Insolvency Act 1986.

[4] Rule 8.9(1) of the Insolvency (England and Wales) Rules 2016.

[5] Rule 8.9(2) of the Insolvency (England and Wales) Rules 2016.

[6] Section 253(3) of the Insolvency Act 1986.

[7] Section 253(4) of the Insolvency Act 1986 and rule 8.8.(4) of the Insolvency (England and Wales) Rules 2016.

application should be made to the court with conduct of his bankruptcy and shall be filed with the bankruptcy proceedings.[8]

A discharged bankrupt cannot apply for an interim order.[9]

The application is made on Form IAA. The application should set out:

- that the application is made under the Insolvency Act 1986 or the Insolvency (England and Wales) Rules 2016 (as the case may be);[10]
- the section number or rule under which relief is sought;[11]
- the name of the parties;[12]
- the name of the bankrupt or debtor;[13]
- the court name;[14]
- the case number;[15]
- the remedy applied for or directions sought;[16]
- the name and address of each person to be served or, if none, stating that that it is intended that no person will be served;[17]
- where there is a requirement for particular persons to be given notice of the application under the Act or Rules, stating the name and address of each such person;[18]
- the applicant's address for service.[19]

The application notice must be authenticated by the applicant or his solicitor.[20]

COURT FEES

Where the application is made by or in respect of an undischarged bankrupt, a court fee of £155 is payable. Otherwise (as fresh proceedings) a court fee of £160 is payable.

---

[8]   Rule 8.9(1)(a) of the Insolvency (England and Wales) Rules 2016.
[9]   *Wright v OR* [2001] BPIR 196.
[10] Rule 1.35(2)(a) of the Insolvency (England and Wales) Rules 2016.
[11] Rule 1.35(2)(b) of the Insolvency (England and Wales) Rules 2016.
[12] Rule 1.35(2)(c) of the Insolvency (England and Wales) Rules 2016.
[13] Rule 1.35(2)(d) of the Insolvency (England and Wales) Rules 2016.
[14] Rule 1.35(2)(e) of the Insolvency (England and Wales) Rules 2016.
[15] Rule 1.35(2)(f) of the Insolvency (England and Wales) Rules 2016.
[16] Rule 1.35(2)(g) of the Insolvency (England and Wales) Rules 2016.
[17] Rule 1.35(2)(h) of the Insolvency (England and Wales) Rules 2016.
[18] Rule 1.35(2)(i) of the Insolvency (England and Wales) Rules 2016.
[19] Rule 1.35(2)(j) of the Insolvency (England and Wales) Rules 2016.
[20] Rule 1.35(3) of the Insolvency (England and Wales) Rules 2016. For what amounts to authentication, see rule 1.5. For hard copy applications, this means signed: rule 1.5(2).

EVIDENCE

The application should be supported by a witness statement. This should address:

- the capacity in which the applicant makes this application;
- who is the debtor in respect of whom the application is being made;
- that an interim order under section 252 of the Insolvency Act 1986 is sought;
- the reasons for making the application;[21]
- particulars of any execution or other legal process or levying of any distress which, to the debtor's knowledge, has been commenced against him;[22]
- whether the debtor is an undischarged bankrupt or (as the case may be) that he is able to petition for his own bankruptcy;[23]
- that no previous application for an interim order has been made by or in respect of the debtor in the period of 12 months ending with the date of the witness statement;[24]
- the name of the nominee under the proposal;
- that the nominee has given written notice under rule 8.4 of his IVA proposal;
- that the nominee under the proposal is willing to act in relation to the proposal;[25]
- that the nominee is a person who is either qualified to act as an insolvency practitioner in relation to the debtor or is authorised to act as nominee in relation to him;
- whether the debtor has submitted to the Official Receiver a document setting out the terms of his IVA proposal[26] and/or the statement of his affairs;[27]
- if so:

  - when such documents were sent;
  - what (if any) the Official Receiver's reaction to these was.

The applicant should exhibit:

- the proposed nominee's consent;[28]
- a copy of the debtor's proposal given to the nominee under rule 8.8(2)(b).[29]

---

[21] Rule 8.8(1)(a) of the Insolvency (England and Wales) Rules 2016.

[22] Rule 8.8(1)(b) of the Insolvency (England and Wales) Rules 2016.

[23] Rule 8.8(1)(c) of the Insolvency (England and Wales) Rules 2016.

[24] Rule 8.8(1)(d) of the Insolvency (England and Wales) Rules 2016.

[25] Rule 8.8(1)(e) of the Insolvency (England and Wales) Rules 2016.

[26] Section 263B(1)(a) of the Insolvency Act 1986.

[27] Section 263B(1)(b) of the Insolvency Act 1986.

[28] Rule 8.8(2)(a) of the Insolvency (England and Wales) Rules 2016.

[29] Rule 8.8(2)(b) of the Insolvency (England and Wales) Rules 2016.

SERVICE

The applicant must give at least 2 business days' notice of the hearing:[30]

- where the debtor is an undischarged bankrupt, to the bankrupt, the Official Receiver and the trustee (whichever of those three is not himself the applicant);
- where the debtor is not an undischarged bankrupt, to any creditor who (to the debtor's knowledge) has presented a bankruptcy petition against him; and
- in either case, to the nominee who has agreed to act in relation to the debtor's proposal.

Service may be effected personally[31] or by post on the respondent (Part 6 of the CPR applies for these purposes)[32] or, where they have authority to accept service, on the respondent's solicitors.[33] Electronic service of documents is now permissible under the Rules, providing the respondent currently consents to service in that way and has provided an email address for service in that way.[34]

STEPS FOLLOWING THE MAKING OF AN INTERIM ORDER

Where an interim order is made, the applicant must serve a sealed copy of the order on the nominee under the debtor's proposal.[35] The applicant shall also, as soon as reasonably practicable, give notice of the making of the order to any person who was given notice of the hearing and was not present or represented at it.[36]

If an interim order has been made, the nominee under the IVA proposal must then file with the court not less than 2 days before the interim order ceases to have effect,[37] a report to the court stating his opinion of whether the voluntary arrangement which the debtor is proposing has a reasonable prospect of being approved and implemented, whether a meeting of the debtor's creditors should be summoned to consider the debtor's proposal and if his opinion is that such a meeting should be summoned, the date on which, and time and place at which, he proposes the meeting should be held.[38]

---

[30] Rule 8.8(4) of the Insolvency (England and Wales) Rules 2016.
[31] Rule 1.44 of the Insolvency (England and Wales) Rules 2016.
[32] Schedule 4, paragraph 1(2) to the Insolvency (England and Wales) Rules 2016.
[33] Rule 1.40 of the Insolvency (England and Wales) Rules 2016.
[34] Rule 1.45 of the Insolvency (England and Wales) Rules 2016.
[35] Rule 8.13(1) of the Insolvency (England and Wales) Rules 2016.
[36] Rule 8.13(2)(b) of the Insolvency (England and Wales) Rules 2016.
[37] Rule 8.15 of the Insolvency (England and Wales) Rules 2016.
[38] Section 256(1) of the Insolvency Act 1986.

FURTHER DIRECTIONS

The court has powers to give directions replacing the nominee, renewing or extending the period during which the interim order has effect or discharging the order.[39]

KEY MATERIALS

Sections 252–256 of the Insolvency Act 1986

252 Interim order of court

(1) In the circumstances specified below, the court may in the case of a debtor (being an individual) make an interim order under this section.

(2) An interim order has the effect that, during the period for which it is in force—

    (a) no bankruptcy petition relating to the debtor may be presented or proceeded with,

    (aa) no landlord or other person to whom rent is payable may exercise any right of forfeiture by peaceable re-entry in relation to premises let to the debtor in respect of a failure by the debtor to comply with any term or condition of his tenancy of such premises, except with the leave of the court and

    (b) no other proceedings, and no execution or other legal process, may be commenced or continued and no distress may be levied against the debtor or his property except with the leave of the court.

253 Application for interim order

(1) Application to the court for an interim order may be made where the debtor intends to make a proposal under this Part, that is, a proposal to his creditors for a composition in satisfaction of his debts or a scheme of arrangement of his affairs (from here on referred to, in either case, as a 'voluntary arrangement').

(2) The proposal must provide for some person ('the nominee') to act in relation to the voluntary arrangement either as trustee or otherwise for the purpose of supervising its implementation and the nominee must be a person who is qualified to act as an insolvency practitioner, or authorised to act as nominee, in relation to the voluntary arrangement.

(3) Subject as follows, the application may be made—

    (a) if the debtor is an undischarged bankrupt, by the debtor, the trustee of his estate, or the official receiver, and

    (b) in any other case, by the debtor.

---

[39] Section 256(3)–(6) of the Insolvency Act 1986.

(4) An application shall not be made under subsection (3)(a) unless the debtor has given notice of the proposal to the official receiver and, if there is one, the trustee of his estate.

(5) An application shall not be made while a bankruptcy petition presented by the debtor is pending, if the court has, under section 273 below, appointed an insolvency practitioner to inquire into the debtor's affairs and report.

254 Effect of application

(1) At any time when an application under section 253 for an interim order is pending:

    (a) no landlord or other person to whom rent is payable may exercise any right of forfeiture by peaceable re-entry in relation to premises let to the debtor in respect of a failure by the debtor to comply with any term or condition of his tenancy of such premises, except with the leave of the court, and

    (b) the court may forbid the levying of any distress on the debtor's property or its subsequent sale, or both, and stay any action, execution or other legal process against the property or person of the debtor.

(2) Any court in which proceedings are pending against an individual may, on proof that an application under that section has been made in respect of that individual, either stay the proceedings or allow them to continue on such terms as it thinks fit.

255 Cases in which interim order can be made

(1) The court shall not make an interim order on an application under section 253 unless it is satisfied—

    (a) that the debtor intends to make a proposal under this Part;

    (b) that on the day of the making of the application the debtor was an undischarged bankrupt or was able to petition for his own bankruptcy;

    (c) that no previous application has been made by the debtor for an interim order in the period of 12 months ending with that day; and

    (d) that the nominee under the debtor's proposal . . . is willing to act in relation to the proposal.

(2) The court may make an order if it thinks that it would be appropriate to do so for the purpose of facilitating the consideration and implementation of the debtor's proposal.

(3) Where the debtor is an undischarged bankrupt, the interim order may contain provision as to the conduct of the bankruptcy, and the administration of the bankrupt's estate, during the period for which the order is in force.

(4) Subject as follows, the provision contained in an interim order by virtue of subsection (3) may include provision staying proceedings in the bankruptcy or modifying any provision in this Group of Parts, and any provision of the rules in their application to the debtor's bankruptcy.

(5) An interim order shall not, in relation to a bankrupt, make provision relaxing or removing any of the requirements of provisions in this Group of Parts, or of the rules, unless the court is satisfied that that provision is unlikely to result in any significant diminution in, or in the value of, the debtor's estate for the purposes of the bankruptcy.

(6) Subject to the following provisions of this Part, an interim order made on an application under section 253 ceases to have effect at the end of the period of 14 days beginning with the day after the making of the order.

256 Nominee's report on debtor's proposal

(1) Where an interim order has been made on an application under section 253, the nominee shall, before the order ceases to have effect, submit a report to the court stating—

(a) whether, in his opinion, the voluntary arrangement which the debtor is proposing has a reasonable prospect of being approved and implemented,

(aa) whether, in his opinion, a meeting of the debtor's creditors should be summoned to consider the debtor's proposal, and

(b) if in his opinion such a meeting should be summoned, the date on which, and time and place at which, he proposes the meeting should be held.

(2) For the purpose of enabling the nominee to prepare his report the debtor shall submit to the nominee—

(a) a document setting out the terms of the voluntary arrangement which the debtor is proposing, and

(b) a statement of his affairs containing—

(i) such particulars of his creditors and of his debts and other liabilities and of his assets as may be prescribed, and

(ii) such other information as may be prescribed.

(3) The court may—

(a) on an application made by the debtor in a case where the nominee has failed to submit the report required by this section or has died, or

(b) on an application made by the debtor or the nominee in a case where it is impracticable or inappropriate for the nominee to continue to act as such,

direct that the nominee shall be replaced as such by another person qualified to act as an insolvency practitioner, or authorised to act as nominee, in relation to the voluntary arrangement.

(3A) The court may, on an application made by the debtor in a case where the nominee has failed to submit the report required by this section, direct that the interim order shall continue, or (if it has ceased to have effect) be renewed, for such further period as the court may specify in the direction.

(4) The court may, on the application of the nominee, extend the period for which the interim order has effect so as to enable the nominee to have more time to prepare his report.

(5) If the court is satisfied on receiving the nominee's report that a meeting of the debtor's creditors should be summoned to consider the debtor's proposal, the court shall direct that the period for which the interim order has effect shall be extended, for such further period as it may specify in the direction, for the purpose of enabling the debtor's proposal to be considered by his creditors in accordance with the following provisions of this Part.

(6) The court may discharge the interim order if it is satisfied, on the application of the nominee—

  (a) that the debtor has failed to comply with his obligations under subsection (2), or

  (b) that for any other reason it would be inappropriate for a meeting of the debtor's creditors to be summoned to consider the debtor's proposal.

Rules 8.8–8.18 of the Insolvency (England and Wales) Rules 2016

Application for interim order

8.8.—(1) An application to the court for an interim order under Part 8 of the Act must be accompanied by a witness statement containing—

  (a) the reasons for making the application;

  (b) information about any action, execution, other legal process or the levying of any distress which, to the debtor's knowledge, has been commenced against the debtor or the debtor's property;

  (c) a statement that the debtor is an undischarged bankrupt or is able to make a bankruptcy application;

  (d) a statement that no previous application for an interim order has been made by or in relation to the debtor in the period of 12 months ending with the date of the witness statement; and

  (e) a statement that a person named in the witness statement is willing to act as nominee in relation to the proposal and is qualified to act as an insolvency practitioner (or is an authorised person) in relation to the debtor.

(2) The witness statement must be accompanied by a copy of—

  (a) the proposal; and

  (b) the notice of the nominee's consent to act.

(3) When the application and the witness statement have been filed, the court must fix a venue for the hearing of the application.

(4) The applicant must deliver a notice of the hearing and the venue at least two business days before the hearing to—

    (a) the nominee;

    (b) the debtor, the official receiver or the trustee (whichever is not the applicant) where the debtor is an undischarged bankrupt; and

    (c) any creditor who (to the debtor's knowledge) has presented a bankruptcy petition against the debtor where the debtor is not an undischarged bankrupt.

(5) A notice under section 253(4) must contain the name and address of the nominee.

Court in which application is to be made

8.9.—(1) An application must be made—

    (a) to the court (and hearing centre if applicable), if any, which has the conduct of the bankruptcy, where the debtor is an undischarged bankrupt; or

    (b) to the court (and hearing centre if applicable) determined in accordance with rule 10.48.

(2) The application must contain sufficient information to establish that it is made to the appropriate court or hearing centre.

Order granting a stay

8.10. A court order under section 254(1)(b) granting a stay pending hearing of an application must identify the proceedings and contain—

    (a) the section number of the Act under which it is made;

    (b) details of the action, execution or other legal process which is stayed;

    (c) the date on which the application for an interim order will be heard; and

    (d) the date that the order granting the stay is made.

Hearing of the application

8.11.—(1) A person to whom a notice of the hearing of the application for an interim order was (or should have been) delivered under rule 8.8(4) may appear or be represented at the hearing.

(2) The court must take into account any representations made by or on behalf of such a person (in particular, as to whether an order should contain such provision as is referred to in section 255(3) (provisions as to the conduct of the bankruptcy etc.) and (4) (provisions staying proceedings in bankruptcy etc.).

(3) If the court makes an interim order, it must fix a venue for consideration of the nominee's report for a date no later than the date on which the order ceases to have effect.

The interim order

8.12. An interim order must contain—

   (a)   identification details for the proceedings;
   (b)   the section number of the Act under which it is made;
   (c)   a statement that the order has effect from its making until the end of the period of 14 days beginning on the day after the date on which it is made;
   (d)   particulars of the effect of the order (as set out in section 252(2));
   (e)   an order that the report of the nominee be delivered to the court no later than two business days before the date fixed for the court's consideration of the report;
   (f)   particulars of any orders made under section 255(3) and (4);
   (g)   where the debtor is an undischarged bankrupt and the applicant is not the official receiver, an order that the applicant delivers, as soon as reasonably practicable, a copy of the interim order to the official receiver;
   (h)   the venue for the court's consideration of the nominee's report; and
   (i)   the date of the order.

Action to follow making of an interim order

8.13.—(1) The court must deliver at least two sealed copies of the interim order to the applicant.

(2)   As soon as reasonably practicable, the applicant must deliver—

   (a)   one copy to the nominee and, where the debtor is an undischarged bankrupt, another copy to the official receiver (unless the official receiver was the applicant); and
   (b)   a notice that the order has been made to any other person to whom a notice of the hearing of the application for an interim order was (or should have been) delivered under rule 8.8(4) and who was not in attendance or represented at the hearing.

Order extending period of an interim order (section 256(4))

8.14. An order under section 256(4) extending the period for which an interim order has effect must contain—

   (a)   identification details for the proceedings;
   (b)   a statement that the application is that of the nominee for an extension of the period under section 256(4) for which an interim order is to have effect;
   (c)   an order that the period for which the interim order has effect is extended to a specified date;
   (d)   particulars of the effect (as set out in section 252(2)) of the interim order;
   (e)   an order that the report of the nominee be delivered to the court no later two business days before the date fixed for the court's consideration of the nominee's report;

(f) particulars of any orders made under section 255(3) or (4);

(g) where the debtor is an undischarged bankrupt and the applicant is not the official receiver, an order that the applicant deliver, as soon as reasonably practicable, a copy of the order to the official receiver;

(h) the venue for the court's consideration of the report; and

(i) the date of the order.

Nominee's report on the proposal

8.15.—(1) The nominee's report under section 256 must be filed with the court not less than two business days before the interim order ceases to have effect, accompanied by—

(a) a copy of the report;

(b) a copy of the proposal (as amended, if applicable, under rule 8.2(2); and

(c) a copy of any statement of affairs or a summary of such a statement.

(2) The nominee must also deliver a copy of the report to the debtor.

(3) The nominee's report must explain whether or not the nominee considers that the proposal has a reasonable prospect of being approved and implemented and whether or not creditors should be invited to consider the proposal.

(4) The court must endorse the nominee's report and the copy of it with the date on which they were filed and return the copy to the nominee.

(5) Where the debtor is an undischarged bankrupt, the nominee must deliver to the official receiver and any trustee, a copy of—

(a) the proposal;

(b) the nominee's report; and

(c) any statement of affairs or summary of such a statement.

(6) Where the debtor is not an undischarged bankrupt, the nominee must deliver a copy of each of those documents to any person who has presented a bankruptcy petition against the debtor.

Order extending period of interim order to enable the creditors to consider the proposal (section 256(5))

8.16. An order under section 256(5) extending the period for which an interim order has effect to enable creditors to consider the proposal must contain—

(a) identification details for the proceedings;

(b) the section number of the Act under which it is made;

(c) the date that the nominee's report was filed;

(d) a statement that for the purpose of enabling the creditors to consider the proposal, the period for which the interim order has effect is extended to a specified date;

(e) a statement that the nominee will be inviting the creditors to consider the proposal and details of the decision procedure the nominee intends to use;

(f) where the debtor is an undischarged bankrupt and the nominee is not the official receiver, an order that the nominee deliver, as soon as reasonably practicable, a copy of the order to the official receiver; and

(g) the date of the order.

Replacement of the nominee (section 256(3))

8.17.—(1) A debtor who intends to apply under section 256(3)(a) or (b) for the nominee to be replaced must deliver a notice to the nominee that such an application is intended to be made at least five business days before filing the application with the court.

(2   A nominee who intends to apply under section 256(3)(b) to be replaced must deliver a notice to the debtor that such an application is intended to be made at least five business days before filing the application with the court.

(3) The court must not appoint a replacement nominee unless the replacement nominee has filed with the court a statement confirming—

(a) that person is qualified to act as an insolvency practitioner (or is an authorised person) in relation to the debtor; and

(b) that person's consent to act.

Consideration of the nominee's report

8.18.—(1) A person to whom a notice was (or should have been) delivered under rule 8.8(4) may appear or be represented at the court's hearing to consider the nominee's report.

(2) Rule 8.13 applies to any order made by the court at the hearing.

13.1 ORDINARY APPLICATION FOR AN INTERIM ORDER

Form IAA **Insolvency Act Application Notice**

IN THE HIGH COURT OF JUSTICE
BUSINESS AND PROPERTY COURTS OF ENGLAND AND WALES
INSOLVENCY AND COMPANIES LIST (ChD)
IN BANKRUPTCY

NO: 666 OF 2020

IN THE MATTER OF IAN FLAKEY
AND IN THE MATTER OF THE INSOLVENCY ACT 1986

BETWEEN:-

IAN FLAKEY

Applicant

and

(1) ANGRY PLC
(2) GILES GRABBER

Respondents

Is this application within existing insolvency proceedings? YES/~~NO~~

I (~~We~~), IAN FLAKEY of 1 Geranium Cottage, London intend to apply to the ~~Judge/District Judge~~/Registrar on:

Date: 1st April 2020

Time: 00:00 hours

Place: Royal Courts of Justice, 7 Rolls Buildings, Fetter Lane, London EC4A 1NL

This application having been issued at the RCJ, 7 Rolls Buildings, Fetter Lane, London, EC4A 1NL will be heard at the time and date pursuant to the endorsement underneath the Court Seal on the front page of this application.

FOR AN ORDER THAT:

1.   An Interim Order in respect of Ian Flakey under section 252 of the Insolvency Act 1986.

2.   Such further and other order and other relief as this Honourable Court thinks fit.

The applicant is resident in and has carried on business in the London Insolvency District for the greater part of the 6 months prior to this application.

The applicant relies on the witness statement of Ian Flakey dated 1st April 2020, which sets out the grounds in support of this application.

THE NAMES AND ADDRESSES OF THE PERSON(S) UPON WHOM IT IS INTENDED TO SERVE THIS APPLICATION ARE:

Name: ANGRY PLC

Address: 1 UNPAID BILL STREET, LONDON

Name: GILES GRABBER

Address: 1 VULTURE STREET, LONDON

~~OR~~

~~IT IS NOT INTENDED TO SERVE ANY PERSON WITH THIS APPLICATION~~

Dated:

Signed: SNARKEY & SNYDE

Solicitors for the applicant ~~or Applicant~~   *This is the address
Address: 1 LAW STREET, LONDON   which will be treated
Telephone: 0207 666 6666   by Court as the
Email: law@snarkeysnyde.com   Petitions address for
                                             service

If you do not attend, the court may make such order as it thinks just.

13.2   WITNESS STATEMENT IN SUPPORT OF AN APPLICATION FOR AN INTERIM ORDER

Applicant: I Flakey: 1st: IF1: [ ] 20[ ]

IN THE HIGH COURT OF JUSTICE
BUSINESS AND PROPERTY COURTS OF ENGLAND AND WALES
INSOLVENCY AND COMPANIES LIST (ChD)

NO: [ ] OF 20[ ]

IN THE MATTER OF IAN FLAKEY
AND IN BANKRUPTCY
AND IN THE MATTER OF THE INSOLVENCY ACT 1986

BETWEEN:-

IAN FLAKEY

Applicant

and

(1) ANGRY PLC
(2) GILES GRABBER

Respondents

1ST WITNESS STATEMENT OF IAN FLAKEY

I, IAN FLAKEY OF 1 Geranium Cottage, London, Businessman, STATE as follows:

1.   I am the Applicant in this application.

2.   The matters set out in this witness statement are true and within my own knowledge except where otherwise indicated, in which case I have explained the source of my information or belief.

3.   There is now produced and shown to me a bundle consisting of true copies of the documents I will refer to in my witness statement marked 'IF1'.

4.   I make this witness statement in support of my application for an Interim Order under section 252 of the Insolvency Act 1986 to allow me to present proposals to my creditors for an individual voluntary arrangement in satisfaction of my debts (which I am unable to pay in full).

5.   An individual voluntary arrangement would allow me to continue to trade as a widget seller which I would wish to do so that I can try to pay off my creditors. My proposals envisage a recovery of 80 pence in the £ for my creditors whilst on my bankruptcy my creditors would be unlikely to receive more than 2 pence in the £. For the reasons set out in my proposal I believe it is likely that my creditors will accept my proposal. I refer to page [ ] of 'IF1' which is a true copy my proposals which I have given to my nominee.

6.   The only proceedings which have been commenced against me are a bankruptcy petition presented by Angry plc. I refer to page [ ] of 'IF1' which is a true copy of

the petition. I am unaware of any other execution or other legal process or other levying of distress against me.

7. I am able to petition for my own bankruptcy and I am resident in and have carried on business in the London Insolvency District.

8. I have made no previous application for an interim order in the last 12 months.

9. Giles Grabber of 1 Vulture Street, London has indicated that he is willing to act as nominee and supervisor in relation to my proposal. I refer to page [ ] of 'IF1' which is a true copy of the notice I sent to Mr Grabber as my intended nominee under Rule 5.4 which has been endorsed by Mr Grabber to the effect that he agrees to act as my nominee.

10. Giles Grabber is a licensed insolvency practitioner and therefore qualified to act. I refer to page [ ] of 'IF1' which is a true copy of his certificate showing his entitlement to practise as a licensed insolvency practitioner.

11. I confirm I have not submitted to the Official Receiver either the document referred to at section 263B(1)(a) or the statement referred to section 263B(1)(b) of the Insolvency Act 1986.

12. In all the circumstances I ask this Honourable Court to grant an Interim Order in the terms sought.

STATEMENT OF TRUTH

I believe that the facts stated in this Witness Statement are true.

Signed [ ]
Full name [*IAN FLAKEY*]
Dated [ ] 20[ ]

13.3 INTERIM ORDER OF COURT UNDER SECTION 252 OF THE INSOLVENCY ACT 1986

IN THE HIGH COURT OF JUSTICE
BUSINESS AND PROPERTY COURTS OF ENGLAND AND WALES
INSOLVENCY AND COMPANIES LIST (ChD)

IN THE MATTER OF IAN FLAKEY
IN BANKRUPTCY
AND IN THE MATTER OF THE INSOLVENCY ACT 1986

NO: [ ] OF 20[ ]

BEFORE MR REGISTRAR WISE
DATED: [ ] OF 20[ ]

BETWEEN:-

IAN FLAKEY

Petitioner

and

(1) ANGRY PLC
(2) GILES GRABBER

Respondents

DRAFT MINUTE OF ORDER

UPON THE APPLICATION OF Ian Flakey of 1 Geranium Cottage, London dated [ ]

AND UPON HEARING Counsel for the Applicant and Counsel for the 1st Respondent and the 2nd Respondent ['the nominee']

AND UPON READING the evidence noted as having been read

IT IS ORDERED THAT:

1. Under section 252 of the Insolvency Act 1986 from the making of this order until the end of the period of [14] days beginning on the day after the date of this order and during any extended period for which this interim order has effect:

    a. no bankruptcy petition relating to the above-named IAN FLAKEY (the debtor) may be presented or proceeded with, and
    b. no landlord or other person to whom rent is payable may exercise any right of forfeiture by peaceable re-entry in relation to premises let to the debtor in respect of a failure by the debtor to comply with any term or condition of his tenancy of such premises, except with permission of the court, and
    c. no other proceedings, and no execution or other legal process, may be commenced or continued and no distress may be levied against the debtor or his property except with the permission of the court.

2. The report of the nominee be submitted and delivered by him to the court not later than [2 business days before the return date].

3.   The application to be adjourned to [ ] at [ ] o'clock for consideration of the
      nominee's report.

4.   [Provision as to costs.]

Dated: [ ] 20[ ]

Service of this order

The Court has provided a sealed copy of this order to the serving party:

SNARKEY & SNYDE
1 LAW STREET
LONDON

Chapter 14

APPLICATION FOR LEAVE TO ENFORCE SECURITY OR SEEK POSSESSION DESPITE AN INTERIM ORDER

OBJECTIVE

The effect of an interim order is to provide a moratorium during which a debtor may make a proposal to his creditors for an IVA, during which no bankruptcy petition may be presented or proceeded with, a landlord cannot forfeit his lease by peaceable re-entry, security cannot be enforced, goods cannot be repossessed, legal proceedings or process cannot be instituted or proceeded with and execution and distress cannot be levied against the debtor or his property.[1]

The exception to this rule is where the court gives leave.

APPLICATION

The application is made by application notice on notice and should be made to the registrar or district judge.

The application is made on Form IAA. The application should set out:

- that the application is made under the Insolvency Act 1986 or the Insolvency (England and Wales) Rules 2016 (as the case may be);[2]
- the section number or rule under which relief is sought;[3]
- the name of the parties;[4]
- the name of the bankrupt or debtor;[5]
- the court name;[6]
- the case number;[7]

---

[1]   Section 252 of the Insolvency Act 1986.
[2]   Rule 1.35(2)(a) of the Insolvency (England and Wales) Rules 2016.
[3]   Rule 1.35(2)(b) of the Insolvency (England and Wales) Rules 2016.
[4]   Rule 1.35(2)(c) of the Insolvency (England and Wales) Rules 2016.
[5]   Rule 1.35(2)(d) of the Insolvency (England and Wales) Rules 2016.
[6]   Rule 1.35(2)(e) of the Insolvency (England and Wales) Rules 2016.
[7]   Rule 1.35(2)(f) of the Insolvency (England and Wales) Rules 2016.

- the remedy applied for or directions sought;[8]
- the name and address of each person to be served or, if none, stating that that it is intended that no person will be served;[9]
- where there is a requirement for particular persons to be given notice of the application under the Act or Rules, stating the name and address of each such person;[10]
- the applicant's address for service.[11]

The application notice must be authenticated by the applicant or his solicitor.[12]

Where no bankruptcy order has been made, the respondents should be the debtor and the nominee only.

Where a bankruptcy order has been made, the respondents should be the undischarged bankrupt, his trustee in bankruptcy or the Official Receiver, the nominee.[13]

COURT FEES

Where the application is made by ordinary application on notice to other parties, a court fee of £155 is payable.[14] Where the application is made by consent or without notice in existing proceedings, a court fee of £50 is payable.[15]

EVIDENCE

The application should be supported by a witness statement. This should address:

- the capacity in which the applicant makes this application;
- who is the debtor in respect of whom the application is being made;
- the nature of the applicant's interest;
- the nature of the security, if any;
- the manner or rights of enforcement that the applicant's interest gives him (so far as it is material to the application);
- what steps the applicant wishes to take;
- the amount of money owed to the applicant;

---

[8]   Rule 1.35(2)(g) of the Insolvency (England and Wales) Rules 2016.

[9]   Rule 1.35(2)(h) of the Insolvency (England and Wales) Rules 2016.

[10] Rule 1.35(2)(i) of the Insolvency (England and Wales) Rules 2016.

[11] Rule 1.35(2)(j) of the Insolvency (England and Wales) Rules 2016.

[12] Rule 1.35(3) of the Insolvency (England and Wales) Rules 2016. For what amounts to authentication, see rule 1.5. For hard copy applications, this means signed: rule 1.5(2).

[13] Section 253(3) of the Insolvency Act 1986.

[14] Paragraph 3.12 of Schedule 1 to the Civil Proceedings Fees (Amendment) Order 2014.

[15] Paragraph 3.11 of Schedule 1 to the Civil Proceedings Fees (Amendment) Order 2014.

- the value of the asset;
- that an interim order has been made under section 252 of the Insolvency Act 1986;
- the name of the nominee under the proposal;
- that there is a moratorium in force;
- that the moratorium created by the interim order prevents his taking the proposed steps without the permission of the court;
- how, but for the moratorium, the applicant would wish to enforce his interest;
- the consequences for the applicant of his being rendered unable to enforce his interest and, in particular, why waiting to see whether the proposals are adopted would be unfair on the applicant;
- the consequences for the applicant and the other creditors of his being allowed to enforce his interest;
- that the applicant seeks permission from the court to enforce.

The applicant should exhibit:

- a copy of the interim order;
- a copy of the arrangement or proposal;
- evidence of the interest that the applicant seeks to enforce;
- evidence showing the entitlement to take the steps proposed by the applicant;
- evidence of the level of debt;
- evidence of the value of the asset (if applicable);
- any documents relevant to the issue;
- any documents relevant to the facts upon which the issue arises.

SERVICE

Service may be effected personally[16] or by post on the respondent (Part 6 of the CPR applies for these purposes)[17] or, where they have authority to accept service, on the respondent's solicitors.[18] Electronic service of documents is now permissible under the Rules, providing the respondent currently consents to service in that way and has provided an email address for service in that way.[19]

---

[16] Rule 1.44 of the Insolvency (England and Wales) Rules 2016.

[17] Schedule 4, paragraph 1(2) to the Insolvency (England and Wales) Rules 2016.

[18] Rule 1.40 of the Insolvency (England and Wales) Rules 2016.

[19] Rule 1.45 of the Insolvency (England and Wales) Rules 2016.

KEY MATERIALS

Section 252 of the Insolvency Act 1986

252 Interim order of court
(1) In the circumstances specified below, the court may in the case of a debtor (being an individual) make an interim order under this section.
(2) An interim order has the effect that, during the period for which it is in force—

(a) no bankruptcy petition relating to the debtor may be presented or proceeded with,
(aa) no landlord or other person to whom rent is payable may exercise any right of forfeiture by peaceable re-entry in relation to premises let to the debtor in respect of a failure by the debtor to comply with any term or condition of his tenancy of such premises, except with the leave of the court and
(b) no other proceedings, and no execution or other legal process, may be commenced or continued and no distress may be levied against the debtor or his property except with the leave of the court.

Rules 8.8–8.13 of the Insolvency (England and Wales) Rules 2016

Application for interim order
8.8.—(1) An application to the court for an interim order under Part 8 of the Act must be accompanied by a witness statement containing—

(a) the reasons for making the application;
(b) information about any action, execution, other legal process or the levying of any distress which, to the debtor's knowledge, has been commenced against the debtor or the debtor's property;
(c) a statement that the debtor is an undischarged bankrupt or is able to make a bankruptcy application;
(d) a statement that no previous application for an interim order has been made by or in relation to the debtor in the period of 12 months ending with the date of the witness statement; and
(e) a statement that a person named in the witness statement is willing to act as nominee in relation to the proposal and is qualified to act as an insolvency practitioner (or is an authorised person) in relation to the debtor.

(2) The witness statement must be accompanied by a copy of—

(a) the proposal; and
(b) the notice of the nominee's consent to act.

(3) When the application and the witness statement have been filed, the court must fix a venue for the hearing of the application.

(4)   The applicant must deliver a notice of the hearing and the venue at least two business days before the hearing to—

(a)   the nominee;

(b)   the debtor, the official receiver or the trustee (whichever is not the applicant) where the debtor is an undischarged bankrupt; and

(c)   any creditor who (to the debtor's knowledge) has presented a bankruptcy petition against the debtor where the debtor is not an undischarged bankrupt.

(5)   A notice under section 253(4) must contain the name and address of the nominee.

Court in which application is to be made

8.9.—(1) An application must be made—

(a)   to the court (and hearing centre if applicable), if any, which has the conduct of the bankruptcy, where the debtor is an undischarged bankrupt; or

(b)   to the court (and hearing centre if applicable) determined in accordance with rule 10.48.

(2)   The application must contain sufficient information to establish that it is made to the appropriate court or hearing centre.

Order granting a stay

8.10. A court order under section 254(1)(b) granting a stay pending hearing of an application must identify the proceedings and contain—

(a)   the section number of the Act under which it is made;

(b)   details of the action, execution or other legal process which is stayed;

(c)   the date on which the application for an interim order will be heard; and

(d)   the date that the order granting the stay is made.

Hearing of the application

8.11.—(1) A person to whom a notice of the hearing of the application for an interim order was (or should have been) delivered under rule 8.8(4) may appear or be represented at the hearing.

(2)   The court must take into account any representations made by or on behalf of such a person (in particular, as to whether an order should contain such provision as is referred to in section 255(3) (provisions as to the conduct of the bankruptcy etc.) and (4) (provisions staying proceedings in bankruptcy etc.).

(3)   If the court makes an interim order, it must fix a venue for consideration of the nominee's report for a date no later than the date on which the order ceases to have effect.

The interim order

8.12. An interim order must contain—

    (a)   identification details for the proceedings;

    (b)   the section number of the Act under which it is made;

    (c)   a statement that the order has effect from its making until the end of the period of 14 days beginning on the day after the date on which it is made;

    (d)   particulars of the effect of the order (as set out in section 252(2));

    (e)   an order that the report of the nominee be delivered to the court no later than two business days before the date fixed for the court's consideration of the report;

    (f)   particulars of any orders made under section 255(3) and (4);

    (g)   where the debtor is an undischarged bankrupt and the applicant is not the official receiver, an order that the applicant delivers, as soon as reasonably practicable, a copy of the interim order to the official receiver;

    (h)   the venue for the court's consideration of the nominee's report; and

    (i)   the date of the order.

Action to follow making of an interim order

8.13.—(1) The court must deliver at least two sealed copies of the interim order to the applicant.

(2)   As soon as reasonably practicable, the applicant must deliver—

    (a)   one copy to the nominee and, where the debtor is an undischarged bankrupt, another copy to the official receiver (unless the official receiver was the applicant); and

    (b)   a notice that the order has been made to any other person to whom a notice of the hearing of the application for an interim order was (or should have been) delivered under rule 8.8(4) and who was not in attendance or represented at the hearing.

14.1 ORDINARY APPLICATION FOR PERMISSION TO ENFORCE SECURITY DESPITE AN INTERIM ORDER

Form IAA   **Insolvency Act Application Notice**

IN THE HIGH COURT OF JUSTICE
BUSINESS AND PROPERTY COURTS OF ENGLAND AND WALES
INSOLVENCY AND COMPANIES LIST (ChD)
IN BANKRUPTCY

NO: 666 OF 2020

IN THE MATTER OF IAN FLAKEY
AND IN THE MATTER OF THE INSOLVENCY ACT 1986

BETWEEN:-

ANGRY PLC

Applicant

and

(1) IAN FLAKEY
(2) GILES GRABBER
(as nominee under a proposal for an
individual voluntary arrangement for IAN FLAKEY)

Respondents

Is this application within existing insolvency proceedings?   YES/~~NO~~

~~I~~(We), ANGRY PLC of 1 Unpaid Bill Street, London intend to apply to the ~~Judge/District Judge~~/Registrar on:

Date: 1st April 2020

Time: 00:00 hours

Place: Royal Courts of Justice, 7 Rolls Buildings, Fetter Lane, London EC4A 1NL

This application having been issued at the RCJ, 7 Rolls Buildings, Fetter Lane, London, EC4A 1NL will be heard at the time and date pursuant to the endorsement underneath the Court Seal on the front page of this application.

FOR AN ORDER THAT:

1.   ANGRY PLC have leave pursuant to section 252(2) of the Insolvency Act 1986 to exercise its right of peaceable re-entry over the premises known as and situate at 1 Poor Street, London pursuant to clause 15 of the lease between Angry plc and Ian Flakey dated 1st April 2019.

2.   The 1st Respondent do pay the Applicant's costs of, and occasioned by, the application.

The grounds of the application are set out in the 1st witness statement of Freddy Furious dated 1st April 2020.

THE NAMES AND ADDRESSES OF THE PERSON(S) UPON WHOM IT IS INTENDED TO SERVE THIS APPLICATION ARE:

Name: IAN FLAKEY

Address: 1 GERANIUM COTTAGE, LONDON

Name: GILES GRABBER

Address: 1 VULTURE STREET, LONDON

~~OR~~

~~IT IS NOT INTENDED TO SERVE ANY PERSON WITH THIS APPLICATION~~

Dated:

Signed: SNARKEY & SNYDE

Solicitors for the applicant ~~or Applicant~~   *This is the address
Address: 1 LAW STREET, LONDON   which will be treated
Telephone: 0207 666 6666   by Court as the
Email: law@snarkeysnyde.com   Petitions address for
                                             service

If you do not attend, the court may make such order as it thinks just.

14.2   WITNESS STATEMENT IN SUPPORT OF AN APPLICATION FOR PERMISSION TO ENFORCE SECURITY DESPITE AN INTERIM ORDER

Applicant: F Furious: 1st: FF1: [ ] 20[ ]

IN THE HIGH COURT OF JUSTICE
BUSINESS AND PROPERTY COURTS OF ENGLAND AND WALES
INSOLVENCY AND COMPANIES LIST (ChD)

NO: [ ] OF 20[ ]

IN THE MATTER OF IAN FLAKEY
AND IN BANKRUPTCY
AND IN THE MATTER OF THE INSOLVENCY ACT 1986

BETWEEN:-

ANGRY PLC

Applicant

and

(1) IAN FLAKEY
(2) GILES GRABBER
(as nominee under a proposal for an
individual voluntary arrangement for IAN FLAKEY)

Respondents

1ST WITNESS STATEMENT OF FREDDY FURIOUS

I, FREDDY FURIOUS, of Angry plc, 1 Unpaid Bill Street, London, Company Director, STATE as follows:

1. I am a director of the Applicant company. I am duly authorised to make this witness statement on its behalf.

2. I make this witness statement in support of the Applicant's application for orders granting leave from this Honourable Court pursuant to section 252(2) of the Insolvency Act 1986 for Angry plc to exercise its right of peaceable re-entry pursuant to clause 15 of the lease between Angry plc and Ian Flakey dated 1st April 2019.

3. The matters stated in this witness statement are true and are made from my own knowledge except where otherwise indicated, in which case I explain the source of my information and belief.

4. There is now produced and shown to me a bundle marked 'FF1' which contains true copies of the documents I will refer to in support of this application.

5. On 1st April 2019, Angry plc granted Ian Flakey a commercial lease of their factory premises at 1 Geranium Cottage, London for £10,000 per calendar month. I refer to page [ ] of 'FF1' which is a true copy of the lease.

6.   Under clause 2 of the lease Ian Flakey agreed to pay the rent each month on the first day of each month. The first rental payment would have fallen due on 1st April 2019.

7.   Under clause 15 of the lease Angry plc are granted the right to retake possession of the premises in the event that Ian Flakey defaults on any payment of his rent.

8.   To date no payments have been made under the lease and Ian Flakey is 12 months in arrears and owes Angry plc £120,000 in unpaid rent.

9.   Angry plc has therefore been entitled under the terms of the lease to take peaceable re-entry of the premises since 1st May 2019.

10.   On 25th February 2020, I wrote to Ian Flakey stating that I intended to take such steps if he did not pay his arrears by the end of the following month.

11.   I was particularly concerned since driving by the property I saw it was vacant and unsecured and therefore at considerable risk of squatters or vandalism.

12.   On 1st March 2020, Ian Flakey obtained an interim order prior to the approval of his individual voluntary arrangement under section 252 of the Insolvency Act 1986. I refer to page [ ] of 'FF1' which is a true copy of the interim order he obtained. This prevents me from obtaining possession.

13.   The proposals under the voluntary arrangement make no provision for the ongoing payment of rent in relation to the premises. I refer to page [ ] of 'FF1' which is a true copy of his proposals.

14.   Given that the property is at immediate risk, forms no part of the IVA proposals and there is no prospect of Angry plc recovering its past or future rent, I would wish to seek possession but am unable to do so because of the moratorium imposed by the interim order.

15.   In all the circumstances, I ask this Honourable Court to grant the relief sought in this application and grant Angry plc permission to exercise its contractual right to peaceable re-entry of the premises.

STATEMENT OF TRUTH

I believe the facts stated in this Witness Statement are true.

Signed [ ]
Full name [*FREDDY FURIOUS*]
Dated [ ] 20[ ]

14.3 ORDER FOR PERMISSION TO ENFORCE SECURITY DESPITE AN INTERIM ORDER

IN THE HIGH COURT OF JUSTICE
BUSINESS AND PROPERTY COURTS OF ENGLAND AND WALES
INSOLVENCY AND COMPANIES LIST (ChD)

NO: [ ] OF 20[ ]

IN THE MATTER OF IAN FLAKEY
AND IN BANKRUPTCY
AND IN THE MATTER OF THE INSOLVENCY ACT 1986

BEFORE MR REGISTRAR WISE
DATED: [ ] OF 20[ ]

BETWEEN:-

ANGRY PLC

Applicant

and

(1) IAN FLAKEY
(2) GILES GRABBER
(as nominee under a proposal for an
individual voluntary arrangement for IAN FLAKEY)

Respondents

_____
DRAFT ORDER
_____

UPON THE APPLICATION of ANGRY PLC, a creditor dated [ ]

AND UPON HEARING counsel for the Respondents and the Applicant

AND UPON reading the evidence noted as being read

IT IS ORDERED THAT:

1. ANGRY PLC have leave pursuant to section 252(2) of the Insolvency Act 1986 to exercise its right of peaceable re-entry over the premises known as and situate at 1 Geranium Cottage, London pursuant to clause 15 of the lease between Angry plc and Ian Flakey dated 1st April 2019

2. The 1st Respondent do pay the Applicant's costs of and occasioned by the application

Service of this order

The Court has provided a sealed copy of this order to the serving party:

SNARKEY & SNYDE
1 LAW STREET
LONDON

Chapter 15

APPLICATION TO CHALLENGE DECISIONS MADE BY A MEETING FOR AN INDIVIDUAL VOLUNTARY ARRANGEMENT

OBJECTIVE

The court has the power to revoke or suspend any approval given by a meeting of creditors for the consideration of a debtor's proposal for an IVA and has a wide discretion to give directions as to how matters should be conducted for the future.[1] The debtor, his creditors (whether or not they had notice of the meeting), the nominee and (if the debtor is an undischarged bankrupt) the trustee in bankruptcy or the Official Receiver each has the right to seek this relief.[2]

Issues that could be challenged in this way include decisions such as the rejection of a creditor's claim to vote,[3] the value to be put on the voting[4] or even as to the voting itself, or a failure to give proper notice.[5]

The court has the power to reverse the decision where there has been unfair prejudice or a material irregularity.[6] Any unfair prejudice must arise from the IVA itself.[7]

APPLICATION

The application is made by application notice on notice using Form IAA. The application should set out:

- that the application is made under the Insolvency Act 1986 or the Insolvency (England and Wales) Rules 2016 (as the case may be);[8]

---

[1] Section 262(4)–(6) of the Insolvency Act 1986.

[2] Section 262(2) of the Insolvency Act 1986.

[3] *Re a Debtor (no 222 of 1990) ex parte Bank of Ireland (No 2)* [1993] BCLC 233.

[4] *National Westminster Bank v Yadgaroff* [2011] EWHC 3711 (Ch), [2012] BPIR 371; *Kapoor v National Westminster Bank* [2011] EWCA Civ 1083, [2011] BPIR 1680.

[5] *Namulas Pension Trustees v Mouzakis* [2011] BPIR 1724.

[6] Section 262(1) of the Insolvency Act 1986.

[7] *Re a Debtor (No 259 of 1990)* [1992] 1 WLR 226.

[8] Rule 1.35(2)(a) of the Insolvency (England and Wales) Rules 2016.

- the section number or rule under which relief is sought;[9]
- the name of the parties;[10]
- the name of the bankrupt or debtor;[11]
- the court name;[12]
- the case number;[13]
- the remedy applied for or directions sought;[14]
- the name and address of each person to be served or, if none, stating that that it is intended that no person will be served;[15]
- where there is a requirement for particular persons to be given notice of the application under the Act or Rules, stating the name and address of each such person;[16]
- the applicant's address for service.[17]

The application notice must be authenticated by the applicant or his solicitor.[18]

The application should be returnable to the registrar in the Bankruptcy Registry or to the district judge in a Chancery District Registry or county court with insolvency jurisdiction.

The application must be made within 28 days of the decision, beginning with the first day upon which the creditors' meeting's report was made to the court, or 28 days from the date the creditor first became aware of the meeting if he was not given notice of the same.[19]

COURT FEES

Where the application is made by ordinary application on notice to other parties, a court fee of £155 is payable.[20] Where the application is made by consent or without notice in existing proceedings, a court fee of £50 is payable.[21]

---

[9] Rule 1.35(2)(b) of the Insolvency (England and Wales) Rules 2016.

[10] Rule 1.35(2)(c) of the Insolvency (England and Wales) Rules 2016.

[11] Rule 1.35(2)(d) of the Insolvency (England and Wales) Rules 2016.

[12] Rule 1.35(2)(e) of the Insolvency (England and Wales) Rules 2016.

[13] Rule 1.35(2)(f) of the Insolvency (England and Wales) Rules 2016.

[14] Rule 1.35(2)(g) of the Insolvency (England and Wales) Rules 2016.

[15] Rule 1.35(2)(h) of the Insolvency (England and Wales) Rules 2016.

[16] Rule 1.35(2)(i) of the Insolvency (England and Wales) Rules 2016.

[17] Rule 1.35(2)(j) of the Insolvency (England and Wales) Rules 2016.

[18] Rule 1.35(3) of the Insolvency (England and Wales) Rules 2016. For what amounts to authentication, see rule 1.5. For hard copy applications, this means signed: rule 1.5(2).

[19] Section 262(3) of the Insolvency Act 1986.

[20] Paragraph 3.12 of Schedule 1 to the Civil Proceedings Fees (Amendment) Order 2014.

[21] Paragraph 3.11 of Schedule 1 to the Civil Proceedings Fees (Amendment) Order 2014.

EVIDENCE

A witness statement should be prepared in support of the application. This should address:

- the identity of the deponent;
- the stage which the IVA has reached;
- what the deponent's interest is in the decision (is he a creditor and what value should be given to his vote and why);
- what decision the meeting made;
- when the decision was made;
- why that decision is wrong;
- that there has been unfair prejudice or a material irregularity and why the deponent says this is so.

And should exhibit:

- a copy of the arrangement or proposal;
- proof of the debt relied on;
- any documents evidencing the decision made and its date;
- any documents relied on as evidencing the unfairness of the decision.

SERVICE

The application and the evidence in support will need to be filed at court and served on the respondents as soon as practicable after it is filed and in any event, unless it is necessary to apply without notice or on short notice, at least 14 days before the date fixed for the hearing.[22]

The usual rule is that, subject to any other express provision, the application must be served at least 14 days before the date fixed for the hearing.[23] However, the court does have power, in cases of urgency, to hear an application immediately with or without notice to the other parties.[24]

Service may be effected personally[25] or by post on the respondent (Part 6 of the CPR applies for these purposes)[26] or, where they have authority to accept service, on the respondent's solicitors.[27] Electronic service of documents is now permissible under the Rules, providing the respondent currently consents to service in that way and has provided an email address for service in that way.[28]

---

[22] Rule 12.9(3) of the Insolvency (England and Wales) Rules 2016.

[23] Rule 12.9(3) of the Insolvency (England and Wales) Rules 2016.

[24] Rule 12.10(1) of the Insolvency (England and Wales) Rules 2016.

[25] Rule 1.44 of the Insolvency (England and Wales) Rules 2016.

[26] Schedule 4, paragraph 1(2) to the Insolvency (England and Wales) Rules 2016.

[27] Rule 1.40 of the Insolvency (England and Wales) Rules 2016.

[28] Rule 1.45 of the Insolvency (England and Wales) Rules 2016.

KEY MATERIALS

Sections 262–262B of the Insolvency Act 1986

262 Challenge of meeting's decision

(1) Subject to this section, an application to the court may be made, by any of the persons specified below, on one or both of the following grounds, namely—

    (a) that a voluntary arrangement approved by a creditors' meeting summoned under section 257 unfairly prejudices the interests of a creditor of the debtor;

    (b) that there has been some material irregularity at or in relation to such a meeting.

(2) The persons who may apply under this section are—

    (a) the debtor;

    (b) a person who—

        (i) was entitled, in accordance with the rules, to vote at the creditors' meeting, or

        (ii) would have been so entitled if he had had notice of it;

    (c) the nominee (or his replacement under section 256(3), 256A(4) or 258(3)); and

    (d) if the debtor is an undischarged bankrupt, the trustee of his estate or the official receiver.

(3) An application under this section shall not be made—

    (a) after the end of the period of 28 days beginning with the day on which the report of the creditors' meeting was made to the court under section 259, or

    (b) in the case of a person who was not given notice of the creditors' meeting, after the end of the period of 28 days beginning with the day on which he became aware that the meeting had taken place,

but (subject to that) an application made by a person within subsection (2)(b)(ii) on the ground that the arrangement prejudices his interests may be made after the arrangement has ceased to have effect, unless it has come to an end prematurely.

(4) Where on an application under this section the court is satisfied as to either of the grounds mentioned in subsection (1), it may do one or both of the following, namely—

    (a) revoke or suspend any approval given by the meeting;

(b)   give a direction to any person for the summoning of a further meeting of the debtor's creditors to consider any revised proposal he may make or, in a case falling within subsection (1)(b), to reconsider his original proposal.

(5)   Where at any time after giving a direction under subsection (4)(b) for the summoning of a meeting to consider a revised proposal the court is satisfied that the debtor does not intend to submit such a proposal, the court shall revoke the direction and revoke or suspend any approval given at the previous meeting.

(6)   Where the court gives a direction under subsection (4)(b), it may also give a direction continuing or, as the case may require, renewing, for such period as may be specified in the direction, the effect in relation to the debtor of any interim order.

(7)   In any case where the court, on an application made under this section with respect to a creditors' meeting, gives a direction under subsection (4)(b) or revokes or suspends an approval under subsection (4)(a) or (5), the court may give such supplemental directions as it thinks fit and, in particular, directions with respect to—

(a)   things done since the meeting under any voluntary arrangement approved by the meeting, and

(b)   such things done since the meeting as could not have been done if an interim order had been in force in relation to the debtor when they were done.

(8)   Except in pursuance of the preceding provisions of this section, an approval given at a creditors' meeting summoned under section 257 is not invalidated by any irregularity at or in relation to the meeting.

262A False representations etc.

(1)   If for the purpose of obtaining the approval of his creditors to a proposal for a voluntary arrangement, the debtor—

(a)   makes any false representation, or

(b)   fraudulently does, or omits to do, anything,

he commits an offence.

(2)   Subsection (1) applies even if the proposal is not approved.

(3)   A person guilty of an offence under this section is liable to imprisonment or a fine, or both.

262B Prosecution of delinquent debtors

(1)   This section applies where a voluntary arrangement approved by a creditors' meeting summoned under section 257 has taken effect.

(2)   If it appears to the nominee or supervisor that the debtor has been guilty of any offence in connection with the arrangement for which he is criminally liable, he shall forthwith—

(a)　report the matter to the Secretary of State, and
(b)　provide the Secretary of State with such information and give the Secretary of State such access to and facilities for inspecting and taking copies of documents (being information or documents in his possession or under his control and relating to the matter in question) as the Secretary of State requires.

(3)　Where a prosecuting authority institutes criminal proceedings following any report under subsection (2), the nominee or, as the case may be, supervisor shall give the authority all assistance in connection with the prosecution which he is reasonably able to give.
For this purpose, 'prosecuting authority' means the Director of Public Prosecutions or the Secretary of State.
(4)　The court may, on the application of the prosecuting authority, direct a nominee or supervisor to comply with subsection (3) if he has failed to do so.

Rules 8.22–8.24 of the Insolvency (England and Wales) Rules 2016

Consideration of the proposal

8.22.—(1) This rule applies where the nominee is required to seek a decision from the debtor's creditors as to whether they approve the debtor's proposal.
(2)　The nominee must deliver to each creditor a notice which complies with rule 15.8 so far as is relevant.
(3)　The notice must also contain—

(a)　identification details for the proceedings;
(b)　where an interim order has not been obtained, details of the court or hearing centre to which an application relating to the proposal or the IVA must be made under rule 8.20(2);
(c)　where an interim order is in force, details of the court or hearing centre in which the nominee's report on the debtor's proposal has been filed under section 256(1);
(d)　a statement as to how a person entitled to vote for the proposal may propose a modification to it, and how the nominee will deal with such a proposal for a modification.

(4)　The notice may contain or be accompanied by a notice that the results of the consideration of the proposal will be made available for viewing and downloading on a website and that no other notice will be delivered to the creditors to whom the notice under this rule was sent.
(5)　Where the results of the consideration of the proposal are to be made available for viewing and downloading on a website the nominee must comply with the requirements for use of a website to deliver a document set out in rule 1.49(2)(a) to (c), (3) and (4) with any necessary adaptations and rule 1.49(5)(a) applies to determine the time of delivery of the document.
(6)　The notice must be accompanied by the following (unless they have been delivered already under rule 8.19)—

(a)   a copy of the proposal;

(b)   a copy of the statement of affairs, or a summary including a list of creditors with the amounts of their debts; and

(c)   a copy of the nominee's report on the proposal.

(7)   The decision date must be not less than 14 days from the date of delivery of the notice and not more than 28 days from the date on which—

(a)   the nominee received the document and statement of affairs referred to in section 256A(2) in a case where an interim order has not been obtained; or

(b)   the nominee's report was considered by the court in a case where an interim order is in force.

Proposals for an alternative supervisor

8.23.—(1) If in response to a notice of a decision procedure to consider the proposal other than at a meeting, a creditor proposes that a person other than the nominee be appointed as supervisor, that person's consent to act and confirmation of being qualified to act as an insolvency practitioner (or being an authorised person) in relation to the debtor must be delivered to the nominee by the creditor.

(2)   If at a creditors' meeting to consider the proposal a resolution is moved for the appointment of a person other than the nominee to be supervisor, that person must produce to the chair at or before the meeting—

(a)   confirmation of being qualified to act as an insolvency practitioner (or being an authorised person) in relation to the debtor; and

(b)   written consent to act (unless the person is present at the meeting and signifies consent).

Report of the creditors' consideration of a proposal

8.24.—(1) A report of the creditors' consideration of a proposal must be prepared by the convener or, if the proposal is considered at a meeting, by the chair.

(2)   The report must—

(a)   state whether the proposal was approved or rejected and, if approved, with what (if any) modifications;

(b)   list the creditors who voted in the decision procedure, setting out with their respective values how they voted on each decision;

(c)   if the proposal was approved, state whether the proceedings are main, territorial or non-EC proceedings and the reasons for so stating; and

(d)   include such further information as the nominee or the chair thinks appropriate.

(3)   Where an interim order was obtained a copy of the report must be filed with the court, within four business days of the decision date.

(4)   The court must endorse the copy of the report with the date of filing.

(5)   The nominee must give notice of the result of the consideration to—

    (a)   everyone who was invited to consider the proposal and to whom notice of the decision procedure was delivered;

    (b)   any other creditor; and

    (c)   where the debtor is an undischarged bankrupt, the official receiver and any trustee.

(6)   The notice must be given—

    (a)   where an interim order was obtained, as soon as reasonably practicable after a copy of the report is filed with the court; or

    (b)   where an interim order was not obtained, within four business days of the decision date.

15.1   APPLICATION FOR AN ORDER REVOKING A DECISION MADE BY THE CREDITORS' MEETING IN AN INDIVIDUAL VOLUNTARY ARRANGEMENT

Form IAA   **Insolvency Act Application Notice**

IN THE HIGH COURT OF JUSTICE
BUSINESS AND PROPERTY COURTS OF ENGLAND AND WALES
INSOLVENCY AND COMPANIES LIST (ChD)
IN BANKRUPTCY

NO: 666 OF 2020

IN THE MATTER OF IAN FLAKEY
AND IN THE MATTER OF THE INSOLVENCY ACT 1986

BETWEEN:-

ANGRY PLC

Applicant

and

(1) IAN FLAKEY
(2) GILES GRABBER
(as nominee under a proposal for an
individual voluntary arrangement for IAN FLAKEY)

Respondents

Is this application within existing insolvency proceedings? YES/~~NO~~

I̶(We), ANGRY PLC of 1 Unpaid Bill Street, London intend to apply to the ~~Judge/District Judge~~/Registrar on:

Date: 1st April 2020

Time: 00:00 hours

Place: Royal Courts of Justice, 7 Rolls Buildings, Fetter Lane, London EC4A 1NL

This application having been issued at the RCJ, 7 Rolls Buildings, Fetter Lane, London, EC4A 1NL will be heard at the time and date pursuant to the endorsement underneath the Court Seal on the front page of this application.

FOR AN ORDER THAT:

1.   The approval of the voluntary arrangement given by the meeting of creditors held on 1st April 2020 in respect of Ian Flakey be revoked.

2.   The 2nd Respondent nominee do within 14 days convene a further meeting of the creditors of the Company to consider the Applicant's proposals filed herein and that the Applicant be permitted to vote in the full amount of his claim in the sum

of £120,000 and that the expense of convening such further meeting and of this application be an expense of the voluntary arrangement.

(3)   [Costs be provided for.]

The grounds of the application are set out in the 1st witness statement of Freddy Furious dated 1st April 2020.

THE NAMES AND ADDRESSES OF THE PERSON(S) UPON WHOM IT IS INTENDED TO SERVE THIS APPLICATION ARE:

Name: IAN FLAKEY

Address: 1 GERANIUM COTTAGE, LONDON

Name: GILES GRABBER

Address: 1 VULTURE STREET, LONDON

~~OR~~

~~IT IS NOT INTENDED TO SERVE ANY PERSON WITH THIS APPLICATION~~

Dated:

Signed: SNARKEY & SNYDE

Solicitors for the applicant ~~or Applicant~~
Address: 1 LAW STREET, LONDON
Telephone: 0207 666 6666
Email: law@snarkeysnyde.com

*This is the address which will be treated by Court as the Petitions address for service

If you do not attend, the court may make such order as it thinks just.

15.2 WITNESS STATEMENT IN SUPPORT OF AN APPLICATION FOR AN ORDER REVOKING A DECISION MADE BY THE CREDITORS' MEETING IN AN INDIVIDUAL VOLUNTARY ARRANGEMENT

Applicant: F Furious: 1st: FF1: [ ] 20[ ]

IN THE HIGH COURT OF JUSTICE
BUSINESS AND PROPERTY COURTS OF ENGLAND AND WALES
INSOLVENCY AND COMPANIES LIST (ChD)

NO: [ ] OF 20[ ]

IN THE MATTER OF IAN FLAKEY
AND IN BANKRUPTCY

BETWEEN:-

ANGRY PLC

Applicant

and

(1) IAN FLAKEY
(2) GILES GRABBER
(as nominee under a proposal for an
individual voluntary arrangement for IAN FLAKEY)

Respondents

_____

1ST WITNESS STATEMENT OF FREDDY FURIOUS

_____

I, FREDDY FURIOUS, of Angry plc, 1 Unpaid Bill Street, London, Company Director, STATE as follows:

1.   I am a director of the Applicant company. I am duly authorised to make this witness statement on its behalf.

2.   I make this witness statement in support of the Applicant's application for an order:

a.   That the approval of the voluntary arrangement given by the meeting of creditors held on 1st April 2020 in respect of Ian Flakey be revoked.

b.   That the 2nd Respondent nominee do within 14 days convene a further meeting of the creditors of the Company to consider the Applicant's proposals filed herein and that the Applicant be permitted to vote in the full amount of his claim in the sum of £120,000 and that the expense of convening such further meeting and of this application be an expense of the voluntary arrangement.

3.   The matters stated in this witness statement are true and made from my own knowledge except where otherwise indicated, in which case I explain the source of my information and belief.

4.   There is now produced and shown to me a bundle marked 'FF1' which contains true copies of the documents I will refer to in support of this application.

5. On 1st April 2019, Angry plc granted Ian Flakey a commercial lease of their factory premises at 1 Geranium Cottage, London for £10,000 per calendar month. I refer to page [ ] of 'FF1' which is a true copy of the lease.

6. Under clause 2 of the lease, Ian Flakey agreed to pay the rent each month on the first day of each month. The first rental payment would have fallen due on 1st April 2019.

7. To date, no payments have been made under the lease and Ian Flakey is 12 months in arrears and owes Angry plc £120,000 in unpaid rent.

8. Angry plc sent in a proof of debt for the £120,000 owed by Mr Flakey. I refer to page [ ] of the exhibit marked 'FF1' which is a true copy of my proof of debt.

9. I attended the meeting of creditors on 1st May 2020. The chairman of the meeting, Mr Grabber, refused to allow the value of my vote to be taken account of for voting purposes on the grounds that he 'didn't trust people with ginger hair'. I refer to page [ ] of my exhibit marked 'FF1' which is a true copy of the minutes of the meeting.

10. I would have wished my alternative proposal for the arrangement to be considered. I refer to page [ ] of my exhibit marked 'FF1' which is a true copy of my alternative proposal which I had hoped to be adopted as a variation.

11. However, the chairman refused to permit the meeting to consider these matters whether as a variation to the arrangement or at all. He stated that as he had decided not to count the money I said I was owed, he was refusing me the right to either speak or vote at the meeting and he would not permit my proposals to be shown to or considered by the other creditors. I refer to page [ ] of my exhibit marked 'FF1' which is a true copy of the minutes of the meeting.

12. I therefore ask this Honourable Court to make the order in the terms sought.

STATEMENT OF TRUTH

I believe the facts stated in this Witness Statement are true.

Signed [ ]
Full name [*FREDDY FURIOUS*]
Dated [ ] 20[ ]

15.3   DRAFT ORDER REVOKING A DECISION MADE BY THE CREDITORS' MEETING IN AN INDIVIDUAL VOLUNTARY ARRANGEMENT

IN THE HIGH COURT OF JUSTICE
BUSINESS AND PROPERTY COURTS OF ENGLAND AND WALES
INSOLVENCY AND COMPANIES LIST (ChD)

NO. [ ] OF 20[ ]

IN THE MATTER OF IAN FLAKEY
AND IN BANKRUPTCY

BEFORE MR REGISTRAR WISE
DATED: [ ] OF 20[ ]

BETWEEN:-

ANGRY PLC

Applicant

and

(1) IAN FLAKEY
(2) GILES GRABBER
(as nominee under a proposal for an
individual voluntary arrangement for IAN FLAKEY)

Respondents

DRAFT ORDER

UPON THE APPLICATION of Angry plc, a creditor

AND UPON HEARING counsel for the parties

AND UPON reading the evidence noted as being read

IT IS ORDERED THAT:

1.   The approval of the voluntary arrangement given by the meeting of creditors held on 1st April 2020 in respect of Ian Flakey be revoked

2.   The 2nd Respondent nominee do within 14 days convene a further meeting of the creditors of the Company to consider the Applicant's proposals filed herein and that the Applicant be permitted to vote in the full amount of his claim in the sum of £120,000 and that the expense of convening such further meeting and of this application be an expense of the voluntary arrangement

3.   [Costs be provided for.]

Service of this order

The Court has provided a sealed copy of this order to the serving party:

SNARKEY & SNYDE
1 LAW STREET
LONDON

Chapter 16

APPLICATION TO CHALLENGE DECISIONS IN RESPECT OF A DEBT RELIEF ORDER

OVERVIEW

Debt relief orders provide an alternative insolvency framework for debtors whose debts are below £15,000 and whose assets are below £300[1] and whose surplus income is below £50. An application for a debt relief order must be made through an approved intermediary and operates as an immediate moratorium against a creditor's bankruptcy petition and other action or legal proceedings.[2]

At the end of the moratorium the debtor is discharged from his liability for unsecured qualifying debts.[3]

Any person may make an application to the court if he is dissatisfied by any act or omission of the Official Receiver in connection with a debt relief order.[4] The same section also gives the Official Receiver power to apply to the court for directions.[5]

APPLICATION

The application is by application on notice on Form IAA.

The application should set out:

- that the application is made under the Insolvency Act 1986 or the Insolvency (England and Wales) Rules 2016 (as the case may be);[6]
- the section number or rule under which relief is sought;[7]
- the name of the parties;[8]

---

[1]   Cars worth under £1,000 are excluded.
[2]   Section 251G of the Insolvency Act 1986.
[3]   Section 251I of the Insolvency Act 1986.
[4]   Section 251M of the Insolvency Act 1986.
[5]   Section 251M of the Insolvency Act 1986.
[6]   Rule 1.35(2)(a) of the Insolvency (England and Wales) Rules 2016.
[7]   Rule 1.35(2)(b) of the Insolvency (England and Wales) Rules 2016.
[8]   Rule 1.35(2)(c) of the Insolvency (England and Wales) Rules 2016.

- the name of the bankrupt or debtor;[9]
- the court name;[10]
- the case number;[11]
- the remedy applied for or directions sought;[12]
- the name and address of each person to be served or, if none, stating that that it is intended that no person will be served;[13]
- where there is a requirement for particular persons to be given notice of the application under the Act or Rules, stating the name and address of each such person;[14]
- the applicant's address for service.[15]

The application notice must be authenticated by the applicant or his solicitor.[16]

The application should stipulate what order is sought from the court. The court has power to:[17]

- quash the whole or part of any act or decision of the Official Receiver;
- give the Official Receiver directions (including a direction that he reconsider any matter in relation to which his act or decision has been quashed under paragraph (a));
- make an order for the enforcement of any obligation on the debtor to provide information, attend on the Official Receiver or do all such things as the Official Receiver may require;[18]
- extend the moratorium period applicable to the debt relief order;
- make an order revoking or amending the debt relief order;
- make an order for an inquiry into the debtor's dealings and property;[19] or
- make such other order as the court thinks fit.

An order for the revocation of a debt relief order may be made during the moratorium period applicable to the debt relief order or at any time after that period has ended, may be made on the court's own motion if the court has made a bankruptcy order in relation to the debtor during that period and may provide for the revocation of the order to take effect on such terms and at such a time as the court may specify.[20]

---

[9] Rule 1.35(2)(d) of the Insolvency (England and Wales) Rules 2016.
[10] Rule 1.35(2)(e) of the Insolvency (England and Wales) Rules 2016.
[11] Rule 1.35(2)(f) of the Insolvency (England and Wales) Rules 2016.
[12] Rule 1.35(2)(g) of the Insolvency (England and Wales) Rules 2016.
[13] Rule 1.35(2)(h) of the Insolvency (England and Wales) Rules 2016.
[14] Rule 1.35(2)(i) of the Insolvency (England and Wales) Rules 2016.
[15] Rule 1.35(2)(j) of the Insolvency (England and Wales) Rules 2016.
[16] Rule 1.35(3) of the Insolvency (England and Wales) Rules 2016. For what amounts to authentication, see rule 1.5. For hard copy applications, this means signed: rule 1.5(2).
[17] Section 251M(6) of the Insolvency Act 1986.
[18] Section 251J of the Insolvency Act 1986.
[19] Section 251N of the Insolvency Act 1986.
[20] Section 251M(7) of the Insolvency Act 1986.

The application must disclose sufficient information to explain why the application is brought in that court.[21]

The application should be returnable to the registrar in the Bankruptcy Registry or to the district judge in a Chancery District Registry or county court with insolvency jurisdiction.

COURT FEES

Where the application is made by ordinary application on notice to other parties, a court fee of £155 is payable.[22] Where the application is made by consent or without notice in existing proceedings, a court fee of £50 is payable.[23]

EVIDENCE

A witness statement should be prepared in support of the application. This should address:

- the identity of the deponent;
- the capacity in which the applicant makes the application;
- what order the applicant seeks;
- the date upon which the debt relief order was made;
- the stage which the debt relief order has reached;
- what order is being sought;
- if a decision is being challenged:

  - when the decision was made;
  - why that decision is wrong;

- that there has been unfairness or an irregularity and why the deponent says this is so.

And should exhibit:

- a copy of the debt relief order and any material disclosed to date;
- proof of the debt relied on;
- any documents evidencing the decision made and its date;
- any documents relied on as evidencing the incorrectness, irregularity and unfairness of the decision.

---

[21] Rule 9.22(5) of the Insolvency (England and Wales) Rules 2016.

[22] Paragraph 3.12 of Schedule 1 to the Civil Proceedings Fees (Amendment) Order 2014.

[23] Paragraph 3.11 of Schedule 1 to the Civil Proceedings Fees (Amendment) Order 2014.

SERVICE

Where an application is made to the court under section 251M of the Insolvency Act 1986 by a person who is dissatisfied by any act, omission or decision of the Official Receiver in connection with a debt relief order or an application for a debt relief order, if the person making the application is the debtor, notice of the application to the court must be sent to the Official Receiver and to any creditor specified in the debt relief order or in the application for a debt relief order.[24]

Where the applicant is a person other than the debtor, notice of the application to the court must be sent to the Official Receiver and to the debtor.[25]

Where the application is made by the Official Receiver for directions or an order in relation to any matter arising in connection with a debt relief order or an application for such an order, notice of the application must be sent by the Official Receiver to the debtor and to any person appearing to the Official Receiver to have an interest in the application.[26]

The application and the evidence in support will need to be filed at court and served on the respondent as soon as practicable after it is filed and in any event, unless it is necessary to apply without notice or on short notice, at least 14 days before the date fixed for the hearing.[27]

The usual rule is that, subject to any other express provision, the application must be served at least 14 days before the date fixed for the hearing.[28] However, the court does have power, in cases of urgency, to hear an application immediately with or without notice to the other parties.[29]

Service may be effected personally[30] or by post on the respondent (Part 6 of the CPR applies for these purposes)[31] or, where they have authority to accept service, on the respondent's solicitors.[32] Electronic service of documents is now permissible under the Rules, providing the respondent currently consents to service in that way and has provided an email address for service in that way.[33]

---

[24]   Rule 9.21(2)(a) of the Insolvency (England and Wales) Rules 2016.
[25]   Rule 9.21(2)(b) of the Insolvency (England and Wales) Rules 2016.
[26]   Rule 9.21(3) of the Insolvency (England and Wales) Rules 2016.
[27]   Rule 12.9(3) of the Insolvency (England and Wales) Rules 2016.
[28]   Rule 12.9(3) of the Insolvency (England and Wales) Rules 2016.
[29]   Rule 12.10(1) of the Insolvency (England and Wales) Rules 2016.
[30]   Rule 1.44 of the Insolvency (England and Wales) Rules 2016.
[31]   Schedule 4, paragraph 1(2) to the Insolvency (England and Wales) Rules 2016.
[32]   Rule 1.40 of the Insolvency (England and Wales) Rules 2016.
[33]   Rule 1.45 of the Insolvency (England and Wales) Rules 2016.

KEY MATERIALS

Sections 251M and 251X of the Insolvency Act 1986

251M Powers of court in relation to debt relief orders

(1)   Any person may make an application to the court if he is dissatisfied by any act, omission or decision of the official receiver in connection with a debt relief order or an application for such an order.

(2)   The official receiver may make an application to the court for directions or an order in relation to any matter arising in connection with a debt relief order or an application for such an order.

(3)   The matters referred to in subsection (2) include, among other things, matters relating to the debtor's compliance with any duty arising under section 251J.

(4)   An application under this section may, subject to anything in the rules, be made at any time.

(5)   The court may extend the moratorium period applicable to a debt relief order for the purposes of determining an application under this section.

(6)   On an application under this section the court may dismiss the application or do one or more of the following—

  (a)   quash the whole or part of any act or decision of the official receiver;
  (b)   give the official receiver directions (including a direction that he reconsider any matter in relation to which his act or decision has been quashed under paragraph (a));
  (c)   make an order for the enforcement of any obligation on the debtor arising by virtue of a duty under section 251J;
  (d)   extend the moratorium period applicable to the debt relief order;
  (e)   make an order revoking or amending the debt relief order;
  (f)   make an order under section 251N; or
  (g)   make such other order as the court thinks fit.

(7)   An order under subsection (6)(e) for the revocation of a debt relief order—

  (a)   may be made during the moratorium period applicable to the debt relief order or at any time after that period has ended;
  (b)   may be made on the court's own motion if the court has made a bankruptcy order in relation to the debtor during that period;
  (c)   may provide for the revocation of the order to take effect on such terms and at such a time as the court may specify.

(8)   An order under subsection (6)(e) for the amendment of a debt relief order may not add any debts that were not specified in the application for the debt relief order to the list of qualifying debts.

251X Interpretation

(1)   In this Part—

'the application date', in relation to a debt relief order or an application for
    a debt relief order, means the date on which the application for the
    order is made to the official receiver;
'approved intermediary' has the meaning given in section 251U(1);
'debt relief order' means an order made by the official receiver under this
    Part;
'debtor' means—

(a)   in relation to an application for a debt relief order, the applicant;
       and
(b)   in relation to a debt relief order, the person in relation to whom
       the order is made;

'debt relief restrictions order' and 'debt relief restrictions undertaking'
    means an order made, or an undertaking accepted, under Schedule
    4ZB;
'the determination date', in relation to a debt relief order or an application
    for a debt relief order, means the date on which the application for the
    order is determined by the official receiver;
'the effective date' has the meaning given in section 251E(7);
'excluded debt' is to be construed in accordance with section 251A;
'moratorium' and 'moratorium period' are to be construed in accordance
    with sections 251G and 251H;
'qualifying debt', in relation to a debtor, has the meaning given in section
    251A(2);
'the register' means the register maintained under section 251W;
'specified qualifying debt' has the meaning given in section 251G(1).

(2)   In this Part references to a creditor specified in a debt relief order as the
       person to whom a qualifying debt is owed by the debtor include a reference
       to any person to whom the right to claim the whole or any part of the debt
       has passed, by assignment or operation of law, after the date of the
       application for the order.

Rules 9.14 and 9.21–9.22 of the Insolvency (England and Wales) Rules 2016

Meaning of 'creditor'
9.14. In this Chapter, 'creditor' means a person specified in a debt relief order as
    a creditor to whom a qualifying debt is owed.

Notice of application to court under section 251M
9.21.—(1) This rule applies to applications to the court under section 251M.
(2)   Where the application is made by a person who is dissatisfied by an act,
       omission or decision of the official receiver in connection with a debt relief
       order or an application for a debt relief order the applicant must deliver
       a notice—

    (a) if the applicant is the debtor, to the official receiver and any creditor specified in the debt relief order or in the application for the debt relief order; or

    (b) if the applicant is a person other than the debtor, to the official receiver and the debtor.

(3)   Where the application is made by the official receiver for directions or an order in relation to a matter arising in connection with a debt relief order or an application for such an order, the official receiver must deliver notice to—

    (a) the debtor; and

    (b) any person appearing to the official receiver to have an interest in the application.

Court in which applications under sections 251M or 251N are to be made

9.22.—(1) An application to the court under section 251M or 251N must be made to—

    (a) the County Court at Central London, where the proceedings are allocated to the London Insolvency District under rule 12.5(a)(i) to (iv);

    (b) the High Court, where the proceedings are allocated to the London Insolvency District under rule 12.5(a)(v);

    (c) the debtor's own hearing centre as determined under paragraph (3) (subject to paragraph (4)), in any other case where the debtor is resident in England and Wales.

(2)   The application may be filed either with the debtor's own hearing centre or with the High Court if—

    (a) the debtor is not resident in England and Wales but was resident or carried on business in England and Wales within the six months immediately before the application is filed with the court; and

    (b) the proceedings are not allocated to the London Insolvency District.

(3)   In this rule the debtor's own hearing centre is—

    (a) where the debtor has carried on business in England and Wales within the six months immediately before the application is filed with the court, the hearing centre which serves the insolvency district where for the longest period during those six months—

        (i) the debtor carried on business, or

        (ii) the principal place of business was located, if business was carried on in more than one insolvency district; or

    (b) where the debtor has not carried on business in England and Wales within the six months immediately before the application is filed with the court, the hearing centre which serves the insolvency district where the debtor resided for the longest period during those six months.

(4)   Where, for whatever reason, it is not possible for the application to be filed with the debtor's own hearing centre, the applicant may, with a view to expediting the application, file the application—

(a)   where paragraph (3)(a) applies, with—

(i)   the hearing centre for the insolvency district in which the debtor resides, or

(ii)   the hearing centre specified in Schedule 6 as the nearest full-time hearing centre to the hearing centre specified in paragraph (3)(a), or paragraph (i) as the case may be; or

(b)   where paragraph (3)(b) applies, with the hearing centre specified in Schedule 6 as being the nearest full-time hearing centre to that specified in paragraph (3)(b).

(5)   The application must contain sufficient information to establish that it is brought in the appropriate court, and where the application is made to the County Court, the appropriate hearing centre.

16.1   ORDINARY APPLICATION FOR AN ORDER REVOKING A DEBT RELIEF ORDER

Form IAA   **Insolvency Act Application Notice**

IN THE HIGH COURT OF JUSTICE
BUSINESS AND PROPERTY COURTS OF ENGLAND AND WALES
INSOLVENCY AND COMPANIES LIST (ChD)
IN BANKRUPTCY

NO: 666 OF 2020

IN THE MATTER OF IAN FLAKEY
AND IN THE MATTER OF THE INSOLVENCY ACT 1986

BETWEEN:-

ANGRY PLC

Applicant

and

(1) IAN FLAKEY
(2) THE OFFICIAL RECEIVER

Respondents

Is this application within existing insolvency proceedings?   YES/~~NO~~

I̶(We), ANGRY PLC of 1 Unpaid Bill Street, London intend to apply to the ~~Judge/District Judge~~/Registrar on:

Date: 1st April 2020

Time: 00:00 hours

Place: Royal Courts of Justice, 7 Rolls Buildings, Fetter Lane, London EC4A 1NL

This application having been issued at the RCJ, 7 Rolls Buildings, Fetter Lane, London, EC4A 1NL will be heard at the time and date pursuant to the endorsement underneath the Court Seal on the front page of this application.

FOR AN ORDER THAT:

1.   The Debt Relief Order made on 1st April 2020 in respect of Ian Flakey be revoked.

2.   Costs be provided for.

3.   Further and other relief under section 251M of the Insolvency Act 1986.

The grounds of the application are set out in the 1st witness statement of Freddy Furious dated 1st April 2020.

The debtor is resident in England and Wales and the debtor has resided or carried on business in the London Insolvency District for the greater part of the 6 months immediately preceding the making of the application and for a longer period in those 6 months than in any other insolvency district.

THE NAMES AND ADDRESSES OF THE PERSON(S) UPON WHOM IT IS INTENDED TO SERVE THIS APPLICATION ARE:

Name: IAN FLAKEY

Address: 1 GERANIUM COTTAGE, LONDON

Name: THE OFFICIAL RECEIVER

Address: 5TH FLOOR, ZONE B, 21 BLOOMSBURY STREET, LONDON WC1B 3SS

~~OR~~

~~IT IS NOT INTENDED TO SERVE ANY PERSON WITH THIS APPLICATION~~

Dated:

Signed: SNARKEY & SNYDE

Solicitors for the applicant ~~or Applicant~~
Address: 1 LAW STREET, LONDON
Telephone: 0207 666 6666
Email: law@snarkeysnyde.com

*This is the address which will be treated by Court as the Petitions address for service

If you do not attend, the court may make such order as it thinks just.

16.2   WITNESS STATEMENT IN SUPPORT OF AN APPLICATION FOR AN ORDER REVOKING A DEBT RELIEF ORDER

Applicant: F Furious: 1st: FF1: [ ] 20[ ]

IN THE HIGH COURT OF JUSTICE
BUSINESS AND PROPERTY COURTS OF ENGLAND AND WALES
INSOLVENCY AND COMPANIES LIST (ChD)

NO: [ ] OF 20[ ]

IN THE MATTER OF IAN FLAKEY
AND IN BANKRUPTCY

BETWEEN:-

ANGRY PLC

Applicant

and

(1) IAN FLAKEY
(2) THE OFFICIAL RECEIVER

Respondents

1ST WITNESS STATEMENT OF FREDDY FURIOUS

I, FREDDY FURIOUS, of Angry plc, 1 Unpaid Bill Street, London, Company Director, STATE as follows:

1. I am a director of the Applicant company. I am duly authorised to make this witness statement on their behalf.

2. I make this witness statement in support of the Applicant's application for an order:

    a. That the Debt Relief Order made on 1st April 2020 in respect of Ian Flakey be revoked.
    b. Provision for costs.
    c. Further and other relief.

3. The matters stated in this witness statement are true and made from my own knowledge except where otherwise indicated, in which case I explain the source of my information and belief.

4. There is now produced and shown to me a bundle marked 'FF1' which contains true copies of the documents I will refer to in support of this application.

5. On 1st April 2019, Angry plc sold Ian Flakey 100 boxes of widgets for £11,100. I refer to page [ ] of 'FF1' which is a true copy of the invoice.

6. To date no payments have been made for the widgets and Ian Flakey owes Angry plc £11,100.

7.   I understand Ian Flakey owns a 1926 Rolls Royce Silver Cough motor car. I refer to page [ ] of 'FF1' which is a true copy of a press clipping showing Mr Flakey in front of the motor car on the Bognor Regis Concours D'Elegance.

8.   Angry plc contacted the Official Receiver and told him that his assets exceeded £300 in value and that the motor car should be counted as being of a value in excess of £1,000. I refer to page [ ] of the exhibit marked 'FF1' which is a true copy of the letter to the Official Receiver. Attached to the letter was an article from 'Collectors Cars' magazine which reported the sale of another 1926 Rolls Royce Silver Cough motor car for £1.25 million. I refer to page [ ] of 'FF1' which is a true copy of the press clipping.

9.   The Official Receiver wrote back to Angry plc, refusing to revoke the Debt Relief Order. The reason given was that Mr Flakey had told him that the car was very old, never started on cold days and was therefore 'not worth a bean'. I refer to page [ ] of my exhibit marked 'FF1' which is a true copy of the letter.

10.   The value of the car is reflected by the fact that it was built in 1926 and one of only two Silver Coughs made. I refer to page [ ] of my exhibit marked 'FF1' which is a true copy of a report on the car's valuation.

11.   In all the circumstances Mr Flakey's assets far exceed the permissible value for a Debt Relief Order to be made.

12.   I therefore ask this Honourable Court to make the order in the terms sought.

STATEMENT OF TRUTH

I believe the facts stated in this Witness Statement are true.

Signed [ ]
Full name [*FREDDY FURIOUS*]
Dated [ ] 20[ ]

16.3   DRAFT ORDER REVOKING A DEBT RELIEF ORDER

IN THE HIGH COURT OF JUSTICE
BUSINESS AND PROPERTY COURTS OF ENGLAND AND WALES
INSOLVENCY AND COMPANIES LIST (ChD)

NO: [ ] OF 20[ ]

IN THE MATTER OF IAN FLAKEY
AND IN BANKRUPTCY

BEFORE MR REGISTRAR WISE
DATED: [ ] OF 20[ ]

BETWEEN:-

ANGRY PLC

Applicant

and

(1) IAN FLAKEY
(2) THE OFFICIAL RECEIVER

Respondents

DRAFT ORDER

UPON THE APPLICATION of Angry plc, a creditor

AND UPON HEARING Counsel for the parties

AND UPON reading the evidence noted as being read

IT IS ORDERED THAT:

1.   The Debt Relief Order made in respect of Ian Flakey be revoked with effect from 10 am on [ ]

2.   [Provision for costs.]

Service of this order

The Court has provided a sealed copy of this order to the serving party:

SNARKEY & SNYDE
1 LAW STREET
LONDON

Chapter 17

APPLICATION FOR AN INCOME PAYMENT ORDER

OBJECTIVE

The trustee in bankruptcy (or the Official Receiver) may apply to the court for an order claiming for the estate in bankruptcy or part of the bankrupt's salary or income for the period from the date of the bankruptcy order to a date fixed by the court, which can be up to 3 years later.[1] The order may either direct the bankrupt to make such payments[2] or direct the person paying the bankrupt (such as his employer) to make the payments to the trustee direct.[3] Both the trustee and the bankrupt may subsequently apply to vary or discharge the order[4] and the trustee (or the Official Receiver) may enter into an agreement instead about the payment of income provided that it is not on terms which are more severe than the court could have ordered.[5] There is no requirement that creditors receive a benefit from the income payment order – defraying the insolvency practitioner's costs may be reason in itself.[6]

The bankrupt, however, will not be required to draw down uncrystallised capital sums in his pension pot.[7]

The income payment order will only be ordered in respect of sums which are surplus to the bankrupt's reasonable domestic needs.[8] Whether private school fees fall within reasonable domestic needs will be determined by reference to the circumstances and whether it will be detrimental to the children.[9]

---

[1]   Section 310 of the Insolvency Act 1986.

[2]   Section 310(3)(a) of the Insolvency Act 1986.

[3]   Section 310(3)(b) of the Insolvency Act 1986.

[4]   Section 310(6A) of the Insolvency Act 1986.

[5]   Section 310A of the Insolvency Act 1986.

[6]   *Official Receiver v Negus* [2011] EWHC 3719 (Ch), [2012] 1 WLR 1598.

[7]   *Re Wotherspoon* [2016] EWHC 621 (Ch), [2016] BPIR 944; *Norton v Henry* [2016] EWCA Civ 989, [2017] 3 All ER 735.

[8]   Section 310(2) of the Insolvency Act 1986; *Boyden v Watson* [2004] BPIR 1131.

[9]   *Re Rayatt* [1998] BPIR 495; *Scott v Davies* [2003] BPIR 1009.

APPLICATION

The application is made by application notice on notice using Form IAA.[10]

Each application should set out:

- that the application is made under the Insolvency Act 1986 or the Insolvency (England and Wales) Rules 2016 (as the case may be);[11]
- the section number or rule under which relief is sought;[12]
- the name of the parties;[13]
- the name of the bankrupt or debtor;[14]
- the court name;[15]
- the case number;[16]
- the remedy applied for or directions sought;[17]
- the name and address of each person to be served or, if none, stating that that it is intended that no person will be served;[18]
- where there is a requirement for particular persons to be given notice of the application under the Act or Rules, stating the name and address of each such person;[19]
- the applicant's address for service.[20]

The application notice must be authenticated by the applicant or his solicitor.[21]

The application should be returnable to the registrar in the Bankruptcy Registry or to the district judge in a Chancery District Registry or county court with insolvency jurisdiction.

---

[10] Rule 10.109 of the Insolvency (England and Wales) Rules 2016.

[11] Rule 1.35(2)(a) of the Insolvency (England and Wales) Rules 2016.

[12] Rule 1.35(2)(b) of the Insolvency (England and Wales) Rules 2016.

[13] Rule 1.35(2)(c) of the Insolvency (England and Wales) Rules 2016.

[14] Rule 1.35(2)(d) of the Insolvency (England and Wales) Rules 2016.

[15] Rule 1.35(2)(e) of the Insolvency (England and Wales) Rules 2016.

[16] Rule 1.35(2)(f) of the Insolvency (England and Wales) Rules 2016.

[17] Rule 1.35(2)(g) of the Insolvency (England and Wales) Rules 2016.

[18] Rule 1.35(2)(h) of the Insolvency (England and Wales) Rules 2016.

[19] Rule 1.35(2)(i) of the Insolvency (England and Wales) Rules 2016.

[20] Rule 1.35(2)(j) of the Insolvency (England and Wales) Rules 2016.

[21] Rule 1.35(3) of the Insolvency (England and Wales) Rules 2016. For what amounts to authentication, see rule 1.5. For hard copy applications, this means signed: rule 1.5(2).

COURT FEES

Where the application is made by ordinary application on notice to other parties, a court fee of £155 is payable.[22] Where the application is made by consent in existing proceedings, a court fee of £50 is payable.[23]

EVIDENCE

The application should be supported by a witness statement. This should address:

- the capacity in which the deponent makes this application;
- the order the deponent seeks;
- the date of the petition;
- the date of the bankruptcy order;
- the details of the bankrupt's current income;
- the particulars of the bankrupt's current outgoings;
- the trustee's assessment of the reasonable domestic needs of the bankrupt and his family;
- whether the trustee considers any of the bankrupt's expenses are excessive (and if so which).

And should exhibit:

- evidence of the trustee's appointment;
- the bankruptcy order;
- the statement of affairs;
- evidence of the bankrupt's income;
- evidence of the bankrupt's outgoings.

SERVICE

The application and the evidence in support will need to be filed at court and should be served on the bankrupt at least 28 days before the date fixed for the hearing.[24]

Service may be effected personally[25] or by post on the respondent (Part 6 of the CPR applies for these purposes)[26] or, where they have authority to accept service, on the respondent's solicitors.[27] Electronic service of documents is now

---

[22] Paragraph 3.12 of Schedule 1 to the Civil Proceedings Fees (Amendment) Order 2014.

[23] Paragraph 3.11 of Schedule 1 to the Civil Proceedings Fees (Amendment) Order 2014.

[24] Rule 10.109(2) of the Insolvency (England and Wales) Rules 2016.

[25] Rule 1.44 of the Insolvency (England and Wales) Rules 2016.

[26] Schedule 4, paragraph 1(2) to the Insolvency (England and Wales) Rules 2016.

[27] Rule 1.40 of the Insolvency (England and Wales) Rules 2016.

permissible under the Rules, providing the respondent currently consents to service in that way and has provided an email address for service in that way.[28]

KEY MATERIALS

Sections 310–310A of the Insolvency Act 1986

310 Income payments orders

(1)　The court may . . . make an order ('an income payments order') claiming for the bankrupt's estate so much of the income of the bankrupt during the period for which the order is in force as may be specified in the order.

(1A) An income payments order may be made only on an application instituted—

　　(a)　by the trustee, and
　　(b)　before the discharge of the bankrupt.

(2)　The court shall not make an income payments order the effect of which would be to reduce the income of the bankrupt when taken together with any payments to which subsection (8) applies below what appears to the court to be necessary for meeting the reasonable domestic needs of the bankrupt and his family.

(3)　An income payments order shall, in respect of any payment of income to which it is to apply, either—

　　(a)　require the bankrupt to pay the trustee an amount equal to so much of that payment as is claimed by the order, or
　　(b)　require the person making the payment to pay so much of it as is so claimed to the trustee, instead of to the bankrupt.

(4)　Where the court makes an income payments order it may, if it thinks fit, discharge or vary any attachment of earnings order that is for the time being in force to secure payments by the bankrupt.

(5)　Sums received by the trustee under an income payments order form part of the bankrupt's estate.

(6)　An income payments order must specify the period during which it is to have effect; and that period—

　　(a)　may end after the discharge of the bankrupt, but
　　(b)　may not end after the period of three years beginning with the date on which the order is made.

(6A) An income payments order may (subject to subsection (6)(b)) be varied on the application of the trustee or the bankrupt (whether before or after discharge).

28　Rule 1.45 of the Insolvency (England and Wales) Rules 2016.

(7) For the purposes of this section the income of the bankrupt comprises every payment in the nature of income which is from time to time made to him or to which he from time to time becomes entitled, including any payment in respect of the carrying on of any business or in respect of any office or employment and (despite anything in section 11 or 12 of the Welfare Reform and Pensions Act 1999) any payment under a pension scheme but excluding any payment to which subsection (8) applies.

(8) This subsection applies to—

    (a) payments by way of guaranteed minimum pension; and

    (b) payments giving effect to the bankrupt's protected rights as a member of a pension scheme.

(9) In this section, 'guaranteed minimum pension' and 'protected rights' have the same meaning as in the Pension Schemes Act 1993.

310A Income payments agreement

(1) In this section 'income payments agreement' means a written agreement between a bankrupt and his trustee or between a bankrupt and the official receiver which provides—

    (a) that the bankrupt is to pay to the trustee or the official receiver an amount equal to a specified part or proportion of the bankrupt's income for a specified period, or

    (b) that a third person is to pay to the trustee or the official receiver a specified proportion of money due to the bankrupt by way of income for a specified period.

(2) A provision of an income payments agreement of a kind specified in subsection (1)(a) or (b) may be enforced as if it were a provision of an income payments order.

(3) While an income payments agreement is in force the court may, on the application of the bankrupt, his trustee or the official receiver, discharge or vary an attachment of earnings order that is for the time being in force to secure payments by the bankrupt.

(4) The following provisions of section 310 shall apply to an income payments agreement as they apply to an income payments order—

    (a) subsection (5) (receipts to form part of estate), and

    (b) subsections (7) to (9) (meaning of income).

(5) An income payments agreement must specify the period during which it is to have effect; and that period—

    (a) may end after the discharge of the bankrupt, but

    (b) may not end after the period of three years beginning with the date on which the agreement is made.

(6)   An income payments agreement may (subject to subsection (5)(b)) be varied—

    (a)   by written agreement between the parties, or

    (b)   by the court on an application made by the bankrupt, the trustee or the official receiver.

(7)   The court—

    (a)   may not vary an income payments agreement so as to include provision of a kind which could not be included in an income payments order, and

    (b)   shall grant an application to vary an income payments agreement if and to the extent that the court thinks variation necessary to avoid the effect mentioned in section 310(2).

Rules 10.109–10.114 of the Insolvency (England and Wales) Rules 2016

Application for income payments order (section 310)

10.109.—(1) Where the trustee applies for an income payments order under section 310, the court must fix a venue for the hearing of the application.

(2)   Notice of the application and the venue must be delivered by the trustee to the bankrupt at least 28 days before the day fixed for the hearing, together with a copy of the trustee's application and a short statement of the grounds on which it is made.

(3)   The notice must inform the bankrupt that—

    (a)   the bankrupt is required to attend the hearing unless at least five business days before the date fixed for the hearing the bankrupt files with the court and delivers to the trustee, consent to an order being made in the terms of the application; and

    (b)   if the bankrupt attends, the bankrupt will be given an opportunity to show cause why the order should not be made, or why a different order should be made to that applied for by the trustee.

(4)   The notice must be authenticated and dated by the trustee.

Order for income payments order

10.110. An order under section 310 must have the title 'Income Payments Order' and must contain—

    (a)   identification details for the proceedings;

    (b)   identification and contact details for the trustee;

    (c)   a statement that the bankrupt has or has not consented to the order (as the case may be);

(d) the order that it appears to the court that the sum which is specified in the order should be paid to the trustee in accordance with the payments schedule detailed in the order until the date specified in the order;

(e) the order that the bankrupt must pay to the trustee the sum referred to in paragraph (e) in accordance with the payments schedule out of the bankrupt's income, the first of such instalments to be made on or before the date specified in the order; and

(f) the date of the order.

Action to follow making of order

10.111.—(1) Where the court makes an income payments order, the trustee must deliver a sealed copy of the order to the bankrupt as soon as reasonably practicable after it is made.

(2) If the order is made under section 310(3)(b), a sealed copy of the order must also be delivered by the trustee to the person to whom the order is directed.

Variation of order

10.112.—(1) If an income payments order is made under section 310(3)(a), and the bankrupt does not comply with it, the trustee may apply to the court for the order to be varied, so as to take effect under section 310(3)(b) as an order to the payer of the relevant income.

(2) The trustee's application under this rule may be made without notice to any other party.

(3) The order must contain—

(a) identification details for the proceedings;

(b) identification and contact details for the trustee who made the application;

(c) the name and address of the payer;

(d) a statement that the applicant is the trustee of the bankrupt;

(e) the date of the income payments order;

(f) a statement that it appears to the court that the bankrupt has failed to comply with the income payments order;

(g) the order that the income payments order be varied to the effect that the payer specified in this order do take payment in accordance with the payments schedule detailed in this order out of the bankrupt's income and that the first instalment must be paid on the date specified in the order; and that the payer must deliver the sums deducted to the trustee; and

(h) the date of the order.

(4) The court must deliver sealed copies of any order made on the application to the trustee and the bankrupt as soon as reasonably practicable after the order is made.

(5) In the case of an order varying or discharging an income payments order made under section 310(3)(b), the court must deliver an additional sealed copy of the order to the trustee, for delivery as soon as reasonably practicable to the payer of the relevant income.

Order to payer of income: administration

10.113.—(1) Where a person receives notice of an income payments order under section 310(3)(b), with reference to income otherwise payable by that person to the bankrupt, that person ('the payer') must make the necessary arrangements for compliance with the order as soon as reasonably practicable.

(2)   When making any payment to the trustee, the payer may deduct the permitted fee towards the clerical and administrative costs of compliance with the income payments order.

(3)   The payer must give to the bankrupt a statement of any amount deducted by the payer under paragraph (2).

(4)   Where a payer receives notice of an income payments order imposing on the payer a requirement under section 310(3)(b), and either—

(a)   the payer is then no longer liable to make to the bankrupt any payment of income; or

(b)   having made payments in compliance with the order, the payer ceases to be so liable;

the payer must as soon as reasonably practicable deliver notice of that fact to the trustee.

Review of order

10.114.—(1) Where an income payments order is in force, either the trustee or the bankrupt may apply to the court for the order to be varied or discharged.

(2)   If the application is made by the trustee, rule 10.109 applies (with any necessary modification) as in the case of an application for an income payments order.

(3)   If the application is made by the bankrupt, it must be accompanied by a short statement of the grounds on which it is made.

(4)   On receipt of an application, the court may, if it is satisfied that no sufficient cause is shown for it, dismiss it without giving notice to any party other than the applicant.

(5)   Unless the application is dismissed, the court must fix a venue for it to be heard.

(6)   The applicant must, at least 28 days before any hearing, deliver to the trustee or the bankrupt (whichever of them is not the applicant) a notice stating the venue with—

(a)   a copy of the application; and

(b)   where the applicant is the bankrupt, a copy of the statement of the grounds for the application referred to in paragraph (3).

(7)   The trustee may do either or both of the following—

(a)   file a report of any matters which the trustee thinks ought to be drawn to the court's attention; or

(b)   appear and be heard on the application.

(8)   The trustee must file a copy of a report under paragraph (7)(a) with the court not less than five business days before the date fixed for the hearing and must deliver a copy of it to the bankrupt.

(9)   The court order must contain—

(a)   identification details for the proceedings;
(b)   the name and title of the judge making the order;
(c)   the name and postal address of the applicant;
(d)   an order that the income payments order specified is varied as specified;
(e)   the date of the income payments order referred to in paragraph (d);
(f)   details of how the income payments order is varied by this order; and
(g)   the date of the order.

(10) Sealed copies of any order made on the application must be delivered by the court to the trustee, the bankrupt and the payer (if other than the bankrupt) as soon as reasonably practicable after the order is made.

17.1   APPLICATION FOR AN INCOME PAYMENT ORDER PURSUANT TO SECTION 310 OF THE INSOLVENCY ACT 1986

Form IAA   **Insolvency Act Application Notice**

IN THE HIGH COURT OF JUSTICE
BUSINESS AND PROPERTY COURTS OF ENGLAND AND WALES
INSOLVENIES AND COMPANIES LIST (ChD)
IN BANKRUPTCY

NO: 666 OF 2020

IN THE MATTER OF IAN FLAKEY
AND IN THE MATTER OF THE INSOLVENCY ACT 1986

BETWEEN:-

GILES GRABBER
(Trustee in Bankruptcy of IAN FLAKEY)

Applicant

and

IAN FLAKEY
(a bankrupt)

Respondent

Is this application within existing insolvency proceedings? YES/~~NO~~

I (~~We~~), GILES GRABBER of 1 Vulture Street, London intend to apply to the ~~Judge/District Judge~~/Registrar on:

Date: 1st April 2020

Time: 00:00 hours

Place: Royal Courts of Justice, 7 Rolls Buildings, Fetter Lane, London EC4A 1NL

This application having been issued at the RCJ, 7 Rolls Buildings, Fetter Lane, London, EC4A 1NL will be heard at the time and date pursuant to the endorsement underneath the Court Seal on the front page of this application.

FOR AN ORDER THAT:

1.   Under Section 310 of the Insolvency Act 1986 for the payment from your income to me as your Trustee in Bankruptcy, of £3,600,000 by monthly instalments of £100,000 (which it is intended will be paid to me) by you or such other order as the court thinks fit.

2.   The Respondent do pay the Applicant's costs of and incidental to this application.

3.   Any costs of the application that are not payable by the Respondent or not recovered from him should be paid to the Applicant as such trustee out of the assets

of the bankruptcy as an expense of the bankruptcy within rule 10.149(a) of the Insolvency (England and Wales) Rules 2016.

4. Further and other relief.

The grounds on which the Applicant claims to be entitled to the Order are set out in the 1st witness statement of Giles Grabber dated 1st April 2020, a copy of which is annexed to this application.

THE NAMES AND ADDRESSES OF THE PERSON(S) UPON WHOM IT IS INTENDED TO SERVE THIS APPLICATION ARE:

Name: IAN FLAKEY

Address: 1 GERANIUM COTTAGE, LONDON

Name:

Address:

~~OR~~

~~IT IS NOT INTENDED TO SERVE ANY PERSON WITH THIS APPLICATION~~

Dated:

Signed: SNARKEY & SNYDE

Solicitors for the applicant ~~or Applicant~~   *This is the address
Address: 1 LAW STREET, LONDON   which will be treated
Telephone: 0207 666 6666   by Court as the
Email: law@snarkeysnyde.com   Petitions address for
                                             service

If you do not attend, the court may make such order as it thinks just.

17.2   WITNESS STATEMENT IN SUPPORT OF AN APPLICATION FOR AN INCOME PAYMENT ORDER

Applicant: G Grabber: 1st: GG1: [ ] 20[ ]

IN THE HIGH COURT OF JUSTICE
BUSINESS AND PROPERTY COURTS OF ENGLAND AND WALES
INSOLVENCY AND COMPANIES LIST (ChD)

NO: [ ] OF 20[ ]

IN THE MATTER OF IAN FLAKEY
IN BANKRUPTCY

BETWEEN:-

GILES GRABBER
(as Trustee in Bankruptcy of IAN FLAKEY)

Applicant

and

IAN FLAKEY

Respondent

1ST WITNESS STATEMENT OF GILES GRABBER

I, GILES GRABBER of Grabbers LLP, of 1 Vulture Street, London, Trustee in Bankruptcy of Ian Flakey, STATE as follows:

1.   I am the Applicant in this application. I am the Trustee in Bankruptcy of Ian Flakey.

2.   I make this witness statement in support of my application for:

    a.   An order under section 310(3)(a) of the Insolvency Act 1986 that Ian Flakey ('the Bankrupt') do pay the sum of £100,000 per month to the Applicant or such other sum as this Honourable Court thinks fit each month for a 3-year period.

    b.   An order that the Respondent do pay the Applicant's costs of and incidental to this application

    c.   An order that any costs of the application that are not payable by the Respondent or not recovered from him should be paid to the Applicant as such trustee out of the assets of the bankruptcy as an expense of the bankruptcy within rule 10.149(a) of the Insolvency (England and Wales) Rules 2016.

    d.   Such further and other order and other relief as this Honourable Court thinks fit.

3.   The matters set out in this witness statement are true and within my own knowledge except where otherwise indicated, in which case I have explained the source of my information or belief.

4.   There is now produced and shown to me a bundle consisting of true copies of the documents I will refer to in my witness statement marked 'GG1'.

5.   A bankruptcy order was made against the Bankrupt on 1st March 2020. I refer to page [ ] of 'GG1' which is a true copy of the bankruptcy order.

6.   I was appointed as the Trustee in Bankruptcy of the Bankrupt on 1st April 2020. I refer to page [ ] of 'GG1' which is a true copy of my certificate of appointment.

7.   The Bankrupt's statement of affairs show that he was insolvent as at 31st December 2019 with a deficiency in the sum of £2,000,000. I refer to page [ ] of 'GG1' which is a true copy of the trading accounts of the Bankrupt and his statement of affairs. Creditors' claims lodged in the bankruptcy amount to £3,500,000. I refer to page [ ] of 'GG1' which is a true copy of the proofs of debt evidencing the creditors' claims.

8.   Following my appointment, I began to investigate the affairs of the Bankrupt. The following matters became apparent.

9.   The Bankrupt lives at 1 Geranium Cottage with his dependent wife, Tabitha Flakey. They have no children.

10. I have learned from the Bankrupt and truly believe that he has since his bankruptcy started business as a self-employed hedge fund manager and earns £110,000 per month.

11. From my interview with the bankrupt I have prepared a schedule of his monthly outgoings. I refer to page [ ] of 'GG1' which is a true copy of these outgoings.

12. I consider that these outgoings exceed the reasonable domestic needs of the Bankrupt and his family. For example:

   a.   The expenditure of £25,000 in vintage champagne for Mrs Flakey's bathing seems excessive. I suggest that a saving of £24,000 per month could be achieved if she bathes in Cava (which I understand from my wife and truly believe is a perfectly acceptable alternative for ablutionary purposes).
   b.   The expenditure of £75,000 per month in first class air fares and five star hotels is excessive. The bankrupt could undertake the same business trips by flying standard class and staying in a motel at a cost of £5,000 per month. It is not immediately apparent why Mr Flakey needs to undertake these trips (other than for the coincidence of sporting fixtures) as he conducts all his business from the kitchen table at 1 Geranium Cottage.
   c.   The expenditure of £7,000 per month on seven dancing girls strikes me as unnecessary luxury. I suggest that Mr Flakey could dispense with this outrageous extravagance and make do with merely one at £1,000 per month.

13. I have prepared a schedule of what I suggest would be a reasonable schedule of outgoings which meet the reasonable domestic needs of Mr Flakey and his wife and allow for the payment envisaged under the order. These total £10,000 per month. I refer to page [ ] of 'GG1' which is a true copy of the schedule. Accordingly, I believe an income payment order of £100,000 per month is the appropriate figure for the order.

14. I therefore ask this Honourable Court to make the order in the terms sought.

STATEMENT OF TRUTH

I believe that the facts stated in this Witness Statement are true.

Signed [ ]
Full name [*GILES GRABBER*]
Dated [ ] 20[ ]

17.3   INCOME PAYMENT ORDER

IN THE HIGH COURT OF JUSTICE
BUSINESS AND PROPERTY COURTS OF ENGLAND AND WALES
INSOLVENCY AND COMPANIES LIST (ChD)

IN THE MATTER OF IAN FLAKEY
IN BANKRUPTCY
AND IN THE MATTER OF THE INSOLVENCY ACT 1988

NO: [ ] OF 20[ ]

BEFORE MR REGISTRAR WISE
DATED: [ ] OF 20[ ]

BETWEEN:-

GILES GRABBER

Petitioner

and

IAN FLAKEY

Respondent

_____

ORDER

_____

UPON the application of Giles Grabber of Grabbers LLP of 1 Vulture Street, London, Trustee in Bankruptcy ('the Trustee') of the above named IAN FLAKEY ('the Bankrupt') dated [ ]

AND UPON HEARING Counsel for the Trustee and Counsel for the Bankrupt

AND UPON the Bankrupt not consenting to this order

AND it appearing to the court that the sum of £3,600,000 should be paid to the trustee in accordance with the payments schedule detailed in the order until the date specified in the order

IT IS ORDERED THAT the sum of £3,600,000 be paid by the Bankrupt to the Trustee by monthly instalments of £100,000 out of the Bankrupt's income, the first of such instalments to be made on or before 1st June 2020.

Dated: [ ] 20[ ]

Service of this order

The Court has provided a sealed copy of this order to the serving party:

SNARKEY & SNYDE
1 LAW STREET
LONDON

Chapter 18

APPLICATION FOR A PRIVATE EXAMINATION

OBJECTIVE

The court has the power to assist a trustee in bankruptcy or Official Receiver in his investigations into a bankrupt's assets and affairs.[1] The court may, on the application of the office-holder, summon to appear before it:

- the bankrupt, the bankrupt's present or former spouse or the bankrupt's present or former civil partner;
- any person known or believed to have in his possession any property comprised in the bankrupt's estate or to be indebted to the bankrupt; or
- any person whom the court thinks capable of giving information concerning the bankrupt or the bankrupt's dealings, affairs or property.

The court can order the respondent to:

- give evidence by witness statement; or
- submit to an oral examination.

The power survives the discharge of the bankruptcy.[2] If the respondent fails to attend or there are reasonable grounds for thinking he will abscond, the court can issue a warrant for his arrest, have his books, papers, money or possessions seized and (if he absconds or there is a real likelihood of him absconding) have him held in custody until the hearing.

It is important to remember that if the court takes the view from the evidence it has heard that the respondent has property comprising part of the bankrupt's estate, it also has power to order it to be delivered up[3] or any debt to be paid.[4]

APPLICATION

The application is by application on notice using Form IAA.

---

[1] Section 366 of the Insolvency Act 1986; *Long v Farrer & Co* [2004] EWHC 1774 (Ch), [2004] BPIR 1218.

[2] *Oakes v Simms* [1997] BPIR 499.

[3] Section 367(1) of the Insolvency Act 1986.

[4] Section 367(2) of the Insolvency Act 1986.

The application should set out:

- that the application is made under the Insolvency Act 1986 or the Insolvency (England and Wales) Rules 2016 (as the case may be);[5]
- the section number or rule under which relief is sought;[6]
- the name of the parties;[7]
- the addresses of the parties;
- the name of the bankrupt or debtor;[8]
- the court name;[9]
- the case number;[10]
- the remedy applied for or directions sought:[11]

  - specifically, whether the person is to attend before the court to be examined; or
  - to submit evidence by witness statement and the subject matter of such evidence.

- the grounds relied upon;[12]
- the name and address of each person to be served or, if none, stating that that it is intended that no person will be served;[13]
- where there is a requirement for particular persons to be given notice of the application under the Act or Rules, stating the name and address of each such person;[14]
- the applicant's address for service.[15]

The application notice must be authenticated by the applicant or his solicitor.[16]

Care should be taken to ensure that the relief sought is specific and clearly identifies what is to be done.[17]

---

[5]   Rule 1.35(2)(a) of the Insolvency (England and Wales) Rules 2016.

[6]   Rule 1.35(2)(b) of the Insolvency (England and Wales) Rules 2016.

[7]   Rule 1.35(2)(c) of the Insolvency (England and Wales) Rules 2016.

[8]   Rule 1.35(2)(d) of the Insolvency (England and Wales) Rules 2016.

[9]   Rule 1.35(2)(e) of the Insolvency (England and Wales) Rules 2016.

[10] Rule 1.35(2)(f) of the Insolvency (England and Wales) Rules 2016.

[11] Rules 1.35(2)(g) and 12.18(1)(b) of the Insolvency (England and Wales) Rules 2016.

[12] Rule 12.18(1)(a) of the Insolvency (England and Wales) Rules 2016.

[13] Rule 1.35(2)(h) of the Insolvency (England and Wales) Rules 2016.

[14] Rule 1.35(2)(i) of the Insolvency (England and Wales) Rules 2016.

[15] Rule 1.35(2)(j) of the Insolvency (England and Wales) Rules 2016.

[16] Rule 1.35(3) of the Insolvency (England and Wales) Rules 2016. For what amounts to authentication, see rule 1.5. For hard copy applications, this means signed: rule 1.5(2).

[17] Rule 1.35 of the Insolvency (England and Wales) Rules 2016.

The application must be accompanied by a brief statement of the grounds upon which it is made.[18] The application can be made without notice,[19] however, this should only be done where there is good reason for doing so.

The respondent should be the person the office holder is seeking relief against.

The application should be returnable to the registrar in the Bankruptcy Registry or to the district judge in a Chancery District Registry or county court with insolvency jurisdiction.

COURT FEES

Where the application is made by ordinary application on notice to other parties, a court fee of £155 is payable.[20] Where the application is made by consent or without notice in existing proceedings, a court fee of £50 is payable.[21]

SERVICE

The application should be served personally unless the court orders otherwise.[22] Travelling expenses should be paid for any person who is to be examined.[23]

The usual rule is that, subject to any other express provision, the application must be served at least 14 days before the date fixed for the hearing.[24] However, the court does have power, in cases of urgency, to hear an application immediately with or without notice to the other parties.[25]

WITNESS STATEMENT

The witness statement should state:

- the applicant's capacity (why the applicant has *locus* to make this application);
- the name of the bankrupt;
- the date of the bankruptcy order;
- what role the respondent played in relation to the bankrupt;
- whether the respondent is under a duty to co-operate, and, if so, why;

---

[18] Rule 12.18(1)(b) of the Insolvency (England and Wales) Rules 2016.

[19] Rule 12.11(4) of the Insolvency (England and Wales) Rules 2016.

[20] Paragraph 3.12 of Schedule 1 to the Civil Proceedings Fees (Amendment) Order 2014.

[21] Paragraph 3.11 of Schedule 1 to the Civil Proceedings Fees (Amendment) Order 2014.

[22] Rule 12.11(4) of the Insolvency (England and Wales) Rules 2016.

[23] Rule 12.22(4) of the Insolvency (England and Wales) Rules 2016.

[24] Rule 12.9(3) of the Insolvency (England and Wales) Rules 2016.

[25] Rule 12.19(2) of the Insolvency (England and Wales) Rules 2016.

- precisely what it is sought that the respondent is to do (thus if documents are to be produced, identifying those documents);
- why the applicant wishes to have the information or documents sought to assist him in the performance of his functions;
- why it is believed that the respondent has the information or documents sought;
- what steps have been taken to encourage the respondent to provide that information and documents voluntarily and why the respondent's reaction to those steps has made the application necessary.

FIRST HEARING

The hearing will be in chambers unless the court directs and will be before a registrar or district judge. The applicant may be represented by counsel or by solicitors.

Where an order is made for the attendance of the respondent before the court, the order must specify a time, date and place for examination not less than 14 days from the date of the order.[26]

Where evidence by witness statement is ordered, the court will specify the matters to be addressed.[27] Where documents are to be produced, the documents will be identified and time and manner of compliance will be specified.

RETURN DATE

On the date fixed for the examination, if it appears to the court that any person has property of the bankrupt, the court may, on the application of the office holder, order the delivery of the property or money to the office holder.[28]

WARRANT FOR ARREST

If the respondent fails to attend at the appointed time, without reasonable excuse, or there are reasonable grounds for belief that he has or is about to abscond to avoid his attendance, the court may issue a warrant for his arrest and for the seizure of any books, papers, records, money or goods in his possession.[29] The court may also authorise the respondent to be kept in custody until he is brought before the court.[30]

---

[26] Rule 12.19(2) of the Insolvency (England and Wales) Rules 2016.
[27] Rule 12.19(3) of the Insolvency (England and Wales) Rules 2016.
[28] Section 367(1)–(2) of the Insolvency Act 1986.
[29] Section 366(3) of the Insolvency Act 1986.
[30] Section 366(4) of the Insolvency Act 1986 and rule 12.22 of the Insolvency (England and Wales) Rules 2016.

KEY MATERIALS

Sections 366–369 of the Insolvency Act 1986

366 Inquiry into bankrupt's dealings and property

(1) At any time after a bankruptcy order has been made the court may, on the application of the official receiver or the trustee of the bankrupt's estate, summon to appear before it—

    (a) the bankrupt or the bankrupt's spouse or former spouse or civil partner or former civil partner,

    (b) any person known or believed to have any property comprised in the bankrupt's estate in his possession or to be indebted to the bankrupt,

    (c) any person appearing to the court to be able to give information concerning the bankrupt or the bankrupt's dealings, affairs or property.

The court may require any such person as is mentioned in paragraph (b) or (c) to submit a witness statement verified by a statement of truth to the court containing an account of his dealings with the bankrupt or to produce any documents in his possession or under his control relating to the bankrupt or the bankrupt's dealings, affairs or property.

(2) Without prejudice to section 364, the following applies in a case where—

    (a) a person without reasonable excuse fails to appear before the court when he is summoned to do so under this section, or

    (b) there are reasonable grounds for believing that a person has absconded, or is about to abscond, with a view to avoiding his appearance before the court under this section.

(3) The court may, for the purpose of bringing that person and anything in his possession before the court, cause a warrant to be issued to a constable or prescribed officer of the court—

    (a) for the arrest of that person, and

    (b) for the seizure of any books, papers, records, money or goods in that person's possession.

(4) The court may authorise a person arrested under such a warrant to be kept in custody, and anything seized under such a warrant to be held, in accordance with the rules, until that person is brought before the court under the warrant or until such other time as the court may order.

367 Court's enforcement powers under s 366

(1) If it appears to the court, on consideration of any evidence obtained under section 366 or this section, that any person has in his possession any property comprised in the bankrupt's estate, the court may, on the application of the official receiver or the trustee of the bankrupt's estate, order that person to deliver the whole or any part of the property to the official receiver or the trustee at such time, in such manner and on such terms as the court thinks fit.

(2) If it appears to the court, on consideration of any evidence obtained under section 366 or this section, that any person is indebted to the bankrupt, the court may, on the application of the official receiver or the trustee of the bankrupt's estate, order that person to pay to the official receiver or trustee, at such time and in such manner as the court may direct, the whole or part of the amount due, whether in full discharge of the debt or otherwise as the court thinks fit.

(3) The court may, if it thinks fit, order that any person who if within the jurisdiction of the court would be liable to be summoned to appear before it under section 366 shall be examined in any part of the United Kingdom where he may be for the time being, or in any place outside the United Kingdom.

(4) Any person who appears or is brought before the court under section 366 or this section may be examined on oath, either orally or by interrogatories, concerning the bankrupt or the bankrupt's dealings, affairs and property.

368 Provision corresponding to s 366, where interim receiver appointed

Sections 366 and 367 apply where an interim receiver has been appointed under section 286 as they apply where a bankruptcy order has been made, as if—

(a) references to the official receiver or the trustee were to the interim receiver, and

(b) references to the bankrupt and to his estate were (respectively) to the debtor and his property.

369 Order for production of documents by inland revenue

(1) For the purposes of an examination under section 290 (public examination of bankrupt) or proceedings under sections 366 to 368, the court may, on the application of the official receiver or the trustee of the bankrupt's estate, order an inland revenue official to produce to the court—

(a) any return, account or accounts submitted (whether before or after the commencement of the bankruptcy) by the bankrupt to any inland revenue official,

(b) any assessment or determination made (whether before or after the commencement of the bankruptcy) in relation to the bankrupt by any inland revenue official, or

(c) any correspondence (whether before or after the commencement of the bankruptcy) between the bankrupt and any inland revenue official.

(2) Where the court has made an order under subsection (1) for the purposes of any examination or proceedings, the court may, at any time after the document to which the order relates is produced to it, by order authorise the disclosure of the document, or of any part of its contents, to the official receiver, the trustee of the bankrupt's estate or the bankrupt's creditors.

(3) The court shall not address an order under subsection (1) to an inland revenue official unless it is satisfied that that official is dealing, or has dealt, with the affairs of the bankrupt.

(4)   Where any document to which an order under subsection (1) relates is not in the possession of the official to whom the order is addressed, it is the duty of that official to take all reasonable steps to secure possession of it and, if he fails to do so, to report the reasons for his failure to the court.

(5)   Where any document to which an order under subsection (1) relates is in the possession of an inland revenue official other than the one to whom the order is addressed, it is the duty of the official in possession of the document, at the request of the official to whom the order is addressed, to deliver it to the official making the request.

(6)   In this section 'inland revenue official' means any inspector or collector of taxes appointed by the Commissioners of Inland Revenue or any person appointed by the Commissioners to serve in any other capacity.

(7)   This section does not apply for the purposes of an examination under sections 366 and 367 which takes place by virtue of section 368 (interim receiver).

Rules 12.17–12.22 of the Insolvency (England and Wales) Rules 2016

12.17.—(1) The rules in this sub-division apply to applications to the court for an order under—

(a)   section 236 (inquiry into company's dealings);

(b)   section 251N (debt relief orders – inquiry into dealings and property of debtor); and

(c)   section 366 (inquiry into bankrupt's dealings and property) including section 366 as it applies by virtue of section 368.

(2)   In this sub-division—

'applicable section' means section 236, 251N or 366; and
'the insolvent' means the company, the debtor or the bankrupt as the case may be.

Contents of application

12.18.—(1) An application to the court under section 236, 251N or 366 must state—

(a)   the grounds on which it is made; and

(b)   which one or more of the following orders is sought—

    (i)   for the respondent to appear before the court,

    (ii)   for the respondent to clarify any matter which is in dispute in the proceedings or to give additional information in relation to any such matter (if so Part 18 CPR (further information) applies to any such order),

    (iii)   for the respondent to submit witness statements (if so, particulars must be given of the matters to be included), or

(iv) for the respondent to produce books, papers or other records (if so, the items in question to be specified).

(2) An application under an applicable section may be made without notice to any other party.
(3) The court may, whatever the order sought in the application, make any order which it has power to make under the applicable section.

Order for examination etc.

12.19.—(1) Where the court orders the respondent to appear before it, it must specify the venue for the appearance.
(2) The date must not be less than 14 days from the date of the order.
(3) If the respondent is ordered to file with the court a witness statement or a written account, the order must specify—

(a) the matters which are to be dealt with in it; and
(b) the time within which it is to be delivered.

(4) If the order is to produce documents or other records, the time and manner of compliance must be specified.
(5) The applicant must serve a copy of the order on the respondent as soon as reasonably practicable.

Procedure for examination

12.20.—(1) The applicant may attend an examination of the respondent, in person, or be represented by an appropriately qualified legal representative, and may put such questions to the respondent as the court may allow.
(2) Unless the applicant objects, the following persons may attend the examination with the permission of the court and may put questions to the respondent (but only through the applicant)—

(a) any person who could have applied for an order under the applicable section; and
(b) any creditor who has provided information on which the application was made under section 236 or 366.

(3) If the respondent is ordered to clarify any matter or to give additional information, the court must direct the respondent as to the questions which the respondent is required to answer, and as to whether the respondent's answers (if any) are to be made in a witness statement.
(4) The respondent may employ an appropriately qualified legal representative at the respondent's own expense, who may—

(a) put to the respondent such questions as the court may allow for the purpose of enabling the respondent to explain or qualify any answers given by the respondent; and
(b) make representations on the respondent's behalf.

(5)   Such written record of the examination must be made as the court thinks proper and such record must be read either to or by the respondent and authenticated by the respondent at a venue fixed by the court.

(6)   The record may, in any proceedings (whether under the Act or otherwise), be used as evidence against the respondent of any statement made by the respondent in the course of the respondent's examination.

Record of examination

12.21.—(1) Unless the court otherwise directs, the record of questions put to the respondent, the respondent's answers and any witness statement or written account delivered to the court by the respondent in compliance with an order of the court under the applicable section are not to be filed with the court.

(2)   The documents listed in paragraph (3) may not be inspected without the permission of the court, except by—

(a)   the applicant for an order under the applicable section; or

(b)   any person who could have applied for such an order in relation to the affairs of the same insolvent.

(3)   The documents are—

(a)   the record of the respondent's examination;

(b)   copies of questions put to the respondent or proposed to be put to the respondent and answers to questions given by the respondent;

(c)   any witness statement by the respondent; and

(d)   any document on the court file that shows the grounds for the application for the order.

(4)   The court may from time to time give directions as to the custody and inspection of any documents to which this rule applies, and as to the provision of copies of, or extracts from, such documents.

Costs of proceedings under sections 236, 251N and 366

12.22.—(1) Where the court has ordered an examination of a person under an applicable section, and it appears to it that the examination was made necessary because information had been unjustifiably refused by the respondent, it may order that the respondent pay the costs of the examination.

(2)   Where the court makes an order against a person under—

(a)   section 237(1) or 367(1) (to deliver up property in any person's possession which belongs to the insolvent estate); or

(b)   section 237(2) or 367(2) (to pay any amount in discharge of a debt due to the insolvent);

the costs of the application for the order may be ordered by the court to be paid by the respondent.

(3) Subject to paragraphs (1) and (2), the applicant's costs must, unless the court orders otherwise, be paid—

   (a) in relation to a company insolvency, as an expense of the insolvency proceedings; and
   (b) in relation to an individual insolvency, but not in proceedings relating to debt relief orders or applications for debt relief orders, out of the bankrupt's estate or (as the case may be) the debtor's property.

(4) A person summoned to attend for examination must be tendered a reasonable sum for travelling expenses incurred in connection with that person's attendance but any other costs falling on that person are at the court's discretion.

(5) Where the examination is on the application of the official receiver otherwise than in the capacity of liquidator or trustee, no order may be made for the payment of costs by the official receiver.

18.1 LETTER REQUESTING DOCUMENTS BEFORE AN APPLICATION IS MADE FOR A PRIVATE EXAMINATION

Dear Sir,

Re: Ian Flakey (a bankrupt)

As you are aware, we act for Giles Grabber, your Trustee in Bankruptcy ('the Trustee'). We are, together with our client, continuing to investigate your affairs.

You are under a statutory duty under section 333 of the Insolvency Act 1986 to:

(a) give to the office holder such information concerning your affairs as the trustee may reasonably require to carry out his functions;

(b) attend on the trustee at such times as the latter may reasonably require;

(c) do all such things as the trustee may reasonably require.

1. Review of your books, papers and records

1.1 We have conducted a detailed review (the 'Review') of all of your and your business's account statements, books, papers and records which have been provided to us to date by you (the 'Documents').

1.2 Following the completion of the Review, it is clear that:

1.2.1 the books, papers and records provided to us, which were in no particular order, are incomplete;

1.2.2 certain documentation which we would reasonably expect to form part of the books, papers and records of a business are not contained, or are contained only to a limited extent, within the Documents (see attached Schedule).

1.3 We write to ask you to deliver up to our offices all of these documents in the Schedule relating to the Company in your possession, power and control (by 4 pm on 1st April 2020). In so far that such documents are not within your possession, power and control or you are unable to deliver them to us we would ask you to write by 4 pm on 1st April 2020 to us to tell us where (to the best of your knowledge) each of the documents listed in the Schedule is and who currently possesses or controls them.

2. Meeting

2.1 We would be grateful if you could attend for interview at 10 am on 1st April 2020 at our offices at 1 Vulture Street, London. A map is enclosed. The nearest tube station is Saint Pools.

2.2 If this appointment is not convenient for you, please could you write back to us by 4 pm on 1st February 2020 to suggest three alternative dates and times, within the next three months, that might be convenient for you to attend.

2.3   Without wishing to limit the agenda of the meeting, we would particularly wish to explore with you at this meeting the following issues:

    2.3.1 Your past and present assets, their current location and any disposals of them in the last 5 years.
    2.3.2 Your dealings in your business, Flakey & Co.
    2.3.3 Where all your business's money has disappeared to.

2.4   You may wish to bring any documents you find helpful to assist you. If you wish to be accompanied to the meeting, you may bring someone to accompany you, however you will be expected to answer the questions asked yourself without interference or prompting.

3. Formal Notice

3.1   This letter is written pursuant to sections 333 and 366 of the Insolvency Act 1986.

3.2   If you fail to attend an appointment, without reasonable excuse, or fail to provide the documents required from you we reserve right to apply to the Court under section 366 of the Insolvency Act 1986 to compel you to do so and for an order that you pay our costs of making that application. Failure to co-operate with an office holder without reasonable excuse is a criminal offence under section 333(4) of the Insolvency Act 1986.

Yours faithfully

Wigg & Co.

SCHEDULE

LIST OF DOCUMENTS EXPECTED TO FORM PART OF BOOKS, PAPERS AND RECORDS

GENERAL DOCUMENTATION

(A)   FINANCE

- Loan agreements
- Details of any mortgages, charges, security granted (if any)
- Documentation evidencing the release of any security (if any)
- Invoices and credit notes
- Any correspondence with your accountants
- Accounts
- Budget
- Cash flow projections
- Business plan
- Journals
- Bank statements

(B)   TAX

- Returns made to any tax authority: (i) of income, profits or gains or of any other amounts; or (ii) in relation to VAT (we have seen some examples of these) ('Returns')
- All records, claims, elections, accounts, computations, invoices or attachments relating to or relevant to any Return
- Returns in respect of PAYE and NIC together with all records, claims, forms, elections, accounts, computations or attachments relating to such returns
- Any notice, demand, assessment, clearance, registration, letter or other document or communication issued by or on behalf of, or addressed to, a tax authority
- Any agreement relating to taxation
- Any professional advice received in relation to taxation

(C)   EMPLOYMENT

- Template/standard form employment contracts
- Confirmation that the following documents exist:

  - list of employees
  - payslips
  - working time regulation opt-out letters
  - payroll and wage records
  - maternity records
  - annual leave records
  - sickness records
  - staff handbooks
  - policies/manuals/guidance for disciplinary proceedings, grievance, whistle-blowing, equal opportunities, data protection, email/internet policies, smoking policy, health and safety manual
  - accident book
  - disciplinary correspondence (if any)
  - details of terminations, redundancies and resignations

— employment contracts and personnel records
— details of pensions/benefits

(D)   ASSETS

- Documents relating to the acquisition and sale of any land or buildings in the last 5 years including TR1s, deeds, correspondence with solicitors
- Leases
- Equipment purchase documentation
- Equipment leases (if any)
- Licences
- Intellectual property rights (if any)

18.2   APPLICATION FOR A PRIVATE EXAMINATION

Form IAA   **Insolvency Act Application Notice**

<u>IN THE HIGH COURT OF JUSTICE</u>
<u>BUSINESS AND PROPERTY COURTS OF ENGLAND AND WALES</u>
<u>INSOLVENCY AND COMPANIES LIST (ChD)</u>
<u>IN BANKRUPTCY</u>

<u>NO: 666 OF 2020</u>

IN THE MATTER OF IAN FLAKEY
AND IN THE MATTER OF THE INSOLVENCY ACT 1986

BETWEEN:-

GILES GRABBER
(Trustee in Bankruptcy of IAN FLAKEY)

<u>Applicant</u>

and

IAN FLAKEY
(a bankrupt)

<u>Respondent</u>

Is this application within existing insolvency proceedings?   YES/~~NO~~

I(We), GILES GRABBER of 1 Vulture Street, London intend to apply to the ~~Judge/District Judge~~/Registrar on:

Date: 1st April 2020

Time: 00:00 hours

Place: Royal Courts of Justice, 7 Rolls Buildings, Fetter Lane, London EC4A 1NL

This application having been issued at the RCJ, 7 Rolls Buildings, Fetter Lane, London, EC4A 1NL will be heard at the time and date pursuant to the endorsement underneath the Court Seal on the front page of this application.

FOR AN ORDER THAT:

1.   The Respondent do attend court to be examined under oath on a date and time to be fixed and that the Applicant be at liberty to examine the Respondent in respect of his assets dealings and affairs under section 366 of the Insolvency Act 1986, and

2.   The Respondent be ordered to produce all his books, correspondence and documents in his custody or power, relating to his dealings, affairs and property, including the documents set out in the attached Schedule under section 366 of the Insolvency Act 1986,

3.   The Respondent be ordered to pay the costs of and occasioned by this application,

4.   Further and other relief.

The grounds on which the Applicant claims to be entitled to the order are set out in the 1st witness statement of Giles Grabber dated 1st April 2020, a copy of which is annexed to this application.

THE NAMES AND ADDRESSES OF THE PERSON(S) UPON WHOM IT IS INTENDED TO SERVE THIS APPLICATION ARE:

Name: IAN FLAKEY

Address: 1 GERANIUM COTTAGE, LONDON

Name:

Address:

OR

~~IT IS NOT INTENDED TO SERVE ANY PERSON WITH THIS APPLICATION~~

Dated:

Signed: SNARKEY & SNYDE

Solicitors for the applicant ~~or Applicant~~
Address: 1 LAW STREET, LONDON
Telephone: 0207 666 6666
Email: law@snarkeysnyde.com

*This is the address which will be treated by Court as the Petitions address for service

If you do not attend, the court may make such order as it thinks just.

SCHEDULE ABOVE REFERRED TO

TR1s
Correspondence with solicitors in relation to the acquisition or sale of any property
Sales ledgers
Bank statements
Cash books
Invoice sales daybooks
Correspondence files

18.3   WITNESS STATEMENT IN SUPPORT OF AN APPLICATION FOR A PRIVATE EXAMINATION

Applicant: G Grabber: 1st: GG1: [ ] 20[ ]

IN THE HIGH COURT OF JUSTICE
BUSINESS AND PROPERTY COURTS OF ENGLAND AND WALES
INSOLVENCY AND COMPANIES LIST (ChD)

NO: [ ] OF 20[ ]

IN THE MATTER OF IAN FLAKEY (A BANKRUPT)
IN BANKRUPTCY
AND IN THE MATTER OF THE INSOLVENCY ACT 1986

BETWEEN:-

GILES GRABBER

Applicant

and

IAN FLAKEY

Respondent

1ST WITNESS STATEMENT OF GILES GRABBER

I, GILES GRABBER of Grabbers LLP, of 1 Vulture Street, London, Insolvency Practitioner, STATE as follows:

1.   I am the Applicant in this application. I am the Trustee in Bankruptcy of the Respondent.

2.   I make this witness statement in support of my application for an order under section 366 of the Insolvency Act 1986:

      (a)   That the Respondent do attend court to be examined under oath on a date and time to be fixed and that I be at liberty to examine the Respondent in respect of his affairs, assets and dealings and property;

      (b)   That the Respondent be ordered to produce all his books, correspondence and documents in his custody or power including the documents set out in the attached Schedule;

      (c)   That the Respondent be ordered to pay the costs of and occasioned by this application.

3.   The matters set out in this witness statement are true and within my own knowledge except where otherwise indicated, in which case I have explained the source of my information or belief.

4.   There is now produced and shown to me a bundle consisting of true copies of the documents I will refer to in my witness statement marked 'GG1'.

5.   A bankruptcy order was made against the Bankrupt on 1st March 2020. I refer to page [ ] of 'GG1' which is a true copy of the bankruptcy order.

6.   I was appointed as the Trustee in Bankruptcy of the Bankrupt on 1st April 2020. I refer to page [ ] of 'GG1' which is a true copy of my certificate of appointment.

7. The Bankrupt's statement of affairs show that he was insolvent as at 31st December 2020 with a deficiency in the sum of £2,000,000. I refer to page [ ] of 'GG1' which is a true copy of the trading accounts of the Bankrupt and his statement of affairs. Creditors' claims lodged in the bankruptcy amount to £3,500,000. I refer to page [ ] of 'GG1' which is a true copy of the proofs of debt evidencing the creditors' claims.

8. Following my appointment, I began to investigate the affairs of the Bankrupt. The following matters became apparent.

9. Upon going through the limited business records of the respondent that I had been provided, I discovered that the correspondence files were missing as well as the bank statements (save one page), VAT returns (save three non-sequential examples), sales ledger and cashbook.

10. The one page of bank statement disclosed includes reference to a direct debit for a mortgage with Salamander Bank. There is no reference to any property with such a mortgage in his statement of affairs to the Official Receiver. I refer to page [ ] of 'GG1' which is a true copy of his statement of affairs. I refer to page [ ] of 'GG1' which is a true copy of the one page from his bank statements.

11. The Respondent has made no serious efforts to contact me with a view to discussing his affairs. As a bankrupt, he is however under a statutory duty to co-operate with his Trustee.

12. I have written to the Respondent requesting this information on numerous occasions but have not yet had a response. I refer to page [ ] of 'GG1' which is a true copy of the letters I have sent the Respondent and page [ ] of 'GG1' which is a true copy of a schedule of documents requested from him but not provided to me.

13. I need this information to reconstitute a picture of the bankrupt's financial affairs and to identify his assets, liabilities and to form a view of the genuineness (or otherwise) of the claims.

14. I therefore ask this Honourable Court to make the order in the terms sought.

STATEMENT OF TRUTH

I believe that the facts stated in this Witness Statement are true.

Signed [ ]
Full name [*GILES GRABBER*]
Dated [ ] 20[ ]

18.4   ORDER FOR PRIVATE EXAMINATION

IN THE HIGH COURT OF JUSTICE
BUSINESS AND PROPERTY COURTS OF ENGLAND AND WALES
INSOLVENCY AND COMPANIES LIST (ChD)

NO: [ ] OF 20[ ]

IN THE MATTER OF IAN FLAKEY (A BANKRUPT)
IN BANKRUPTCY
AND IN THE MATTER OF THE INSOLVENCY ACT 1986

BEFORE MR REGISTRAR WISE
DATED: [ ] 20[ ]

BETWEEN:-

GILES GRABBER

Applicant

and

IAN FLAKEY

Respondent

ORDER

UPON THE APPLICATION OF Giles Grabber dated [ ]

AND UPON READING the evidence filed

IT IS ORDERED THAT Ian Flakey of 1 Geranium Cottage, London, the Respondent, do attend at the Chambers of the Registrar, Room No. TM101 Thomas More Building, Royal Courts of Justice, 7 Rolls Buildings, Fetter Lane, London EC4A 1NL on [ ] 20[ ] at [ ] am/pm to be examined on oath in the above matter

AND IT IS ORDERED THAT Ian Flakey do deliver up to the Applicant by 4 pm on [ ] all books, papers and records in his possession or under his power or control relating to his assets, property dealings and affairs and in particular those set out in the schedule hereto

Dated: [ ] 20[ ]

NOTE:

IAN FLAKEY, IF YOU FAIL TO COMPLY WITH THIS ORDER WITHOUT REASONABLE EXCUSE HAVING BEEN GIVEN TO AND ACCEPTED BY THE COURT A WARRANT MAY BE ISSUED FOR YOU TO BE ARRESTED AND BROUGHT TO THE COURT FOR EXAMINATION.

Service of this order

The Court has provided a sealed copy of this order to the serving party:

SNARKEY & SNYDE
1 LAW STREET
LONDON

SCHEDULE OF DOCUMENTS

TR1s
Correspondence with solicitors in relation to the acquisition or sale of any property
Sales ledgers
Bank statements
Cash books
Invoice sales daybooks
Correspondence files

18.5   WARRANT FOR THE ARREST OF THE EXAMINEE ON HIS FAILURE TO ATTEND A PRIVATE EXAMINATION

IN THE HIGH COURT OF JUSTICE
BUSINESS AND PROPERTY COURTS OF ENGLAND AND WALES
INSOLVENCY AND COMPANIES LIST (ChD)

NO: [ ] OF 20[ ]

BEFORE MR REGISTRAR WISE
DATED: [ ] 20[ ]

IN THE MATTER OF IAN FLAKEY (A BANKRUPT)
IN BANKRUPTCY

AND IN THE MATTER OF THE INSOLVENCY ACT 1986

To the Tipstaff and his assistances of this Court and to every constable within his jurisdiction and to the Governor of Brixton Prison.

IAN FLAKEY was required by an order of this Court dated [ ] 20[ ] to attend at this Court to be examined on oath and to produce documents in his possession or under his control namely his books and records.

The said Ian Flakey of 1 Geranium Cottage, London has failed to attend at the appointed time and produce the required documents.

You the Tipstaff and his assistances of this Court and others are required to seize any books, papers, records, money or goods in the possession of Ian Flakey and to arrest Ian Flakey and to bring him before this Court for examination at such time and place as the Court directs. In the meantime, he shall be detained and delivered to the Governor of Her Majesty's Prison at Brixton. This shall be reported to the Court and its directions sought.

Anything you seize you are required safely to keep in your possession to await the written orders of the Court as to its disposal *or* to deliver to or otherwise deal with as directed by the judge of this Court.

And you, the Governor of Brixton Prison are required to receive Ian Flakey and keep him in custody to await the direction or order of this Court.

Dated: [ ] 20[ ]

Chapter 19

APPLICATION FOR A DECLARATION THAT A TRANSACTION IS INVALIDATED BY VIRTUE OF SECTION 284 OF THE INSOLVENCY ACT 1986

OBJECTIVE

In a bankruptcy, any disposition of the bankrupt's property made after the date of the presentation of the bankruptcy petition until the property vests in his trustee is, unless the court otherwise orders, void.[1] A defence exists, however, for third parties where the payment or property is received before the commencement of the bankruptcy in good faith, for value and without notice of the presentation of the petition.[2]

Where a trustee in bankruptcy wishes to challenge such a transfer, the remedy is to seek a declaration and an order to restore the position.

APPLICATION

The application is by application on notice using Form IAA for a declaration and an order restoring the position to what it would have been had the transaction not been entered into.

The application should set out:

- that the application is made under the Insolvency Act 1986 or the Insolvency (England and Wales) Rules 2016 (as the case may be);[3]
- the section number or rule under which relief is sought;[4]
- the name of the parties;[5]
- the name of the bankrupt or debtor;[6]

---

[1] Section 284(1)–(3) of the Insolvency Act 1986; *Official Receiver v Bathurst* [2008] BPIR 1548.

[2] Section 284(4) of the Insolvency Act 1986; *Sands and Treharne v Wright* [2010] BPIR 1437.

[3] Rule 1.35(2)(a) of the Insolvency (England and Wales) Rules 2016.

[4] Rule 1.35(2)(b) of the Insolvency (England and Wales) Rules 2016.

[5] Rule 1.35(2)(c) of the Insolvency (England and Wales) Rules 2016.

[6] Rule 1.35(2)(d) of the Insolvency (England and Wales) Rules 2016.

- the court name;[7]
- the case number;[8]
- the remedy applied for or directions sought;[9]
- the name and address of each person to be served or, if none, stating that that it is intended that no person will be served;[10]
- where there is a requirement for particular persons to be given notice of the application under the Act or Rules, stating the name and address of each such person;[11]
- the applicant's address for service.[12]

The application notice must be authenticated by the applicant or his solicitor.[13]

The application should be returnable to the registrar in the Bankruptcy Registry or to the district judge in a Chancery District Registry or county court with insolvency jurisdiction.

The respondent should be the person who made the transfer and any other party to the transaction which the applicant is seeking to set aside.

COURT FEES

Where the application is made by ordinary application on notice to other parties, a court fee of £155 is payable.[14] Where the application is made by consent or without notice in existing proceedings, a court fee of £50 is payable.[15]

EVIDENCE

The application should be supported by a witness statement. This should address:

- the capacity in which the deponent makes this application;
- the order he seeks;
- the date of the petition;
- the date of the bankruptcy order;
- the date of the transaction subject to challenge;
- the particulars of the transaction subject to challenge;

---

[7] Rule 1.35(2)(e) of the Insolvency (England and Wales) Rules 2016.

[8] Rule 1.35(2)(f) of the Insolvency (England and Wales) Rules 2016.

[9] Rule 1.35(2)(g) of the Insolvency (England and Wales) Rules 2016.

[10] Rule 1.35(2)(h) of the Insolvency (England and Wales) Rules 2016.

[11] Rule 1.35(2)(i) of the Insolvency (England and Wales) Rules 2016.

[12] Rule 1.35(2)(j) of the Insolvency (England and Wales) Rules 2016.

[13] Rule 1.35(3) of the Insolvency (England and Wales) Rules 2016. For what amounts to authentication, see rule 1.5. For hard copy applications, this means signed: rule 1.5(2).

[14] Paragraph 3.12 of Schedule 1 to the Civil Proceedings Fees (Amendment) Order 2014.

[15] Paragraph 3.11 of Schedule 1 to the Civil Proceedings Fees (Amendment) Order 2014.

- the fact that no validation or other order was made which permitted the transaction;
- any matters that might rebut the suggestion that the payment or property was received before the commencement of the bankruptcy in good faith, for value and without notice of the presentation of the petition.

And should exhibit:

- evidence of the trustee's appointment;
- the bankruptcy order;
- the statement of affairs;
- evidence of the transaction subject to challenge;
- evidence of the date of the transfer and the consideration (if any) paid.

SERVICE

The application and the evidence in support will need to be filed at court and served on the respondent as soon as practicable after it is filed and in any event, unless it is necessary to apply without notice or on short notice, at least 14 days before the date fixed for the hearing.[16]

The usual rule is that, subject to any other express provision, the application must be served at least 14 days before the date fixed for the hearing.[17] However, the court does have power, in cases of urgency, to hear an application immediately with or without notice to the other parties.[18]

Service may be effected personally[19] or by post on the respondent (Part 6 of the CPR applies for these purposes)[20] or, where they have authority to accept service, on the respondent's solicitors.[21] Electronic service of documents is now permissible under the Rules, providing the respondent currently consents to service in that way and has provided an email address for service in that way.[22]

FIRST HEARING

At the first hearing, the registrar or district judge will give directions as to whether points of claim are needed and for the filing of evidence. He may also require the application to be served on other people. He may give directions as to whether

---

[16] Rule 12.9(3) of the Insolvency (England and Wales) Rules 2016.

[17] Rule 12.9(3) of the Insolvency (England and Wales) Rules 2016.

[18] Rule 12.10(1) of the Insolvency (England and Wales) Rules 2016.

[19] Rule 1.44 of the Insolvency (England and Wales) Rules 2016.

[20] Schedule 4, paragraph 1(2) to the Insolvency (England and Wales) Rules 2016.

[21] Rule 1.40 of the Insolvency (England and Wales) Rules 2016.

[22] Rule 1.45 of the Insolvency (England and Wales) Rules 2016.

witnesses are to attend for cross examination. The first hearing is likely to be heard in chambers and the advocates are not expected to robe.

KEY MATERIALS

Section 284 of the Insolvency Act 1986

284 Restrictions on dispositions of property

(1) Where a person is adjudged bankrupt, any disposition of property made by that person in the period to which this section applies is void except to the extent that it is or was made with the consent of the court, or is or was subsequently ratified by the court.

(2) Subsection (1) applies to a payment (whether in cash or otherwise) as it applies to a disposition of property and, accordingly, where any payment is void by virtue of that subsection, the person paid shall hold the sum paid for the bankrupt as part of his estate.

(3) This section applies to the period beginning with the day of the presentation of the petition for the bankruptcy order and ending with the vesting, under Chapter IV of this Part, of the bankrupt's estate in a trustee.

(4) The preceding provisions of this section do not give a remedy against any person—

    (a) in respect of any property or payment which he received before the commencement of the bankruptcy in good faith, for value and without notice that the petition had been presented, or

    (b) in respect of any interest in property which derives from an interest in respect of which there is, by virtue of this subsection, no remedy.

(5) Where after the commencement of his bankruptcy the bankrupt has incurred a debt to a banker or other person by reason of the making of a payment which is void under this section, that debt is deemed for the purposes of any of this Group of Parts to have been incurred before the commencement of the bankruptcy unless—

    (a) that banker or person had notice of the bankruptcy before the debt was incurred, or

    (b) it is not reasonably practicable for the amount of the payment to be recovered from the person to whom it was made.

(6) A disposition of property is void under this section notwithstanding that the property is not or, as the case may be, would not be comprised in the bankrupt's estate; but nothing in this section affects any disposition made by a person of property held by him on trust for any other person.

19.1   APPLICATION FOR A DECLARATION OF INVALIDITY OF A TRANSFER PURSUANT TO SECTION 284 OF THE INSOLVENCY ACT 1986

Form IAA   **Insolvency Act Application Notice**

IN THE HIGH COURT OF JUSTICE
BUSINESS AND PROPERTY COURTS OF ENGLAND AND WALES
INSOLVENCY AND COMPANIES LIST (ChD)
IN BANKRUPTCY

NO: 666 OF 2020

IN THE MATTER OF IAN FLAKEY
AND IN THE MATTER OF THE INSOLVENCY ACT 1986

BETWEEN:-

GILES GRABBER
(Trustee in Bankruptcy of IAN FLAKEY)

Applicant

and

(1) IAN FLAKEY
(2) MRS TABITHA FLAKEY

Respondents

Is this application within existing insolvency proceedings?   YES/~~NO~~

I (~~We~~), GILES GRABBER of 1 Vulture Street, London intend to apply to the ~~Judge/District Judge~~/Registrar on:

Date: 1st April 2020

Time: 00:00 hours

Place: Royal Courts of Justice, 7 Rolls Buildings, Fetter Lane, London EC4A 1NL

This application having been issued at the RCJ, 7 Rolls Buildings, Fetter Lane, London, EC4A 1NL will be heard at the time and date pursuant to the endorsement underneath the Court Seal on the front page of this application.

FOR AN ORDER THAT:

1. A declaration that the payment of £250,000 by Ian Flakey ('the Bankrupt') to the 2nd Respondent on or around 1st January 2020 is void against the Applicant as his Trustee in Bankruptcy pursuant to section 284 of the Insolvency Act 1986.

2. The 2nd Respondent do pay to the Applicant the sum of £250,000 and/or such other sum as this Honourable Court thinks fit to restore the position to what it would have been if the Bankrupt had not entered into the transaction.

3. The 2nd Respondent do pay the Applicant's costs of and incidental to this application.

4. Any costs of the application that are not payable by the 2nd Respondent or not recovered from her should be paid to the Applicant as such trustee out of the assets of the bankruptcy as an expense of the bankruptcy pursuant to rule 10.149(a) of the Insolvency (England and Wales) Rules 2016.

5. Such further and other order and other relief as this Honourable Court thinks fit.

The grounds upon which the Applicant relies are set out in the 1st witness statement of Giles Grabber dated 1st April 2020, a true copy of which is served herewith.

THE NAMES AND ADDRESSES OF THE PERSON(S) UPON WHOM IT IS INTENDED TO SERVE THIS APPLICATION ARE:

Name: IAN FLAKEY

Address: 1 GERANIUM COTTAGE, LONDON

Name: TABITHA FLAKEY

Address: 1 GERANIUM COTTAGE, LONDON

~~OR~~

~~IT IS NOT INTENDED TO SERVE ANY PERSON WITH THIS APPLICATION~~

Dated:

Signed: SNARKEY & SNYDE

Solicitors for the applicant ~~or Applicant~~
Address: 1 LAW STREET, LONDON
Telephone: 0207 666 6666
Email: law@snarkeysnyde.com

*This is the address which will be treated by Court as the Petitions address for service

If you do not attend, the court may make such order as it thinks just.

19.2 WITNESS STATEMENT FOR A DECLARATION THAT THE TRANSACTION IS INVALIDATED BY SECTION 284 OF THE INSOLVENCY ACT 1986

Applicant: G Grabber: 1st: GG1: [ ] 20[ ]

IN THE HIGH COURT OF JUSTICE
BUSINESS AND PROPERTY COURTS OF ENGLAND AND WALES
INSOLVENCY AND COMPANIES LIST (ChD)

NO: [ ] OF 20[ ]

IN THE MATTER OF IAN FLAKEY
IN BANKRUPTCY
AND IN THE MATTER OF THE INSOLVENCY ACT 1986

BETWEEN:-

GILES GRABBER
(as Trustee in Bankruptcy of IAN FLAKEY)

Applicant

and

(1) IAN FLAKEY
(2) TABITHA FLAKEY

Respondents

1ST WITNESS STATEMENT OF GILES GRABBER

I, GILES GRABBER of Grabbers LLP, of 1 Vulture Street, London, Trustee in Bankruptcy of Ian Flakey, STATE as follows:

1.   I am the Applicant in this application. I am the Trustee in Bankruptcy of Ian Flakey.

2.   I make this witness statement in support of my application for:

   a.   A declaration that the payment of £250,000 by Ian Flakey ('the Bankrupt') to the 2nd Respondent on or around 1st January 2020 is void against the Applicant as his Trustee in Bankruptcy pursuant to section 284 of the Insolvency Act 1986.

   b.   An order that the 2nd Respondent do pay to the Applicant the sum of £250,000 and/or such other sum as this Honourable Court thinks fit to restore the position to what it would have been if the Bankrupt had not entered into the transaction.

   c.   An order that the 2nd Respondent do pay the Applicant's costs of and incidental to this application.

   d.   Any costs of the application that are not payable by the 2nd Respondent or not recovered from her should be paid to the Applicant as such trustee out of the assets of the bankruptcy as an expense of the bankruptcy within rule 10.149(a) of the Insolvency (England and Wales) Rules 2016.

   e.   Such further and other order and other relief as this Honourable Court thinks fit.

3.   The matters set out in this witness statement are true and within my own knowledge except where otherwise indicated, in which case I have explained the source of my information or belief.

4.   There is now produced and shown to me a bundle consisting of true copies of the documents I will refer to in my witness statement marked 'GG1'.

5.   On 1st November 2010, a bankruptcy petition was presented in respect of the Bankrupt.

6.   A bankruptcy order was made against the Bankrupt on 1st March 2020. I refer to page [ ] of 'GG1' which is a true copy of the bankruptcy order.

7.   I was appointed as the Trustee in Bankruptcy of the Bankrupt on 1st April 2020. I refer to page [ ] of 'GG1' which is a true copy of my certificate of appointment.

8.   Following my appointment, I began to investigate the affairs of the Bankrupt. The following matters became apparent.

9.   On 1st January 2020, there was a bank transfer in the sum of £250,000 from the Bankrupt to Mrs Flakey. I refer to page [ ] of 'GG1' which is a true copy of the bank statement of the Bankrupt showing the transfer of £250,000 from the Bankrupt to Mrs Flakey.

10.   Further, in the circumstances, it is clear that the payment took place in the period after the presentation of the petition and in the period leading up the bankruptcy order.

11.   I believe that Mrs Flakey would, at the time of payment, have been well aware of the existence of the Bankruptcy petition against her husband. Indeed, I understand and truly believe from a witness statement filed by Mr Flingitt-Anrun, a process server, that Mrs Flakey was present at the time when the bankruptcy petition was served on her husband. I refer to page [ ] of 'GG1' which is a true copy of the evidence of service of the petition filed by the process server.

12.   I have written to Mrs Flakey inviting her to return the £250,000 and explaining the effect of section 284. In the same letter, I gave Mrs Flakey notice of my intention to apply for this order if she failed to make the payment but, to date, Mrs Flakey has not extended the courtesy of a reply to my letter. I refer to page [ ] of 'GG1' which is a true copy of the letter I sent.

13.   I therefore ask this Honourable Court to make the order in the terms sought.

STATEMENT OF TRUTH

I believe that the facts stated in this Witness Statement are true.

Signed [ ]
Full name [*GILES GRABBER*]
Dated [ ] 20[ ]

19.3   DECLARATION THAT A TRANSACTION IS INVALIDATED PURSUANT TO SECTION 284 OF THE INSOLVENCY ACT 1986

IN THE HIGH COURT OF JUSTICE
BUSINESS AND PROPERTY COURTS OF ENGLAND AND WALES
INSOLVENCY AND COMPANIES LIST (ChD)

NO: [ ] OF 20[ ]

IN THE MATTER OF IAN FLAKEY
IN BANKRUPTCY
AND IN THE MATTER OF THE INSOLVENCY ACT 1986

BEFORE MR REGISTRAR WISE
DATED:

BETWEEN:-

GILES GRABBER
(as Trustee in Bankruptcy of IAN FLAKEY)

Applicant

and

(1) IAN FLAKEY
(2) TABITHA FLAKEY

Respondents

DRAFT MINUTE OF ORDER

UPON THE APPLICATION of Giles Grabber of Grabbers LLP, Trustee in Bankruptcy of the above named IAN FLAKEY ('the Bankrupt')

UPON HEARING Counsel for the Applicant and Counsel for the Respondents

AND UPON READING the evidence noted as being read

IT IS DECLARED THAT the payment of £250,000 by Ian Flakey ('the Bankrupt') to the 2nd Respondent on or around 1st January 2020 is void against the Applicant as his Trustee in Bankruptcy pursuant to section 284 of the Insolvency Act 1986

IT IS ORDERED THAT the 2nd Respondent do pay to the Applicant the sum of £250,000

IT IS ORDERED THAT the 2nd Respondent do pay to the Applicant the costs of and occasioned by the Applicant such costs to be assessed if not agreed

AND IT IS ORDERED THAT any costs of the application that are not payable by the 2nd Respondent or not recovered from her should be paid to the Applicant as such trustee out of the assets of the bankruptcy as an expense of the bankruptcy pursuant to rule 10.149(a) of the Insolvency (England and Wales) Rules 2016

Service of this order

The Court has provided a sealed copy of this order to the serving party:

SNARKEY & SNYDE
1 LAW STREET
LONDON

Chapter 20

APPLICATION TO SET ASIDE A TRANSACTION AT AN UNDERVALUE

OBJECTIVE

The court has wide powers on the application of the trustee in bankruptcy to rewind transfers of the bankrupt's property which have been undertaken during the relevant period prior to bankruptcy for no consideration or for significantly less than the value in money or money's worth provided by the bankrupt.[1] 'Significantly less' involves a 'substantial element of bounty'.[2]

The relevant time means in the case of a transaction at an undervalue, at a time in the period of 5 years ending with the day of the presentation of the bankruptcy petition on which the individual is adjudged bankrupt.[3] This is subject to the proviso that, where the transaction at an undervalue is at a time over 2 years before the bankruptcy, it is not deemed to be within the relevant time unless the bankrupt was either insolvent at that time or became insolvent in consequence of the transaction. The requirements are presumed to be satisfied, unless the contrary is shown, in relation to any transaction at an undervalue which is entered into by an individual with a person who is an associate[4] of his (otherwise than by reason only of being his employee).[5] For these purposes, an individual is insolvent if either he is unable to pay his debts as they fall due or the value of his assets is less than the amount of his liabilities, taking into account his contingent and prospective liabilities.[6]

APPLICATION

The application is by application on notice using Form IAA for a declaration and an order restoring the position to what it would have been had the transaction not been entered into.

---

[1] Section 339 of the Insolvency Act 1986.

[2] *Re Kumar* [1993] BCLC 548.

[3] Section 341(1) of the Insolvency Act 1986.

[4] As defined under section 435 of the Insolvency Act 1986.

[5] Section 341(2) of the Insolvency Act 1986.

[6] Section 341(3) of the Insolvency Act 1986.

Each application should set out:

- that the application is made under the Insolvency Act 1986 or the Insolvency (England and Wales) Rules 2016 (as the case may be);[7]
- the section number or rule under which relief is sought;[8]
- the name of the parties;[9]
- the name of the bankrupt or debtor;[10]
- the court name;[11]
- the case number;[12]
- the remedy applied for or directions sought;[13]
- the name and address of each person to be served or, if none, stating that that it is intended that no person will be served;[14]
- where there is a requirement for particular persons to be given notice of the application under the Act or Rules, stating the name and address of each such person;[15]
- the applicant's address for service.[16]

The application notice must be authenticated by the applicant or his solicitor.[17]

The application should be returnable to the registrar in the Bankruptcy Registry or to the district judge in a Chancery District Registry or county court with insolvency jurisdiction.

The respondent should be the person who made the transfer and any other party to the transaction that the applicant is seeking to set aside.

COURT FEES

Where the application is made on notice to other parties, a court fee of £155 is payable.[18] Where the application is made by consent or without notice in existing proceedings, a court fee of £50 is payable.[19]

---

[7] Rule 1.35(2)(a) of the Insolvency (England and Wales) Rules 2016.
[8] Rule 1.35(2)(b) of the Insolvency (England and Wales) Rules 2016.
[9] Rule 1.35(2)(c) of the Insolvency (England and Wales) Rules 2016.
[10] Rule 1.35(2)(d) of the Insolvency (England and Wales) Rules 2016.
[11] Rule 1.35(2)(e) of the Insolvency (England and Wales) Rules 2016.
[12] Rule 1.35(2)(f) of the Insolvency (England and Wales) Rules 2016.
[13] Rule 1.35(2)(g) of the Insolvency (England and Wales) Rules 2016.
[14] Rule 1.35(2)(h) of the Insolvency (England and Wales) Rules 2016.
[15] Rule 1.35(2)(i) of the Insolvency (England and Wales) Rules 2016.
[16] Rule 1.35(2)(j) of the Insolvency (England and Wales) Rules 2016.
[17] Rule 1.35(3) of the Insolvency (England and Wales) Rules 2016. For what amounts to authentication, see rule 1.5. For hard copy applications, this means signed: rule 1.5(2).
[18] Paragraph 3.12 of Schedule 1 to the Civil Proceedings Fees (Amendment) Order 2014.
[19] Paragraph 3.11 of Schedule 1 to the Civil Proceedings Fees (Amendment) Order 2014.

EVIDENCE

The application should be supported by a witness statement. This should address:

- the capacity in which the deponent makes this application;
- the order the deponent seeks;
- the date of the petition;
- the date of the bankruptcy order;
- the date of the transaction subject to challenge;
- the particulars of the transaction subject to challenge;
- the value of the assets transferred under the transaction;
- the fact that the asset was transferred for no consideration or identifying the price it was being transferred for and stating that this was significantly less than its value in money or money's worth;
- whether the respondent is an associate of the bankrupt and, if so, why it is said so;
- that the bankrupt was insolvent (or is to be presumed to have been insolvent) at the time of the transaction or was rendered insolvent by the transaction.

And should exhibit:

- evidence of the trustee's appointment;
- the bankruptcy order;
- the statement of affairs;
- evidence of the transaction subject to challenge;
- evidence of the date of the transfer and the consideration (if any) paid;
- evidence that the respondent is an associate (if applicable);
- evidence to show the insolvency of the bankrupt at the time of the transaction;
- an independent valuation of the property disposed of;
- evidence of the bankrupt's ownership of the asset transferred.

SERVICE

The application and the evidence in support will need to be filed at court and served on the respondent as soon as practicable after it is filed and in any event, unless it is necessary to apply without notice or on short notice, at least 14 days before the date fixed for the hearing.[20]

The usual rule is that, subject to any other express provision, the application must be served at least 14 days before the date fixed for the hearing.[21] However, the court does have power, in cases of urgency, to hear an application immediately with or without notice to the other parties.[22]

---

[20] Rule 12.9(3) of the Insolvency (England and Wales) Rules 2016.

[21] Rule 12.9(3) of the Insolvency (England and Wales) Rules 2016.

[22] Rule 12.10(1) of the Insolvency (England and Wales) Rules 2016.

Service may be effected personally[23] or by post on the respondent (Part 6 of the CPR applies for these purposes)[24] or, where they have authority to accept service, on the respondent's solicitors.[25] Electronic service of documents is now permissible under the Rules, providing the respondent currently consents to service in that way and has provided an email address for service in that way.[26]

FIRST HEARING

At the first hearing, the registrar or district judge will give directions as to whether points of claim are needed and for the filing of evidence. He may also require the application to be served on other people. He may give directions as to whether witnesses are to attend for cross examination. The first hearing is likely to be heard in chambers and the advocates are not expected to robe.

KEY MATERIALS

Sections 339, 341–342 and 435 of the Insolvency Act 1986

339 Transactions at an undervalue
(1) Subject as follows in this section and sections 341 and 342, where an individual is adjudged bankrupt and he has at a relevant time (defined in section 341) entered into a transaction with any person at an undervalue, the trustee of the bankrupt's estate may apply to the court for an order under this section.
(2) The court shall, on such an application, make such order as it thinks fit for restoring the position to what it would have been if that individual had not entered into that transaction.
(3) For the purposes of this section and sections 341 and 342, an individual enters into a transaction with a person at an undervalue if—

(a) he makes a gift to that person or he otherwise enters into a transaction with that person on terms that provide for him to receive no consideration,
(b) he enters into a transaction with that person in consideration of marriage or the formation of a civil partnership, or
(c) he enters into a transaction with that person for a consideration the value of which, in money or money's worth, is significantly less than the value, in money or money's worth, of the consideration provided by the individual.

---

[23] Rule 1.44 of the Insolvency (England and Wales) Rules 2016.
[24] Schedule 4, paragraph 1(2) to the Insolvency (England and Wales) Rules 2016.
[25] Rule 1.40 of the Insolvency (England and Wales) Rules 2016.
[26] Rule 1.45 of the Insolvency (England and Wales) Rules 2016.

341 'Relevant time' under ss 339, 340

(1)   Subject as follows, the time at which an individual enters into a transaction at an undervalue or gives a preference is a relevant time if the transaction is entered into or the preference given—

    (a)   in the case of a transaction at an undervalue, at a time in the period of 5 years ending with the day of the presentation of the bankruptcy petition on which the individual is adjudged bankrupt,

    (b)   in the case of a preference which is not a transaction at an undervalue and is given to a person who is an associate of the individual (otherwise than by reason only of being his employee), at a time in the period of 2 years ending with that day, and

    (c)   in any other case of a preference which is not a transaction at an undervalue, at a time in the period of 6 months ending with that day.

(2)   Where an individual enters into a transaction at an undervalue or gives a preference at a time mentioned in paragraph (a), (b) or (c) of subsection (1) (not being, in the case of a transaction at an undervalue, a time less than 2 years before the end of the period mentioned in paragraph (a)), that time is not a relevant time for the purposes of sections 339 and 340 unless the individual—

    (a)   is insolvent at that time, or

    (b)   becomes insolvent in consequence of the transaction or preference;

but the requirements of this subsection are presumed to be satisfied, unless the contrary is shown, in relation to any transaction at an undervalue which is entered into by an individual with a person who is an associate of his (otherwise than by reason only of being his employee).

(3)   For the purposes of subsection (2), an individual is insolvent if—

    (a)   he is unable to pay his debts as they fall due, or

    (b)   the value of his assets is less than the amount of his liabilities, taking into account his contingent and prospective liabilities.

(4)   A transaction entered into or preference given by a person who is subsequently adjudged bankrupt on a petition under section 264(1)(d) (criminal bankruptcy) is to be treated as having been entered into or given at a relevant time for the purposes of sections 339 and 340 if it was entered into or given at any time on or after the date specified for the purposes of this subsection in the criminal bankruptcy order on which the petition was based.

(5)   No order shall be made under section 339 or 340 by virtue of subsection (4) of this section where an appeal is pending (within the meaning of section 277) against the individual's conviction of any offence by virtue of which the criminal bankruptcy order was made.

342 Orders under ss 339, 340

(1)   Without prejudice to the generality of section 339(2) or 340(2), an order under either of those sections with respect to a transaction or preference

entered into or given by an individual who is subsequently adjudged
bankrupt may (subject as follows)—

(a) require any property transferred as part of the transaction, or in
     connection with the giving of the preference, to be vested in the trustee
     of the bankrupt's estate as part of that estate;
(b) require any property to be so vested if it represents in any person's
     hands the application either of the proceeds of sale of property so
     transferred or of money so transferred;
(c) release or discharge (in whole or in part) any security given by the
     individual;
(d) require any person to pay, in respect of benefits received by him from
     the individual, such sums to the trustee of his estate as the court may
     direct;
(e) provide for any surety or guarantor whose obligations to any person
     were released or discharged (in whole or in part) under the transaction
     or by the giving of the preference to be under such new or revived
     obligations to that person as the court thinks appropriate;
(f) provide for security to be provided for the discharge of any obligation
     imposed by or arising under the order, for such an obligation to be
     charged on any property and for the security or charge to have the same
     priority as a security or charge released or discharged (in whole or in
     part) under the transaction or by the giving of the preference; and
(g) provide for the extent to which any person whose property is vested by
     the order in the trustee of the bankrupt's estate, or on whom obligations
     are imposed by the order, is to be able to prove in the bankruptcy for
     debts or other liabilities which arose from, or were released or
     discharged (in whole or in part) under or by, the transaction or the
     giving of the preference.

(2) An order under section 339 or 340 may affect the property of, or impose any
     obligation on, any person whether or not he is the person with whom the
     individual in question entered into the transaction or, as the case may be, the
     person to whom the preference was given; but such an order—

(a) shall not prejudice any interest in property which was acquired from a
     person other than that individual and was acquired in good faith and
     for value, or prejudice any interest deriving from such an interest, and
(b) shall not require a person who received a benefit from the transaction
     or preference in good faith and for value to pay a sum to the trustee of
     the bankrupt's estate, except where he was a party to the transaction or
     the payment is to be in respect of a preference given to that person at a
     time when he was a creditor of that individual.

(2A) Where a person has acquired an interest in property from a person other than
     the individual in question, or has received a benefit from the transaction or
     preference, and at the time of that acquisition or receipt—

(a) he had notice of the relevant surrounding circumstances and of the
     relevant proceedings, or

(b)   he was an associate of, or was connected with, either the individual in question or the person with whom that individual entered into the transaction or to whom that individual gave the preference,

then, unless the contrary is shown, it shall be presumed for the purposes of paragraph (a) or (as the case may be) paragraph (b) of subsection (2) that the interest was acquired or the benefit was received otherwise than in good faith.

(3)   Any sums required to be paid to the trustee in accordance with an order under section 339 or 340 shall be comprised in the bankrupt's estate.

(4)   For the purposes of subsection (2A)(a), the relevant surrounding circumstances are (as the case may require)—

(a)   the fact that the individual in question entered into the transaction at an undervalue; or
(b)   the circumstances which amounted to the giving of the preference by the individual in question.

(5)   For the purposes of subsection (2A)(a), a person has notice of the relevant proceedings if he has notice—

(a)   of the fact that the petition on which the individual in question is adjudged bankrupt has been presented; or
(b)   of the fact that the individual in question has been adjudged bankrupt.

(6)   Section 249 in Part VII of this Act shall apply for the purposes of subsection (2A)(b) as it applies for the purposes of the first Group of Parts.

435 Meaning of 'associate'
(1)   For the purposes of this Act any question whether a person is an associate of another person is to be determined in accordance with the following provisions of this section (any provision that a person is an associate of another person being taken to mean that they are associates of each other).
(2)   A person is an associate of an individual if that person is—

(a)   the individual's husband or wife or civil partner,
(b)   a relative of—

(i)   the individual, or
(ii)   the individual's husband or wife or civil partner, or

(c)   the husband or wife or civil partner of a relative of—

(i)   the individual, or
(ii)   the individual's husband or wife or civil partner.

(3)   A person is an associate of any person with whom he is in partnership, and of the husband or wife or civil partner or a relative of any individual with whom he is in partnership; and a Scottish firm is an associate of any person who is a member of the firm.

(4)   A person is an associate of any person whom he employs or by whom he is employed.

(5)   A person in his capacity as trustee of a trust other than—

(a)   a trust arising under any of the second Group of Parts or the Bankruptcy (Scotland) Act 1985, or

(b)   a pension scheme or an employees' share scheme . . . ,

is an associate of another person if the beneficiaries of the trust include, or the terms of the trust confer a power that may be exercised for the benefit of, that other person or an associate of that other person.

(6)   A company is an associate of another company—

(a)   if the same person has control of both, or a person has control of one and persons who are his associates, or he and persons who are his associates, have control of the other, or

(b)   if a group of two or more persons has control of each company, and the groups either consist of the same persons or could be regarded as consisting of the same persons by treating (in one or more cases) a member of either group as replaced by a person of whom he is an associate.

(7)   A company is an associate of another person if that person has control of it or if that person and persons who are his associates together have control of it.

(8)   For the purposes of this section a person is a relative of an individual if he is that individual's brother, sister, uncle, aunt, nephew, niece, lineal ancestor or lineal descendant, treating—

(a)   any relationship of the half blood as a relationship of the whole blood and the stepchild or adopted child of any person as his child, and

(b)   an illegitimate child as the legitimate child of his mother and reputed father;

and references in this section to a husband or wife include a former husband or wife and a reputed husband or wife and references to a civil partner include a former civil partner and a reputed civil partner.

(9)   For the purposes of this section any director or other officer of a company is to be treated as employed by that company.

(10) For the purposes of this section a person is to be taken as having control of a company if—

(a)   the directors of the company or of another company which has control of it (or any of them) are accustomed to act in accordance with his directions or instructions, or

(b)   he is entitled to exercise, or control the exercise of, one third or more of the voting power at any general meeting of the company or of another company which has control of it;

and where two or more persons together satisfy either of the above conditions, they are to be taken as having control of the company.

(11) In this section 'company' includes any body corporate (whether incorporated in Great Britain or elsewhere); and references to directors and other officers of a company and to voting power at any general meeting of a company have effect with any necessary modifications.

20.1   APPLICATION FOR A DECLARATION THAT A PAYMENT IS A TRANSACTION AT AN UNDERVALUE PURSUANT TO SECTION 339 OF THE INSOLVENCY ACT 1986

Form IAA   **Insolvency Act Application Notice**

IN THE HIGH COURT OF JUSTICE
BUSINESS AND PROPERTY COURTS OF ENGLAND AND WALES
INSOLVENCY AND COMPANIES LIST (ChD)
IN BANKRUPTCY

NO: 666 OF 2020

IN THE MATTER OF IAN FLAKEY
AND IN THE MATTER OF THE INSOLVENCY ACT 1986

BETWEEN:-

GILES GRABBER
(Trustee in Bankruptcy of IAN FLAKEY)

Applicant

and

(1) IAN FLAKEY
(2) MRS TABITHA FLAKEY

Respondents

Is this application within existing insolvency proceedings?   YES/~~NO~~

I (~~We~~), GILES GRABBER of 1 Vulture Street, London intend to apply to the ~~Judge/District Judge~~/Registrar on:

Date: 1st April 2020

Time: 00:00 hours

Place: Royal Courts of Justice, 7 Rolls Buildings, Fetter Lane, London EC4A 1NL

This application having been issued at the RCJ, 7 Rolls Buildings, Fetter Lane, London, EC4A 1NL will be heard at the time and date pursuant to the endorsement underneath the Court Seal on the front page of this application.

FOR AN ORDER THAT:

1.   A declaration that the payment of £250,000 by the Bankrupt to the 2nd Respondent on or around 1st January 2020 is void against the Applicant as trustee and that the same constituted a transaction at an undervalue within the meaning of section 339 of the Insolvency Act 1986.

2.   The 2nd Respondent do pay to the Applicant the sum of £250,000 and/or such other sum as this Honourable Court thinks fit to restore the position to what it would have been if the Bankrupt had not entered into the transaction.

3.   The 2nd Respondent do pay the Applicant's costs of and incidental to this application.

4.   Any costs of the application that are not payable by the 2nd Respondent or not recovered from her should be paid to the Applicant as such trustee out of the assets of the bankruptcy as an expense of the bankruptcy within rule 10.149(a) of the Insolvency (England and Wales) Rules 2016.

5.   Such further and other order and other relief as this Honourable Court thinks fit.

The grounds upon which the Applicant relies are set out in the 1st Witness statement of Giles Grabber dated 1st April 2020, a true copy of which is served herewith.

THE NAMES AND ADDRESSES OF THE PERSON(S) UPON WHOM IT IS INTENDED TO SERVE THIS APPLICATION ARE:

Name: IAN FLAKEY

Address: 1 GERANIUM COTTAGE, LONDON

Name: TABITHA FLAKEY

Address: 1 GERANIUM COTTAGE, LONDON

OR

IT IS NOT INTENDED TO SERVE ANY PERSON WITH THIS APPLICATION

Dated:

Signed: SNARKEY & SNYDE

Solicitors for the applicant or Applicant
Address: 1 LAW STREET, LONDON
Telephone: 0207 666 6666
Email: law@snarkeysnyde.com

*This is the address which will be treated by Court as the Petitions address for service

If you do not attend, the court may make such order as it thinks just.

20.2   WITNESS STATEMENT TO SET ASIDE A TRANSACTION AT AN UNDERVALUE PURSUANT TO SECTION 339 OF THE INSOLVENCY ACT 1986

Applicant: G Grabber: 1st: GG1: [ ] 20[ ]

IN THE HIGH COURT OF JUSTICE
BUSINESS AND PROPERTY COURTS OF ENGLAND AND WALES
INSOLVENCY AND COMPANIES LIST (ChD)

NO: [ ] OF 20[ ]

IN THE MATTER OF IAN FLAKEY
IN BANKRUPTCY
AND IN THE MATTER OF THE INSOLVENCY ACT 1986

BETWEEN:-

GILES GRABBER
(as Trustee in Bankruptcy of IAN FLAKEY)

Applicant

and

(1) IAN FLAKEY
(2) TABITHA FLAKEY

Respondents

1ST WITNESS STATEMENT OF GILES GRABBER

I, GILES GRABBER of Grabbers LLP, of 1 Vulture Street, London, Trustee in Bankruptcy of Ian Flakey, STATE as follows:

1.   I am the Applicant in this application. I am the Trustee in Bankruptcy of Ian Flakey.

2.   I make this witness statement in support of my application for:

   a.   A declaration that the payment of £250,000 by Ian Flakey ('the Bankrupt') to the 2nd Respondent on or around 1st January 2020 is void against the Applicant as his Trustee in Bankruptcy and that the same constituted a transaction at an undervalue within the meaning of section 339 of the Insolvency Act 1986.
   b.   An order that the 2nd Respondent do pay to the Applicant the sum of £250,000 and/or such other sum as this Honourable Court thinks fit to restore the position to what it would have been if the Bankrupt had not entered into the transaction.
   c.   An order that the 2nd Respondent do pay the Applicant's costs of and incidental to this application.
   d.   Any costs of the application that are not payable by the 2nd Respondent or not recovered from her should be paid to the Applicant as such trustee out of the assets of the bankruptcy as an expense of the bankruptcy within rule 10.149(a) of the Insolvency (England and Wales) Rules 2016.
   e.   Such further and other order and other relief as this Honourable Court thinks fit.

3.   The matters set out in this witness statement are true and within my own knowledge except where otherwise indicated, in which case I have explained the source of my information or belief.

4.   There is now produced and shown to me a bundle consisting of true copies of the documents I will refer to in my witness statement marked 'GG1'.

5.   A bankruptcy order was made against the Bankrupt on 1st March 2020. I refer to page [ ] of 'GG1' which is a true copy of the bankruptcy order.

6.   I was appointed as the Trustee in Bankruptcy of the Bankrupt on 1st April 2020. I refer to page [ ] of 'GG1' which is a true copy of my certificate of appointment.

7.   The Bankrupt's statement of affairs show that he was insolvent as at 31st December 2010 with a deficiency in the sum of £2,000,000. I refer to page [ ] of 'GG1' which is a true copy of the trading accounts of the Bankrupt and his statement of affairs. Creditors' claims lodged in the bankruptcy amount to £3,500,000. I refer to page [ ] of 'GG1' which is a true copy of the proofs of debt evidencing the creditors' claims.

8.   Following my appointment, I began to investigate the affairs of the Bankrupt. The following matters became apparent.

9.   On 1st January 2020, there was a bank transfer in the sum of £250,000 from the Bankrupt to Mrs Flakey. I refer to page [ ] of 'GG1' which is a true copy of the bank statement of the Bankrupt showing the transfer of £250,000 from the Bankrupt to Mrs Flakey. This appears in the accounts as payment for a gobstopper bought from Mrs Flakey. I refer to page [ ] of 'GG1' which is a true copy of the accounts of Mr Flakey showing the entry for the purchase.

10.   Mrs Flakey is the Bankrupt's wife and therefore his associate within the meaning of section 435 of the Insolvency Act 1986.

11.   The true value of the gobstopper (even when not partially sucked) is 5 pence. This is a mere fraction of the £250,000 paid to Mrs Flakey for this. I refer to page [ ] of 'GG1' which is a true copy of the price list of Toothy Sweets showing the retail price of their gobstoppers to be 5 pence each.

12.   The money paid represented the whole of the Bankrupt's available money in the bank. By making the payment, the monies left in the Bankrupt's account were dissipated. By making the transfer the Bankrupt rendered himself unable to pay his debts as they fell due and therefore insolvent. This, in practice, meant that creditors in the bankruptcy can hope for a dividend of no more than 1 pence for each £1 owed to them.

13.   Further, in the circumstances, it is clear that the transaction took place within the relevant period of 5 years leading up to the bankruptcy order within the meaning of the Act.

14.   I therefore ask this Honourable Court to make the order in the terms sought.

STATEMENT OF TRUTH

I believe that the facts stated in this Witness Statement are true.

Signed [ ]
Full name [*GILES GRABBER*]
Dated [ ] 20[ ]

20.3   DECLARATION THAT A PAYMENT IS A TRANSACTION AT AN UNDERVALUE PURSUANT TO SECTION 339 OF THE INSOLVENCY ACT 1986

IN THE HIGH COURT OF JUSTICE
BUSINESS AND PROPERTY COURTS OF ENGLAND AND WALES
INSOLVENCY AND COMPANIES LIST (ChD)

NO: [ ] OF 20[ ]

IN THE MATTER OF IAN FLAKEY
IN BANKRUPTCY
AND IN THE MATTER OF THE INSOLVENCY ACT 1986

BEFORE MR REGISTRAR WISE
DATED:

BETWEEN:-

GILES GRABBER
(as Trustee in Bankruptcy of IAN FLAKEY)

Applicant

and

(1) IAN FLAKEY
(2) TABITHA FLAKEY

Respondents

DRAFT MINUTE OF ORDER

UPON THE APPLICATION of Giles Grabber of Grabbers LLP, Trustee in Bankruptcy of the above named IAN FLAKEY ('the Bankrupt')

UPON HEARING Counsel for the Applicant and Counsel for the Respondents

AND UPON READING the evidence noted as being read

IT IS DECLARED THAT the payment of £250,000 by the Bankrupt to the 2nd Respondent on or around 1st January 2020 is void against the Applicant as Trustee in Bankruptcy of the Bankrupt and that the same constituted a transaction at an undervalue within the meaning of section 339 of the Insolvency Act 1986

IT IS ORDERED THAT the 2nd Respondent do pay to the Applicant the sum of £250,000

IT IS ORDERED THAT the 2nd Respondent do pay to the Applicant the costs of and occasioned by the Applicant such costs to be assessed if not agreed

AND IT IS ORDERED THAT any costs of the application that are not payable by the 2nd Respondent or not recovered from her should be paid to the Applicant as such trustee out of the assets of the bankruptcy as an expense of the bankruptcy within rule 10.149(a) of the Insolvency (England and Wales) Rules 2016

Service of this order

The Court has provided a sealed copy of this order to the serving party:

SNARKEY & SNYDE
1 LAW STREET
LONDON

Chapter 21

APPLICATION TO SET ASIDE A PREFERENCE

OBJECTIVE

The court has wide powers on the application of the trustee in bankruptcy to rewind arrangements which have been undertaken during the relevant period prior to bankruptcy to prefer one of the bankrupt's creditors, sureties or guarantors.[1]

The relevant time means in the case of a preference, at a time in the period of 6 months ending with the day of the presentation of the bankruptcy petition on which the individual is adjudged bankrupt or 2 years where the person preferred is an associate.[2] This is subject to the proviso that a preference is not deemed to be within the relevant time unless the bankrupt was either insolvent at that time or became insolvent in consequence of the transaction. The requirements are presumed to be satisfied, unless the contrary is shown, in relation to any preference which is entered into by an individual with a person who is an associate[3] of his (otherwise than by reason only of being his employee).[4] For these purposes an individual is insolvent if either he is unable to pay his debts as they fall due or the value of his assets is less than the amount of his liabilities, taking into account his contingent and prospective liabilities.[5] Similarly, the court will not make an order unless the bankrupt acted with the dominant purpose of preferring the creditor. Again, this is presumed where the creditor is an associate.

APPLICATION

The application is by application on notice using Form IAA for a declaration and an order restoring the position to what it would have been had the arrangement not been entered into.

---

[1] Section 340 of the Insolvency Act 1986.

[2] Section 341(1) of the Insolvency Act 1986.

[3] As defined under section 435 of the Insolvency Act 1986.

[4] Section 341(2) of the Insolvency Act 1986.

[5] Section 341(3) of the Insolvency Act 1986.

Each application should set out:

- that the application is made under the Insolvency Act 1986 or the Insolvency (England and Wales) Rules 2016 (as the case may be);[6]
- the section number or rule under which relief is sought;[7]
- the name of the parties;[8]
- the name of the bankrupt or debtor;[9]
- the court name;[10]
- the case number;[11]
- the remedy applied for or directions sought;[12]
- the name and address of each person to be served or, if none, stating that that it is intended that no person will be served;[13]
- where there is a requirement for particular persons to be given notice of the application under the Act or Rules, stating the name and address of each such person;[14]
- the applicant's address for service.[15]

The application notice must be authenticated by the applicant or his solicitor.[16]

The application should be returnable to the registrar in the Bankruptcy Registry or to the district judge in a Chancery District Registry or county court with insolvency jurisdiction.

The respondents should be the person who made the arrangement and any other party to the arrangement that the applicant is seeking to set aside.

COURT FEES

Where the application is made on notice to other parties, a court fee of £155 is payable.[17] Where the application is made by consent or without notice in existing proceedings, a court fee of £50 is payable.[18]

---

[6]   Rule 1.35(2)(a) of the Insolvency (England and Wales) Rules 2016.

[7]   Rule 1.35(2)(b) of the Insolvency (England and Wales) Rules 2016.

[8]   Rule 1.35(2)(c) of the Insolvency (England and Wales) Rules 2016.

[9]   Rule 1.35(2)(d) of the Insolvency (England and Wales) Rules 2016.

[10] Rule 1.35(2)(e) of the Insolvency (England and Wales) Rules 2016.

[11] Rule 1.35(2)(f) of the Insolvency (England and Wales) Rules 2016.

[12] Rule 1.35(2)(g) of the Insolvency (England and Wales) Rules 2016.

[13] Rule 1.35(2)(h) of the Insolvency (England and Wales) Rules 2016.

[14] Rule 1.35(2)(i) of the Insolvency (England and Wales) Rules 2016.

[15] Rule 1.35(2)(j) of the Insolvency (England and Wales) Rules 2016.

[16] Rule 1.35(3) of the Insolvency (England and Wales) Rules 2016. For what amounts to authentication, see rule 1.5. For hard copy applications, this means signed: rule 1.5(2).

[17] Paragraph 3.12 of Schedule 1 to the Civil Proceedings Fees (Amendment) Order 2014.

[18] Paragraph 3.11 of Schedule 1 to the Civil Proceedings Fees (Amendment) Order 2014.

EVIDENCE

The application should be supported by a witness statement. This should address:

- the capacity in which the deponent makes this application;
- the order the deponent seeks;
- the date of the petition;
- the date of the bankruptcy order;
- that the respondent is a creditor, guarantor or surety of the company;
- particulars of the respondent's loan, indemnity or guarantee;
- the date of the transaction subject to challenge;
- the particulars of the arrangement subject to challenge;
- that the arrangement operated to prefer the position of the respondent in the event of the bankruptcy;
- why it is said that the arrangement operated to prefer the position of the respondent in the event of the bankruptcy;
- that in entering the arrangement the bankrupt had been influenced by a desire to put the respondent in a better position in the event of his bankruptcy;
- whether the respondent is an associate of the bankrupt and, if so, why it is said so;
- that the bankrupt was insolvent (or is to be presumed to have been insolvent) at the time of the transaction or was rendered insolvent by the transaction;
- the order the respondent seeks.

And should exhibit:

- evidence of the trustee's appointment;
- the bankruptcy order;
- the statement of affairs;
- the respondent's loan, indemnity or guarantee;
- evidence of the arrangement subject to challenge;
- evidence that the respondent is an associate (if applicable);
- evidence tending to show the insolvency of the bankrupt at the time of the transaction.

SERVICE

The application and the evidence in support will need to be filed at court and served on the respondent as soon as practicable after it is filed and in any event, unless it is necessary to apply without notice or on short notice, at least 14 days before the date fixed for the hearing.[19]

---

[19] Rule 12.9(3) of the Insolvency (England and Wales) Rules 2016.

The usual rule is that, subject to any other express provision, the application must be served at least 14 days before the date fixed for the hearing.[20] However, the court does have power, in cases of urgency, to hear an application immediately with or without notice to the other parties.[21]

Service may be effected personally[22] or by post on the respondent (Part 6 of the CPR applies for these purposes)[23] or, where they have authority to accept service, on the respondent's solicitors.[24] Electronic service of documents is now permissible under the Rules, providing the respondent currently consents to service in that way and has provided an email address for service in that way.[25]

FIRST HEARING

At the first hearing, the registrar or district judge will give directions as to whether points of claim are needed and for the filing of evidence. He may also require the application to be served on other people. He may give directions as to whether witnesses are to attend for cross examination. The first hearing is likely to be heard in chambers and the advocates are not expected to robe.

KEY MATERIALS

Sections 340–342 and 435 of the Insolvency Act 1986

340 Preferences

(1)   Subject as follows in this and the next two sections, where an individual is adjudged bankrupt and he has at a relevant time (defined in section 341) given a preference to any person, the trustee of the bankrupt's estate may apply to the court for an order under this section.

(2)   The court shall, on such an application, make such order as it thinks fit for restoring the position to what it would have been if that individual had not given that preference.

(3)   For the purposes of this and the next two sections, an individual gives a preference to a person if—

      (a)   that person is one of the individual's creditors or a surety or guarantor for any of his debts or other liabilities, and

      (b)   the individual does anything or suffers anything to be done which (in either case) has the effect of putting that person into a position which,

---

20   Rule 12.9(3) of the Insolvency (England and Wales) Rules 2016.

21   Rule 12.10(1) of the Insolvency (England and Wales) Rules 2016.

22   Rule 1.44 of the Insolvency (England and Wales) Rules 2016.

23   Schedule 4, paragraph 1(2) to the Insolvency (England and Wales) Rules 2016.

24   Rule 1.40 of the Insolvency (England and Wales) Rules 2016.

25   Rule 1.45 of the Insolvency (England and Wales) Rules 2016.

in the event of the individual's bankruptcy, will be better than the position he would have been in if that thing had not been done.

(4) The court shall not make an order under this section in respect of a preference given to any person unless the individual who gave the preference was influenced in deciding to give it by a desire to produce in relation to that person the effect mentioned in subsection (3)(b) above.

(5) An individual who has given a preference to a person who, at the time the preference was given, was an associate of his (otherwise than by reason only of being his employee) is presumed, unless the contrary is shown, to have been influenced in deciding to give it by such a desire as is mentioned in subsection (4).

(6) The fact that something has been done in pursuance of the order of a court does not, without more, prevent the doing or suffering of that thing from constituting the giving of a preference.

341 'Relevant time' under ss 339, 340

(1) Subject as follows, the time at which an individual enters into a transaction at an undervalue or gives a preference is a relevant time if the transaction is entered into or the preference given—

(a) in the case of a transaction at an undervalue, at a time in the period of 5 years ending with the day of the presentation of the bankruptcy petition on which the individual is adjudged bankrupt,

(b) in the case of a preference which is not a transaction at an undervalue and is given to a person who is an associate of the individual (otherwise than by reason only of being his employee), at a time in the period of 2 years ending with that day, and

(c) in any other case of a preference which is not a transaction at an undervalue, at a time in the period of 6 months ending with that day.

(2) Where an individual enters into a transaction at an undervalue or gives a preference at a time mentioned in paragraph (a), (b) or (c) of subsection (1) (not being, in the case of a transaction at an undervalue, a time less than 2 years before the end of the period mentioned in paragraph (a)), that time is not a relevant time for the purposes of sections 339 and 340 unless the individual—

(a) is insolvent at that time, or

(b) becomes insolvent in consequence of the transaction or preference;

but the requirements of this subsection are presumed to be satisfied, unless the contrary is shown, in relation to any transaction at an undervalue which is entered into by an individual with a person who is an associate of his (otherwise than by reason only of being his employee).

(3) For the purposes of subsection (2), an individual is insolvent if—

(a) he is unable to pay his debts as they fall due, or

    (b)   the value of his assets is less than the amount of his liabilities, taking into account his contingent and prospective liabilities.

(4)   A transaction entered into or preference given by a person who is subsequently adjudged bankrupt on a petition under section 264(1)(d) (criminal bankruptcy) is to be treated as having been entered into or given at a relevant time for the purposes of sections 339 and 340 if it was entered into or given at any time on or after the date specified for the purposes of this subsection in the criminal bankruptcy order on which the petition was based.

(5)   No order shall be made under section 339 or 340 by virtue of subsection (4) of this section where an appeal is pending (within the meaning of section 277) against the individual's conviction of any offence by virtue of which the criminal bankruptcy order was made.

342 Orders under ss 339, 340

(1)   Without prejudice to the generality of section 339(2) or 340(2), an order under either of those sections with respect to a transaction or preference entered into or given by an individual who is subsequently adjudged bankrupt may (subject as follows)—

    (a)   require any property transferred as part of the transaction, or in connection with the giving of the preference, to be vested in the trustee of the bankrupt's estate as part of that estate;

    (b)   require any property to be so vested if it represents in any person's hands the application either of the proceeds of sale of property so transferred or of money so transferred;

    (c)   release or discharge (in whole or in part) any security given by the individual;

    (d)   require any person to pay, in respect of benefits received by him from the individual, such sums to the trustee of his estate as the court may direct;

    (e)   provide for any surety or guarantor whose obligations to any person were released or discharged (in whole or in part) under the transaction or by the giving of the preference to be under such new or revived obligations to that person as the court thinks appropriate;

    (f)   provide for security to be provided for the discharge of any obligation imposed by or arising under the order, for such an obligation to be charged on any property and for the security or charge to have the same priority as a security or charge released or discharged (in whole or in part) under the transaction or by the giving of the preference; and

    (g)   provide for the extent to which any person whose property is vested by the order in the trustee of the bankrupt's estate, or on whom obligations are imposed by the order, is to be able to prove in the bankruptcy for debts or other liabilities which arose from, or were released or discharged (in whole or in part) under or by, the transaction or the giving of the preference.

(2)   An order under section 339 or 340 may affect the property of, or impose any obligation on, any person whether or not he is the person with whom the

individual in question entered into the transaction or, as the case may be, the person to whom the preference was given; but such an order—

(a) shall not prejudice any interest in property which was acquired from a person other than that individual and was acquired in good faith and for value, or prejudice any interest deriving from such an interest, and

(b) shall not require a person who received a benefit from the transaction or preference in good faith and for value to pay a sum to the trustee of the bankrupt's estate, except where he was a party to the transaction or the payment is to be in respect of a preference given to that person at a time when he was a creditor of that individual.

(2A) Where a person has acquired an interest in property from a person other than the individual in question, or has received a benefit from the transaction or preference, and at the time of that acquisition or receipt—

(a) he had notice of the relevant surrounding circumstances and of the relevant proceedings, or

(b) he was an associate of, or was connected with, either the individual in question or the person with whom that individual entered into the transaction or to whom that individual gave the preference,

then, unless the contrary is shown, it shall be presumed for the purposes of paragraph (a) or (as the case may be) paragraph (b) of subsection (2) that the interest was acquired or the benefit was received otherwise than in good faith.

(3) Any sums required to be paid to the trustee in accordance with an order under section 339 or 340 shall be comprised in the bankrupt's estate.

(4) For the purposes of subsection (2A)(a), the relevant surrounding circumstances are (as the case may require)—

(a) the fact that the individual in question entered into the transaction at an undervalue; or

(b) the circumstances which amounted to the giving of the preference by the individual in question.

(5) For the purposes of subsection (2A)(a), a person has notice of the relevant proceedings if he has notice—

(a) of the fact that the petition on which the individual in question is adjudged bankrupt has been presented; or

(b) of the fact that the individual in question has been adjudged bankrupt.

(6) Section 249 in Part VII of this Act shall apply for the purposes of subsection (2A)(b) as it applies for the purposes of the first Group of Parts.

435 Meaning of 'associate'

(1) For the purposes of this Act any question whether a person is an associate of another person is to be determined in accordance with the following

provisions of this section (any provision that a person is an associate of another person being taken to mean that they are associates of each other).

(2)   A person is an associate of an individual if that person is—

(a)   the individual's husband or wife or civil partner,
(b)   a relative of—

(i)   the individual, or
(ii)   the individual's husband or wife or civil partner, or

(c)   the husband or wife or civil partner of a relative of—

(i)   the individual, or
(ii)   the individual's husband or wife or civil partner.

(3)   A person is an associate of any person with whom he is in partnership, and of the husband or wife or civil partner or a relative of any individual with whom he is in partnership; and a Scottish firm is an associate of any person who is a member of the firm.

(4)   A person is an associate of any person whom he employs or by whom he is employed.

(5)   A person in his capacity as trustee of a trust other than—

(a)   a trust arising under any of the second Group of Parts or the Bankruptcy (Scotland) Act 1985, or
(b)   a pension scheme or an employees' share scheme . . . ,

is an associate of another person if the beneficiaries of the trust include, or the terms of the trust confer a power that may be exercised for the benefit of, that other person or an associate of that other person.

(6)   A company is an associate of another company—

(a)   if the same person has control of both, or a person has control of one and persons who are his associates, or he and persons who are his associates, have control of the other, or
(b)   if a group of two or more persons has control of each company, and the groups either consist of the same persons or could be regarded as consisting of the same persons by treating (in one or more cases) a member of either group as replaced by a person of whom he is an associate.

(7)   A company is an associate of another person if that person has control of it or if that person and persons who are his associates together have control of it.

(8)   For the purposes of this section a person is a relative of an individual if he is that individual's brother, sister, uncle, aunt, nephew, niece, lineal ancestor or lineal descendant, treating—

(a)   any relationship of the half blood as a relationship of the whole blood and the stepchild or adopted child of any person as his child, and

(b)   an illegitimate child as the legitimate child of his mother and reputed father;

and references in this section to a husband or wife include a former husband or wife and a reputed husband or wife and references to a civil partner include a former civil partner and a reputed civil partner.

(9)   For the purposes of this section any director or other officer of a company is to be treated as employed by that company.

(10) For the purposes of this section a person is to be taken as having control of a company it—

(a)   the directors of the company or of another company which has control of it (or any of them) are accustomed to act in accordance with his directions or instructions, or

(b)   he is entitled to exercise, or control the exercise of, one third or more of the voting power at any general meeting of the company or of another company which has control of it;

and where two or more persons together satisfy either of the above conditions, they are to be taken as having control of the company.

(11) In this section 'company' includes any body corporate (whether incorporated in Great Britain or elsewhere); and references to directors and other officers of a company and to voting power at any general meeting of a company have effect with any necessary modifications.

21.1   APPLICATION FOR A DECLARATION OF A PREFERENCE PURSUANT TO SECTION 340 OF THE INSOLVENCY ACT 1986

Form IAA   **Insolvency Act Application Notice**

IN THE HIGH COURT OF JUSTICE
BUSINESS AND PROPERTY COURTS OF ENGLAND AND WALES
INSOLVENCY AND COMPANIES LIST (ChD)
IN BANKRUPTCY

NO: 666 OF 2020

IN THE MATTER OF IAN FLAKEY
AND IN THE MATTER OF THE INSOLVENCY ACT 1986

BETWEEN:-

GILES GRABBER
(Trustee in Bankruptcy of IAN FLAKEY)

Applicant

and

(1) IAN FLAKEY
(2) MRS TABITHA FLAKEY

Respondents

Is this application within existing insolvency proceedings?   YES/~~NO~~

I (~~We~~), GILES GRABBER of 1 Vulture Street, London intend to apply to the ~~Judge/District Judge~~/Registrar on:

Date: 1st April 2020

Time: 00:00 hours

Place: Royal Courts of Justice, 7 Rolls Buildings, Fetter Lane, London EC4A 1NL

This application having been issued at the RCJ, 7 Rolls Buildings, Fetter Lane, London, EC4A 1NL will be heard at the time and date pursuant to the endorsement underneath the Court Seal on the front page of this application.

FOR AN ORDER THAT:

1.   A declaration that the payment of £250,000 by the Bankrupt to the 2nd Respondent on or around 1st January 2020 is void against the Applicant as the Bankrupt's Trustee in Bankruptcy and that the same constituted a preference within the meaning of section 340 of the Insolvency Act 1986.

2.   The 2nd Respondent do pay to the Applicant the sum of £250,000 and/or such other sum as this Honourable Court thinks fit to restore the position to what it would have been if the Bankrupt had not entered into the transaction and protecting the interests of the victims of the same.

3.   The 2nd Respondent do pay the Applicant's costs of and incidental to this application.

4.   Any costs of the application that are not payable by the 2nd Respondent or not recovered from her should be paid to the Applicant as such trustee out of the assets of the bankruptcy as an expense of the bankruptcy within rule 10.149(a) of the Insolvency (England and Wales) Rules 2016.

5.   Such further and other order and other relief as this Honourable Court thinks fit.

The grounds upon which the Applicant relies are set out in the 1st witness statement of Giles Grabber dated 1st April 2020, a true copy of which is served herewith.

THE NAMES AND ADDRESSES OF THE PERSON(S) UPON WHOM IT IS INTENDED TO SERVE THIS APPLICATION ARE:

Name: IAN FLAKEY

Address: 1 GERANIUM COTTAGE, LONDON

Name: TABITHA FLAKEY

Address: 1 GERANIUM COTTAGE, LONDON

OR

IT IS NOT INTENDED TO SERVE ANY PERSON WITH THIS APPLICATION

Dated:

Signed: SNARKEY & SNYDE

Solicitors for the applicant or Applicant   *This is the address
Address: 1 LAW STREET, LONDON   which will be treated
Telephone: 0207 666 6666   by Court as the
Email: law@snarkeysnyde.com   Petitions address for
                                              service

If you do not attend, the court may make such order as it thinks just.

21.2   WITNESS STATEMENT FOR A DECLARATION OF A PREFERENCE PURSUANT TO SECTION 340 OF THE INSOLVENCY ACT 1986

Applicant: G Grabber: 1st: GG1: [ ] 20[ ]

IN THE HIGH COURT OF JUSTICE
BUSINESS AND PROPERTY COURTS OF ENGLAND AND WALES
INSOLVENCY AND COMPANIES LIST (ChD)

NO: [ ] OF 20[ ]

IN THE MATTER OF IAN FLAKEY
IN BANKRUPTCY
AND IN THE MATTER OF THE INSOLVENCY ACT 1986

BETWEEN:-

GILES GRABBER
(as Trustee in Bankruptcy of IAN FLAKEY)

Applicant

and

(1) IAN FLAKEY
(2) TABITHA FLAKEY

Respondents

1ST WITNESS STATEMENT OF GILES GRABBER

I, GILES GRABBER of Grabbers LLP, of 1 Vulture Street, London, Trustee in Bankruptcy of Ian Flakey, STATE as follows:

1.   I am the Applicant in this application. I am the Trustee in Bankruptcy of Ian Flakey.

2.   I make this witness statement in support of my application for:

   a.   A declaration that the payment of £250,000 by the Bankrupt to the 2nd Respondent on or around 1st January 2020 is void against the Applicant as the Bankrupt's Trustee in Bankruptcy and that the same constituted a preference within the meaning of section 340 of the Insolvency Act 1986.

   b.   An order that the 2nd Respondent do pay to the Applicant the sum of £250,000 and/or such other sum as this Honourable Court thinks fit to restore the position to what it would have been if the Bankrupt had not entered into the transaction and to protect the interests of the victims of the same.

   c.   An order that the 2nd Respondent do pay the Applicant's costs of and incidental to this application.

   d.   That any costs of the application that are not payable by the 2nd Respondent or not recovered from her should be paid to the Applicant as such trustee out of the assets of the bankruptcy as an expense of the bankruptcy within rule 10.149(a) of the Insolvency (England and Wales) Rules 2016.

   e.   Such further and other order and other relief as this Honourable Court thinks fit.

3. The matters set out in this witness statement are true and within my own knowledge except where otherwise indicated, in which case I have explained the source of my information or belief.

4. There is now produced and shown to me a bundle consisting of true copies of the documents I will refer to in my witness statement marked 'GG1'.

5. A bankruptcy order was made against the Bankrupt on 1st March 2020. I refer to page [ ] of 'GG1' which is a true copy of the bankruptcy order.

6. I was appointed as the Trustee in Bankruptcy of the Bankrupt on 1st April 2020. I refer to page [ ] of 'GG1' which is a true copy of my certificate of appointment.

7. The Bankrupt's statement of affairs show that he was insolvent as at 31st December 2020 with a deficiency in the sum of £2,000,000. I refer to page [ ] of 'GG1' which is a true copy of the trading accounts of the Bankrupt and his statement of affairs. Creditors' claims lodged in the bankruptcy amount to £3,500,000. I refer to page [ ] of 'GG1' which is a true copy of the proofs of debt evidencing the creditors' claims.

8. Following my appointment, I began to investigate the affairs of the Bankrupt. The following matters became apparent.

9. On 1st January 2020, there was a bank transfer in the sum of £250,000 from the Bankrupt to Mrs Flakey. I refer to page [ ] of 'GG1' which is a true copy of the bank statement of the Bankrupt showing the transfer of £250,000 from the Bankrupt to Mrs Flakey.

10. This was the repayment of an unsecured loan from Mrs Flakey. I refer to page [ ] of 'GG1' which is a true copy of the loan agreement.

11. Mrs Flakey is the Bankrupt's wife and therefore his associate within the meaning of section 435 of the Insolvency Act 1986.

12. The payment operated to fully satisfy the Bankrupt's indebtedness to Mrs Flakey.

13. The money paid represented the whole of the Bankrupt's available money in the bank. By making the payment, creditors in the bankruptcy can hope for a dividend of no more than 1 penny for each £ owed to them.

14. On 2nd January 2020, a bankruptcy petition was presented by HM Revenue & Customs for £1 million in unpaid VAT. I refer to page [ ] of 'GG1' which is a true copy of the petition.

15. Due to the proximity of the payments and the onset of insolvency, it is inconceivable that the Bankrupt was solvent at the date of the payment.

16. In the light of the above, I consider that the payment to the 2nd Respondent constituted a voidable preference within the meaning of section 340 of the Act in that the payments occurred at a relevant time and at the date of payment the Bankrupt was unable to pay his debts and/or became so unable as a consequence of the preference.

17.   In the circumstances as described above, it may be inferred that the Bankrupt, in making the payment to Mrs Flakey was influenced by a desire to put her into a better position in the event of his bankruptcy than if the payment had not been made.

18.   I therefore ask this Honourable Court to make the order in the terms sought.

STATEMENT OF TRUTH

I believe that the facts stated in this Witness Statement are true.

Signed [ ]
Full name [*GILES GRABBER*]
Dated [ ] 20[ ]

21.3   DECLARATION OF A PREFERENCE PURSUANT TO SECTION 340 OF THE INSOLVENCY ACT 1986

IN THE HIGH COURT OF JUSTICE
BUSINESS AND PROPERTY COURTS OF ENGLAND AND WALES
INSOLVENCY AND COMPANIES LIST (ChD)

NO: [ ] OF 20[ ]

IN THE MATTER OF IAN FLAKEY
IN BANKRUPTCY
AND IN THE MATTER OF THE INSOLVENCY ACT 1986

BEFORE MR REGISTRAR WISE
DATED:

BETWEEN:-

GILES GRABBER
(as Trustee in Bankruptcy of IAN FLAKEY)

Applicant

and

(1) IAN FLAKEY
(2) TABITHA FLAKEY

Respondents

DRAFT MINUTE OF ORDER

UPON THE APPLICATION of Giles Grabber of Grabbers LLP, Trustee in Bankruptcy of the above named IAN FLAKEY ('the Bankrupt')

UPON HEARING Counsel for the Applicant and Counsel for the Respondents

AND UPON READING the evidence noted as being read

IT IS DECLARED THAT the payment of £250,000 by the Bankrupt to the 2nd Respondent on or around 1st January 2020 is void against the Applicant as the Bankrupt's Trustee in Bankruptcy and that the same constituted a preference within the meaning of section 340 of the Insolvency Act 1986

IT IS ORDERED THAT the 2nd Respondent do pay to the Applicant the sum of £250,000

IT IS ORDERED THAT the 2nd Respondent do pay to the Applicant the costs of and occasioned by the Applicant such costs to be assessed if not agreed

AND IT IS ORDERED THAT any costs of the application that are not payable by the 2nd Respondent or not recovered from her should be paid to the Applicant as such trustee out of the assets of the bankruptcy as an expense of the bankruptcy within rule 10.149(a) of the Insolvency (England and Wales) Rules 2016

Service of this order

The Court has provided a sealed copy of this order to the serving party:

SNARKEY & SNYDE
1 LAW STREET
LONDON

Chapter 22

APPLICATION TO SET ASIDE A TRANSACTION DEFRAUDING CREDITORS

OBJECTIVE

The court has wide powers to rewind transfers of a debtor's property which have been undertaken for no consideration or for significantly less than the value in money or money's worth provided by the debtor where the transaction has been entered into for the purpose of either putting assets beyond the reach of a person who is making or may make a claim against the debtor or otherwise prejudicing such a person's interests in such a claim.[1] This does not need to be the sole or main purpose of the transfer but should be shown to be a real and substantial purpose behind the transaction.[2]

'Transaction' is flexibly interpreted and covers arrangements spanning from formal contracts to informal understandings, and can in certain circumstances be used to challenge a dividend to shareholders.[3] Fraud does not need to be shown. Nor does the debtor need to be insolvent at the time of the transaction.

APPLICATION

The application is by application notice on notice using Form IAA for a declaration and an order restoring the position to what it would have been had the transaction not been entered into.

Each application should set out:

- that the application is made under the Insolvency Act 1986 or the Insolvency (England and Wales) Rules 2016 (as the case may be);[4]
- the section number or rule under which relief is sought;[5]
- the name of the parties;[6]

---

[1]   Section 423 of the Insolvency Act 1986.

[2]   *Hashmi v IRC* [2002] EWCA Civ 981, [2002] BCC 943.

[3]   *Feakins v DEFRA* [2005] EWCA Civ 1513, [2006] BPIR 895; *BTI 2014 LLC v Sequana SA* [2016] EWHC 1686 (Ch), [2017] Bus LR 82.

[4]   Rule 1.35(2)(a) of the Insolvency (England and Wales) Rules 2016.

[5]   Rule 1.35(2)(b) of the Insolvency (England and Wales) Rules 2016.

[6]   Rule 1.35(2)(c) of the Insolvency (England and Wales) Rules 2016.

- the name of the bankrupt or debtor;[7]
- the court name;[8]
- the case number;[9]
- the remedy applied for or directions sought;[10]
- the name and address of each person to be served or, if none, stating that that it is intended that no person will be served;[11]
- where there is a requirement for particular persons to be given notice of the application under the Act or Rules, stating the name and address of each such person;[12]
- the applicant's address for service.[13]

The application notice must be authenticated by the applicant or his solicitor.[14]

The application should be returnable to the registrar in the Bankruptcy Registry or to the district judge in a Chancery District Registry or county court with insolvency jurisdiction.

The applicant can be the Official Receiver, the trustee in bankruptcy or a victim of the debtor. Where the debtor is a bankrupt, a victim will need the permission of the court to make this application. Victim is flexibly interpreted.[15] A creditor can be a victim for these purposes.[16] HM Revenue & Customs can be a victim for these purposes where the purpose of the transaction was to mislead them as to the tax liability.[17]

The respondent should be the person who made the transfer and any other party to the transaction that the applicant is seeking to set aside.

COURT FEES

Where the application is made by ordinary application on notice to other parties, a court fee of £155 is payable.[18] Where the application is made by consent or without notice in existing proceedings, a court fee of £50 is payable.[19]

---

[7]   Rule 1.35(2)(d) of the Insolvency (England and Wales) Rules 2016.

[8]   Rule 1.35(2)(e) of the Insolvency (England and Wales) Rules 2016.

[9]   Rule 1.35(2)(f) of the Insolvency (England and Wales) Rules 2016.

[10] Rule 1.35(2)(g) of the Insolvency (England and Wales) Rules 2016.

[11] Rule 1.35(2)(h) of the Insolvency (England and Wales) Rules 2016.

[12] Rule 1.35(2)(i) of the Insolvency (England and Wales) Rules 2016.

[13] Rule 1.35(2)(j) of the Insolvency (England and Wales) Rules 2016.

[14] Rule 1.35(3) of the Insolvency (England and Wales) Rules 2016. For what amounts to authentication, see rule 1.5. For hard copy applications, this means signed: rule 1.5(2).

[15] *Hill v Spread Trustee Co Ltd* [2006] EWCA Civ 542, [2006] BPIR 789.

[16] *Re Ayala Holdings Ltd* [1993] BCLC 256.

[17] *Hill v Spread Trustee Co Ltd* [2006] EWCA Civ 542, [2006] BPIR 789.

[18] Paragraph 3.12 of Schedule 1 to the Civil Proceedings Fees (Amendment) Order 2014.

[19] Paragraph 3.11 of Schedule 1 to the Civil Proceedings Fees (Amendment) Order 2014.

EVIDENCE

The application should be supported by a witness statement. This should address:

- the capacity in which the deponent makes this application (e.g. victim, trustee, etc.);
- the order the deponent seeks;
- the date of the petition;
- the date of the bankruptcy order;
- the date of the transaction subject to challenge;
- the particulars of the transaction subject to challenge;
- the value of the assets transferred under the transaction;
- that the asset was transferred for no consideration or identifying the price it was being transferred for and stating that this was significantly less than its value in money or money's worth;
- why it is said that the transaction has been entered into for the purpose of either putting assets beyond the reach of a person who is making or may make a claim against the bankrupt or otherwise prejudicing such a person's interests in such a claim;
- (in so far that there is an application to set aside the transaction) that the proposed order will not prejudice any interest in property that was acquired in good faith, for value and without notice of the relevant circumstances;[20]
- (in so far that there is an application to set aside the transaction) that the proposed order will not require a person who has received a benefit from the transaction in good faith, for value and without notice of the relevant circumstances to pay any sum unless he was a party to the transaction.[21]

And should exhibit:

- (as applicable) evidence of the trustee's appointment or of the basis upon which the applicant asserts he was a victim of the transaction;
- (as applicable) a copy of the bankruptcy order;
- evidence of the transaction subject to challenge;
- evidence of the bankrupt's ownership of the asset transferred;
- evidence of the transaction under which the bankrupt's asset was transferred and of its date and the consideration (if any) paid;
- an independent valuation of the property disposed of.

SERVICE

The application and the evidence in support will need to be filed at court and served on the respondent as soon as practicable after it is filed and in any event,

---

[20] Pre-empting the possible defence under section 425(2) of the Insolvency Act 1986.

[21] Pre-empting the possible defence under section 425(2) of the Insolvency Act 1986.

unless it is necessary to apply without notice or on short notice, at least 14 days before the date fixed for the hearing.[22]

The usual rule is that, subject to any other express provision, the application must be served at least 14 days before the date fixed for the hearing.[23] However, the court does have power, in cases of urgency, to hear an application immediately with or without notice to the other parties.[24]

Service may be effected personally[25] or by post on the respondent (Part 6 of the CPR applies for these purposes)[26] or, where they have authority to accept service, on the respondent's solicitors.[27] Electronic service of documents is now permissible under the Rules, providing the respondent currently consents to service in that way and has provided an email address for service in that way.[28]

FIRST HEARING

At the first hearing, the registrar or district judge will give directions as to whether points of claim are needed and for the filing of evidence. He may also require the application to be served on other people. He may give directions as to whether witnesses are to attend for cross examination. The first hearing is likely to be heard in chambers and the advocates are not expected to robe.

KEY MATERIALS

Sections 423–425 of the Insolvency Act 1986

423 Transactions defrauding creditors

(1)   This section relates to transactions entered into at an undervalue; and a person enters into such a transaction with another person if—

(a)   he makes a gift to the other person or he otherwise enters into a transaction with the other on terms that provide for him to receive no consideration;

(b)   he enters into a transaction with the other in consideration of marriage or the formation of a civil partnership; or

(c)   he enters into a transaction with the other for a consideration the value of which, in money or money's worth, is significantly less than the

---

[22]   Rule 12.9(3) of the Insolvency (England and Wales) Rules 2016.

[23]   Rule 12.9(3) of the Insolvency (England and Wales) Rules 2016.

[24]   Rule 12.10(1) of the Insolvency (England and Wales) Rules 2016.

[25]   Rule 1.44 of the Insolvency (England and Wales) Rules 2016.

[26]   Schedule 4, paragraph 1(2) to the Insolvency (England and Wales) Rules 2016.

[27]   Rule 1.40 of the Insolvency (England and Wales) Rules 2016.

[28]   Rule 1.45 of the Insolvency (England and Wales) Rules 2016.

value, in money or money's worth, of the consideration provided by himself.

(2) Where a person has entered into such a transaction, the court may, if satisfied under the next subsection, make such order as it thinks fit for—

    (a)   restoring the position to what it would have been if the transaction had not been entered into, and

    (h)   protecting the interests of persons who are victims of the transaction.

(3) In the case of a person entering into such a transaction, an order shall only be made if the court is satisfied that it was entered into by him for the purpose—

    (a)   of putting assets beyond the reach of a person who is making, or may at some time make, a claim against him, or

    (b)   of otherwise prejudicing the interests of such a person in relation to the claim which he is making or may make.

(4) In this section 'the court' means the High Court or—

    (a)   if the person entering into the transaction is an individual, any other court which would have jurisdiction in relation to a bankruptcy petition relating to him;

    (b)   if that person is a body capable of being wound up under Part IV or V of this Act, any other court having jurisdiction to wind it up.

(5) In relation to a transaction at an undervalue, references here and below to a victim of the transaction are to a person who is, or is capable of being, prejudiced by it; and in the following two sections the person entering into the transaction is referred to as 'the debtor'.

424 Those who may apply for an order under s 423

(1) An application for an order under section 423 shall not be made in relation to a transaction except—

    (a)   in a case where the debtor has been adjudged bankrupt or is a body corporate which is being wound up or is in administration, by the official receiver, by the trustee of the bankrupt's estate or the liquidator or administrator of the body corporate or (with the leave of the court) by a victim of the transaction;

    (b)   in a case where a victim of the transaction is bound by a voluntary arrangement approved under Part I or Part VIII of this Act, by the supervisor of the voluntary arrangement or by any person who (whether or not so bound) is such a victim; or

    (c)   in any other case, by a victim of the transaction.

(2) An application made under any of the paragraphs of subsection (1) is to be treated as made on behalf of every victim of the transaction.

425 Provision which may be made by order under s 423

(1) Without prejudice to the generality of section 423, an order made under that section with respect to a transaction may (subject as follows)—

    (a) require any property transferred as part of the transaction to be vested in any person, either absolutely or for the benefit of all the persons on whose behalf the application for the order is treated as made;

    (b) require any property to be so vested if it represents, in any person's hands, the application either of the proceeds of sale of property so transferred or of money so transferred;

    (c) release or discharge (in whole or in part) any security given by the debtor;

    (d) require any person to pay to any other person in respect of benefits received from the debtor such sums as the court may direct;

    (e) provide for any surety or guarantor whose obligations to any person were released or discharged (in whole or in part) under the transaction to be under such new or revived obligations as the court thinks appropriate;

    (f) provide for security to be provided for the discharge of any obligation imposed by or arising under the order, for such an obligation to be charged on any property and for such security or charge to have the same priority as a security or charge released or discharged (in whole or in part) under the transaction.

(2) An order under section 423 may affect the property of, or impose any obligation on, any person whether or not he is the person with whom the debtor entered into the transaction; but such an order—

    (a) shall not prejudice any interest in property which was acquired from a person other than the debtor and was acquired in good faith, for value and without notice of the relevant circumstances, or prejudice any interest deriving from such an interest, and

    (b) shall not require a person who received a benefit from the transaction in good faith, for value and without notice of the relevant circumstances to pay any sum unless he was a party to the transaction.

(3) For the purposes of this section the relevant circumstances in relation to a transaction are the circumstances by virtue of which an order under section 423 may be made in respect of the transaction.

(4) In this section 'security' means any mortgage, charge, lien or other security.

22.1 ORDINARY APPLICATION FOR A DECLARATION THAT A PAYMENT IS A TRANSACTION DEFRAUDING CREDITORS PURSUANT TO SECTION 423 OF THE INSOLVENCY ACT 1986

Form IAA   **Insolvency Act Application Notice**

IN THE HIGH COURT OF JUSTICE
BUSINESS AND PROPERTY COURTS OF ENGLAND AND WALES
INSOLVENCY AND COMPANIES LIST (ChD)
IN BANKRUPTCY

NO: 666 OF 2020

IN THE MATTER OF IAN FLAKEY
AND IN THE MATTER OF THE INSOLVENCY ACT 1986

BETWEEN:-

GILES GRABBER
(Trustee in Bankruptcy of IAN FLAKEY)

Applicant

and

(1) IAN FLAKEY
(a bankrupt)
(2) MRS TABITHA FLAKEY

Respondents

Is this application within existing insolvency proceedings? YES/~~NO~~

I (~~We~~), GILES GRABBER of 1 Vulture Street, London intend to apply to the ~~Judge/District Judge~~/Registrar on:

Date: 1st April 2020

Time: 00:00 hours

Place: Royal Courts of Justice, 7 Rolls Buildings, Fetter Lane, London EC4A 1NL

This application having been issued at the RCJ, 7 Rolls Buildings, Fetter Lane, London, EC4A 1NL will be heard at the time and date pursuant to the endorsement underneath the Court Seal on the front page of this application.

FOR AN ORDER THAT:

1. A declaration that the payment of £250,000 by the Bankrupt to the 2nd Respondent on or around 1st January 2020 is void against the Applicant as trustee and that the same:

    a. constituted a transaction at an undervalue within the meaning of section 423 of the Insolvency Act 1986,

b.   was entered into for the purpose of either putting assets beyond the reach of the Bankrupt's creditors or otherwise prejudicing the interests of the Bankrupt's creditors in relation to the claims which they were making or might make.

2.   The 2nd Respondent do pay to the Applicant the sum of £250,000 and/or such other sum as this Honourable Court thinks fit to restore the position to what it would have been if the Bankrupt had not entered into the transaction and to protect the interests of the victims of the same.

3.   The 2nd Respondent do pay the Applicant's costs of and incidental to this application.

4.   Any costs of the application that are not payable by the 2nd Respondent or not recovered from her should be paid to the Applicant as such trustee out of the assets of the bankruptcy as an expense of the bankruptcy within rule 10.149(a) of the Insolvency (England and Wales) Rules 2016.

5.   Such further and other order and other relief as this Honourable Court thinks fit.

The applicant relies on the witness statement of Giles Grabber dated 1st April 2020.

THE NAMES AND ADDRESSES OF THE PERSON(S) UPON WHOM IT IS INTENDED TO SERVE THIS APPLICATION ARE:

Name: IAN FLAKEY

Address: 1 GERANIUM COTTAGE, LONDON

Name: TABITHA FLAKEY

Address: 1 GERANIUM COTTAGE, LONDON

~~OR~~

~~IT IS NOT INTENDED TO SERVE ANY PERSON WITH THIS APPLICATION~~

Dated:

Signed: SNARKEY & SNYDE

Solicitors for the applicant ~~or Applicant~~   *This is the address
Address: 1 LAW STREET, LONDON   which will be treated
Telephone: 0207 666 6666   by Court as the
Email: law@snarkeysnyde.com   Petitions address for
                                             service

If you do not attend, the court may make such order as it thinks just.

22.2 WITNESS STATEMENT TO SET ASIDE A FRAUDULENT TRANSACTION PURSUANT TO SECTION 423 OF THE INSOLVENCY ACT 1986

Applicant: G Grabber: 1st: GG1: [ ] 20[ ]

IN THE HIGH COURT OF JUSTICE
BUSINESS AND PROPERTY COURTS OF ENGLAND AND WALES
INSOLVENCY AND COMPANIES LIST (ChD)

NO: [ ] OF 20[ ]

IN THE MATTER OF IAN FLAKEY
IN BANKRUPTCY
AND IN THE MATTER OF THE INSOLVENCY ACT 1986

BETWEEN:-

GILES GRABBER
(as Trustee in Bankruptcy of IAN FLAKEY)

Applicant

and

(1) IAN FLAKEY
(2) TABITHA FLAKEY

Respondents

1ST WITNESS STATEMENT OF GILES GRABBER

I, GILES GRABBER of Grabbers LLP, of 1 Vulture Street, London, Trustee in Bankruptcy of Ian Flakey, STATE as follows:

1. I am the Applicant in this application. I am the Trustee in Bankruptcy of Ian Flakey.

2. I make this witness statement in support of my application for:

   a. A declaration that the payment of £250,000 by Ian Flakey ('the Bankrupt') to the 2nd Respondent on or around 1st January 2020 is void against the Applicant as his Trustee in Bankruptcy and that the same:

      i. constituted a transaction at an undervalue within the meaning of section 423 of the Insolvency Act 1986;
      ii. was entered into for the purpose of either putting assets beyond the reach of the Bankrupt's creditors or otherwise prejudicing the interests of the Bankrupt's creditors in relation to the claims which they were making or might make.

   b. An order that the 2nd Respondent do pay to the Applicant the sum of £250,000 and/or such other sum as this Honourable Court thinks fit to restore the position to what it would have been if the Bankrupt had not entered into the transaction and to protect the interests of the victims of the same.

   c. An order that the 2nd Respondent do pay the Applicant's costs of and incidental to this application.

    d.   Any costs of the application that are not payable by the 2nd Respondent or not recovered from her should be paid to the Applicant as such trustee out of the assets of the bankruptcy as an expense of the bankruptcy within rule 10.149(a) of the Insolvency (England and Wales) Rules 2016.

    e.   Such further and other order and other relief as this Honourable Court thinks fit.

3.   The matters set out in this witness statement are true and within my own knowledge except where otherwise indicated, in which case I have explained the source of my information or belief.

4.   There is now produced and shown to me a bundle consisting of true copies of the documents I will refer to in my witness statement marked 'GG1'.

5.   A bankruptcy order was made against the Bankrupt on 1st March 2020. I refer to page [ ] of 'GG1' which is a true copy of the bankruptcy order.

6.   I was appointed as the Trustee in Bankruptcy of the Bankrupt on 1st April 2020. I refer to page [ ] of 'GG1' which is a true copy of my certificate of appointment.

7.   The Bankrupt's statement of affairs show that he was insolvent as at 31st December 2020 with a deficiency in the sum of £2,000,000. I refer to page [ ] of 'GG1' which is a true copy of the trading accounts of the Bankrupt and his statement of affairs. Creditors' claims lodged in the bankruptcy amount to £3,500,000. I refer to page [ ] of 'GG1' which is a true copy of the proofs of debt evidencing the creditors' claims.

8.   Following my appointment, I began to investigate the affairs of the Bankrupt. The following matters became apparent.

9.   On 1st January 2020, there was a bank transfer in the sum of £250,000 from the Bankrupt to Mrs Flakey. I refer to page [ ] of 'GG1' which is a true copy of the bank statement of the Bankrupt showing the transfer of £250,000 from the Bankrupt to Mrs Flakey. This appears in the accounts as payment for a gobstopper bought from Mrs Flakey. I refer to page [ ] of 'GG1' which is a true copy of the accounts of the bankrupt trading as Flakey & Co showing the entry evidencing the purchase.

10.   The true value of the gobstopper (even when not partially sucked) is 5 pence. This is a mere fraction of the £250,000 paid to Mrs Flakey for this. I refer to page [ ] of 'GG1' which is a true copy of the price list of Toothy Sweets showing the retail price of their gobstoppers to be 5 pence each.

11.   The money paid represented the whole of the Bankrupt's available money in the bank. By making the payment, the monies left in the Bankrupt's account were dissipated. This meant that creditors in the bankruptcy can hope for a dividend of no more than 1 pence for each £1 owed to them.

12.   On 2nd January 2020, a bankruptcy petition was presented by HM Revenue & Customs for £1 million in unpaid VAT. I refer to page [ ] of 'GG1' which is a true copy of the petition. The petition had been preceded by a number of letters by HMRC warning that unless they were paid they intended to issue a petition on 2nd January 2020. I refer to page [ ] of 'GG1' which is a true copy of the letters.

13. In the light of the above, the payment to the Respondent was at a significant undervalue to the Bankrupt and, given the circumstances and timing of the purchase, it is to be inferred that the payment was made with the sole purpose of putting the Bankrupt's money beyond the reach of HMRC and its other creditors.

14. I therefore ask this Honourable Court to make the order in the terms sought.

STATEMENT OF TRUTH

I believe that the facts stated in this Witness Statement are true.

Signed [ ]
Full name [*GILES GRABBER*]
Dated [ ] 20[ ]

22.3   DECLARATION THAT A PAYMENT IS A TRANSACTION DEFRAUDING CREDITORS PURSUANT TO SECTION 423 OF THE INSOLVENCY ACT 1986

IN THE HIGH COURT OF JUSTICE
BUSINESS AND PROPERTY COURTS OF ENGLAND AND WALES
INSOLVENCY AND COMPANIES LIST (ChD)

NO: [ ] OF 20[ ]

IN THE MATTER OF IAN FLAKEY
IN BANKRUPTCY
AND IN THE MATTER OF THE INSOLVENCY ACT 1986

BEFORE MR REGISTRAR WISE
DATED:

BETWEEN:-

GILES GRABBER
(as Trustee in Bankruptcy of IAN FLAKEY)

Applicant

and

(1) IAN FLAKEY
(2) TABITHA FLAKEY

Respondents

_____

DRAFT MINUTE OF ORDER
_____

UPON THE APPLICATION of Giles Grabber of Grabbers LLP, Trustee in Bankruptcy of the above named IAN FLAKEY ('the Bankrupt')

UPON HEARING Counsel for the Applicant and the Respondents

AND UPON READING the evidence noted as being read

IT IS DECLARED THAT the payment of £250,000 by the Bankrupt to the 2nd Respondent on or around 1st January 2020 is void against the Applicant as Trustee in Bankruptcy of the Bankrupt and that the same constituted a transaction at an undervalue within the meaning of section 423 of the Insolvency Act 1986 AND was entered into for the purpose of either putting assets beyond the reach of the Bankrupt's creditors or otherwise prejudicing the interests of the Bankrupt's creditors in relation to the claims which they were making or might make

IT IS ORDERED THAT the 2nd Respondent do pay to the Applicant the sum of £250,000

IT IS ORDERED THAT the 2nd Respondent do pay to the Applicant the costs of and occasioned by the Applicant such costs to be assessed if not agreed

AND IT IS ORDERED THAT any costs of the application that are not payable by the 2nd Respondent or not recovered from her should be paid to the Applicant as such trustee out of the assets of the bankruptcy as an expense of the bankruptcy within rule 10.149(a) of the Insolvency (England and Wales) Rules 2016

Service of this order

The Court has provided a sealed copy of this order to the serving party:

SNARKEY & SNYDE
1 LAW STREET
LONDON

Chapter 23

APPEAL AGAINST THE ORDER OF A REGISTRAR

OBJECTIVE

An appeal from a district judge is to a registrar in bankruptcy or high court judge, depending on the court hearing the case.[1] An appeal from a registrar of the bankruptcy court or a district judge or circuit judge is to a High Court judge.[2] Permission needs to be sought from the judge being appealed or (if refused) from the appellate judge. The appeal is a true appeal limited to a review of the decision of the lower court[3] and will only be allowed if the decision was wrong or unjust because of a serious procedural irregularity or other irregularity in the proceedings.

APPEAL NOTICE

The appellant's notice must be filed within 21 days after the date of the decision under appeal.[4] The appeal should be filed in the High Court or the Chancery District Registry with jurisdiction for that area. There are no longer special forms for insolvency appeals, and so the ordinary notice of appeal, N161, should be used. Sufficient copies should be prepared to allow one for the appellant, two for the court and one for each respondent to the appeal.

The appellant should also file:

- a copy of the order under appeal;
- a time estimate;
- a chronology of events;
- an approved transcript or note of judgment; and
- a skeleton argument.

Where it is impractical to serve the skeleton argument at the same time as the appellant's notice, it should be filed within 14 days of filing the notice.

---

[1]   Rule 12.59 of, and Schedule 10 to, the Insolvency (England and Wales) Rules 2016. Paragraphs 24.14–24.15 of the Chancery Guide 2016 (as amended October 2017).

[2]   Paragraph 19.1 of the CPR Practice Direction – Insolvency Proceedings. Paragraphs 24.14–24.15 of the Chancery Guide 2016 (as amended October 2017).

[3]   *Vadher v Wesigard* [1997] BCC 219.

[4]   Rule 12.61 of the Insolvency (England and Wales) Rules 2016.

COURT FEE

A court fee of £480 is payable if permission to appeal is required. A fee of £1,090 is charged for the full appeal.

SERVICE

The appeal notice should be served on the respondents within 7 days of the notice of appeal being filed.

RESPONDENT'S NOTICE

A respondent to an appeal may file a respondent's notice. The respondent's notice must be filed at court no later than 14 days after the date on which the respondent is served with the appellant's notice. The respondent's notice will need to be served on the appellants within 7 days of the respondent's notice being filed.

APPEAL BUNDLE

The appellant needs to prepare, file and serve his appeal bundle not later than 7 days before the hearing of the appeal.

TIME LIMITS

The time limits are strict and can only be extended by order of the court. They cannot be extended by agreement with the other side.

KEY MATERIALS

Rules 12.58 and 12.61 of the Insolvency (England and Wales) Rules 2016

12.58. —CPR Part 52 (appeals) applies to appeals under this Chapter as varied by any applicable Practice Direction.

Procedure on appeal
12.61.—(1) An appeal against a decision at first instance may be brought only with the permission of the court which made the decision or of the court that has jurisdiction to hear the appeal.
(2) An appellant must file an appellant's notice within 21 days after the date of the decision of the court that the appellant wishes to appeal.

Schedule 10 to the Insolvency (England and Wales) Rules 2016

Schedule 10
Rule 12.59
Destination of appeals from decisions of District Judges in corporate insolvency matters

County court hearing centre	Destination of Appeal
Aberystwyth	Cardiff or Caernarfon District Registry
Banbury	Birmingham District Registry
Barnsley	Leeds District Registry
Barnstaple	Bristol District Registry
Barrow-in-Furness	Liverpool District Registry or Manchester District Registry
Bath	Bristol District Registry
Bedford	Birmingham District Registry
Birkenhead	Liverpool District Registry or Manchester District Registry
Birmingham	Birmingham District Registry
Blackburn	Liverpool District Registry or Manchester District Registry
Blackpool	Liverpool District Registry or Manchester District Registry
Blackwood	Cardiff District Registry
Bolton	Liverpool District Registry or Manchester District Registry
Boston	Birmingham District Registry
Bournemouth and Poole	Registrar in Bankruptcy
Bradford	Leeds District Registry
Brighton	Registrar in Bankruptcy
Bristol	Bristol District Registry
Burnley	Liverpool District Registry or Manchester District Registry
Bury	Liverpool District Registry or Manchester District Registry
Bury St. Edmunds	Registrar in Bankruptcy

County court hearing centre	Destination of Appeal
Caernarfon	Cardiff District Registry
Cambridge	Registrar in Bankruptcy
Canterbury	Registrar in Bankruptcy
Cardiff	Cardiff District Registry
Carlisle	Liverpool District Registry or Manchester District Registry
Caernarfon	Cardiff District Registry or Caernarfon District Registry
County Court at Central London	Registrar in Bankruptcy
Chelmsford	Registrar in Bankruptcy
Chester	Liverpool District Registry or Manchester District Registry
Chesterfield	Leeds District Registry
Colchester	Registrar in Bankruptcy
Coventry	Birmingham District Registry
Crewe	Liverpool District Registry or Manchester District Registry
Croydon	Registrar in Bankruptcy
Darlington	Newcastle District Registry
Derby	Birmingham District Registry
Doncaster	Leeds District Registry
Dudley	Birmingham District Registry
Durham	Leeds District Registry or Newcastle District Registry
Eastbourne	Registrar in Bankruptcy
Exeter	Bristol District Registry
Gloucester and Cheltenham	Bristol District Registry
Great Grimsby	Leeds District Registry
Guildford	Registrar in Bankruptcy
Halifax	Leeds District Registry
Harrogate	Leeds District Registry
Hastings	Registrar in Bankruptcy

County court hearing centre	Destination of Appeal
Haverfordwest	Cardiff District Registry
Hereford	Bristol District Registry
Hertford	Registrar in Bankruptcy
Huddersfield	Leeds District Registry
Ipswich	Registrar in Bankruptcy
Kendal	Liverpool District Registry or Manchester District Registry
Kingston-upon-Hull	Leeds District Registry
Kingston-upon-Thames	Registrar in Bankruptcy
Lancaster	Liverpool District Registry or Manchester District Registry
Leeds	Leeds District Registry
Leicester	Birmingham District Registry
Lincoln	Leeds District Registry or Birmingham District Registry
Liverpool	Liverpool District Registry or Manchester District Registry
Llangefni	Cardiff District Registry or Caernarfon District Registry
Luton	Registrar in Bankruptcy
Maidstone	Registrar in Bankruptcy
Manchester	Manchester District Registry
Merthyr Tydfil	Cardiff District Registry
Middlesbrough	Newcastle District Registry
Milton Keynes	Birmingham District Registry
Newcastle upon Tyne	Newcastle District Registry
Newport (Gwent)	Cardiff District Registry
Newport (Isle of Wight)	Registrar in Bankruptcy
Northampton	Birmingham District Registry
Norwich	Registrar in Bankruptcy
Nottingham	Birmingham District Registry
Oldham	Liverpool District Registry or Manchester District Registry

County court hearing centre	Destination of Appeal
Oxford	Registrar in Bankruptcy
Peterborough	Registrar in Bankruptcy
Plymouth	Bristol District Registry
Pontypridd	Cardiff District Registry
Portsmouth	Registrar in Bankruptcy
Port Talbot	Cardiff District Registry
Prestatyn	Cardiff District Registry or Caernarfon District Registry
Preston	Liverpool District Registry or Manchester District Registry
Reading	Registrar in Bankruptcy
Rhyl	Cardiff District Registry or Caernarfon District Registry
Romford	Registrar in Bankruptcy
Salisbury	Registrar in Bankruptcy
Scarborough	Leeds District Registry
Scunthorpe	Leeds District Registry
Sheffield	Leeds District Registry
Slough	Registrar in Bankruptcy
Southampton	Registrar in Bankruptcy
Southend-on-Sea	Registrar in Bankruptcy
Stafford	Birmingham District Registry
St Albans	Registrar in Bankruptcy
Stockport	Liverpool District Registry or Manchester District Registry
Stoke-on-Trent	Manchester District Registry
Sunderland	Newcastle District Registry
Swansea	Cardiff District Registry
Swindon	Bristol District Registry
Taunton	Bristol District Registry
Telford	Birmingham District Registry
Torquay & Newton Abbot	Bristol District Registry
Truro	Bristol District Registry

County court hearing centre	Destination of Appeal
Tunbridge Wells	Registrar in Bankruptcy
Wakefield	Leeds District Registry
Walsall	Birmingham District Registry
Warwick	Birmingham District Registry
Welshpool & Newton	Cardiff District Registry
West Cumbria	Liverpool District Registry or Manchester District Registry
Wigan	Liverpool District Registry or Manchester District Registry
Winchester	Registrar in Bankruptcy
Wolverhampton	Birmingham District Registry
Worcester	Birmingham District Registry
Wrexham	Cardiff District Registry or Caernarfon District Registry
Yeovil	Bristol District Registry
York	Leeds District Registry

Chapter 24

TOOLKIT

ISSUING PROCEEDINGS IN THE ROYAL COURTS OF JUSTICE

Proceedings under the Insolvency Act 1986 are instituted by either a petition or application. The new Form IAA application replaces the old ordinary and originating applications.

The Bankruptcy Registry has a separate administrative procedure. Proceedings are issued in the Bankruptcy Registry Office and they are dealt with by the Registrars. Proceedings in bankruptcy under a particular statute should be entitled accordingly, thus: 'In the matter of [name] and In Bankruptcy' and 'In the matter of the [name of statute as appropriate]'.

COURTS ELECTRONIC FILING – CE-FILE

From 25 April 2017, it has not been possible to issue applications in paper form at the Rolls Buildings. Any person wishing to file documents, start a claim, conduct a public search or order office copies in the Bankruptcy Court in the Rolls Buildings jurisdictions needs to do so electronically on the CE-File website at https://efile.cefile-app.com.

To obtain a username and password to get access to the CE-File website, click on the registration link 'Register as an E-Filer' on the home page.

The Court 'Bankruptcy and Companies' should be selected. Documents can be uploaded as Word or PDF files up to a maximum of 50MB (larger documents should be split using the 'add' button, although it would be wise to alert the court of this by using the 'comments' box).

Fees can be paid by credit card or Payment on Account (PBA). Information about court fees can be found at http://hmctsformfinder.justice.gov.uk/HMCTS/GetLeaflet.do?court_leaflets_id=264.

When an urgent application is filed, the filing party will need to upload a letter with the claim form outlining the reason(s) why a case must be dealt with urgently. The filing party must also place a comment in the 'comments' box stating that the filing is urgent.

Information on Payment on Account (PBA) can be found in the leaflet *Fee Account – the Easy Way to Pay Fees*, at http://hmctsformfinder.justice. gov.uk/HMCTS/GetLeaflet.do?court_leaflets_id=4780. The application form to open your own PBA may be downloaded from http://hmctsformfinder. justice.gov.uk/HMCTS/GetLeaflet.do?court_leaflets_id=4780.

The contact number for queries regarding online filing is 0207 947 6725.

COUNTY COURT OR HIGH COURT?

Petitions can be presented in the Bankruptcy Registry; the Royal Courts of Justice, 7 Rolls Buildings, Fetter Lane, London EC4A 1NL; a Chancery District Registry; or at a county court.

Where the proceedings are allocated to the London Insolvency District,[1] the creditor must present the petition to the High Court where the petition debt is £50,000 or more and the Central London County Court if the petition debt is under £50,000.[2] Confusingly, the Central London County Court for bankruptcy is situated at the Royal Courts of Justice, Strand, London on the 1st Floor of the Thomas More Building where the High Court Bankruptcy Registry used to be. Where the debtor is resident in England and Wales and the proceedings are not allocated to the London Insolvency District, the creditor must present the petition to the debtor's own county court.

The debtor's own county court is:

- where the debtor has carried on business in England and Wales within the 6 months immediately preceding the presentation of the petition, the county court for the insolvency district where for the longest period during those 6 months:

  - the debtor carried on business, or
  - the principal place of business was located, if business was carried on in more than one insolvency district; or

- where the debtor has not carried on business in England and Wales within the 6 months immediately preceding the presentation of the petition, the county court for the insolvency district where the debtor resided for the longest period during those 6 months.

If the debtor is not resident in England and Wales but was resident or carried on business in England and Wales within the 6 months immediately preceding the presentation of the petition and the proceedings are not allocated to the London

---

[1]   Rule 12.5 of the Insolvency (England and Wales) Rules 2016.
[2]   Rule 10.11 of the Insolvency (England and Wales) Rules 2016.

Insolvency District, the petition may be presented either to the debtor's own county court or to the High Court.

The county court may also transfer proceedings to the High Court generally just as the High Court similarly has power to transfer proceedings to the county court.[3]

REGISTRAR OR JUDGE?

Most applications should be commenced before a registrar or district judge who may, if he sees fit, remit the matter to a High Court judge. However, the following applications must be made direct to the judge and, unless otherwise ordered, shall be heard in public:[4]

- applications to commit any person to prison for contempt;
- applications for urgent interim relief (e.g. applications for validation orders before a bankruptcy order is made);
- appeals from a decision made by a district judge in a county court or by a Registrar of the High Court.

URGENT APPLICATIONS

A registrar is available at 2 pm each Tuesday and Thursday during term to hear urgent applications or time-critical applications. Parties seeking to list an urgent bankruptcy application should do so with a certificate signed by the advocate attending explaining the urgency of the application (see 24.2 for a precedent).

EVIDENCE

Evidence in insolvency proceedings may be given by witness statement.[5]

The Official Receiver or a deputy Official Receiver may file his evidence by way of a report.[6] There is a similar exception to allow an administrator, liquidator, trustee in bankruptcy, provisional liquidator or interim receiver, a special manager or an insolvency practitioner appointed under section 273(2) of the Insolvency Act 1986 to also file their evidence by way of a report. However, this right is limited to applications which do not involve other parties and, even then, the court may direct otherwise.[7]

---

[3] Rule 12.30 of the Insolvency (England and Wales) Rules 2016.
[4] Practice Note – The Hearing of Insolvency Proceedings, 23 May 2005 [2005] BCC 456.
[5] Rule 12.28(1) of the Insolvency (England and Wales) Rules 2016.
[6] Rule 12.29(2) of the Insolvency (England and Wales) Rules 2016.
[7] Rule 12.28(1)(b) of the Insolvency (England and Wales) Rules 2016.

Where a party wishes to cross examine a witness (e.g. if there is a substantial dispute of fact on his written evidence) he should seek a direction from the court that the witness should attend for cross examination at the hearing and an order that, absent which, his evidence would not be received other than with the permission of the court.[8]

BUNDLES

The applicant will normally be expected to prepare a bundle of documents for use in court whenever the documents involved are more than 30 pages long.[9] Failure to properly prepare the bundle may be punished by a special costs order.[10] There is a strict policy of 'no bundle, no hearing'.[11]

The bundle should be arranged in the following order:

- the application notice or statements of case in 'chapter' format (any back sheets and superseded documents (e.g. particulars of claim overtaken by amendments, requests for further information recited in the answers given) should be omitted);
- any court orders;
- the witness statements, affidavits and expert reports for the applicant (the witness statements should have written on them the page for that document in the bundles in manuscript; exhibits should appear separately; back sheets should be omitted);
- the witness statements, affidavits and expert reports for the respondent;
- the documents (these should be arranged in chronological order);
- the correspondence (the inter-solicitor correspondence should be included only if and to the extent it is strictly necessary and should be placed in a separate bundle).

Where the volume of documents is large, a separate core bundle should be prepared for the trial, containing only those documents likely to be referred to most frequently.

It is of paramount importance that the preparation of bundles is commenced in good time. A common mistake by solicitors is to fail to allow sufficient time to begin the preparation of the bundles: to enable the bundles to be agreed with the other parties; for the cross-referencing to the bundles in respect of any evidence referred to in skeleton arguments (the bundle needs to be delivered to counsel in sufficient time for this work to be done, which needs to be taken into account for the time limits for delivery of skeleton arguments); and for the bundles to be delivered to the court at the required time. The required time means:

---

[8]   Rule 12.28(3)–(4) of the Insolvency (England and Wales) Rules 2016.

[9]   Paragraph 24.14 of the Chancery Guide 2016 (as amended October 2017).

[10]   Paragraph 21.84 of the Chancery Guide 2016 (as amended October 2017).

[11]   Paragraph 24.14 of the Chancery Guide 2016 (as amended October 2017).

- before a trial or application by order not less than 3 clear days and not more than 7 days where listed before a judge and not less than 2 clear days and not more than 7 days where listed before a registrar;[12]
- for applications (other than applications by order) by 10 am on the morning preceding the day of the hearing.[13]

The bundle should be clearly marked with the name and number of the case and the words, 'For hearing on [date] before [Registrar/Judge]'.

The bundle should be paginated in bold at the bottom of the document (tabs are also useful):

- the documents wherever possible should be in A4 format;
- no more than one copy of any one document should be included;[14]
- documents should be arranged in date order starting with the earliest document;
- documents in manuscript, or not easily legible, should be transcribed; the transcription should be marked and placed adjacent to the document transcribed;
- documents in a foreign language should be translated (the translation should be marked and placed adjacent to the document translated, the translation should be agreed or, if it cannot be agreed, each party's proposed translation should be included);
- no bundle should contain more than 300 pages;
- binders and files must be strong enough to withstand heavy use;
- all staples, heavy metal clips, etc. should be removed.

The bundle should be accompanied by the following documents which should be signed by the parties' advocates:[15]

- an agreed time estimate;
- an agreed reading list;
- an agreed time estimate in respect of that reading list.

In the Royal Courts of Justice, bundles should be delivered to the Bankruptcy Court Issue Section.

Failure to lodge bundles on time may result in the matter not being heard on the date in question, the costs of preparation being disallowed or an adverse costs order.[16] A log is maintained in the Royal Courts of Justice of late bundles.

---

[12] Paragraph 21.70 of the Chancery Guide 2016 (as amended October 2017).

[13] Paragraph 21.77 of the Chancery Guide 2016 (as amended October 2017).

[14] If the same document is included in the chronological bundles and is also an exhibit to an affidavit or witness statement, it should be included in the chronological bundle and where it would otherwise appear as an exhibit a sheet should instead be inserted. This sheet should state the page and bundle number in the chronological bundles where the document can be found.

[15] Paragraphs 21.25 and 21.82 of the Chancery Guide 2016 (as amended October 2017).

[16] Paragraph 21.84 of the Chancery Guide 2016 (as amended October 2017).

TIME ESTIMATES

Realistic estimates of the length of time a hearing is expected to take must be given. In estimating the length of a hearing, sufficient time must be allowed for reading the documents and for judgment, together with the summary assessment of costs and any application for permission to appeal.[17] The parties must inform the court and each other immediately of any material change in a time estimate.[18] Failure to give an accurate time estimate may result in the hearing being adjourned and the party at fault ordered to pay the costs thrown away.[19]

SKELETON ARGUMENTS

A skeleton should include:

- a *dramatis personae*;
- time estimates for both the hearing and reading time;
- a reading list of documents the judge should read before the hearing;
- the facts of the case;
- a chronology (which should be expressed in neutral terms and agreed if possible);
- a list of issues.

The skeleton should briefly set out on double spaced A4 in numbered paragraphs:

- the nature of the case generally and the background facts;
- the propositions of law relied on with references to the relevant authorities;
- the submissions of fact to be made with reference to the evidence;
- the name (and contact details) of the advocate who prepared it.

Skeleton arguments should be delivered:

- on trials and applications by order not less than 2 clear days before the date or first date on which the application or trial is due to come on for hearing[20] (that is to say the first day it is to come on the warned list);
- on judge's applications without notice with the papers which the judge is asked to read on the application;[21]
- on all other applications, including interim applications, as soon as possible and not later than 10 am on the day preceding the hearing.[22]

---

[17] Paragraph 21.21 of the Chancery Guide 2016 (as amended October 2017).
[18] Paragraph 21.22 of the Chancery Guide 2016 (as amended October 2017).
[19] Paragraph 21.26 of the Chancery Guide 2016 (as amended October 2017).
[20] Paragraph 21.77 of the Chancery Guide 2016 (as amended October 2017).
[21] Paragraph 21.77 of the Chancery Guide 2016 (as amended October 2017).
[22] Paragraph 21.77 of the Chancery Guide 2016 (as amended October 2017).

Advocates should attempt to agree and provide a single joint bundle of authorities and, even where separate bundles are prepared, care should be taken to avoid duplication of authorities.[23]

Excessive citation of legal authority should be avoided, and care should be taken when citing authority to comply with Practice Direction (Judgments: Neutral Citations).[24]

USEFUL EMAIL ADDRESSES

The Royal Courts of Justice

For lodging skeleton arguments, chronologies, reading lists, list of issues, lists of authorities (but not the authorities themselves):

Judge: rcjchancery.judgeslisting@hmcourts-service.gsi.gov.uk
             chancery.applications.skeletons@hmcts.gsi.gov.uk
             chancery.general.skeletons@hmcts.gsi.gov.uk
Registrar: rcjcompanies.orders@hmcourts-service.gsi.gov.uk

For lodging the agreed terms of an Order which is ready to be sealed:

Judge: rcjchancery.ordersandaccounts@hmcourts-service.gsi.gov.uk
Registrar: rcjcompanies.orders@hmcourts-service.gsi.gov.uk

The County Court at Central London

For lodging skeleton arguments, chronologies, reading lists, list of issues, lists of authorities (but not the authorities themselves) and orders:

RCJBankCLCCDJhearings@hmcts.gsi.gov.uk

COURT DRESS

Advocates are expected to robe for appeals and contempt hearings (or any hearing where the liberty of the subject is in issue). Otherwise, advocates should wear a dark business suit for court hearings.

---

[23] Paragraph 21.86 of the Chancery Guide 2016 (as amended October 2017).

[24] Practice Direction (Judgments: Neutral Citations) [2002] 1 WLR 346. Paragraph 21.87 of the Chancery Guide 2016 (as amended October 2017).

COURT FEES

General fees: High Court and county court	Fee
General application (on notice)	£155
Bankruptcy/Insolvency	
Petition for bankruptcy (presented by debtor)	£180
Petition for bankruptcy (presented by creditor/other person)	£280
Any other petition	£280
Request for a certificate of discharge from bankruptcy	£70
Copy of a certificate of discharge from bankruptcy	£10
Insolvency – other application	£280
Filing insolvency documents	£50
Application within proceedings (by consent/without notice)	£50
Application within proceedings (with notice)	£155
Search of bankruptcy and company records (county court)	£45
Court of Appeal fees	
Application – permission to appeal/extension of time	£480
General application (on notice)	£155
General application (by consent/without notice)	£50
Permission to appeal is not required or has been granted	£1,090
Appellant/respondent filing an appeal questionnaire	£1,090

KEY MATERIALS

Rules 1.5, 1.6, 1.35, 10.11 and 12.5 of the Insolvency (England and Wales) Rules 2016

Authentication

1.5.—(1) A document in electronic form is sufficiently authenticated—

    (a)   if the identity of the sender is confirmed in a manner specified by the recipient; or

    (b)   where the recipient has not so specified, if the communication contains or is accompanied by a statement of the identity of the sender and the recipient has no reason to doubt the truth of that statement.

(2) A document in hard-copy form is sufficiently authenticated if it is signed.

(3) If a document is authenticated by the signature of an individual on behalf of—

   (a) a body of persons, the document must also state the position of that individual in relation to the body;

   (b) a body corporate of which the individual is the sole member, the document must also state that fact.

Information required to identify persons and proceedings etc.

1.6.—(1) Where the Act or these Rules require a document to identify, or to contain identification details in respect of, a person or proceedings, or to provide contact details for an office-holder, the information set out below must be given.

(2) Where a requirement relates to a proposed office-holder, the information set out below in respect of an office-holder must be given with any necessary adaptations.

Bankrupt	(a) full name; and (b) residential address (subject to any order for limited disclosure made under Part 20).

Company where it is the subject of the proceedings	In the case of a registered company—
	
	(c) the registered name;
	
	(d) for a company incorporated in England and Wales under the Companies Act or a previous Companies Act, its registered number;
	
	(e) for a company incorporated outside the United Kingdom—
	
	   (i) the country or territory in which it is incorporated,
	
	   (ii) the number, if any, under which it is registered, and
	
	   (iii) the number, if any, under which it is registered as an overseas company under Part 34 of the Companies Act.
	
	In the case of an unregistered company—
	
	(f) its name; and
	
	(g) the postal address of any principal place of business.

Company other than one which is the subject of the proceedings	In the case of a registered company— (h) the registered name; (i) for a company incorporated in any part of the United Kingdom under the Companies

		Act or a previous Companies Act, its registered number;
	(j)	for a company incorporated outside the United Kingdom—
		(i) the country or territory in which it is incorporated,
		(ii) the number, if any, under which it is registered; and
	(k)	the number, if any, under which it is registered as an overseas company under Part 34 of the Companies Act;
	(l)	In the case of an unregistered company—
		(i) its name, and
		(ii) the postal address of any principal place of business.
Debtor	(m)	full name; and
	(n)	residential address (subject to any order for limited disclosure made under Part 20).
Office-holder	(o)	the name of the office-holder; and
	(p)	the nature of the appointment held by the office-holder.
Contact details for an office-holder	(q)	a postal address for the office-holder; and
	(r)	either an email address, or a telephone number, through which the office-holder may be contacted.
Proceedings	(s)	for proceedings relating to a company, the information identifying the company;
	(t)	for proceedings relating to an individual, the full name of the bankrupt or debtor;
	(u)	the full name of the court or hearing centre in which the proceedings are, or are to be, conducted or where documents relating to the proceedings have been or will be filed; and, if applicable,
	(v)	any number assigned to those proceedings by the court, the hearing centre or the adjudicator.

Standard contents and authentication of applications to the court under Parts 1 to 11 of the Act

1.35.—(1) This rule applies to applications to court under Parts 1 to 11 of the Act (other than an application for an administration order, a winding up petition or a bankruptcy petition).

(2) The application must state—

    (a) that the application is made under the Act or these Rules (as applicable);

    (b) the section of the Act or paragraph of a Schedule to the Act or the number of the rule under which it is made;

    (c) the names of the parties;

    (d) the name of the bankrupt, debtor or company which is the subject of the insolvency proceedings to which the application relates;

    (e) the court (and where applicable, the division or district registry of that court) or hearing centre in which the application is made;

    (f) where the court has previously allocated a number to the insolvency proceedings within which the application is made, that number;

    (g) the nature of the remedy or order applied for or the directions sought from the court;

    (h) the names and addresses of the persons on whom it is intended to serve the application or that no person is intended to be served;

    (i) where the Act or Rules require that notice of the application is to be delivered to specified persons, the names and addresses of all those persons (so far as known to the applicant); and

    (j) the applicant's address for service.

(3) The application must be authenticated by or on behalf of the applicant or the applicant's solicitor.

Court in which petition is to be presented

10.11.—(1) Where the proceedings are allocated to the London Insolvency District under rule 12.5(a)(i) to (iv) or (b), the creditor must present the petition to—

    (a) the High Court where the debt is £50,000 or more; or

    (b) the County Court at Central London where the debt is less than £50,000.

(2) Where the proceedings are allocated to the London Insolvency District under rule 12.5(a)(v), (c) or (d), the creditor must present the petition to the High Court.

(3) Where the debtor is resident in England and Wales and the proceedings are not allocated to the London Insolvency District, the creditor must present the petition to the debtor's own hearing centre.

(4) The debtor's own hearing centre is—

    (a) where the debtor has carried on business in England and Wales within the six months immediately preceding the presentation of the petition, the hearing centre for the insolvency district where for the longest period during those six months—

        (i) the debtor carried on business, or

        (ii) the principal place of business was located, if business was carried on in more than one insolvency district; or

(b)   where the debtor has not carried on business in England and Wales within the six months immediately preceding the presentation of the petition, the hearing centre for the insolvency district where the debtor resided for the longest period during those six months.

(5)   If the debtor is not resident in England and Wales but was resident or carried on business in England and Wales within the six months immediately preceding the presentation of the petition and the proceedings are not allocated to the London Insolvency District, the petition may be presented either to the debtor's own hearing centre or to the High Court.

(6)   Unless paragraph (2) applies, where to the petitioner's knowledge there is in force for the debtor an IVA under Part 8 of the Act, the petition must be presented to the court or hearing centre—

(a)   to which the nominee's report under section 256 was submitted;
(b)   to which an application has been made, where a nominee has made a report under section 256A(3); or
(c)   as determined under paragraphs (1) to (5) in any other case.

(7)   The petition must contain sufficient information to establish that it is presented in the appropriate court and, where the court is the County Court, the appropriate hearing centre.

Allocation of proceedings to the London Insolvency District
12.5.   The following proceedings are allocated to the London Insolvency District—

(a)   bankruptcy petitions or applications in relation to a debt relief order under section 251M (powers of court in relation to debt relief orders) or 251N (inquiry into debtor's dealings and property) where—

(i)   the debtor is resident in England and Wales and within the six months immediately preceding the presentation of the petition or the making of the application the debtor carried on business within the area of the London Insolvency District—

(aa)   for the greater part of those six months, or
(bb)   for a longer period in those six months than in any other insolvency district,

(ii)   the debtor is resident in England and Wales and within the six months immediately preceding the presentation of the petition or the making of the application the debtor did not carry on business in England and Wales but resided within the area of the London Insolvency District for—

        (aa)   the greater part of those six months, or

        (bb)   a longer period in those six months than in any other insolvency district,

    (iii) the debtor is not resident in England and Wales but within the six months immediately preceding the presentation of the petition or the making of the application carried on business within the area of the London Insolvency District,

    (iv) the debtor is not resident in England and Wales and within the 6 months immediately preceding the presentation of the petition or the making of the application did not carry on business in England and Wales but resided within the area of the London Insolvency District, or

    (v) the debtor is not resident in England and Wales and within the 6 months immediately preceding the presentation of the petition or the making of the application the debtor neither carried on business nor resided in England and Wales;

(b)   creditors' bankruptcy petitions presented by a Minister of the Crown or a Government Department, where either—

    (i)   in any statutory demand on which the petition is based the creditor has indicated the intention to present a bankruptcy petition to a court exercising jurisdiction in relation to the London Insolvency District, or

    (ii) the petition is presented under section 267(2)(c) on the grounds specified in section 268(1)(b);

(c)   bankruptcy petitions—

    (i)   where the petitioner is unable to ascertain the place where the debtor resides or, if the debtor carries on business in England and Wales, both where the debtor resides and where the debtor carries on business, or

    (ii) where the debtor is a member of a partnership and—

        (aa)   the partnership is being wound up by the High Court sitting in London; or

        (bb)   a petition for the winding up of the partnership has been presented to the High Court sitting in London and at the time of the presentation of the bankruptcy petition, the petition for the winding up of the partnership has not been fully disposed of; and

(d)   bankruptcy petitions based on criminal bankruptcy orders under section 264(1)(d).

Schedule 4 to the Insolvency (England and Wales) Rules 2016

Service of documents

1.—(1) This Schedule sets out the requirements for service where a document is required to be served.

(2) Service is to be carried out in accordance with Part 6 of the CPR as that Part applies to either a 'claim form' or a 'document other than the claim form' except where this Schedule provides otherwise or the court otherwise approves or directs.

(3) However, where a document is required or permitted to be served at a company's registered office service may be effected at a previous registered office in accordance with section 87(2) of the Companies Act.

(4) In the case of an overseas company service may be effected in any manner provided for by section 1139(2) of the Companies Act.

(5) If for any reason it is impracticable to effect service as provided for in paragraphs (2) to (4) then service may be effected in such other manner as the court may approve or direct.

(6) The third column of the table below sets out which documents are treated as 'claim forms' for the purposes of applying Part 6 of the CPR and which are 'documents other than the claim form' (called in this Schedule 'other documents').

(7) The fourth column of the table sets out modifications to Part 6 of the CPR which apply to the service of documents listed in the first and second columns.

(8) Part 6 of the CPR applies to the service of documents outside the jurisdiction with such modifications as the court may approve or direct.

...

Table of Requirements for Service

Rule (or section)	Document	Whether treated as claim form or other document	Modifications to Part 6 of the CPR which apply unless the court directs otherwise
...			
10.2	Statutory demand (bankruptcy)	Other document	Service in accordance with rule 10.2.
10.14	Bankruptcy Petition (creditor's)	Claim form	Personal service. The petitioner must serve the petition.
10.29	Court order – change of carriage of petition	Other document	

10.50	Court order for additional deposit to be paid – interim receiver	Other document	
10.99	Court order for public examination served on bankrupt	Other document	
10.119	Court order for disclosure by HMRC	Other document	
10.126	Notice to recipient of after acquired property	Other document	
10.166	Court order for post direction	Other document	
11.3	Application for debt relief restrictions order (DRRO) or bankruptcy restrictions order (BRO)	Claim form	The applicant must serve the application.
11.4	Service of evidence for DRRO or BRO	Other document	
12.9	Applications to court generally (where service required)	Claim form	The applicant must serve the application.
12.19	Court order for private examination	Other document	Personal service. The applicant must serve the order.
12.28(2)	Witness statement of evidence	Other document	
12.37(7)	Application for block transfer order	Claim form	The applicant must serve the application.
12.42	Notice requiring person to assess costs by detailed assessment	Other document	
12.48	Application for costs	Claim form	The applicant must serve the application.
19.4 (& sections 179 and 317)	Notice of disclaimer (leasehold property)		
19.5 (& section 318)	Notice of disclaimer (dwelling house)		
21.2	Application for conversion into winding up/bankruptcy under EU regulation	Claim form	The applicant must serve the application.
Paragraph 5(1) of this Schedule	Order staying proceedings		The applicant must serve the order.

Schedule 5 to the Insolvency (England and Wales) Rules 2016

Calculation of time periods

[Note: section 376 of the Act contains a power for the court to extend the time for doing anything required by the Act or these Rules under the Second Group of Parts (Insolvency of Individuals; bankruptcy).]

1. The rules in CPR 2.8 with the exception of paragraph (4) apply for the calculation of periods expressed in days in the Act and these Rules.
2.— (1) This paragraph applies for the calculation of periods expressed in months.

   (2) The beginning and the end of a period expressed in months is to be determined as follows—

   (a) if the beginning of the period is specified—

   (i) the month in which the period ends is the specified number of months after the month in which it begins, and
   (ii) the date in the month on which the period ends is—

   (aa) the date corresponding to the date in the month on which it begins, or
   (bb) if there is no such date in the month in which it ends, the last day of that month;

   (b) if the end of the period is specified—

   (i) the month in which the period begins is the specified number of months before the month in which it ends, and
   (ii) the date in the month on which the period begins is—

   (aa) the date corresponding to the date in the month on which it ends, or
   (bb) if there is no such date in the month in which it begins, the last day of that month.

3. The provisions of CPR rule 3.1(2)(a) (the court's general powers of management) apply so as to enable the court to extend or shorten the time for compliance with anything required or authorised to be done by these Rules.
4. Paragraph 3 is subject to any time limits expressly stated in the Act and to any specific powers in the Act or these Rules to extend or shorten the time for compliance.

Schedule 6 to the Insolvency (England and Wales) Rules 2016

Insolvency jurisdiction of county court hearing centres

[Note: where the entry 'London Insolvency District' appears in this table, jurisdiction under Parts 1 to 7 of the Act is conferred on the High Court as a result of article 6B of the High Court and County Courts Jurisdiction Order 1991 (S.I. 1991/724) which was inserted by the High Court and County Courts Jurisdiction (Amendment) Order 2014 (S.I. 2014/821).]

Name of county court hearing centre	Parts of the Insolvency Act under which proceedings may be commenced at a county court hearing centre or the alternative court or county court hearing centre where proceedings may be commenced	Nearest full time court or hearing centre
Aberystwyth	Parts 1 to 11	Cardiff
Aldershot & Farnham	Guildford	
Banbury	Parts 1 to 11	Luton, Gloucester or Reading
Barnet	London Insolvency District – High Court for Parts 1 to 7 (see head note); County Court at Central London for Parts 7A to 11	
Barnsley	Parts 1 to 11	Sheffield
Barnstaple	Parts 1 to 11	Exeter
Barrow-in-Furness	Parts 1 to 11	Blackpool or Preston
Basildon	Southend-on-Sea	
Basingstoke	Reading	
Bath	Parts 1 to 11	Bristol
Bedford	Parts 1 to 11	Luton
Birkenhead	Parts 1 to 11	
Birmingham	Parts 1 to 11	
Blackburn	Parts 1 to 11	Preston
Blackpool	Parts 1 to 11	
Blackwood	Parts 1 to 11	Cardiff
Bodmin	Truro	
Bolton	Parts 1 to 11	

Boston	Parts 1 to 11	Nottingham
Bournemouth and Poole	Parts 1 to 11	
Bow	London Insolvency District – High Court for Parts 1 to 7 (see head note); County Court at Central London for Parts 7A to 11	
Bradford	Parts 1 to 11	
Brentford	London Insolvency District – High Court for Parts 1 to 7 (see head note); County Court at Central London for Parts 7A to 11	
Brighton	Parts 1 to 11	
Bristol	Parts 1 to 11	
Bromley	Croydon	
Burnley	Parts 1 to 11	Bolton or Preston
Bury	Parts 1 to 11	Bolton
Bury St. Edmunds	Parts 1 to 11	Cambridge
Caernarfon	Parts 1 to 11	
Cambridge	Parts 1 to 11	
Canterbury	Parts 1 to 11	Croydon or the High Court (London)
Cardiff	Parts 1 to 11	
Carlisle	Parts 1 to 11	Preston or Blackpool
Carmarthen	Parts 1 to 11	Cardiff
County Court at Central London	London Insolvency District – High Court for Parts 1 to 7 (see head note); County Court at Central London for Parts 7A to 11	
Chelmsford	Parts 1 to 11	Southend or the High Court (London)
Chester	Parts 1 to 11	
Chesterfield	Parts 1 to 11	Sheffield
Chichester	Brighton	
Chippenham and Trowbridge	Bath	

Clerkenwell and Shoreditch	London Insolvency District – High Court for Parts 1 to 7 (see head note); County Court at Central London for Parts 7A to 11	
Colchester	Parts 1 to 11	Southend or the High Court (London)
Conwy and Colwyn	Caernarfon	
Coventry	Parts 1 to 11	Birmingham
Crewe	Parts 1 to 11	Stoke or Chester
Croydon	Parts 1 to 11	
Darlington	Parts 1 to 11	Middlesbrough
Dartford	Medway	
Derby	Parts 1 to 11	
Doncaster	Parts 1 to 11	Sheffield
Dudley	Parts 1 to 11	Birmingham
Durham	Parts 1 to 11	Newcastle
Eastbourne	Parts 1 to 11	Brighton
Edmonton	London Insolvency District – High Court for Parts 1 to 7 (see head note); County Court at Central London for Parts 7A to 11	
Exeter	Parts 1 to 11	
Gateshead	Newcastle upon Tyne	
Gloucester and Cheltenham	Parts 1 to 11	
Great Grimsby	Parts 1 to 11	Hull
Guildford	Parts 1 to 11	Croydon
Halifax	Parts 1 to 11	Leeds
Harrogate	Parts 1 to 11	Leeds
Hartlepool	Middlesbrough	
Hastings	Parts 1 to 11	Brighton
Haverfordwest	Parts 1 to 11	Cardiff
Hereford	Parts 1 to 11	Gloucester
Hertford	Parts 1 to 11	Luton

High Wycombe	Aylesbury	
Horsham	Brighton	
Huddersfield	Parts 1 to 11	Leeds
Ipswich	Parts 1 to 11	Norwich or Southend
Kendal	Parts 1 to 11	Blackpool or Preston
Kettering	Northampton	
Kings Lynn	Norwich or Peterborough	
Kingston-upon-Hull	Parts 1 to 11	
Kingston-upon-Thames	Parts 1 to 11	
Lambeth	London Insolvency District – High Court for Parts 1 to 7 (see head note); County Court at Central London for Parts 7A to 11	
Lancaster	Parts 1 to 11	Blackpool or Preston
Leeds	Parts 1 to 11	
Leicester	Parts 1 to 11	
Lewes	Brighton	
Lincoln	Parts 1 to 11	Nottingham
Liverpool	Parts 1 to 11	
Llanelli	Swansea	
Llangefni	Parts 1 to 11	
Luton	Parts 1 to 11	
Maidstone	Parts 1 to 11	Croydon or the High Court (London)
Manchester	Parts 1 to 11	
Mansfield	Nottingham	
Mayor's and City of London	London Insolvency District – High Court for Parts 1 to 7 (see head note); County Court at Central London for Parts 7A to 11	
Medway	Canterbury	Croydon or the High Court (London)
Merthyr Tydfil	Parts 1 to 11	Cardiff
Middlesbrough	Parts 1 to 11	

Milton Keynes	Parts 1 to 11	Luton
Mold	Wrexham	Wrexham
Newcastle upon Tyne	Parts 1 to 11	
Newport (Gwent)	Parts 1 to 11	Cardiff
Newport (Isle of Wight)	Parts 1 to 11	Southampton or Portsmouth
Northampton	Parts 1 to 11	Luton
North Shields	Newcastle upon Tyne	
Norwich	Parts 1 to 11	
Nottingham	Parts 1 to 11	
Nuneaton	Coventry	
Oldham	Parts 1 to 11	
Oxford	Parts 1 to 11	Reading
Peterborough	Parts 1 to 11	Cambridge
Plymouth	Parts 1 to 11	
Pontypridd	Parts 1 to 11	Cardiff
Portsmouth	Parts 1 to 11	
Port Talbot	Parts 1 to 11	
Prestatyn	Parts 1 to 11	
Preston	Parts 1 to 11	
Reading	Parts 1 to 11	
Reigate	Guildford	
Rhyl	Parts 1 to 11	Birkenhead or Chester
Romford	Parts 1 to 11	
Salisbury	Parts 1 to 11	Bournemouth or Southampton
Scarborough	Parts 1 to 11	York, Hull or Middlesbrough
Scunthorpe	Parts 1 to 11	Hull or Sheffield
Sheffield	Parts 1 to 11	
Skipton	Bradford	
Slough	Parts 1 to 11	
Southampton	Parts 1 to 11	

Southend-on-Sea	Parts 1 to 11	
South Shields	Newcastle upon Tyne	
Stafford	Parts 1 to 11	Stoke
Staines	Guildford	
St Albans	Parts 1 to 11	Luton
St Helens	Liverpool	
Stockport	Parts 1 to 11	Manchester
Stoke-on-Trent	Parts 1 to 11	
Sunderland	Parts 1 to 11	Newcastle
Swansea	Parts 1 to 11	Cardiff
Swindon	Parts 1 to 11	Gloucester or Reading
Taunton	Parts 1 to 11	Exeter or Bristol
Telford	Parts 1 to 11	
Thanet	Canterbury	
Torquay & Newton Abbot	Parts 1 to 11	Exeter
Truro	Parts 1 to 11	Plymouth
Tunbridge Wells	Parts 1 to 11	Croydon
Uxbridge	The County Court at Central London	
Wakefield	Parts 1 to 11	Leeds
Walsall	Parts 1 to 11	
Wandsworth	London Insolvency District – High Court for Parts 1 to 7 (see head note); County Court at Central London for Parts 7A to 11	
Warwick	Parts 1 to 11	Birmingham
Watford	Luton	
Welshpool & Newton	Parts 1 to 11	Stoke or Chester
West Cumbria	Parts 1 to 11	
Weston Super Mare	Bristol	
Weymouth	Bournemouth	Bournemouth
Wigan	Parts 1 to 11	Bolton, Manchester or Preston

Willesden	London Insolvency District – High Court for Parts 1 to 7 (see head note); County Court at Central London for Parts 7A to 11	
Winchester	Parts 1 to 11	Southampton
Wolverhampton	Parts 1 to 11	
Woolwich	Croydon	
Worcester	Parts 1 to 11	Gloucester
Worthing	Brighton	
Wrexham	Parts 1 to 11	Birkenhead, Stoke or Chester
Yeovil	Parts 1 to 11	Exeter or Bristol
York	Parts 1 to 11	

Practice Note: Relating to the Insolvency Proceedings Practice Direction

1. Following the making and coming into effect of

   - The Insolvency (England and Wales) Rules 2016
   - The Insolvency (Amendment) Rules 2016
   - The Insolvency (Amendment) (No.2) Rules 2016
   - The Insolvency (England and Wales) Amendment Rules 2017
   - The Insolvency (England and Wales) Rules 2016 (Consequential Amendments and Savings) Rules 2017 (together, 'the new rules')

   significant amendments are required to the Insolvency Proceedings Practice Direction ('IPPD').
2. In the near future the IPPD will be revoked, and an interim Practice Direction will be made pending the making of a substantially revised IPPD in due course.
3. Pending the revocation of the IPPD

   a. The new rules are to be given effect;
   b. The IPPD is to be treated as not in effect where it contradicts the new rules, but the practices set out in the IPPD may continue to be followed as sound guidance to the extent possible.

Made with the authority of the Chancellor of the High Court
6 April 2017

Part One of the CPR Practice Direction – Insolvency Proceedings

Part One: General Provisions

1. Definitions
1.1 In this Practice Direction:

(1) 'The Act' means the Insolvency Act 1986 and includes the Act as applied to limited liability partnerships by the Limited Liability Partnerships Regulations 2001 or to any other person or body by virtue of the Act or any other legislation;
(2) 'The Insolvency Rules' means the rules for the time being in force and made under s.411 and s.412 of the Act in relation to insolvency proceedings, and, save where otherwise provided, any reference to a rule is to a rule in the Insolvency Rules;
(3) 'CPR' means the Civil Procedure Rules and 'CPR' followed by a Part or rule identified by number means the Part or rule with that number in those Rules;

(4) 'EC Regulation on Insolvency Proceedings' means Council Regulation (EC) No. 1346/2000 of 29 May 2000 on Insolvency Proceedings;[25]

(5) 'Service Regulation' means Council Regulation (EC) No. 1393/2007 of 13 November 2007 on the service in the Member States of judicial and extra-judicial documents in civil and commercial matters (service of documents);

(6) 'Insolvency proceedings' means:

    (a) any proceedings under the Act, the Insolvency Rules, the Administration of Insolvent Estates of Deceased Persons Order 1986 (S.I. 1986 No. 1999), the Insolvent Partnerships Order 1994 (S.I. 1994 No. 2421) or the Limited Liability Partnerships Regulations 2001;

    (b) any proceedings under the EC Regulation on Insolvency Proceedings or the Cross-Border Insolvency Regulations 2006 (S.I. 2006/1030);

(7) References to a 'company' include a limited liability partnership and references to a 'contributory' include a member of a limited liability partnership;

(8) References to a 'Registrar' are to a Registrar in Bankruptcy of the High Court and (save in cases where it is clear from the context that a particular provision applies only to the Royal Courts of Justice) include a District Judge in a District Registry of the High Court and in any county court hearing centre having relevant insolvency jurisdiction;

(9) 'Court' means the High Court or any county court hearing centre having relevant insolvency jurisdiction;

(10) 'Royal Courts of Justice' means the Royal Courts of Justice, 7 Rolls Buildings, Fetter Lane, London EC4A 1NL or such other place in London where the Registrars sit;

(11) In Part Six of this Practice Direction:

    (a) 'appointee' means:

        (i) a provisional liquidator appointed under section 135 of the Act;

        (ii) a special manager appointed under section 177 or section 370 of the Act;

        (iii) a liquidator appointed by the members of a company or partnership or by the creditors of a company or partnership or by the Secretary of State pursuant to section 137 of the Act, or by the court pursuant to section 140 of the Act;

        (iv) an administrator of a company appointed to manage the property, business and affairs of that company under the Act or other enactment and to which the provisions of the Act are applicable;

        (v) a trustee in bankruptcy (other than the Official Receiver) appointed under the Act;

        (vi) a nominee or supervisor of a voluntary arrangement under Part I or Part VIII of the Act;

---

25 Replaced by the recast EU Regulation from June 2017: Insolvency Amendment (EU 2015/848) Regulations 2017 (SI 2017/702).

   (vii) a licensed insolvency practitioner appointed by the court pursuant to section 273 of the Act;

   (viii) an interim receiver appointed by the court pursuant to section 286 of the Act;

 (b) 'assessor' means a person appointed in accordance with CPR 35.15;

 (c) 'remuneration application' means any application to fix, approve or challenge the remuneration or expenses of an appointee or the basis of remuneration;

 (d) 'remuneration' includes expenses (where the Act or the Insolvency Rules give the court jurisdiction in relation thereto) and, in the case of an administrator, any pre-appointment administration costs or remuneration.

2. Coming into force

2.1 This Practice Direction shall come into force on 29 July 2014 and shall replace all previous Practice Directions, Practice Statements and Practice Notes relating to insolvency proceedings. For the avoidance of doubt, this Practice Direction does not affect the Practice Direction relating to contributories' winding up petitions (Practice Direction 49B—Order under section 127 Insolvency Act 1986).

3. Distribution of business

3.1 As a general rule all petitions and applications (except those listed in paragraphs 3.2 and 3.3 below) should be listed for initial hearing before a Registrar in accordance with rule 7.6A(2) and (3).

3.2 The following applications relating to insolvent companies should always be listed before a Judge:

(1) applications for committal for contempt;

(2) applications for an administration order;

(3) applications for an injunction pursuant to the Court's inherent jurisdiction (e.g. to restrain the presentation or advertisement of a winding up petition) or pursuant to section 37 of the Senior Courts Act 1981 or section 38 of the County Courts Act 1984 but not applications for any order to be made pursuant to the Act or the Rules;

(4) applications for the appointment of a provisional liquidator;

(5) interim applications and applications for directions or case management after any proceedings have been referred or adjourned to the Judge (except where liberty to apply to the Registrar has been given).

3.3 The following applications relating to insolvent individuals should always be listed before a Judge:

(1) applications for committal for contempt;

(2) applications for an injunction pursuant to the Court's inherent jurisdiction (e.g. to restrain the presentation of a bankruptcy petition) or pursuant to section 37 of the Senior Courts Act 1981 or section 38 of the County Courts

Act 1984 but not applications for any order to be made pursuant to the Act or the Rules;

(3)   interim applications and applications for directions or case management after any proceedings have been referred or adjourned to the Judge (except where liberty to apply to the Registrar has been given).

3.4 When deciding whether to hear proceedings or to refer or adjourn them to the Judge, the Registrar should have regard to the following factors:

(1)   the complexity of the proceedings;
(2)   whether the proceedings raise new or controversial points of law,
(3)   the likely date and length of the hearing;
(4)   public interest in the proceedings.

4. Court documents

4.1 All insolvency proceedings should be commenced and applications in proceedings should be made using the forms prescribed by the Act, the Insolvency Rules or other legislation under which the same is or are brought or made and/or should contain the information prescribed by the Act, the Insolvency Rules or other legislation.

4.2 Every court document in insolvency proceedings under Parts I to VII of the Act shall be headed:

IN THE HIGH COURT OF JUSTICE
CHANCERY DIVISION
[DISTRICT REGISTRY] or in the Royal Courts of Justice
    [COMPANIES COURT]

or

IN THE COUNTY COURT AT [   ]

followed by

IN THE MATTER OF [name of company]
AND IN THE MATTER OF THE INSOLVENCY ACT 1986

...

4.4 Every court document in proceedings to which the Act applies by virtue of other legislation should also be headed:

IN THE MATTER OF [THE FINANCIAL SERVICES AND MARKETS
ACT 2000 or as the case may be]
AND IN THE MATTER OF THE INSOLVENCY ACT 1986

5. Evidence
5.1 Subject to the provisions of rule 7.9 or any other provisions or directions as to the form in which evidence should be given, written evidence in insolvency proceedings must be given by witness statement.

6. Service of court documents in insolvency proceedings
6.1 Except where the Insolvency Rules otherwise provide (and, in this regard, the attention of practitioners is particularly drawn to rule 12A.16(2)), CPR Part 6 applies to the service of court documents both within and out of the jurisdiction as modified by this Practice Direction or as the court may otherwise direct.

6.2 Except where the Insolvency Rules otherwise provide, or as may be required under the Service Regulation, service of documents in insolvency proceedings will be the responsibility of the parties and will not be undertaken by the court.

6.3 A document which, pursuant to rule 12A.16(3)(b), is treated as a claim form, is deemed to have been served on the date specified in CPR Part 6.14, and any other document (including any document which is treated as a claim form pursuant to rule 12A.16(3)(a) but which is not a document of a type specified in rule 12A.16(2)) is deemed to have been served on the date specified in CPR Part 6.26, unless the court otherwise directs. (Pursuant to rule 12A.16(2), the provisions of CPR Part 6 do not apply to the service of any of the following documents within the jurisdiction: (a) a winding-up petition; (b) a bankruptcy petition; (c) any document relating to such a petition; or (d) any administration, winding-up or bankruptcy order.)

6.4 Except as provided below, service out of the jurisdiction of an application which is to be treated as a claim form under rule 12A.16(3) requires the permission of the court.

6.5 An application which is to be treated as a claim form under rule 12A.16(3) may be served out of the jurisdiction without the permission of the court if:

(1) the application is by an office-holder appointed in insolvency proceedings in respect of an individual or company with its centre of main interests within the jurisdiction exercising a statutory power under the Act, and the person to be served is to be served within the EU; or
(2) it is a copy of an application, being served on a Member State liquidator (as defined by Article 2 of the EC Regulation on Insolvency Proceedings).

6.6 An application for permission to serve out of the jurisdiction must be supported by a witness statement setting out:

(1) the nature of the claim or application and the relief sought;
(2) that the applicant believes that the claim has a reasonable prospect of success; and

(3) the address of the person to be served or, if not known, in what place or country that person is, or is likely, to be found.

6.7 CPR 6.36 and 6.37(1) and (2) do not apply in insolvency proceedings.

7. Jurisdiction
7.1 Where CPR 2.4 provides for the court to perform any act, that act may be performed by a Registrar.

8. Drawing up of orders
8.1 The court will draw up all orders except orders on the application of the Official Receiver or for which the Treasury Solicitor is responsible or where the court otherwise directs.

9. Urgent applications
9.1 In the Royal Courts of Justice the Registrars (and in other courts exercising insolvency jurisdiction the District Judges) operate urgent applications lists for urgent and time-critical applications and may be available to hear urgent applications at other times. Parties asking for an application to be dealt with in the urgent applications lists or urgently at any other time must complete the certificate below:

No:

Heading of action

I estimate that this matter is likely to occupy the court for .... mins/hours.

I certify that it is urgent for the following reasons:

....

[name of representative]

....

[telephone number]

Counsel/Solicitor for the ....

WARNING. If, in the opinion of the Registrar/District Judge, the application is not urgent then such sanction will be applied as is thought appropriate in all the circumstances.

Part Three of the CPR Practice Direction – Insolvency Proceedings

Part Three: Personal Insolvency

13. Statutory demands

13.1 Service abroad of statutory demands

13.1.1 A statutory demand is not a document issued by the court. Permission to serve out of the jurisdiction is not, therefore, required.

13.1.2 Rule 6.3(2) ('Requirements as to service') applies to service of the statutory demand whether within or out of the jurisdiction.

13.1.3 A creditor wishing to serve a statutory demand out of the jurisdiction in a foreign country with which a civil procedure convention has been made (including the Hague Convention) may and, if the assistance of a British Consul is desired, must adopt the procedure prescribed by CPR Part 6.42 and 6.43. In the case of any doubt whether the country is a 'convention country', enquiries should be made of the Queen's Bench Masters' Secretary Department, Royal Courts of Justice, Strand, London WC2A 2LL.

13.1.4 In all other cases, service of the demand must be effected by private arrangement in accordance with rule 6.3(2) and local foreign law.

13.1.5 When a statutory demand is to be served out of the jurisdiction, the time limits of 21 days and 18 days respectively referred to in the demand must be amended as provided in the next paragraph. For this purpose reference should be made to the table set out in the practice direction supplementing Section IV of CPR Part 6.

13.1.6 A creditor should amend the statutory demand as follows:

(1) for any reference to 18 days there must be substituted the appropriate number of days set out in the table plus 4 days;

(2) for any reference to 21 days there must be substituted the appropriate number of days in the table plus 7 days.

13.1.7 Attention is drawn to the fact that in all forms of the statutory demand the figure 18 and the figure 21 occur in more than one place.

13.2 Substituted service of statutory demands

13.2.1 The creditor is under an obligation to do all that is reasonable to bring the statutory demand to the debtor's attention and, if practicable, to cause personal service to be effected (rule 6.3(2)).

13.2.2 In the circumstances set out in rule 6.3(3) the demand may instead be advertised. As there is no statutory form of advertisement, the court will accept an advertisement in the following form:

STATUTORY DEMAND
(Debt for liquidated sum payable immediately following a judgment or order of the court)

To (Block letters)

of

TAKE NOTICE that a statutory demand has been issued by·

Name of Creditor:

Address:

The creditor demands payment of £ the amount now due on a judgment or order of the (High Court of Justice Division) (County Court at) dated the [day] of [month] 20[ ].

The statutory demand is an important document and it is deemed to have been served on you on the date of the first appearance of this advertisement. You must deal with this demand within 21 days of the service upon you or you could be made bankrupt and your property and goods taken away from you. If you are in any doubt as to your position, you should seek advice immediately from a solicitor or your nearest Citizens Advice Bureau. The statutory demand can be obtained or is available for inspection and collection from:

Name:

Address:

(Solicitor for) the creditor

Tel. No. Reference:

You have only 21 days from the date of the first appearance of this advertisement before the creditor may present a bankruptcy petition. You have only 18 days from the date of the first appearance of this advertisement within which to apply to the court to set aside the demand.

13.2.3 Where personal service is not effected or the demand is not advertised in the limited circumstances permitted by rule 6.3(3), substituted service is permitted, but the creditor must have taken all those steps which would justify the court making an order for substituted service of a petition. The steps to be taken to obtain an order for substituted service of a petition are set out below. Failure to comply with these requirements may result in the court declining to issue the petition (rule 6.11(9)) or dismissing it.

13.2.4 In most cases, evidence of the following steps will suffice to justify acceptance for presentation of a petition where the statutory demand has been served by substituted service (or to justify making an order for substituted service of a petition):

(1) One personal call at the residence and place of business of the debtor where both are known or at either of such places as is known. Where it is known that the debtor has more than one residential or business address, personal calls should be made at all the addresses.

(2) Should the creditor fail to effect personal service, a letter should be written to the debtor referring to the call(s), the purpose of the same and the failure to meet the debtor, adding that a further call will be made for the same purpose on the [day] of [month] 20[ ] at [ ] hours at [place]. Such letter may be sent by first class prepaid post or left at or delivered to the debtor's address in such a way as it is reasonably likely to come to the debtor's attention. At least two business days' notice should be given of the appointment and copies of the letter sent to or left at all known addresses of the debtor. The appointment letter should also state that:

   (a) in the event of the time and place not being convenient, the debtor should propose some other time and place reasonably convenient for the purpose;

   (b) (In the case of a statutory demand) if the debtor fails to keep the appointment the creditor proposes to serve the debtor by [advertisement] [post] [insertion through a letter box] or as the case may be, and that, in the event of a bankruptcy petition being presented, the court will be asked to treat such service as service of the demand on the debtor;

   (c) (In the case of a petition) if the debtor fails to keep the appointment, application will be made to the Court for an order for substituted service either by advertisement, or in such other manner as the court may think fit.

(3) When attending any appointment made by letter, inquiry should be made as to whether the debtor has received all letters left for him. If the debtor is away, inquiry should also be made as to whether or not letters are being forwarded to an address within the jurisdiction (England and Wales) or elsewhere.

(4) If the debtor is represented by a solicitor, an attempt should be made to arrange an appointment for personal service through such solicitor.

The Insolvency Rules enable a solicitor to accept service of a statutory demand on behalf of his client but there is no similar provision in respect of service of a bankruptcy petition.

(5) The certificate of service of a statutory demand filed pursuant to rule 6.11 should deal with all the above matters including all relevant facts as to the debtor's whereabouts and whether the appointment letter(s) have been returned. It should also set out the reasons for the belief that the debtor resides at the relevant address or works at the relevant place of business and whether, so far as is known, the debtor is represented by a solicitor.

13.3 Setting aside a statutory demand

13.3.1 The application (Form 6.4) and witness statement in support (Form 6.5) exhibiting a copy of the statutory demand must be filed in court within 18 days of service of the statutory demand on the debtor. Where service is effected by advertisement the period of 18 days is calculated from the date of the first appearance of the advertisement. Three copies of each document must be lodged with the application to enable the court to serve notice of the hearing date on the applicant, the creditor and the person named in Part B of the statutory demand.

13.3.2 Where copies of the documents are not lodged with the application, any order of the Registrar fixing a venue is conditional upon copies of the documents being lodged on the next business day after the Registrar's order otherwise the application will be deemed to have been dismissed.

13.3.3 Where the debt claimed in the statutory demand is based on a judgment, order, liability order, costs certificate, tax assessment or decision of a tribunal, the court will not at this stage inquire into the validity of the debt nor, as a general rule, will it adjourn the application to await the result of an application to set aside the judgment, order decision, costs certificate or any appeal.

13.3.4 Where the debtor (a) claims to have a counterclaim, set-off or cross demand (whether or not he could have raised it in the action in which the judgment or order was obtained) which equals or exceeds the amount of the debt or debts specified in the statutory demand or (b) disputes the debt (not being a debt subject to a judgment, order, liability order, costs certificate or tax assessment) the court will normally set aside the statutory demand if, in its opinion, on the evidence there is a genuine triable issue.

13.3.5 A debtor who wishes to apply to set aside a statutory demand after the expiration of 18 days from the date of service of the statutory demand must apply for an extension of time within which to apply. If the applicant wishes to apply for an injunction to restrain presentation of a petition the application must be made to the Judge. Paragraphs 1 and 2 of Form 6.5 (witness statement in support of application to set aside statutory demand) should be used in support of the application for an extension of time with the following additional paragraphs:

'(3) To the best of my knowledge and belief the creditor(s) named in the demand has/have not presented a petition against me.
(4) The reasons for my failure to apply to set aside the demand within 18 days after service are as follows: ...'

If application is made to restrain presentation of a bankruptcy petition the following additional paragraph should be added:

'(5) Unless restrained by injunction the creditor(s) may present a bankruptcy petition against me'.

14. Bankruptcy petitions

14.1 Listing of petitions

14.1.1 All petitions presented will be listed under the name of the debtor unless the court directs otherwise.

14.2 Content of petitions

14.2.1 The attention of practitioners is drawn to the following points:

(1) A creditor's petition does not require dating, signing or witnessing but must be verified in accordance with rule 6.12.
(2) In the heading it is only necessary to recite the debtor's name e.g. Re John William Smith or Re J W Smith (Male). Any alias or trading name will appear in the body of the petition.

14.2.2 Where the petition is based solely on a statutory demand, only the debt claimed in the demand may be included in the petition.
14.2.3 The attention of practitioners is also drawn to rules 6.7 and 6.8, and in particular to rule 6.8(1) where the 'aggregate sum' is made up of a number of debts.
14.2.4 The date of service of the statutory demand should be recited as follows:

(1) In the case of personal service, the date of service as set out in the certificate of service should be recited and whether service is effected before/after 16.00 hours on Monday to Friday or before/after 12.00 hours on a Saturday.
(2) In the case of substituted service (other than by advertisement), the date alleged in the certificate of service should be recited.
(3) In the strictly limited case of service by advertisement under rule 6.3, the date to be alleged is the date of the advertisement's appearance or, as the case may be, its first appearance (see rules 6.3(3) and 6.11(8)).

14.3 Searches

14.3.1 The petitioning creditor shall, before presenting a petition, conduct an Official Search with the Chief Land Registrar in the register of pending actions for pending petitions presented against the debtor and shall include the following certificate at the end of the petition:

> 'I/we certify that within 7 days ending today I/we have conducted a search for pending petitions presented against the debtor and that to the best of my/our knowledge information and belief [no prior petitions have been presented which are still pending] [a prior petition (No [ ]) has been presented and is/may be pending in the [Court] and I/we am/are issuing this petition at risk as to costs].
>
> Signed….. Dated….'.

14.4 Deposit

14.4.1 The deposit will be taken by the court and forwarded to the Official Receiver. In the Royal Courts of Justice the petition fee and deposit should be paid in the Fee Room, which will record the receipt and will impress two entries on the original petition, one in respect of the court fee and the other in respect of the deposit. In a District Registry or a county court hearing centre, the petition fee and deposit should be handed to the duly authorised officer of the court's staff who will record its receipt.

14.4.2 In all cases cheque(s) for the whole amount should be made payable to 'HM Courts and Tribunals Service' or 'HMCTS'.

14.5 Certificates of continuing debt and of notice of adjournment

14.5.1 On the hearing of a petition where a bankruptcy order is sought, in order to satisfy the court that the debt on which the petition is founded has not been paid or secured or compounded for the court will normally accept as sufficient a certificate signed by the person representing the petitioning creditor in the following form:

> 'I certify that I have/my firm has made enquiries of the petitioning creditor(s) within the last business day prior to the hearing/adjourned hearing and to the best of my knowledge and belief the debt on which the petition is founded is still due and owing and has not been paid or secured or compounded for save as to …
>
> Signed ……… Dated ……'

14.5.2 For convenience, in the Royal Courts of Justice this certificate is incorporated in the attendance sheet for the parties to complete when they come to court and which is filed after the hearing. A fresh certificate will be required on each adjourned hearing.

14.5.3 On any adjourned hearing of a petition where a bankruptcy order is sought, in order to satisfy the court that the petitioner has complied with rule 6.29, the petitioner will be required to file evidence of the date on which, manner in which and address to which notice of the making of the order of adjournment and of the venue for the adjourned hearing has been sent to:

(1)   the debtor, and
(2)   any creditor who has given notice under rule 6.23 but was not present
      at the hearing when the order for adjournment was made or was present
      at the hearing but the date of the adjourned hearing was not fixed at
      that hearing. For convenience, in the Royal Courts of Justice this
      certificate is incorporated in the attendance sheet for the parties to
      complete when they come to court and which is filed after the hearing
      and is as follows:

> 'I certify that the petitioner has complied with rule 6.29 by sending
> notice of adjournment to the debtor [supporting/opposing
> creditor(s)] on [date] at [address]'.

A fresh certificate will be required on each adjourned hearing.

14.6 Extension of hearing date of petition

14.6.1 Late applications for extension of hearing dates under rule 6.28, and failure
to attend on the listed hearing of a petition, will be dealt with as follows:

(1)   If an application is submitted less than two clear working days before
      the hearing date (for example, later than Monday for Thursday, or
      Wednesday for Monday) the costs of the application will not be
      allowed under rule 6.28(3).
(2)   If the petition has not been served and no extension has been granted
      by the time fixed for the hearing of the petition, and if no one attends
      for the hearing, the petition may be dismissed or re-listed for hearing
      about 21 days later. The court will notify the petitioning creditor's
      solicitors (or the petitioning creditor in person), and any known
      supporting or opposing creditors or their solicitors, of the new date and
      times. Written evidence should then be filed on behalf of the
      petitioning creditor explaining fully the reasons for the failure to apply
      for an extension or to appear at the hearing, and (if appropriate) giving
      reasons why the petition should not be dismissed.
(3)   On the re-listed hearing the court may dismiss the petition if not
      satisfied it should be adjourned or a further extension granted.

14.6.2 All applications for an extension should include a statement of the date
fixed for the hearing of the petition.
14.6.3 The petitioning creditor should contact the court (by solicitors or in person)
on or before the hearing date to ascertain whether the application has reached
the file and been dealt with. It should not be assumed that an extension will
be granted.

14.7 Substituted service of bankruptcy petitions

14.7.1 In most cases evidence that the steps set out in paragraph 13.3.4 have
been taken will suffice to justify an order for substituted service of a
bankruptcy petition.

14.8 Validation orders

14.8.1 A person against whom a bankruptcy petition has been presented ('the debtor') may apply to the court after presentation of the petition for relief from the effects of section 284(1) – (3) of the Act by seeking an order that any disposition of his assets or payment made out of his funds, including any bank account (whether it is in credit or overdrawn) shall not be void in the event of a bankruptcy order being made on the petition (a 'validation order').

14.8.2 Save in exceptional circumstances, notice of the making of the application should be given to (a) the petitioning creditor(s) or other petitioner, (b) any creditor who has given notice to the petitioner of his intention to appear on the hearing of the petition pursuant to rule 6.23 1986, (c) any creditor who has been substituted as petitioner pursuant to rule 6.30 Insolvency Rules 1986 and (d) any creditor who has carriage of the petition pursuant to rule 6.31 Insolvency Rules 1986.

14.8.3 The application should be supported by a witness statement which, save in exceptional circumstances, should be made by the debtor. If appropriate, supporting evidence in the form of a witness statement from the debtor's accountant should also be produced.

14.8.4 The extent and contents of the evidence will vary according to the circumstances and the nature of the relief sought, but in a case where the debtor is trading or carrying on business it should include, as a minimum, the following information:

(1) when and to whom notice has been given in accordance with paragraph 14.8.2 above;

(2) brief details of the circumstances leading to presentation of the petition;

(3) how the debtor became aware of the presentation of the petition;

(4) whether the petition debt is admitted or disputed and, if the latter, brief details of the basis on which the debt is disputed;

(5) full details of the debtor's financial position including details of his assets (including details of any security and the amount(s) secured) and liabilities, which should be supported, as far as possible, by documentary evidence, e.g. accounts, draft accounts, management accounts or estimated statement of affairs;

(6) a cash flow forecast and profit and loss projection for the period for which the order is sought;

(7) details of the dispositions or payments in respect of which an order is sought;

(8) the reasons relied on in support of the need for such dispositions or payments to be made;

(9) any other information relevant to the exercise of the court's discretion;

(10) details of any consents obtained from the persons mentioned in paragraph 14.8.2 above (supported by documentary evidence where appropriate);

(11) details of any relevant bank account, including its number and the address and sort code of the bank at which such account is held and the

amount of the credit or debit balance on such account at the time of making the application.

14.8.5 Where an application is made urgently to enable payments to be made which are essential to continued trading (e.g. wages) and it is not possible to assemble all the evidence listed above, the court may consider granting limited relief for a short period, but there must be sufficient evidence to satisfy the court that the interests of creditors are unlikely to be prejudiced.

14.8.6 Where the debtor is not trading or carrying on business and the application relates only to a proposed sale, mortgage or re-mortgage of the debtor's home evidence of the following will generally suffice:

(1) when and to whom notice has been given in accordance with 14.8.2 above;

(2) whether the petition debt is admitted or disputed and, if the latter, brief details of the basis on which the debt is disputed;

(3) details of the property to be sold, mortgaged or re-mortgaged (including its title number);

(4) the value of the property and the proposed sale price, or details of the mortgage or re-mortgage;

(5) details of any existing mortgages or charges on the property and redemption figures;

(6) the costs of sale (e.g. solicitors' or agents' costs);

(7) how and by whom any net proceeds of sale (or sums coming into the debtor's hands as a result of any mortgage or re-mortgage) are to be held pending the final hearing of the petition;

(8) any other information relevant to the exercise of the court's discretion;

(9) details of any consents obtained from the persons mentioned in 14.8.2 above (supported by documentary evidence where appropriate).

14.8.7 Whether or not the debtor is trading or carrying on business, where the application involves a disposition of property the court will need to be satisfied that any proposed disposal will be at a proper value. Accordingly an independent valuation should be obtained and exhibited to the evidence.

14.8.8 The court will need to be satisfied by credible evidence that the debtor is solvent and able to pay his debts as they fall due or that a particular transaction or series of transactions in respect of which the order is sought will be beneficial to or will not prejudice the interests of all the unsecured creditors as a class (*Denney v John Hudson & Co Ltd* [1992] BCLC 901, [1992] BCC 503, CA; *Re Fairway Graphics Ltd* [1991] BCLC 468).

14.8.9 A draft of the order sought should be attached to the application.

14.8.10 Similar considerations to those set out above are likely to apply to applications seeking ratification of a transaction or payment after the making of a bankruptcy order.

15. Applications

15.1 In accordance with rule 13.2(2), in the Royal Courts of Justice the member of court staff in charge of the winding up list has been authorised to deal with applications:

(1) by petitioning creditors to extend the time for hearing petitions (rule 6.28);

(2) by the Official Receiver:

    (a) to transfer proceedings from the High Court to a county court hearing centre (rule 7.13);

    (b) to amend the title of the proceedings (rules 6.35 and 6.47).

15.2 In District Registries or the County Court such applications must be made to the District Judge.

16. Orders without attendance

16.1 In suitable cases the court will normally be prepared to make orders under Part VIII of the Act (Individual Voluntary Arrangements), without the attendance of the parties, provided there is no bankruptcy order in existence and (so far as is known) no pending petition. The orders are:

(1) A 14 day interim order adjourning the application for 14 days for consideration of the nominee's report, where the papers are in order, and the nominee's signed consent to act includes a waiver of notice of the application or the consent by the nominee to the making of an interim order without attendance.

(2) A standard order on consideration of the nominee's report, extending the interim order to a date seven weeks after the date of the proposed meeting, directing the meeting to be summoned and adjourning to a date about three weeks after the meeting. Such an order may be made without attendance if the nominee's report has been delivered to the court and complies with section 256(1) of the Act and rule 5.11(2) and (3) and proposes a date for the meeting not less than 14 days from that on which the nominee's report is filed in court under rule 5.11 nor more than 28 days from that on which that report is considered by the court under rule 5.13.

(3) A 'concertina' order, combining orders as under (1) and (2) above. Such an order may be made without attendance if the initial application for an interim order is accompanied by a report of the nominee and the conditions set out in (1) and (2) above are satisfied.

(4) A final order on consideration of the chairman's report. Such an order may be made without attendance if the chairman's report has been filed and complies with rule 5.27(1). The order will record the effect of the chairman's report and may discharge the interim order.

16.2 Provided that the conditions under sub-paragraphs (2) and (4) above are satisfied and that the appropriate report has been lodged with the court in due time the parties need not attend or be represented on the adjourned hearing for consideration of the nominee's report or of the chairman's report (as the case may be) unless they are notified by the court that attendance is required. Sealed copies of the order made (in all four cases as above) will be posted by the court to the applicant or his solicitor and to the nominee.

16.3 In suitable cases the court may also make consent orders without attendance by the parties. The written consent of the parties will be required. Examples of such orders are as follows:

   (1)   on applications to set aside a statutory demand, orders:

      (a)   dismissing the application, with or without an order for costs as may be agreed (permission will be given to present a petition on or after the seventh day after the date of the order, unless a different date is agreed);

      (b)   setting aside the demand, with or without an order for costs as may be agreed; or

   (2)   On petitions where there is a negative list of supporting or opposing creditors in Form 6.21, or a statement signed by or on behalf of the petitioning creditor that no notices have been received from supporting or opposing creditors, orders:

      (a)   dismissing the petition, with or without an order for costs as may be agreed; or

      (b)   if the petition has not been served, giving permission to withdraw the petition (with no order for costs).

   (3)   On other applications, orders:

      (a)   for sale of property, possession of property, disposal of proceeds of sale;

      (b)   giving interim directions;

      (c)   dismissing the application, with or without an order for costs as may be agreed;

      (d)   giving permission to withdraw the application, with or without an order for costs as may be agreed.

16.4 If, as may often be the case with orders under subparagraphs 3(a) or (b) above, an adjournment is required, whether generally with liberty to restore or to a fixed date, the order by consent may include an order for the adjournment. If adjournment to a date is requested, a time estimate should be given and the court will fix the first available date and time on or after the date requested.

16.5 The above lists should not be regarded as exhaustive, nor should it be assumed that an order will be made without attendance as requested.

16.6 Applications for consent orders without attendance should be lodged at least two clear working days (and preferably longer) before any hearing date.

16.7 Whenever a document is lodged or a letter sent, the correct case number should be quoted. A note should also be given of the date and time of the next hearing (if any).

17. Bankruptcy restrictions undertakings

17.1 Where a bankrupt has given a bankruptcy restrictions undertaking, the Secretary of State or official receiver must file a copy in court and send a copy to the bankrupt as soon as reasonably practicable (rule 6.250). In addition the Secretary of State must notify the court immediately that the bankrupt has given such an undertaking in order that any hearing date can be vacated.

18. Persons at risk of violence

18.1 Where an application is made pursuant to rule 5.67, 5.68, 5A 18, or 6.235B or otherwise to limit disclosure of information as to a person's current address by reason of the possibility of violence, the relevant application should be accompanied by a witness statement which includes the following:

(1) The grounds upon which it is contended that disclosure of the current address as defined by the Insolvency Rules might reasonably be expected to lead to violence against the debtor or a person who normally resides with him or her as a member of his or her family or where appropriate any other person.

(2) Where the application is made in respect of the address of the debtor, the debtor's proposals with regard to information which may safely be given to potential creditors in order that they can recognise that the debtor is a person who may be indebted to them, in particular the address at which the debtor previously resided or carried on business and the nature of such business.

(3) The terms of the order sought by the applicant by reference to the court's particular powers as set out in the rule under which the application is made and, unless impracticable, a draft of the order sought.

(4) Where the application is made by the debtor in respect of whom a nominee or supervisor has been appointed or against whom a bankruptcy order has been made, evidence of the consent of the nominee/supervisor, or, in the case of bankruptcy, the trustee in bankruptcy, if one has been appointed, and the official receiver if a trustee in bankruptcy has not been appointed. Where such consent is not available the statement must indicate whether such consent has been refused.

The application shall in any event make such person a respondent to the application.

18.2 The application shall be referred to the Registrar who will consider it without a hearing in the first instance but without prejudice to the right of the court to list it for hearing if:

(1) the court is minded to refuse the application;
(2) the consent of any respondent is not attached;
(3) the court is of the view that there is another reason why listing is appropriate.

24.1 BLANK APPLICATION FORM

Form IAA **Insolvency Act Application Notice**

<u>IN THE HIGH COURT OF JUSTICE</u>
<u>BUSINESS AND PROPERTY COURTS OF ENGLAND AND WALES</u>
<u>INSOLVENCY AND COMPANIES LIST (ChD)</u>
<u>IN BANKRUPTCY</u>

<u>NO: [ ] OF 20[ ]</u>

IN THE MATTER OF [insert name of Debtor]
AND IN THE MATTER OF THE INSOLVENCY ACT 1986

BETWEEN:-

<u>Applicant(s)</u>

and

<u>Respondent(s)</u>

Is this application within existing insolvency proceedings?   YES/NO

I (We), [insert name and address of applicant] intend to apply to the Judge/District Judge/Registrar on:

Date:

Time:

Place:

This application having been issued at the RCJ, 7 Rolls Buildings, Fetter Lane, London, EC4A 1NL will be heard at the time and date pursuant to the endorsement underneath the Court Seal on the front page of this application.

FOR AN ORDER THAT:

[(a)STATE CLEARLY WHAT ORDER YOU ARE SEEKING; (b) BRIEFLY SET OUT WHY YOU ARE SEEKING THE ORDER; (c) THE SECTION(S) OF THE INSOLVENCY ACT OR NUMBER(S) OF THE INSOLVENCY RULES UNDER WHICH YOU ARE APPLYING; (d) WHAT EVIDENCE YOU RELY ON IN SUPPORT OF THIS APPLICATION – BY WAY OF WITNESS STATEMENT]

THE NAMES AND ADDRESSES OF THE PERSON(S) UPON WHOM IT IS INTENDED TO SERVE THIS APPLICATION ARE:

Name:

Address:

Name:

Address:

OR

IT IS NOT INTENDED TO SERVE ANY PERSON WITH THIS APPLICATION

Dated:

Signed:

Solicitors for the applicant or Applicant
Address:
Telephone:
Email:

*This is the address which will be treated by Court as the Petitions address for service

If you do not attend, the court may make such order as it thinks just.

24.2   CERTIFICATE OF URGENCY

IN THE HIGH COURT OF JUSTICE
BUSINESS AND PROPERTY COURTS OF ENGLAND AND WALES
INSOLVENCY AND COMPANIES LIST (ChD)

NO: [ ] OF [ ]

IN THE MATTER OF IAN FLAKEY
IN BANKRUPTCY

CERTIFICATE OF URGENCY

This is an application for: [ ]. A draft order is attached.

A hearing of this application is required by no later than: [am/pm on   th
of   20]

I estimate that this matter is likely to occupy the court for [ ] mins/hours.

I estimate that pre-reading is likely to occupy the court for [ ] mins / hours.

I certify that it is urgent for the following reasons: [ ]

[ ] [name of representative]

[ ] [telephone number]

Counsel/Solicitor for the [ ]

WARNING. If, in the opinion of the Registrar, the application is not urgent then such
sanction will be applied as is thought appropriate in all the circumstances.

24.3   BANKRUPTCY PETITION ON DEFAULT OF A VOLUNTARY ARRANGEMENT

Rules 10.7–10.9   **Bankruptcy Petition for Default in Connection with**
Form Bank 4   **Voluntary Arrangement**

IN THE HIGH COURT OF JUSTICE
IN BANKRUPTCY

IN THE MATTER OF [Insert name Debtor]
AND IN THE MATTER OF THE INSOLVENCY ACT 1986

(a) Insert full name(s) and   I/We (a)
address(es) of petitioner(s)

(b) Insert full name, place of   petition the court that a bankruptcy order may be
residence and occupation (if any)   made against (b)
of debtor

(c) Insert in full any other   [also known as (c)
name(s) by which the debtor is or
has been known

                                         ]
(d) Insert trading name (adding   [and carrying on business as (d)
'with another or others', if this is
so), business address and nature
of business

                                         ]
(e) Insert any other address or   [and lately residing at (e)
addresses at which the debtor
has resided at or after the time
the petition debt was incurred

                                         ]
(f) Give the same details as   [and lately carrying on business as (f)
specified in note (d) above for
any other businesses which have
been carried on at or after the
time the petition debt was   ]
incurred

                                         and say as follows:–

(g) Delete as applicable   1. (g) [the debtor's centre of main interests is in
                                         England and Wales][the debtor has an establishment
                                         in England and Wales.]

                                         OR

The debtor carries on business as an insurance undertaking; a credit institution; an investment undertaking providing services involving the holding of funds or securities for third parties; or a collective investment undertaking as referred to in Article 2.2 of the EU Regulation on Insolvency Proceedings

OR

The debtor's centre of main interests is not within a member State

2. The debtor is (g)[not] resident in England and Wales. I am presenting this petition to the (g)[High Court][Central London County Court] because (g)[the proceedings are allocated to the London Insolvency District as][(g)Rule 10.11 [(1)[(a)][(b)]][(2)][(5)][(6)] applies][and the petition debt is (g)[£50,000 or more][less than £50,000]][and within the 6 months immediately preceding its presentation (g)[the debtor carried on business in England and Wales and the debtor carried on business within the area of the London Insolvency District (g)[for the greater part of that period of 6 months][for a longer period than in any other insolvency district]][the debtor has not carried on business in England and Wales but has resided in England and Wales and the debtor resided within the area of the London Insolvency District (g)[for the greater part of that period of 6 months][for a longer period than in any other insolvency district]].

OR

The debtor is (g)[not] resident in England and Wales. I am presenting this petition to this county court because (g)Rule 10.11[(3)][(4)] [(a)] [(b)] applies [and within the 6 months immediately preceding its presentation (g)[the debtor has carried on business in England and Wales and for the longest part of the period during which the debtor carried on business within that period of 6 months, the [principal] place of business has been situated in the district of this county court][the debtor has not carried on business in England and Wales, but has resided in England and Wales and for the longest part of the period during which the debtor was resident in England and Wales within that period of 6 months, the debtor resided in the insolvency district of this county court]].

(j) Insert date the debtor entered into voluntary arrangement
(k) Insert name of supervisor.

3. On (j)   a voluntary arrangement proposed by the debtor was approved by his creditors and I am (g) [a person who is for the time being bound by the said voluntary arrangement and (k)
is the supervisor] [(k)
the supervisor of the said voluntary arrangement]

(l) Give details of the default in connection with the composition or scheme, being the grounds under section 276(1) IA86 upon which the bankruptcy order is sought

4. (l)

Endorsement
This Petition having been issued at the RCJ, 7 Rolls Buildings, Fetter Lane, London, EC4A 1NL will be heard at the time and date pursuant to the endorsement underneath the Court Seal on the front page of this Petition

OR

This petition having been presented to the court on
it is ordered that the petition shall be heard as follows:–
Date
Time   hours
Place

(m) Insert name of debtor

and you, the above-named (m)
, are to take notice that if you intend to oppose the petition you must not later than 7 days before the day fixed for the hearing:
(i)   file in court a notice specifying the grounds on which you object to the making of a bankruptcy order; and
(ii)   send a copy of the notice to the petitioner or his solicitor.

(n) Only to be completed where the petitioning creditor is represented by a solicitor

The solicitor to the petitioning creditor is:– (n)
Name
Address

Email
Telephone Number
Reference

24.4 CREDITOR'S BANKRUPTCY PETITION ON FAILURE TO COMPLY WITH A STATUTORY DEMAND FOR A LIQUIDATED SUM PAYABLE AT A FUTURE DATE

Rules 10.7–10.9
Form Bank 2

Creditor's Bankruptcy Petition on Failure to Comply with a Statutory Demand for a Liquidated Sum Payable at a Future Date

IN THE HIGH COURT OF JUSTICE
IN BANKRUPTCY

IN THE MATTER OF [Insert name Debtor]
AND IN THE MATTER OF THE INSOLVENCY ACT 1986

(a) Insert full name(s) and address(es) of petitioner(s)

I/We (a)

(b) Insert full name, place of residence and occupation (if any) of debtor

petition the court that a bankruptcy order may be made against (b)

(c) Insert in full any other name(s) by which the debtor is or has been known

[also known as (c)

]

(d) Insert trading name (adding 'with another or others', if this is so), business address and nature of business

[and carrying on business as (d)

]

(e) Insert any other address or addresses at which the debtor has resided at or after the time the petition debt was incurred

[and lately residing at (e)

]

(f) Give the same details as specified in note (d) above for any other businesses which have been carried on at or after the time the petition debt was incurred

[and lately carrying on business as (f)

]

and say as follows:

(g) Delete as applicable

1. (g) [the debtor's centre of main interests is in England and Wales][the debtor has an establishment in England and Wales.]

OR

The debtor carries on business as an insurance undertaking; a credit institution; an investment undertaking providing services involving the holding of funds or securities for third parties; or a collective investment undertaking as referred to in Article 2.2 of the EU Regulation on Insolvency Proceedings

OR

The debtor's centre of main interests is not within a member State.

2. The debtor is (g)[not] resident in England and Wales. I am presenting this petition to the (g)[High Court][Central London County Court] because (g)[the proceedings are allocated to the London Insolvency District as][(g)Rule 10.11[(1)][(a)][(b)]][(2)][(5)][(6)] applies][and the petition debt is (g)[£50,000 or more][less than £50,000]][and within the 6 months immediately preceding its presentation (g)[the debtor carried on business in England and Wales and the debtor carried on business within the area of the London Insolvency District (g)[for the greater part of that period of 6 months][for a longer period than in any other insolvency district]][the debtor has not carried on business in England and Wales but has resided in England and Wales and the debtor resided within the area of the London Insolvency District (g)[for the greater part of that period of 6 months][for a longer period than in any other insolvency district]].

OR

The debtor is (g)[not] resident in England and Wales. I am presenting this petition to this county court because (g)Rule 10.11[(3)][(4)][(a)][b)] applies [and within the 6 months immediately preceding its presentation (g)[the debtor has carried on business in England and Wales and for the longest part of the period during which the debtor carried on business within that period of 6 months, the [principal] place of business has been situated in the district of this county court][the debtor has not carried on business in England and Wales, but has resided in England and Wales and for the longest part of the period during which the debtor was resident in England and Wales within that period of 6 months, the debtor resided in the Insolvency district of this county court]].

(j) Please give the amount of debt(s), what they relate to and when they were incurred. Please show separately the amount or rate of any interest or other charge not previously notified to the debtor and the reasons why you are claiming it

3. The debtor is justly and truly indebted to me[us] in the aggregate sum of

£(j)

(k) Insert date or dates when the debt becomes payable

4. The above-mentioned debt is for a liquidated sum payable on (k)
and the debtor appears to have no reasonable prospect of being able to pay it

(l) Insert date of service of a statutory demand

5. On (l)
a statutory demand was served on the debtor by

(m) State manner of service of demand

(m)

in respect of the above-mentioned debt. To the best of my knowledge and belief the demand has neither been complied with nor set aside in accordance with the Insolvency Rules and no application to set it aside is outstanding

(n) If 3 weeks have not elapsed since service of statutory demand give reasons for earlier presentation of petition

(n)

6. I/We do not, nor does any person on my/our behalf, hold any security on the debtor's estate, or any part thereof, for the payment of the above-mentioned sum

OR

I/We hold security for the payment of (g) [part of] the above-mentioned sum.
I/We will give up such security for the benefit of all the creditors in the event of a bankruptcy order being made.

OR

I/We hold security for the payment of part of the above-mentioned sum and I/we estimate the value of such security to be £   .
This petition is not made in respect of the secured part of my/our debt.

Endorsement

This Petition having been issued at the RCJ, 7 Rolls Buildings, Fetter Lane, London, EC4A 1NL will be heard at the time and date pursuant to the endorsement underneath the Court Seal on the front page of this Petition

OR

This petition having been presented to the court on it is ordered that the petition shall be heard as follows:
Date
Time   hours
Place

(o) Insert name of debtor

and you, the above-named (o)   , are to take notice that if you intend to oppose the petition you must not later than 7 days before the day fixed for the next hearing
(i)   file in court a notice specifying the grounds on which you object to the making of a bankruptcy order; and
(ii)   send a copy of the notice to the petitioner or his solicitor.

(p) This is the address which will be treated by Court as the Petitions address for service.

The solicitor to the petitioning creditor is:(p)
Name
Address

Email
Telephone Number
Reference

24.5 CREDITOR'S BANKRUPTCY PETITION ON FAILURE TO COMPLY WITH A STATUTORY DEMAND FOR A LIQUIDATED SUM PAYABLE IMMEDIATELY

Rules 10.7–10.9
Form Bank 1

Creditor's Bankruptcy Petition on Failure to Comply with a Statutory Demand for a Liquidated Sum Payable Immediately

IN THE HIGH COURT OF JUSTICE
IN BANKRUPTCY

IN THE MATTER OF [Insert name Debtor]
AND IN THE MATTER OF THE INSOLVENCY ACT 1986

(a) Insert full name(s) and address(es) of petitioner(s)

I/We (a)

(b) Insert full name, place of residence and occupation (if any) of debtor

petition the court that a bankruptcy order may be made against (b)

(c) Insert in full any other name(s) by which the debtor is or has been known
(d) Insert trading name (adding 'with another or others', if this is so), business address and nature of business
(e) Insert any other address or addresses at which the debtor has resided at or after the time the petition debt was incurred
(f) Give the same details as specified in note (d) above for any other businesses which have been carried on at or after the time the petition debt was incurred
(g) Delete as applicable
(h) State how the test in s265(2) of the IA86 is met

[also known as (c)   ]
[and carrying on business as (d)   ]

[and lately residing at (e)   ]
[and lately carrying on business as (f)

and say as follows:—
1. (g) [the debtor's centre of main interests is in England and Wales][the debtor has an establishment in England and Wales.]
OR
The debtor carries on business as an insurance undertaking; a credit institution; an investment undertaking providing services involving the holding of funds or securities for third parties; or a collective investment undertaking as referred to in Article 2.2 of the EU Regulation on Insolvency Proceedings
OR
The debtor's centre of main interests is not within a member State(h)

2. The debtor is (g)[not] resident in England and Wales. I am presenting this petition to the (g)[High Court][Central London County Court] because (g)[the proceedings are allocated to the London Insolvency District as][(g)Rule 10.11[(1)[(a)][(b)]][(2)][(5)][(6)] applies][and the petition debt is (g)[£50,000 or more][less than £50,000]][and within the 6 months immediately preceding its presentation (g)[the debtor carried on business in England and Wales and the debtor carried on business within the area of the London Insolvency District (g)[for the greater part of that period of 6 months][for a longer period than in any other insolvency district]][the debtor has not carried on business in England and Wales but has resided in England and Wales and the debtor resided within the area of the London Insolvency District (g)[for the greater part of that period of 6 months][for a longer period than in any other insolvency district]].

OR

The debtor is (g)[not] resident in England and Wales. I am presenting this petition to this county court because (g)Rule 10.11[(3)][(4)][(a)][(b)] applies [and within the 6 months immediately preceding its presentation (g)[the debtor has carried on business in England and Wales and for the longest part of the period during which the debtor carried on business within that period of 6 months, the [principal] place of business has been situated in the district of this county court][the debtor has not carried on business in England and Wales, but has resided in England and Wales and for the longest part of the period during which the debtor was resident in England and Wales within that period of 6 months, the debtor resided in the Insolvency district of this county court]].

(j) Please give the amount of debt(s), what they relate to and when they were incurred. Please show separately the amount or rate of any interest or other charge not previously notified to the debtor **and the reasons why you are claiming it**

(k) Insert date of service of a statutory demand

(l) State manner of service of demand

(m) If 3 weeks have not elapsed since service of statutory demand give reasons for earlier presentation of petition

3. The debtor is justly and truly indebted to us in the aggregate sum of £(j)

4. The above-mentioned debt is for a liquidated sum payable immediately and the debtor appears to be unable to pay it.

5. On (k)

a statutory demand was served upon the debtor by (l)

in respect of the above-mentioned debt. To the best of my knowledge and belief the demand has neither been complied with nor set aside in accordance with the Insolvency Rules and no application to set it aside is outstanding

(m)

6. I/We do not, nor does any person on our behalf, hold any security on the debtor's estate, or any part thereof, for the payment of the above-mentioned sum

OR

I/We hold security for the payment of (g) [part of] the above-mentioned sum.

I/We will give up such security for the benefit of all the creditors in the event of a bankruptcy order being made.

OR

I/We hold security for the payment of part of the above-mentioned sum and we estimate the value of such security to be £   . This petition is not made in respect of the secured part of our debt.

Endorsement

This Petition having been issued at the RCJ, 7 Rolls Buildings, Fetter Lane, London, EC4A 1NL will be heard at the time and date pursuant to the endorsement underneath the Court Seal on the front page of this Petition

OR

This petition having been presented to the court on it is ordered that the petition shall be heard as follows:—

Date

Time   hours

Place

(n) Insert name of debtor

and you, the above-named (n)   , are to take notice that if you intend to oppose the petition you must not later than 7 days before the day fixed for the next hearing

(i)   file in court a notice specifying the grounds on which you object to the making of a bankruptcy order; and

(ii)   send a copy of the notice to the petitioner or his solicitor.

(o) This is the address which will be treated by Court as the Petitions address for service.

The solicitor to the petitioning creditor is:—(o)

Name

Address

Email

Telephone Number

Reference

24.6 CREDITOR'S BANKRUPTCY PETITION WHERE EXECUTION OR OTHER PROCESS ON A JUDGMENT HAS BEEN RETURNED IN WHOLE OR PART

Rules 10.7–10.9
Form Bank 3

Creditor's Bankruptcy Petition Where Execution or Other Process on a Judgment has been Returned in Whole or Part

IN THE HIGH COURT OF JUSTICE
IN BANKRUPTCY

IN THE MATTER OF [Insert name Debtor]
AND IN THE MATTER OF THE INSOLVENCY ACT 1986

(a) Insert full name(s) and address(es) of petitioner(s)

I/We (a)

(b) Insert full name, place of residence and occupation (if any) of debtor

petition the court that a bankruptcy order be made against (b)

(c) Insert in full any other name(s) by which the debtor is or has been known

[also known as (c)

]

(d) Insert trading name (adding 'with another or others', if this is so), business address and nature of business

[and carrying on business as (d)

]

(e) Insert any other address or addresses at which the debtor has resided at or after the time the petition debt was incurred

[and lately residing at (e)

]

(f) Give the same details as specified in note (d) above for any other businesses which have been carried on at or after the time the petition debt was incurred

[and lately carrying on business as (f)

]
and say as follows:–

(g) Delete as applicable

1. (g) [the debtor's centre of main interests is in England and Wales][the debtor has an establishment in England and Wales.]
OR

The debtor carries on business as an insurance undertaking; a credit institution; an investment undertaking providing services involving the holding of funds or securities for third parties; or a collective investment undertaking as referred to in Article 2.2 of the EU Regulation on Insolvency Proceedings
OR
The debtor's centre of main interests is not within a member State
2. The debtor is (g)[not] resident in England and Wales. I am presenting this petition to the (g)[High Court][Central London County Court] because (g)[the proceedings are allocated to the London Insolvency District as][(g)Rule 10.11[(1)[(a)][(b)]]][(2)][(5)][(6)] applies][and the petition debt is (g)[£50,000 or more][less than £50,000]][and within the 6 months immediately preceding its presentation (g)[the debtor carried on business in England and Wales and the debtor carried on business within the area of the London Insolvency District (g)[for the greater part of that period of 6 months][for a longer period than in any other insolvency district]][the debtor has not carried on business in England and Wales but has resided in England and Wales and the debtor resided within the area of the London Insolvency District (g)[for the greater part of that period of 6 months][for a longer period than in any other insolvency district]].
OR
The debtor is (g)[not] resident in England and Wales. I am presenting this petition to this county court because (g)Rule 10.11[(3)][(4)][(a)] [(b)] applies [and within the 6 months immediately preceding its presentation (g)[the debtor has carried on business in England and Wales and for the longest part of the period during which the debtor carried on business within that period of 6 months, the [principal] place of business has been situated in the district of this county court][the debtor has not carried on business in England and Wales, but has resided in England and Wales and for the longest part of the period during which the debtor was resident in England and Wales within that period of 6 months, the debtor resided in the Insolvency district of this county court]].

Under the EU Regulation on Insolvency Proceedings:

(i) The centre of main interests should correspond to the place where the debtor conducts the administration of his interests on a regular basis.
(ii) Establishment is defined as 'any place of operations where the debtor carries out a non-transitory economic activity with human means and goods'.

(j) Please give the amount of debt(s), what they relate to and when they were incurred. Please show separately the amount or rate of any interest or other charge not previously notified to the debtor **and the reasons why you are claiming it**

(k) Insert date on which judgment was obtained

(l) Insert date of execution

(m) Delete as applicable

3. The debtor is justly and truly indebted to me[us] in the aggregate sum of
£(j)

4. The above-mentioned debt is for a liquidated sum payable immediately and the debtor appears to be unable to pay it.

5. On (k) judgment was obtained in (g) [The High Court of Justice _____ Division]
[_____ County Court] [or as the case may be] on an action the short title and reference to the record whereof is
'∕\   V   ∩   ' Number
in the sum of £   following which execution was issued at the
              court in respect of the debt and on (l)
the sheriff/county court (g) [made a return]
[endorsed upon the writ a statement] to the effect that the execution was unsatisfied (g) [as to the whole] [as to part] and the above-mentioned debt represents the amount by which the execution was returned unsatisfied.

6. I/We do not, nor does any person on my/our behalf, hold any security on the debtor's estate, or any part thereof, for the payment of the above-mentioned sum.
OR
I/We hold security for the payment of (m) [part of] the above-mentioned sum.
I/We will give up such security for the benefit of all the creditors in the event of a bankruptcy order being made.
OR
I/We hold security for the payment of part of the above-mentioned sum and I/we estimate the value of such security to be £   . This petition is not made in respect of the secured part of my/our debt.

Endorsement

This Petition having been issued at the RCJ, 7 Rolls Buildings, Fetter Lane, London, EC4A 1NL will be heard at the time and date pursuant to the endorsement underneath the
Court Seal on the front page of this Petition
OR
This petition having been presented to the court on it is ordered that the petition shall be heard as follows:–
Date
Time   hours
Place
and you, the above-named (n)
, are to take notice that if you intend to oppose the petition you must not later than 7 days before the day fixed for the hearing:
(i)   file in court a notice (in Form 6.19) specifying the grounds on which you object to the making of a bankruptcy order, and
(ii)   send a copy of the notice to the petitioner or his solicitor.

The solicitor to the petitioning creditor is:– (o)
Name
Address

Email
Telephone Number
Reference

24.7 DEBTOR'S NOTICE OF OPPOSITION

Rule 10.18
Form Bank 6

Debtor's notice of opposition to petition

<u>IN THE HIGH COURT OF JUSTICE</u>
<u>IN BANKRUPTCY</u>

IN THE MATTER OF [NAME OF DEBTOR]

AND

IN THE MATTER OF THE INSOLVENCY ACT 1986

(a) Insert name and address
which will be used for service by
the court

Take not that I (a)
intend to oppose the application to make a
bankruptcy order on the following grounds:–

Dated _____

To   court
the
and to the [solicitors for] the petitioner.

24.8   LIST OF APPEARANCES

Rule 10.20   **List of Appearances**
Form Bank 8

<u>IN THE HIGH COURT OF JUSTICE</u>
<u>IN BANKRUPTCY</u>

IN THE MATTER OF [INSERT DEBTOR'S NAME]

AND

IN THE MATTER OF THE INSOLVENCY ACT 1986

Bankruptcy Petition presented on

To be heard on

The following persons have given notice that they intend to appear on the hearing of the above-mentioned petition

Name and Address	Name and Address of Solicitors if any	Amount owed to Creditor £	Whether supporting or opposing the petition

24.9   NOTICE OF PERSONS INTENDING TO APPEAR

Rule 10.19   **Notice of Persons Intending to Appear**
Form Bank 7

IN THE HIGH COURT OF JUSTICE
IN BANKRUPTCY

IN THE MATTER OF [INSERT DEBTOR'S NAME]

AND

IN THE MATTER OF THE INSOLVENCY ACT 1986

(a) Insert date

Bankruptcy petition presented on (a)

to be heard on (a)

(b) Insert full name and
address, or if a firm, the
name of the firm and address

Take notice that (b)

(c) Delete as applicable

a creditor of the above-named debtor intends to
appear on the hearing of the above-mentioned
petition to (c) [support] [oppose] it.

Signed _____

(d) Address

(d) If creditor solicitor or
other agent please give name
and address of firm and
insert name(s) and
address(es) of petitioner(s) or
petitioner(s) solicitor

Telephone No_____
Reference No _____
To (d)

Dated

24.10   STATUTORY DEMAND UNDER SECTION 268(1)(A) OF THE INSOLVENCY ACT 1986. DEBT FOR LIQUIDATED SUM PAYABLE IMMEDIATELY FOLLOWING A JUDGMENT OR ORDER OF THE COURT

Rule 10.1 Form SD4	**Statutory Demand under Section 268(1)(a) of the Insolvency Act 1986. Debt for Liquidated Sum Payable Immediately Following a Judgment or Order of the Court**

Warning

- This is an **important** document. You should refer to the notes below entitled 'How to comply with a statutory demand or have it set aside.'
- If you wish to have this demand set aside you must make application to do so **within 18 days** from its service on you.
- If you do not apply to set aside **within 18 days** or otherwise deal with this demand as set out in the notes **within 21 days** after its service on you, you could be made bankrupt and your property and goods taken away from you.
- Please read the demand and notes very carefully. If you are in doubt about your position you should seek advice **immediately** from a solicitor, a Citizens Advice Bureau or a licensed insolvency practitioner.

Notes for Creditor

- If the Creditor is entitled to the debt by way of assignment, details of the original creditor and any **intermediary** assignees should be given in part B.
- If the amount of debt includes interest not previously notified to the company as included in its liability, details should be given, including the grounds upon which interest is charged. The amount of interest must be shown separately.
- Any other charge accruing due from time to time may be claimed. The amount **or** rate of the charge must be identified and the grounds on which it is claimed must be stated.
- In either case the amount claimed must be limited to that which has accrued due at the date of the demand.
- If signatory of the demand is a solicitor or other agent of the creditor the name of his/her firm should be given

---

Demand

To _____

_____

Address _____

This demand is served on you by the creditor:

Name _____

Address _____

_____

The creditor claims that you own the sum of £ _____, full particulars of which are set out on page 2, and that it is payable immediately and, to the extent of the sum demanded, is unsecured.

By Judgment/Order of the _____ court in proceedings entitled (Case) Number

_____ between _____ claimant and

_____ Defendant it was adjudged/ordered that you pay to the creditor the sum of

£ _____ and £ _____ for costs.

The creditor demands that you pay the above debt or secure or compound for it to the creditor's satisfaction.

[The creditor making this demand is a Minister of the Crown or a Government Department, and it is intended to present a bankruptcy petition in the [High Court][County Court at Central London] [Delete as appropriate].

Signature of individual _____

Name _____
      BLOCK LETTERS

Date _____

*Position with or relationship to creditor _____

* I am authorised to make this demand on the creditor's behalf. [* Delete if signed by the creditor]

N.B. The person making this demand must complete the whole of pages 1, 2 and parts A, B and C (as applicable) on page 3
* This is the address to which the court or the creditor will send any documents relating to this demand.

Address _____

_____

Tel. Nº _____

Ref. _____

Details of Debt
(These details must include (a) when the debt was incurred, (b) the consideration for the debt (or if there is no consideration the way in which it arose) and (c) the amount due as at the date of this demand.)

Note: If there is insufficient space, please continue on a separate sheet and clearly indicate on this page that you are doing so.

Part A
Appropriate Court for Setting Aside Demand

Rule 10.4(4) and 10.4(8) of the Insolvency Rules 2016 sets out the way of determining the appropriate court or hearing centre to which the Application should be sent.

Where the statutory demand is served by a Minister of the Crown or a Government Department you may choose the court to which to make your application. You may choose the court in Rule 10.4 or the court which the Minister of the Crown or Government Department has indicated as the court to which it intends to present a bankruptcy petition against you (the High Court, or the County Court at Central London).

In accordance with those rules the appropriate court is [The High Court] [the County Court at Central London]

[or] [_____County Court hearing centre]. (address)

Any application by you to set aside this demand should be made to that court.

Part B
The individual or individuals to whom any communication regarding this demand may be addressed is/are:

Name _____
    (BLOCK LETTERS)
Address _____

_____

Telephone Number _____

Reference _____

Part C
For completion if the creditor is entitled to the debt by way of assignment.

	Name	Date(s) of Assignment
Original Creditor		
Assignees		

How to comply with a statutory demand or have it set aside (ACT WITHIN 18 DAYS)
If you wish to avoid a bankruptcy petition being presented against you, you must pay the debt shown on page 1, details of which are set out on page 2 of this notice, within the period of 21 days after its service upon you. Alternatively, you can attempt to come to a settlement with the creditor. To do this you should:

- Inform the individual (or one of the individuals) named in Part B above immediately that you are willing and able to offer security for the debt to the creditor's satisfaction; or
- Inform the individual (or one of the individuals) named in Part B immediately that you are willing and able to compound for the debt to the creditor's satisfaction.

If you dispute the demand in whole or in part you should:

- Contact the individual (or one of the individuals) named in Part B immediately.

If you consider that you have grounds to have this demand set aside or you do not quickly receive a satisfactory written reply from the individual named in Part B whom you have contacted, you should **apply within 18 days** from the date of service of this demand on you to the appropriate court shown in Part A above to have the demand set aside.

Any application to set aside the demand should be made within 18 days from the date of service upon you and be supported by a witness statement stating the grounds on which the demand be set aside. The forms may be obtained from the appropriate court when you attend to make the application.
REMEMBER! From the date of service on you of this document

(a)   you have only 18 days to apply to this court to have the demand set aside, and
(b)   you have only 21 days before the creditor may present a bankruptcy petition.

24.11   STATUTORY DEMAND FOR A LIQUIDATED SUM

Rule 10.1	**Statutory Demand under Section 268(1)(a) of the**
Form SD2	**Insolvency Act 1986. Debt for Liquidated Sum**
	Payable Immediately

Warning

- This is an **important** document. You should refer to the notes below entitled 'How to comply with a statutory demand or have it set aside.'
- If you wish to have this demand set aside you must make application to do so **within 18 days** from its service on you.
- If you do not apply to set aside **within 18 days** or otherwise deal with this demand as set out in the notes **within 21 days** after its service on you, you could be made bankrupt and your property and goods taken away from you.
- Please read the demand and notes very carefully. If you are in doubt about your position you should seek advice **immediately** from a solicitor, a Citizens Advice Bureau or a licensed insolvency practitioner.

Notes for Creditor

- If the Creditor is entitled to the debt by way of assignment, details of the original creditor and any **intermediary** assignees should be given in part B on page 3.
- If the amount of debt includes interest not previously notified to the company as included in its liability, details should be given, including the grounds upon which interest is charged. The amount of interest must be shown separately.
- Any other charge accruing due from time to time may be claimed. The amount **or** rate of the charge must be identified and the grounds on which it is claimed must be stated.
- In either case the amount claimed must be limited to that which has accrued due at the date of the demand.
- If signatory of the demand is a solicitor or other agent of the creditor the name of his/her firm should be given

---

Demand

To _____

_____

Address _____

_____

This demand is served on you by the creditor:

Name _____

Address _____

_____

The creditor claims that you own the sum of £ _____, full particulars of which are set out on page 2, and that it is payable immediately and, to the extent of the sum demanded, is unsecured.

The creditor demands that you pay the above debt or secure or compound for it to the creditor's satisfaction.

[The creditor making this demand is a Minister of the Crown or a Government Department, and it is intended to present a bankruptcy petition in the [High Court][County Court at Central London] [Delete as appropriate].

* Delete if signed by the creditor himself.

Signature of individual _____

Name _____
          BLOCK LETTERS

Date _____

*Position with or relationship to creditor _____

* I am authorised to make this demand on the creditor's behalf.

N.B. The person making this demand must complete the whole of pages 1, 2 and parts A, B and C (as applicable) on page 3.

* This is the address to which the court or the creditor will send any documents relating to this demand

Address _____

_____
Tel. Nº _____

Ref. _____

Details of Debt
(These details must include (a) when the debt was incurred, (b) the consideration for the debt (or if there is no consideration the way in which it arose) and (c) the amount due as at the date of this demand.)

Note: If there is insufficient space, please continue on a separate sheet and clearly indicate on this page that you are doing so.

Part A
Appropriate Court for Setting Aside Demand

Rule 10.4(4) and 10.4(8) of the Insolvency Rules 2016 states that the appropriate court is the court to which you would have to present your own bankruptcy petition in accordance with Rule XXXXX. In accordance with those rules on present information the appropriate court is [the High Court] [the County Court at Central London] [or] [County Court Hearing Centre]
(address)

Any application by you to set aside this demand should be made to that court.

Part B
The individual or individuals to whom any communication regarding this demand may be addressed is/are:

Name _____
    (BLOCK LETTERS)
Address _____

_____

Telephone Number _____

Reference _____

Part C
For completion if the creditor is entitled to the debt by way of assignment.

	Name	Date(s) of Assignment
Original Creditor		
Assignees		

How to comply with a statutory demand or have it set aside (ACT WITHIN 18 DAYS)

If you wish to avoid a bankruptcy petition being presented against you, you must pay the debt shown on page 1, details of which are set out on page 2 of this notice, within the period of 21 days after its service upon you. Alternatively, you can attempt to come to a settlement with the creditor. To do this you should:

- Inform the individual (or one of the individuals) named in Part B above immediately that you are willing and able to offer security for the debt to the creditor's satisfaction; or
- Inform the individual (or one of the individuals) named in Part B immediately that you are willing and able to compound for the debt to the creditor's satisfaction.

If you dispute the demand in whole or in part you should:

- Contact the individual (or one of the individuals) named in Part B immediately.

If you consider that you have grounds to have this demand set aside or you do not quickly receive a satisfactory written reply from the individual named in Part B whom you have contacted, you should **apply within 18 days** from the date of service of this demand on you to the appropriate court shown in Part A above to have the demand set aside.

Any application to set aside the demand should be made within 18 days from the date of service upon you and be supported by a witness statement stating the grounds on which the demand be set aside. The forms may be obtained from the appropriate court when you attend to make the application.

REMEMBER! From the date of service on you of this document

(a)   you have only 18 days to apply to this court to have the demand set aside, and
(b)   you have only 21 days before the creditor may present a bankruptcy petition.

24.12 STATUTORY DEMAND FOR A DEBT PAYABLE AT A FUTURE DATE

Rule 10.1
Form SD3

Statutory Demand under Section 268(1)(a) of the Insolvency Act 1986. Debt Payable at Future Date

Warning
- This is an important document. You should refer to the notes below entitled 'How to comply with a statutory demand or have it set aside.'
- If you wish to have this demand set aside you must make application to do so within 18 days from its service on you.
- If you do not apply to set aside within 18 days or otherwise deal with this demand as set out in the notes within 21 days after its service on you, you could be made bankrupt and your property and goods taken away from you.
- Please read the demand and notes very carefully. If you are in doubt about your position you should seek advice immediately from a solicitor, a Citizens Advice Bureau or a licensed insolvency practitioner.

Notes for Creditor
- If the Creditor is entitled to the debt by way of assignment, details of the original creditor and any intermediary assignees should be given in part B on page 3.
- If the amount of debt includes interest not previously notified to the company as included in its liability, details should be given, including the grounds upon which interest is charged. The amount of interest must be shown separately.
- Any other charge accruing due from time to time may be claimed. The amount or rate of the charge must be identified and the grounds on which it is claimed must be stated.
- In either case the amount claimed must be limited to that which has accrued due at the date of the demand.
- If signatory of the demand is a solicitor or other agent of the creditor the name of his/her firm should be given.

_____

Demand

To _____

_____

Address _____

_____

This demand is served on you by the creditor:

Name _____

Address _____

_____

The creditor claims that you own the sum of £ _____, full particulars of which are set out on page 2, and that it is payable immediately and, to the extent of the sum demanded, is unsecured.

The creditor is of the opinion that you have no reasonable prospect of paying this debt when it falls due because _____

The creditor demands that you pay the above debt or secure or compound for it to the creditor's satisfaction.

[The creditor making this demand is a Minister of the Crown or a Government Department, and it is intended to present a bankruptcy petition in the [High Court][County Court at Central London] [Delete as appropriate].]

Signature of individual _____

Name _____
       BLOCK LETTERS

Date _____

*Position with or relationship to creditor _____

* I am authorised to make this demand on the creditor's behalf. [* Delete if signed by the creditor]

N.B. The person making this demand must complete the whole of pages 1, 2 and parts A, B and C (as applicable) on page 3
* This is the address to which the court or the creditor will send any documents relating to this demand.

Address _____

_____

Tel. Nº _____

Ref. _____

Details of Debt
(These details must include (a) when the debt was incurred, (b) the consideration for the debt (or if there is no consideration the way in which it arose) and (c) the amount due as at the date of this demand.)

Note: If there is insufficient space, please continue on a separate sheet and clearly indicate on this page that you are doing so.

Part A
Appropriate Court for Setting Aside Demand

Rule 10.4(4) and 10.4(8) of the Insolvency Rules 2016 sets out the way of determining the appropriate court or hearing centre to which the Application should be sent.

Where the statutory demand is served by a Minister of the Crown or a Government Department you may choose the court to which to make your application. You may choose the court in Rule 10.4 or the court which the Minister of the Crown or Government Department has indicated as the court to which it intends to present a bankruptcy petition against you (the High Court, or the County Court at Central London).

In accordance with those rules the appropriate court is [The High Court] [the County Court at Central London] [or] [County Court hearing centre]. (address)

Any application by you to set aside this demand should be made to that court.

Part B
The individual or individuals to whom any communication regarding this demand may be addressed is/are:

Name _____
        (BLOCK LETTERS)
Address _____

_____

Telephone Number _____

Reference _____

Part C
For completion if the creditor is entitled to the debt by way of assignment.

	Name	Date(s) of Assignment
Original Creditor		
Assignees		

How to comply with a statutory demand or have it set aside (ACT WITHIN 18 DAYS)
If you wish to avoid a bankruptcy petition being presented against you, you must pay the debt shown on page 1, details of which are set out on page 2 of this notice, within the period of **21 days** after its service upon you. Alternatively, you can attempt to come to a settlement with the creditor. To do this you should:

- Inform the individual (or one of the individuals) named in Part B above immediately that you are willing and able to offer security for the debt to the creditor's satisfaction; or
- Inform the individual (or one of the individuals) named in Part B immediately that you are willing and able to compound for the debt to the creditor's satisfaction.

If you dispute the demand in whole or in part you should:

- Contact the individual (or one of the individuals) named in Part B immediately.

If you consider that you have grounds to have this demand set aside or you do not quickly receive a satisfactory written reply from the individual named in Part B whom you have contacted, you should **apply within 18 days** from the date of service of this demand on you to the appropriate court shown in Part A above to have the demand set aside.

Any application to set aside the demand should be made within 18 days from the date of service upon you and be supported by a witness statement stating the grounds on which the demand be set aside. The forms may be obtained from the appropriate court when you attend to make the application.
REMEMBER! From the date of service on you of this document

(a)   you have only 18 days to apply to this court to have the demand set aside, and
(b)   you have only 21 days before the creditor may present a bankruptcy petition.

Index